Adventuring in Arizona

The Sierra Club Adventure Travel Guides

Adventuring in Arizona

John Annerino

Sierra Club Books · San Francisco

The Sierra Club, founded in 1892 by John Muir, has devoted itself to the study and protection of the earth's scenic and ecological resources—mountains, wetlands, woodlands, wild shores and rivers, deserts and plains. The publishing program of the Sierra Club offers books to the public as a nonprofit educational service in the hope that they may enlarge the public's understanding of the Club's basic concerns. The point of view expressed in each book, however, does not necessarily represent that of the Club. The Sierra Club has some sixty chapters coast to coast, in Canada, Hawaii, and Alaska. For information about how you may participate in its programs to preserve wilderness and the quality of life, please address inquiries to Sierra Club, 730 Polk Street, San Francisco, CA 94109.

Library of Congress Cataloging in Publication Data

Annerino, John.
    Adventuring in Arizona : the Sierra Club travel guide to the Grand
Canyon state / John Annerino.
        p. cm.
    Includes bibliographical references and index.
    ISBN 0-87156-681-8
    1. Arizona—Description and travel—1981–   Guide-books.
I. Sierra Club. II. Title.
F809.3.A45   1991
917.9104'53—dc20   91-14186
                                                           CIP

Production by Lynne O'Neil

Cover design by Bonnie Smetts

Book design by Linda Herman + Company

Maps by Hilda Chen

Photos by John Annerino

Printed in the United States of America on acid-free paper containing 50% recovered fiber, of which 10% is post-consumer waste

10 9 8 7 6 5 4 3 2

To Mom and Dad, who first introduced me to
this wonderful, lifelong adventure called Arizona.

Contents

About the Author

John Annerino is a Tucson-based photojournalist whose work has been published in magazines such as *LIFE, Time,* and *Newsweek,* among many others; he is represented by the Gamma-Liaison picture agency in New York and Paris and the Marks agency in Milano. Annerino is the author and photographer of five books, including *High Risk Photography: the Adventure Behind the Image* (American & World Geographic Publishing). He is currently photographing *Canyons of the Southwest* for Sierra Club Books.

Acknowledgments

When the idea for this book was first conceived, it seemed simple enough: Peruse a few historic accounts and archeological surveys to follow the historic and prehistoric trails of Arizona's earliest travelers; divide the state into thirds; then subdivide the adventures in those sections into car touring, trekking, canyoneering, river running, and climbing. Thus organized, I could wrap the whole thing up as a tidy yearlong project—and salt away enough of my advance to rest my weary bones on a beach in sunny Baja.

I thought.

However, once I actually set out to follow the early routes and trails of Arizona's Indians, Spanish missionaries, prospectors, explorers, river runners, and adventurers into Arizona's seldom-traveled mountains, deserts, and canyons, I knew I'd bitten off far more than I could chew by myself. This book would not have been possible without the friends who accompanied me on those exciting, sometimes difficult, adventures; nor would it have been possible for me to sift through the labyrinth of historic documents and research material without the help of many professionals and scholars along the way.

I'd like to thank those who actually accompanied me on the adventures described in this book: the entire Wolf Pack of Dave Ganci, Randy Mulkey, Richard Nebeker, Michael Thomas, Tony Mangine and Bob Farrell for embarking on some of the most difficult adventures; the Arizona Raft Adventures crew of Rob Elliott, Louise Teal, Martha Clark, Renny Sumner, and Suzanne Jordon for the timeless journeys we made together down the Colorado River; the late Robin Lange for climbing Baboquivari with me and the "Mulkster"; Maj. Bruce Lohman and the late David Roberson for following me on a midsummer trek across *El Camino del Diablo*—and Bill Broyles for providing the historic setting and moral support to complete that dangerous trek; George Bain and Craig Newman for scrambling up Shiva Temple with me, and Larry "Captain SWAT" Seligman for his sense of humor when I needed it most; Mike Young for exploring the length of Kanab Creek with me when I knew he would have preferred staying home and milking his cows; and Pat Orozco, Jack Cartier, Christine Keith, Gary Drysmala, Carmen Faucon, Don Meyers, Val Annerino, Janey Roberson, Kathleen Pecuch, Eric Lohman, and Bernard Donuhue for sharing all the other adventures with me. And Elizabeth Alcoverde for her courage.

The field work for this project was the easy part; the hard part was going back into the research catacombs to ferret out exactly which Indian tribe or early adventurer really might have made the first ascent of, say, Baboquivari Peak, or who first crossed the Devil's Highway, or who really was the first man to run the Colorado River. Many times I actually succeeded in discovering the facts; other times I was forced to make educated guesses. Either way, I always wanted to know more: What did these early adventurers see during their travels, and did their descriptions still apply today?

But conducting research is like climbing a large cottonwood tree; you start at its base in hopes of getting to the root of the matter, but the tree continually branches and subbranches into a hundred different—always alluring—directions. . . . Needless to say, my tidy yearlong project quickly ballooned into a 2½-year journey I'd still be locked into were it not for the invaluable assistance of the following people: research librarian Riva Dean and the rest of the kind staff at the Arizona Historical Society (Tucson); the librarians and assistants at the University of Arizona's Special Collections Library and Map Department; archeologists Simone Bruder, Patricia Gillman, Pat Spoerl, and Rich Malcolmson; anthropologist Robert C. Euler; curator Norm Tessman; rangers Terry Cleland, Cindy Swing, Caroline Wilson, and Holly Williams; and Dan Davis, Bob Dowling, and Doug Kasian.

Last, but not least, I would not have considered undertaking this mammoth research project—nor would I have completed it—without the patience and guidance of Sierra Club Books editor Jim Cohee.

Thank you everyone.

✤

The Arizona
Adventure

The Lay of the Land

Comprising 113,956 square miles, modern Arizona lays claim to the most extraordinary mix of deserts in North America—as well as to the most famous canyon on Earth. Yet few people realize that Arizona also has the largest ponderosa pine forest in the contiguous United States and virtually every life zone found between Mexico and Canada—including alpine tundra. The reason for the state's incongruous yet awe-inspiring environmental diversity is simple: Two major physiographic provinces collide about midway across Arizona to form a third province.

Totaling 130,000 square miles, the heart-shaped *Colorado Plateau Province* lies atop huge tracts of Utah, Colorado, New Mexico, and Arizona like a gargantuan slab of multicolored rock. First noted on explorer Lt. Joseph C. Ives' map in 1858, Arizona's slice of the 6,000-foot-high Colorado Plateau Province totals some 45,000 square miles and is characterized by cold, wind-whipped deserts, cloud-piercing volcanic peaks, and mile-deep canyons. The *Basin and Range Province*, on the other hand, stretches all the way from southern Oregon to western Texas; it covers most of southern Arizona and is characterized by rugged, northwest-trending mountain ranges spanned by fierce, low-lying deserts. Where the southwestern arch of the Colorado Plateau sloughs off into the Basin and Range Province below, it forms a statewide brink popularly known as the Mogollon Rim; this awesome escarpment and the spectacular canyons that drain it and its adjoining mountain ranges comprise the state's Mogollon Rim and central Arizona highland country, what some call the *Intermontane Province*.

Landforms

Deserts

Of the world's twelve great desert regions, the North American Desert ranks fifth in size behind the Sahara, Australian, Arabian, and Turkestan deserts. Comprising some 500,000 square miles, the North American Desert is actually made up of four distinct deserts: the Chihuahuan, the Mojave, the Great Basin, and the Sonoran. Only in Arizona do all four of these deserts converge.

Roughly totaling 140,000 square miles, the Chihuahuan Desert is located primarily in Mexico; it ranges in elevation from 3,000 to 5,000 feet and snakes its way into southeastern Arizona near the Chiricahua Mountains. The Mojave Desert, the smallest in North America—and totaling approximately 40,000 square miles—ranges in elevation from 2,000 to 4,000 feet; emanating from its core in Death Valley, the Mojave Desert works its way eastward across southeastern California, into Arizona near Topock Gorge, and up the Colorado River as far as the Grand Canyon. Linked to the Sonoran Desert by the Mojave, the mile-high Great Basin Desert totals 210,000 square miles and is North America's largest and coldest desert; it stretches south from Oregon, blankets most of Nevada, and creeps into northeastern Arizona as far south as Petrified Forest National Park and the surrounding El Desierto Pintado, or Painted Desert.

Lastly, encompassing 120,000 square miles, the Sonoran Desert region includes virtually all of southwestern Arizona, a piece of southeastern California, most of the Baja Peninsula, the state of Sonora, Mexico, and the midriff islands of the Sea of Cortez. Of the four North American deserts, the Sonoran is, on the average, the hottest; it is also far and away the most diverse, ranging in elevation from sea level to 3,500 feet. No other region in North America offers such a broad spectrum of life zones—and the native plants, animals, and people that inhabit them. Five of the world's six principal biotic communities can be found on the Santa Catalina Mountains, a single, mountainous "sky island" looming out of the floor of the lower Sonoran Desert near Tucson. (See entry for Life Zones in this chapter.)

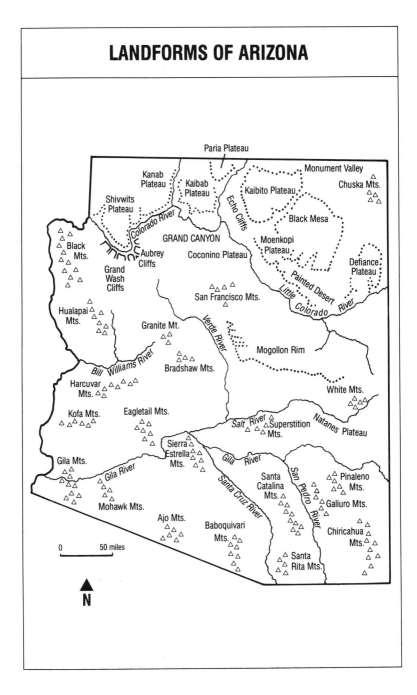

LANDFORMS OF ARIZONA

Paria Plateau

Monument Valley

Kanab Plateau

Kaibab Plateau

Kaibito Plateau

Chuska Mts.

Shivwits Plateau

Echo Cliffs

Black Mesa

Black Mts.

Colorado River

GRAND CANYON

Moenkopi Plateau

Aubrey Cliffs

Coconino Plateau

Grand Wash Cliffs

Defiance Plateau

Painted Desert

San Francisco Mts.

Little Colorado River

Hualapai Mts.

Granite Mt.

Verde River

Mogollon Rim

Bill Williams River

Bradshaw Mts.

White Mts.

Harcuvar Mts.

Kofa Mts.

Eagletail Mts.

Salt River

Superstition Mts.

Natanes Plateau

Sierra Estrella Mts.

Gila River

Gila Mts.

Gila River

Santa Catalina Mts.

San Pedro River

Pinaleno Mts.

Galiuro Mts.

Mohawk Mts.

Ajo Mts.

Baboquivari Mts.

Santa Cruz River

Chiricahua Mts.

Santa Rita Mts.

0   50 miles

N

Canyons

Billed as one of the Seven Natural Wonders of the World, the Grand Canyon, its seventy-odd tributary drainages, and its Brobdingnagian tributary canyons only hint at the spectacular array of canyons awaiting modern adventurers throughout the rest of Arizona. Principally, Arizona has three kinds of canyons: Plateau canyons, canyons of the Colorado Plateau; rim canyons, which drain the Mogollon Rim; and mountain canyons, which drain Arizona's nearly two hundred mountain ranges. As early as 1948, scientist Edwin D. McKee noted the differences between Arizona's canyons. In *The Inverted Mountains,* McKee wrote: "Canyons in the Plateau Country are legion. Some big, some small, they are like the ranges, peaks, and foothills of a great mountain system in reverse. . . . Along the southern margin of the Colorado Plateau south . . . of Flagstaff, Arizona, a large series of canyons has been cut back from the surrounding low country like scallops in lace. Most of these canyons are several thousand feet deep at their lowest ends and colorful throughout." Of the latter, McKee wrote of the rim canyons, which bridge the threshold between the Colorado Plateau Province and the Basin and Range Province below.

Mountains

Surrounded by seemingly nothing but desert and a few odd crags and peaks, we tend to overlook one of Arizona's most valuable natural assets: its 193 mountain ranges, which invite modern exploration. Thundering summer monsoons and deep winter snows unload precious moisture on these ranges, and the runoff continues to carve Arizona's legendary canyons and bring life to its harsh deserts.

Arizona has five kinds of mountains: plateau ranges, whose bases are formed atop the Colorado Plateau; highland ranges, which occupy the Intermontane Province; sky islands, high-altitude ranges generally crowned with ponderosa pine and with their bases formed on the desert floor; desert ranges, low-altitude ranges located primarily in the desert; and landmarks, which include spires, needles, buttes, mesas, and single mountains. Of these, the plateau ranges and sky islands rank as Arizona's loftiest.

Sky islands and ranges.   At 10,720 feet above sea level, the Pinaleno Mountain Range is the third highest in the state; it encompasses a 300-square-mile area and has the greatest vertical relief of any range in Arizona, more than 7,000 vertical feet. First climbed by members of the Mogollon culture perhaps as early as A.D. 900, the Pinalenos are the premier example of southern Arizona's sky islands, which thrust up out of the floor of the Sonoran and Chihuahuan deserts for thousands of vertical feet and provide unique biological islands for flora and fauna isolated from the deserts below. The most dramatic view from southern Arizona's dozen or so sky islands is the uninterrupted 360-degree panorama you find atop 9,453-foot Mount Wrightson, high point of the Santa Rita Mountains.

Plateau ranges. At 12,633 feet, Humphreys Peak is the highest summit in Arizona; it and nearby 12,356-foot Agassiz Peak and 11,969-foot Fremont Peak (Arizona's second and third highest peaks) form the tundra-covered summit crest of the San Francisco Mountains. While the Pinaleno Mountains' base is formed near the 3,000-foot level, the base of the San Francisco Mountains sits atop northern Arizona's 7,000-foot-high Coconino Plateau—so they don't offer the relentless vertical relief encountered in the Pinalenos. What the San Francisco Mountains do offer, most notably, is "tundra in the desert," the only place subalpine tundra can be found in Arizona.

Rivers

Draining Arizona's deserts, canyons, and mountains are three principal river systems. Most notable is the Colorado River, which helped cut the Grand Canyon and forms the border between western Arizona and southern California. According to the *Historical Atlas of Arizona*, "Over 90% of the land area of Arizona drains eventually into the Colorado River, which empties into the Gulf of California some eighty miles south of Yuma." The Colorado River's principal tributary is the Gila River; the Gila, in turn, is fed by southern Arizona's Santa Cruz and San Pedro rivers, and by central Arizona's Salt and Verde river systems from the north and east. Smaller tributary rivers like the Bill Williams drain directly into the Colorado in west-central Arizona, while the Little Colorado River empties into the Colorado River in the eastern Grand Canyon.

Life Zones

According to Charles H. Lowe's *Arizona's Natural Environment*, the state's life zones are generally recognized by the following divisions:

- **Lower Sonoran Desert Zone.** Sea level to 4,000 feet (creosote bush, desert scrub, and desert grassland)

- **Upper Sonoran Desert Zone.** 4,000 to 7,000 feet (oak woodland and chaparral, oak-pine woodland, and juniper-pinyon woodland)

•**Mountain Transition Zone.** 7,000 to 8,000 feet (ponderosa pine forest)

•**Canadian Zone.** 8,000 to 10,000-plus feet (fir forest)

•**Hudsonian Zone.** 9,000 to 11,000-plus feet (spruce-fir forest)

•**Timberline.** around 11,000 feet (Engelmann spruce and bristlecone pine)

•**Arctic-Alpine Zone.** 11,000-plus to 12,633 feet (alpine tundra)

Climate

Unlike the climate and weather of many other geographical regions in the United States, which are controlled largely by latitude and longitude, Arizona's climate zones and weather patterns are shaped by topography and physiography. The most striking example of this is in Phoenix and Flagstaff. Situated in the Lower Sonoran Desert Zone near 1,200 feet above sea level in central Arizona's Basin and Range Province, Phoenix has summertime temperatures peaking at 112–121 degrees Fahrenheit. But Flagstaff, 135 miles north, averages 20–25 degrees cooler because it's located in northern Arizona's Colorado Plateau Province in the Mountain Transition Zone near 7,000 feet. According to Henry P. Walker and Don Bufkin's *Historical Atlas of Arizona*, you can generally count on a 3½-degree drop in temperature for every thousand feet of elevation gained, and a 1½- to 2½-degree drop for every degree in latitude, or 70 miles, you travel from south to north. In the wintertime, the temperature difference between Flagstaff and Phoenix is even more striking: While Phoenicians may lie poolside under clear blue skies and spring warm temperatures, Flagstaffians are oftentimes shoveling snow from their driveways. A more localized example of this same phenomenon can be found in Tucson and the Santa Catalina Mountains that tower above it. Located in the lower Sonoran Desert near the 2,000-foot level in southern Arizona's Basin and Range Province, Tucson is generally 20 degrees warmer than 9,157-foot Mount Lemmon, located atop the Santa Catalinas in the Canadian Life Zone.

Arizona receives most of its precipitation during its July and August "monsoons"; these occur when tropical storms emanating from warm Gulf and Pacific waters create spectacular localized thunderstorms that might dump several inches of rain on one section of parched desert in a matter of hours. At the same time, an adjacent tract of desert might not receive any precipitation for the entire year. Monsoon precipitation is even more dramatic in the Intermontane and Colorado Plateau provinces, which can receive up to 25 inches of rain annually, or five times the average for the lower

Sonoran Desert. There monsoon weather can lead to flash floods, lightning, and firestorms even more life threatening than those pummeling the deserts below. Arizona's second wet season generally occurs during January and February, when masses of Arctic air drift south across the Rockies and dump snow or rain on the state's varied physiographic provinces and life zones.

So to plan an adventure in Arizona, when you might have the best weather, use this rule of thumb: Go high or north in the summer or low or south during the winter.

The People of Arizona

Arizona's Natives

Forefathers of Arizona's modern Indian tribes, the prehistoric Sinagua, Anasazi, Mogollon, and Hohokam Indians occupied Arizona more than a thousand years ago. Principal linguistic groupings further defined these early inhabitants as Yumans, Pimans, Apachean, Hopi, Navajo, and Southern Paiute.

Circa A.D. 1600, Arizona's Native peoples prospered by adapting hunting, gathering, and flood-water agriculture to the environmental demands imposed on them by the ancestral territories they inhabited. But the immigration of Europeans to the New World brought the Indians' natural lifeways to a tragic conclusion. By the end of the nineteenth century, most of these Native peoples were placed on reservations—by Congressional order. Today an estimated 200,000 Indian residents representing seventeen tribes live on twenty reservations on nearly 20 million acres—or some 27 percent of Arizona's total land area.

Arizona's principal Indian tribes, and sections of the ancestral lands they still inhabit, include:

Northern Arizona

• Kaibab Paiute Indians—Arizona Strip

• Hopi Indians—First, Second, and Third mesas

• Navajo Indians—Colorado Plateau country encircling the Hopi

• Havasupai Indians—Supai (near the confluence of Cataract Canyon) and Havasu Creek, Grand Canyon

• Hualapai Indians — Peach Springs and the South Rim of the western Grand Canyon

Central Arizona
• Mojave Indians — Lower Colorado River

• Chemehuevi Indians (originally from California's Mojave Desert) — Lower Colorado River

• Yavapai Indians — Prescott and Camp Verde

• Apache Indians — White Mountain and San Carlos

Southern Arizona
• Cocopa Indians — Yuma

• Tohono O'Odham Indians (Papago) — Papagueria

• Pima Indians — Gila River

• Maricopa Indians — Gila River

• Yaqui Indians (from the Rio Yaqui region of Sonora, Mexico) — Tucson and Phoenix

Prior to the Gadsden Purchase of 1854, most of the land south of the Gila River was part of Mexico and was inhabited by Mexicans and Papago Indians. But with ratification of the treaty on June 24, the United States gained 45,535 square miles — for $10 million. Of that, 27,305 square miles would eventually become part of Arizona; and Mexico's Native peoples would become Arizonans. There's no better example of the state's rich Mexican heritage than in Tucson, where generations of Mexican families have resided since before the Gadsden Purchase. As one bemused visitor was overheard asking a Tucson native: "What part of Mexico are you from, amigo?"
"You're standing in it."

A Colorful History

Located in the heart of the arid Southwest, Arizona has long been thought of as a godforsaken wasteland of sun-scorched desert that was better left alone if you could help it — but most early travelers couldn't. Bordered on the east by the tail end of the Rocky Mountains, on the north by the largely impregnable Grand Canyon and Colorado Plateau region, on the south by Mexico's fearsome El Gran Desierto and the frontier of Sonora, and on the west by the Lower Colorado River and Mojave Desert beyond, frontier Arizona presented a formidable barrier for most early travelers, including the tenacious procession of Spanish explorers who first ventured across this *despoblado* ("uninhabited land") as early as 1540. That was the year Francisco Vásquez de Coronado headed north across eastern Arizona to look for the fabled Seven Cities of Cibola, but the expedition was a bust. Another expedition led that same year by García López de Cárdenas, however, "discovered" the Grand Canyon; only Cárdenas' men couldn't find a way to the bottom of the canyon after 3 days of struggling. A century and a half later, Don Juan de Oñate crossed Arizona from the Hopi villages southwest to the Lower Colorado River and journeyed all the way to the Sea of Cortez in search of mineral wealth.

But until the tireless Jesuit missionary Padre Eusebio Francisco Kino proved he could travel this harsh land—not once, but many, many times—no Spanish explorer had discovered the great wealth he had come looking for. And Kino came in search of souls, not gold. Except possibly for the native Papago Indians Kino tried to convert, no early traveler knew Arizona—or the Sonoran desert—better than he did; between 1693 and 1701 he traveled an estimated 7,500 miles of "unexplored trails" across the harshest stretches of southern Arizona and northern Sonora. One of the keys to his success, and to the successes of Capt. Juan Bautista de Anza and Fray Francisco Garces, who later followed his route along the Santa Cruz and Gila rivers in 1775, was that he followed the proven routes and pathways of the native Pima and Papago.

The ancient Indian routes Padre Kino and other Spanish explorers "pioneered" were used later by an endless parade of Arizona immigrants. First traveled centuries before Kino first set foot on it by the Sand Papago—and perhaps earlier by the Hohokams or San Diguetos—El Camino del Diablo ("highway of the devil") was later followed by prospectors en route to the California goldfields, hundreds of whom died along the way. Major immigrant trails like the Gila Trail, as well as the Butterfield Overland Mail, also followed Kino's routes along the Santa Cruz and Gila rivers to California, and today Interstates 19, 10, and 8 memorialize them.

While Kino's routes and the settlements that sprang up along them traversed southern Arizona, other travel corridors and settlement patterns were established throughout much of frontier Arizona. Spanish and Anglo explorers in many instances followed the routes of Indians, which were later followed by surveyors, immigrant trails, stagecoach lines, and railroads among military forts and towns. Ironically, Phoenix, which first took seed near the fertile confluence of the Salt, Verde and Gila rivers, now needs to pipe water 150 miles across the western Arizona desert from the Colorado River, a river first boated by Maj. John Wesley Powell a century before the modern megalopolis developed its unslakable thirst for the state's most precious natural resource.

Situated west of the 100th meridian, between the 31st and 37th parallels, the Arizona territory that gave birth to Phoenix, Tucson, and Yuma was considered a hell on Earth, stoked by furnace winds and crawling with rattlesnakes, scorpions, and savage "apaches" who, many settlers believed, would just as soon cut your heart out as not: You either crossed this deadly barrier, survived in it, or died in it—with or without your boots on. Those who stayed behind to fulfill their vision of "manifest destiny" did so at the expense of the region's native Indian people who were destroyed or subjugated during the territory's bloody reign of terror. While there was never one great Indian war, massacres like those at Camp Grant, Canyon de Chelly, and Skeleton Cave, to name a few, remain gruesome mileposts of the sacrifice of Indian lives and ancestral lands to ranching, farming, lumber, and mining interests.

By the time Arizona finally achieved statehood in 1912, wagon roads and railroads had ushered in a flood of East Coast immigrants who enjoyed a frontier state that would fence off its Native peoples and dam its wild rivers. Urban growth mushroomed like a cataclysmic cloud. The population of Phoenix, located in an ancient Hohokam village site and trade crossroads, jumped from five hundred people in 1870 to half a million people a century later; it was sustained by a complex irrigation system, oftentimes following the ancient Hohokam's hand-dug canals, which supported an artificial greenbelt and water-hungry crops like cotton. Many of the new settlers, however, wanted out—at least on the weekends and during summer vacations. The federal government recognized that fact and established the Grand Canyon as Arizona's first national park in 1919; what was once utilized by the Anasazi ("ancient ones") and is still occupied, in part, by the Havasupai, formed Arizona's license-plate motto, "the Grand Canyon State."

Contrary to popular belief, though, the "big ditch" is not Arizona's sole point of interest—and that's what *Adventuring in Arizona* will show you: the prehistoric and historic routes that still penetrate its seldom-explored deserts, canyons, and mountains, which remain, in many respects, as wild and untamed as they were when Arizona's Native peoples and early explorers first traveled there.

The Experience of Arizona

Contemporary Arizona is a place of contradictions. Its two great urban centers, Phoenix and Tucson, are replete with the problems of all urban areas: crime, foul air, and the bleak architecture of the shopping mall and the housing tract. Both cities are surrounded by wilderness: protected wilderness and parkland. I've written this book to encourage you to find this other Arizona—to discover its breath-catching beauty and its history. I've tried to choose the widest possible range of adventures to suit every taste and every level of skill. I've written for the peak bagger and for the family out for a Sunday drive. And I've described the widest possible diversity of terrain. Following are a few suggestions for the newcomer—a quick overview of Arizona's better-known canyons, mountains, and deserts. Read it through before you immerse yourself in the detail of the touring chapters.

Arizona's Canyons

The single biggest destination on most visitors' whistle-stop tours of Arizona is the Grand Canyon, which a record 4 million people visited in 1989. By the year 2005, an estimated 8 million people a year will visit the "big ditch." Of those modern adventurers, about twenty-five thousand to thirty thousand will follow in the wake of one-armed explorer Gen. John Wesley Powell, who first ran the Colorado River in a wooden boat in 1869. Even fewer will venture beyond the South Rim's heavily beaten trails to scramble in the footsteps of the Anasazi, ancient canyoneers who trekked in and out of the Grand Canyon as early as A.D. 1100. And fewer still will explore the Canyon's spectacular temples, first climbed by Pueblo Indians a thousand years ago. Most people who do venture beyond the scenic vistas will make a skull-numbing midsummer plod down the Bright Angel Trail; local tourist brokers would still like you to believe that's the perfect time to explore this inverted desert mountain range. It's not . . . but, unfortunately, most hikers who survive that trek will never think about exploring the Grand Canyon's awesome tributary canyons.

Sixty-mile-long Kanab Creek, for example, is well worth a visit. Next to the Little Colorado River Gorge, it's the longest tributary canyon draining into the Grand Canyon. Major Powell and his men trekked out Kanab Creek at the end of their second Colorado River expedition in 1871, just about the time that some five hundred prospectors piled down that same

creek to the Colorado River in hopes of hitting the mother lode rumored
to be near the river's edge.

Eighty-two river miles upstream from the confluence of Kanab Creek
and the Colorado River the 57-mile-long Little Colorado River Gorge enters
the Grand Canyon; historically, Hopi Indians followed this immense gorge
on their sacred salt pilgrimages into the Grand Canyon.

Paria Canyon, located 61 river miles upstream from the mouth of the
Little Colorado River Gorge, is a 35-mile-long slick-walled canyon carved
into the Colorado Plateau when dinosaurs roamed the Earth; Pueblo Indians first used it as a prehistoric migration route, and later, in 1871, Mormon polygamist John D. Lee somehow managed to drive an entire herd
of cattle through its narrow confines. In Paria's tributary drainage of Buckskin Gulch, modern canyoneers come to grips with the longest, narrowest
canyon known: a 12-mile-long gash in the earth hundreds of feet deep,
frequently no more than 15 feet wide.

Undoubtedly first explored by the ancient Sinagua circa A.D. 600, several
rim canyons also make outstanding adventures today, among them Sycamore
Canyon and Wet Beaver Creek. Each offers its own unique brand of
canyoneering: from pleasant day hikes through deciduous riparian communities to end-to-end treks and nonstop scrambles and swims through
canyon passageways that seem as if they'll lead you on a "Journey to the
Center of the Earth." With canyons so diverse and spectacular, there's little reason that the Grand Canyon should attract all the interest, leaving
unexplored the untold hundreds of plateau, rim, and mountain canyons,
gorges, creeks, fissures, and earth cracks that drain Arizona's high country
from the Utah border south through the Mogollon Rim and all the way
to Old Mexico.

High Adventure

In "The Mountains of Arizona," Weldon F. Heald wrote: "Although it's
true that all the highest summits may be reached by simply walking uphill, there is no region in the country which offers a greater variety of
rock climbings, canyon crawling, acrobatic escalades, and hardware adventures. In fact, to climb all of Arizona's cliffs, towers, buttes, spires, and
mesas would take a Methuselan mountaineer centuries to accomplish."

Arizona peak bagger extraordinaire Doug Kasian recently completed
a 4-year odyssey to climb the highest points of all of Arizona's mountain
ranges, from the lower Sonoran Desert to alpine tundra. But before he

could do so, he had to compile an accurate, comprehensive list, which, so far as is known, had not been done before . . . and that alone was a Methuselan undertaking. The geologist-turned-full-time climber meticulously scoured all of Arizona's eighteen-hundred-odd U.S. Geological Survey (USGS) topographical maps for each and every named mountain range; single mountains did not qualify; mountain ranges not entirely located within Arizona did. In fact, nine separate ranges crossed the border into Mexico, Nevada, Utah, or New Mexico; Kasian included those ranges on his list, and then set out to climb the high points on each side of the border.

Kasian journeyed from jagged desert ranges like the 2,764-foot-high Tinajas Altas on the U.S.-Mexico border to sky islands like the 9,759-foot-high Chiricahua Mountains once roamed by Geronimo, and from remote plateau ranges like the 8029-foot-high Uinkaret Mountains first climbed by Major Powell to popular highland ranges like the 7,903-foot-high Mazatzal Mountains poised below the Mogollon Rim. Some, like the 1,794-foot-high Bryan Mountains, were so isolated in the Cabeza Prieta National Wildlife Refuge that Kasian pedaled a mountain bike through 15 miles of hot sand just to reach their base with enough water to actually climb to their high points and make it back to his truck. On the other hand, ranges like the Pinal, the Sierra Ancha, the Salt River, the Seven Mile, and the Black Jack were so accessible by vehicle that Kasian managed to climb all five (a total of 6,820 vertical feet) in a single 24-hour push.

That the tenacious, Canadian-born mountaineer actually accomplished his epic adventure isn't nearly as amazing as the fact that, outside of Phoenix's crowded Squaw Peak, Kasian only met nine other hikers during the 162 days he spent climbing. This would be easier to understand had Kasian's climbs been monstrous, week-long ascents involving spools of ropes and all the jungle gym equipment one associates with serious rock or alpine climbing. But Kasian did almost all of Arizona's high points as day climbs! That fact underscores the accessibility of Arizona's mountains for the average adventure traveler.

Nor do you have to be a rock climber to climb nearly all of Arizona's highest summits. Plateau ranges like the San Francsico Peaks, for instance, are enticing day hikes requiring no special gear. The site of Arizona's most popular "high-altitude" climb, the San Francisco Mountains have long been revered as sacred by the Navajo, Hopi, and Havasupai Indians; there's little doubt that Arizona's Indians, possibly the ancient Sinagua or Anasazi, climbed them during sacred pilgrimages long before the Spaniards named them after Saint Francis of Assisi in 1629. The first recorded winter ascent of the San Franciscos' Humphreys Peak was made on February 12,

1912, during an all-night climb by pioneer Arizonans Lilo Perrin and Milton Farnsworth. And San Francisco Peaks is not the only plateau range worth exploring. Others, like the 9,407-foot-high Carrizo Mountains and the 9,466-foot-high Lukachukai Mountains in the Four Corners region (where Arizona, Utah, Colorado, and New Mexico meet) beg to be climbed. So do the Uinkaret Mountains on the Arizona Strip, first climbed by Major Powell on September 22, 1870. Nor are the San Francisco Mountains the only sacred summits revered by Arizona's Indians. Located in the forested highlands of eastern Arizona, 11,403-foot-high Mount Baldy is the high point of the White Mountains and forms the headwaters of the Little Colorado River, which drains into the Grand Canyon more than 200 miles downstream. To the White Mountain Apaches, it is *dzil ligai* (white mountain); the last quarter-mile below its summit is off-limits to non-Indians because traditional Apaches still make sacred pilgrimages up Arizona's fourth highest summit. But there are plenty of other highland ranges to explore. If you feel like kicking back, for example, try the Bradshaw Mountains. You can virtually drive to their 7,979-foot high point of Mount Union via a car tour off the historic Senator road. (See entry for Senator Road.) Or you can hike any of a number of trails to reach the northern 7,903-foot-high point of the Mazatzal (mäz-at-säl) Mountains, perhaps the most mispronounced and misspelled mountain range in the state. There you can hike, scramble, or rock climb up to its 7,657-foot southern high point at Four Peaks. Nearly 50 miles end to end, the Mazatzals are the longest highland range.

Long revered by traditional Tohono O'Odham Indians (formerly called Papago) as the dwelling place of I'itoi, the 7,734-foot-high Baboquivari Mountains are the only sky island that normally requires ropes to climb; after five previous attempts, territorial climbers Dr. R. H. Forbes and Jesus Montoya made the first recorded ascent of Baboquivari's "huge obelish of granite" on July 13, 1893. Aside from Baboquivari Peak, the only Arizona mountain ranges that require roped climbing to reach thier highest summits are, according to Doug Kasian, the 2,506-foot-high Tank Mountains and the 3,300-foot-high Eagletail Mountains. In his 1923 survey, *The Lower Gila Region, Arizona,* Clyde P. Ross noted that the peak of the Eagletail Mountains "is reported to have been scaled, truly a worthwhile bit of mountain climbing." Incredibly, the Tank Mountains reportedly weren't climbed until November 20, 1989, when Doug Kasian, accompanied by senior desert peak baggers Barbara Lilly and Gordon McCloud, made what they all believed was the first ascent of Arizona's last unclimbed mountain range.

Other desert ranges among many worth climbing are the twenty-five Basin and Range mountains located in the 4,100-square-mile Barry M. Goldwater Range; the 4,877-foot-high Kofa Mountains, whose "Forbidding West Face" was reportedly first climbed in 1941; and the 25-mile-long Sierra Estrella Mountains, undoubtedly the most rugged and least explored range in Arizona. The same cannot be said of the nearby Phoenix Mountains; 2,608-foot-high Squaw Peak is the high point of this small range, also the most climbed desert range—with the most heavily hiked trail—in Arizona. According to Phoenix Parks and Recreation statistics, an average of one thousand people climb Squaw Peak each day. With numbers like that, you would think that the lowly desert crag was the only mountain in Arizona. On the contrary, it's simply the most accessible "climb" for Arizona's largest metropolitan population, and dedicated Phoenicians, who use the 1,200 vertical feet they gain during the short, mile-long trek as a stepping-stone to more challenging outings at places like the Grand Canyon, San Francisco Peaks, Mexico's volcanoes, Mount McKinley, Aconcagua, and even Mount Everest, as one real estate broker claimed.

In this brief overview of day hiking opportunities in Arizona's mountain ranges, it would be impossible to capsulize Arizona's incredible rock climbing history and opportunities (but see "Weaver's Needle" in Central Arizona's climbing section). Suffice it to say that, between the huge granite domes adorning the Santa Catalina Mountains, those comprising the historic stronghold of Cochise in the 7,500-foot-high Dragoon Mountains, and others that form Granite Dells in Prescott, there's enough hard rock in Arizona to keep you busy for the rest of your life. We won't venture into Paradise Forks at the headwaters of Sycamore Canyon Wilderness, list all the temples you can climb in the Grand Canyon or even get within earshot of the spires, faces, buttes, and mesas of Sedona's redrock country and Monument Valley. We've left out the Hualapai Wall shielding the western front of the 8,417-foot-high Hualapai Mountains, the endless procession of "magic lines" waiting to be climbed on Echo Cliffs and the Vermilion Cliffs . . . there's too much out there that hasn't even been touched.

Deserts

Only 40 percent (or 46,600 square miles) of Arizona is actually desert—and, even today, that outback remains largely unexplored and seldom traveled. That's surprising, since much of this wild desert butts up against former cow towns turned Sunbelt boomtowns. These are cities now, bustling with transplanted natives beating the drums of a new civilization. Ricocheting along coal black ribbons of glimmering asphalt from one whistle-stop destination to the next, most people don't see the inextricable link between Arizona's deserts, canyons, and mountains.

Historically, Arizona's sun-scorched Yuma, Tule, and Lechuguilla deserts comprised the ancestral lands for a small band of intrepid Indians called the Sand Papago. But this tract of lower Sonoran Desert proved too hostile even for the native Sand Papago; many believed the Sand Papago marched into extinction in the late 1800s after spending centuries eking out a hard-scrabble existence in one of the driest and most forbidding desert regions in North America. But small, scattered settlements of Sand Papago still exist today outside the Barry M. Goldwater Range. Forty-Niners, who later followed in the bold footsteps of Spanish missionary Padre Kino across El Camino del Diablo, fared even worse than the hardy Sand Papago. Historians believe that during the 1850s alone more than four hundred gold seekers died of thirst in this unforgiving corner of territorial Arizona.

Today, this same region of the lower Sonoran Desert occupies parts of Organ Pipe Cactus National Monument, the Cabeza Prieta National Wild-life Refuge, and the Barry M. Goldwater Range, and you can explore it on foot or from the saddle of your pickup truck. You can drive El Camino del Diablo, which crosses each of these areas; trek up Organ Pipe's loftiest summits, or walk about anywhere that experience and common sense dic-tate in this vast region (with certain limited restrictions imposed by each managing agency).

In the southeast corner of Arizona, on the other hand, you can explore the Chihuahuan Desert, which many believe was first crossed by Fray Marcos de Niza in 1539. The car tour along the modern Couts Trail crosses this tongue of Chihuahuan Desert, which was also traversed by the 1852 Boundary Survey when expedition members tried to ride down two Sonoran grizzly bears on horseback. Or you can explore on foot the canyons of the Galiuro Wilderness near the northern fringe of this high desert.

When Charles F. Lummis crossed northern Arizona during his epic cross-country walk in 1885, he traversed a sliver of the Great Basin Desert that pokes its way south out of Utah and forms, among other natural features, El Desierto Pintado, "the Painted Desert." Lummis later described this small desert as "the most enchanted wood-pile he ever walked on." Today, it's still possible to day hike this charming desert, which now forms Petrified Forest National Park.

The best way to explore the Mojave Desert where it laps over the western border of Arizona is by canoe; Quechan and Mojave Indians used reed rafts to float the Colorado River that Spaniard Capt. Melchior Diaz first called the Rio del Tizon, "firebrand river," in 1541. The Havasu National Wildlife Refuge protects Topock Gorge, the most spectacular remnant of this prehistoric waterway, which some also like to call "Arizona's Everglades." No matter where you go in Arizona's deserts, though, you usually come back to the Sonoran Desert—simply because it's the state's largest. There are so many ways to explore the far reaches of it—from rock climbing the free-standing feathers of the Eagletail Mountains to trekking the Sierra Estrella crest to day hiking Palm Canyon in the Kofa Mountains. Like Arizona's mountains and canyons, the rhythms of the ancient desert still beckon the adventuresome beyond the neon-lit fringes of modern Arizona.

How To Use This Book

The tours in *Adventuring in Arizona* have been divided into southern, central, and northern Arizona. Each section is further divided by the means of exploration:

• **Car tours.** Most follow dirt roads and can be driven in a stout two-wheel-drive vehicle.

• **River expeditions.** Both flatwater canoe trips that you can embark on with your own party and 1- to 2-week whitewater river expeditions that you may prefer to do with a reputable commercial outfitter.

• **Canyoneering.** From day hikes in Arizona's gentlest canyons to week-long treks.

• **Climbing.** Generally those historic mountain summits that can be reached with rudimentary climbing skills, though several more demanding climbs have been salted in for veteran rock climbers.

• **Trekking.** Day hikes and extended peak ascents and traverses of Arizona's trailless mountain ranges.

Something for Everybody

If you're a dedicated armchair adventurer, this book is written with you in mind: Read about what Arizona's earliest travelers experienced. Then, if you're tempted to embark on, say, a day hike along one of those routes, this book will tell you how. As Doug Kasian has proven, with the dilemma of access now solved by modern transportation and good orientation skills, you can experience much of Arizona—and most of the adventures described in this book—by day hiking. On the other hand, if you're a veteran backcountry traveler, this book will show you how to explore the most exciting and challenging historic routes known today. For example, if a 60-mile-long canyon trek is described, *Adventuring in Arizona* will provide you with the resources to (1) read about what the earliest travelers experienced, (2) day hike a mile of it, or (3) explore it for a week. You decide how much of each adventure you want to bite off based on your personal desires, experience, level of fitness, and time.

Arizona's Top Adventures

If I were forced to pick the top ten adventures in Arizona—as my editor assures me I am—I would have difficulty complying, because our perceptions change with each environment we explore. However, a handful of adventures come immediately to mind: rafting the Grand Canyon by paddleboat; hiking Buckskin Gulch; walking through the desert—any desert—on a moonlit night when the buzzworms (rattlesnakes) are hibernating; climbing Baboquivari Peak; driving out to Toroweap Overlook. . . . But that list changes month to month, and season to season. That's why I have featured three dozen wildly diverse, historical adventures. It's an arbitrary number, to be sure, but it comes closer to representing what adventuring in Arizona once was—and still is.

Come explore it through these pages, and if you have a mind to emulate Arizona's earliest travelers, we'll show you how.

Southern Arizona

Car Tours

El Camino del Diablo

The Devil's Highway, Ajo to Wellton via the Yuma Wagon Road and the ancient El Camino: car tour, with notes on trekking

Landform

Included on the National Register of Historic Places, the 108-mile-long leg of El Camino del Diablo, described here, traverses the vast, uninhabited corner of southwestern Arizona that comprises Organ Pipe Cactus National Monument, the Cabeza Prieta National Wildlife Refuge, and the Barry M. Goldwater Range. Bordered on the south by Mexico's El Gran Desierto, on the west by the Lower Colorado River, on the north by the Gila River, and on the east by the sprawling desert lands of the Tohono O'Odham (formerly called the Papago Indians), this 4,100-square-mile despoblado forms what some justifiably believe is the heart of the Sonoran Desert and " . . . one of America's and Mexico's last frontiers." Threading two dozen seldom-explored Basin and Range–type mountain ranges, El Camino del Diablo generally avoided these Northwest-trending sierra- and mesa-type mountains and traversed the broad intervening valleys and deserts in between. The few spur trails that branched off the main east-west leg of El Camino and penetrated these rugged mountains made use of the route's few dependable water sources. Except for two key springs on opposite ends of El Camino del Diablo, however, rain catchments, called tinajas, found in the steep drainages of several prominent ranges provided the only water for the Sand Papago and, later, other survivors. Most years, however, those life-saving tinajas could be counted on one hand instead of two; consequently, much of El Camino's "colorful" history concerns unwitting players who depended on two hands when they were only dealt one.

Historical Overview

In more than 450 years of recorded travel along El Camino del Diablo, no writer described the hazards of following this infamous desert track better than Capt. D. D. Gaillard, a member of the International Boundary Commission that surveyed the U.S.-Mexico border west of the Rio Grande between 1891 and 1896; Gaillard wrote an account of his adventure, for an 1896 issue of *Cosmopolitan*, called "The Perils and Wonders of a True Desert." But you have to go back to the original Report of the Boundary Commission to find his famous passage intact: "It is hard to imagine a more desolate or depressing ride. Mile after mile the journey stretches through this land of 'silence, solitude, and sunshine,' with little to distract the eye from the awful surrounding dreariness and desolation except the bleeching skeletons of horses and the painfully frequent crosses which mark the graves of those who perished of thirst."

In those days, you didn't follow El Camino del Diablo because you wanted to take in the scenery; most people took it because it was the shortest route across southern Arizona to California and because they thought it safe from attack by hostile Indians. Records show, however, that parties using El Camino were raided by both the Sand Papago and Mexican contrabandistas, as well as by Apaches, who normally worked the more commonly traveled route along the Gila River to the north. Compound those threats with the hazards of trying to cross a virtually waterless desert and you had the makings of a life-or-death adventure.

Melchior Diaz made the first recorded traverse of El Camino del Diablo in the winter of 1540. A Spanish soldier, Diaz can also lay claim to one of the most bizarre deaths on El Camino to date: "While on horseback Diaz had thrown his lance at a dog that was bothering some sheep. The lance stuck in the ground and his horse ran over it. The butt end pierced Diaz in the lower abdomen."

Archaeological evidence found at Tule Tanks, Cabeza Prieta Tanks, and Tinajas Altas—three principal waterholes along El Camino—indicates that

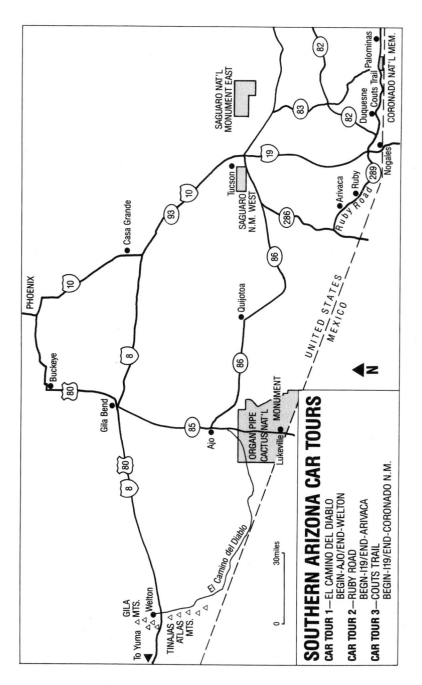

SOUTHERN ARIZONA CAR TOURS

CAR TOUR 1—EL CAMINO DEL DIABLO
BEGIN-AJO/END-WELTON

CAR TOUR 2—RUBY ROAD
BEGN-I19/END-ARIVACA

CAR TOUR 3—COUTS TRAIL
BEGIN-I19/END-CORONADO N.M.

the Areneños, or Sand Papago, first used the route Diaz was following to traverse this desert long before it earned its reputation as the Devil's Highway. The Piman-speaking Sand Papago roamed much of the desolate region surrounding El Camino del Diablo in an unending quest for food. But even in the best of times, it is believed that this austere desert was home to no more than 150 Sand Papago. One of the only eyewitness accounts of the Sand Papago and their spartan, nomadic existence comes from Juan Mateo Manje, who camped at Tinajas Altas with Padre Eusebio Kino in 1699. In *Rim of Christendom,* Kino historian H. E. Bolton wrote, "Here Manje counted 'thirty naked and poverty stricken Indians who lived solely on roots, lizards and other wild foods,' a testimony to the harsh life the Sand Papago faced in the northern corner of what the Spaniards then called Pimeria Alta."

Despite his hardships, however, Father Kino, popularly known as the Padre on Horseback, seemed to thrive where others perished, making many trips without incident along the Devil's Highway between 1698 and 1701. Kino wasn't the only Spanish padre who mastered an inferno that would soon become the killing field for less experienced desert travelers; in August 1779, Fray Francisco Garces made the first recorded traverse of El Camino in the summertime, when air temperatures undoubtedly pushed 120 degrees Fahrenheit and when ground temperatures could melt the soles off his shoes. Like Kino, Garces traveled the "path of the devil" in quest of souls, not gold.

The same could not be said of the thousands of Forty-Niners who later struggled along this path en route to the California goldfields. Historians believe that more than four hundred gold seekers—many Mexican nationals—died of thirst in this unforgiving corner of territorial Arizona during the 1850s alone.

Surveyors from the Texas Western Railroad and the International Boundary Commission traveled El Camino during the 1850s and 1860s with greater success than did the Forty-Niners, and at the turn of the century man first visited this desert to study its natural resources. Anthropologists like William J. McGee came to study meteorology, but McGee's most significant contribution to science may have been his classic paper on the ordeal of prospector Pablo Valencia, "Desert Thirst as a Disease." During one 5-year period, several other noted naturalists visited the region and wrote books that remain invaluable guides today: William T. Hornaday wrote about the 1907 expedition to map the neighboring Pinacate region in *Campfires on Desert and Lava;* anthropologist Carl Lumholtz penned *New Trails in Mexico* after his 1910 visit to collect geographic information, which he also used in his outstanding map on the region; hunter and conservationist Charles Sheldon, the best writer of the lot, wrote *The Wilderness of Desert Bighorns and Seri Indians*; and geologist Kirk Bryan, who in 1917 traveled much of the southwestern Arizona desert, including El Camino del Diablo, produced the single most important source for desert travelers, *The Papago Country, Arizona: A Geographic, Geologic, and Hydrologic Reconnaissance, With a Guide to Desert Watering Places*.

Not until 78-year-old Ralph Pumpelly returned to the scene in 1915 did man travel El Camino del Diablo for what might be called recreational reasons; wrote Pumpelly: "In the shadow of the loss of wife and mother, we sought the healing influence of the desert. For my children this journey was a pilgrimage to the scenes of my early adventures." Pumpelly's early adventures had been across El Camino del Diablo by horseback in midsummer as part of his world tour for his book *Across America and Asia*. Accompanied by his grown children in 1915, the retired Harvard professor made the first traverse of El Camino del Diablo by automobile. The title of a magazine account later written by Harold O. Weight sums up Pumpelly's adventures during that spring Model T expedition: "Tin Lizzies and Iron Men."

If you want to explore El Camino and you're not looking for a near-death experience, use a dependable four-wheel-drive vehicle and go in the winter, as Captain Gaillard suggested: "In the winter . . . the desert is at its best; the air then is clear and crisp, invigorating and stimulating. . . . The nights are perfect and the stars shine with a dazzling brilliancy peculiar to the desert." If you'd rather emulate Padre Kino and Fray Garces, see Notes on Trekking, following the El Camino del Diablo Road Log.

Directions

From Gila Bend, drive south on Highway 85 42 miles to the Cabeza Prieta National Wildlife Refuge in Ajo. From the Refuge headquarters, continue south on Highway 85 through Ajo 4 miles to the Darby Wells Road. Turn right (west) and begin tour.

Road Log

Yuma Wagon Road. From Highway 85 to Las Playas 50 miles southwest you will follow the historic leg of El Camino del Diablo. Travelers used this leg of El Camino, also known as the Jaeger Wagon Road for freighter Louis F. Jaeger, as early as 1854 between the port of Yuma on the Lower Colorado River and the new mines in Ajo. The ancient El

During the 50th Anniversary celebration of the Cabeza Prieta National Wildlife Refuge, historians and history buffs portrayed many of the Devil's Highway's early adventurers. Photo by John Annerino.

Camino del Diablo parallels the U.S.-Mexico border most of the way from Sonoita, Mexico, to Yuma, and at the time, anyone traveling via Ajo could cut off 40 miles of hard desert by using the Yuma Wagon Road.

Mile 0 to 2. Highway 85 to Darby Wells. Before Pumpelly's Model T expedition puttered down this stretch of El Camino in March 1915, its members laid over in Ajo until they could load up with enough gas to reach Yuma. While there, the enterprising Pumpelly bought shares in the New Cornelia Copper Mine, which he "later sold at a profit that more than twice paid for his trip." Unfortunately, you won't get that opportunity today. The price fell out of the world copper market in the early 1980s and the historic Ajo mines closed in a storm of violence and protest, turning the once-bustling mining community into a near ghost town overnight. Vacationing snowbirds who normally roost in nearby Organ Pipe Cactus National Monument and Rocky Point, Mexico, however, have begun buying up scores of quaint homes dumped on the local housing market at bargain prices as hundreds of Ajo miners and their families have been forced to fold up their tents and fade into the night. Only time will tell what that will mean for a historic mining community once populated by generations of closely knit Hispanic families.

Mile 2 to 3. Darby Wells to Locomotive Rock. Beyond Darby Wells, you'll contour the northwest flanks of 3,008-foot Black Mountain, a lone, sprawling mountain covered with heaps of volcanic rubble. At Mile 3 you'll reach the turnoff to Locomotive Rock, which Kirk Bryan described as "a hill with fantastic pinnacles and boulders said to look like a locomotive."

Mile 12.7 to 13.7. Organ Pipe Cactus National Monument Boundary to Cuerda de Lena Wash. A mile south of "ORPI's" northern boundary, you'll cross the main stem of Cuerda de Lena, which means "cord of wood." The story is that Mexican woodcutters who harvested wood nearby to stoke the smelters at the New Cornelia Copper Mine named the wash at the turn of the century.

Mile 14.8, BM 1,487 feet. Better known as Growler Pass, this low desert pass between the Growler Mountains and the Bates Mountains is the first of four that El Camino crosses.

Mile 16.9, Bates Well. A National Monument sign at Bates Well reads, in part, "The development of water made Bates Well a 'place'—worthy of a name on a map—and a place with a story to tell." You can read some of those tales when you get there: of the gunfights; of the vital role Bates Well played for those traveling the Yuma Wagon Road; and of rancher Henry Gray, who, until his death in 1976, maintained his right to run cattle where the National Park would someday count visitors.

But the real stories are behind the signs, and one hot, suffocatingly humid August day in 1988, ol' Ray Camper was telling them. Camper and his sister had worked as volunteer caretakers of the Gray homestead for Organ Pipe Cactus National Monument since 1976, and during those 12 years, Ray had seen a wider diversity of desert wildlife than you'll see in most Arizona zoos today. He reported he'd seen as many as fourteen deer at one time, an uncommon occurrence in this parched desert. There was a bobcat once, more javelina than he can remember, and, strangest of all, a white wolf eating out of the garbage can behind his trailer. Ray called it a "fish wolf" for reasons he didn't explain, and said he tried to make friends with it to no avail. There was another wolf, a Mexican lobo, he'd seen at Bonita Well just this side of the U.S.-Mexico border, and a jaguar he caught prowling near Growler Wash, which he described as having "a thick neck and strong, stout legs."

The area of many of Ray Camper's sightings falls within the peripheral habitat of the Sonoran pronghorn antelope, which roams much of the El Camino region and is believed to number no more than two hundred animals on both sides of the U.S.-Mexico border. Biologists still aren't certain if the endangered Sonoran pronghorn needs to drink water in order to survive or if it processes enough moisture from the browse and forbes they eat. When Ray heard of the $2,500 reward rumored to be offered by the Game and Fish people for a photo of a Sonoran pronghorn drinking water, his eyes rolled back in his head as he related sighting three Sonoran pronghorns drinking water from the trough behind his trailer.

In the next breath, though, Ray Camper talks of other riches: the two 5-gallon copper washbasins bulging with silver and gold coins thought to be buried within sight of Gray's house next door to Ray's trailer; the 5-gallon water jug Ray leaves out for fearless, hard-working Mexican nationals who trek across Organ Pipe's deadly desert midsummer for the storied treasures awaiting them in El Norte; and the drug smugglers who use Quitobaquito Springs and Organ Pipe's border roads, including the Yuma Wagon Road in front of Bates Well, to run loads of dope across the Tohono O'Odham lands into Phoenix. When I hear his stories, I realize that this wily, half-deaf old man has fewer fears than most men half his age. Until Ray Camper's recent retirement, Bates Well was still "a place with a story to tell."

Mile 17. From Bates Well, the two-lane road you've been tooling along since Highway 85 becomes a sandy 4WD track worthy of the name Yuma Wagon Road. On the left (south), 3,197-foot-high Kino Peak rears its craggy, volcanic massif; high point of the Bates Mountains, the cross-country route up Kino Peak is a challenging all-day or overnight round-trip trek from Bates Well.

Mile 22, Growler Wash. If you haven't already, lock in your 4WD for the deep sand and trenchlike track beyond.

Mile 23.3. On the left (south), Organ Pipe's Western Boundary Jeep Trail snakes in from Quitobaquito Springs. This is also a known smuggler's route. (Refer to Border Travel Warning.)

Mile 26. The Yuma Wagon Road enters Cabeza Prieta National Wildlife Refuge and the Barry M. Goldwater Range. Once the domain of the hardy Sand Papago, the boundless desert region beyond Organ Pipe Cactus National Monument is still home to two highly endangered species: the Sonoran pronghorn antelope, believed to number no more than a hundred animals on the U.S. side of the border; and America's premiere figher jocks, who hone combat flying skills by engaging in mock battles with Harrier IIs (jets that can take off like helicopters). Now Harrier IIs and F-14s may seem like strange bedfellows for the Sonoran pronghorn, but word among some Sonoran Desert cognoscenti is that the Sonoran pronghorn would have marched into extinction long ago if this corner of the Gadsden Purchase hadn't been isolated from the general public and maintained as bombing range since 1941.

Mile 28.8, San Cristobal Wash. Difficult to fathom in a desert that averages 0 to 5 inches of rain a year, standing water, sometimes hip deep, collects in San Cristobal Wash during heavy July–August monsoon weather. Whether you're driving or trekking, that can make a challenging obstacle – if you don't drown. (See O'Neill's Grave, Mile 44.)

Somewhere to the north lies "Lost City," the first recorded archaeological site on the Barry M. Goldwater Range. Renowned archaeologist Bernard L. Fontana conducted his own archaeological survey of Cabeza Prieta National Wildlife Refuge between November 11 and 21, 1962, and according to his report, "Lost City is a misnomer for this important Hohokam site." Hohokam are believed to have laid over at Lost City after returning from shell-gathering expeditions to the Gulf of California; they would "rough out" shell ornaments there before continuing their seasonal journeys north to the Gila River. That's approximately the same distance people traveled east to west along El Camino del Diablo — but the prehistoric Hohokam, and later the Sand Papago, followed a route that traversed this desert from north to south and had as its major obstacle Mexico's 1,700-square-mile El Gran Desierto, the driest and largest desert in North America. Most modern athletes and outdoor enthusiasts would be hard-pressed to survive a journey that once was commonplace for Native Americans.

Mile 31.3, Papago Well. One of Kirk Bryan's historic trail signs is still here in the middle of nowhere to show the way; if you're traveling by 4WD, you'll find that comforting. But if you're struggling in the footsteps of Kino, shouldering 30 to 40 pounds of water, you may find it debilitating: "Papago Well 9M. Tule Well 40M. Tinajas Altas 59M."

From Kirk Bryan's bullet-riddled milepost, two roads lead to Papago Well; give or take a few tenths, both are 9 miles long. The right fork, the original, more commonly traveled route, crosses Cholla Pass and Chinamen flat before skirting the north side of 1,974-foot Sheep Mountain. The left fork, the alternate route, is considerably rougher, slower going, and harder to follow. It crosses the Agua Dulce Mountains and Davidson Canyon before contouring the steep southern flanks of 2,000-foot Papago Mountain.

(While Bruce Lohman, David Roberson, and I were trekking El Camino del Diablo on August 23, 1988, six Sonoran pronghorns jumped out in front of us no more than 50 yards away and raced across Cholla Pass. Standing in stifling monsoon heat, awestruck, we knew we were lucky; few people get the opportunity to see wild Sonoran pronghorns, and if they do, it's usually from the air. Seeing those majestic animals bounding through the greasewood and ocotillo remains one of the lifelong payoffs for the difficulties the three of us would have to overcome in order to reach Yuma on foot 5 days later.)

Mile 40, Papago Well. Unlike Tule Tank and Tinajas Altas, Papago Well didn't exist in the days of the Forty-Niners; it was dug around the turn of the century to furnish the nearby Papago Mine with water. Anyone who traveled the ancient El Camino, or Yuma Wagon Road, before then had to make the 60- or 75-mile pull into Tule Tank — or die trying. Today, the Arizona Game and Fish Department has improved the original 235-foot-deep well as a water source for deer and Sonoran pronghorn.

Mile 44, O'Neil's Grave and O'Neil's Pass. If spearing yourself in the groin seems like a bizarre way to die on El Camino del Diablo, imagine how prospector Dave O'Neil must have felt in 1916, when he became the only known person to drown in this virtually waterless desert. One of many historic accounts suggests that O'Neil drowned after he literally fell down drunk; Kirk Bryan's more reliable account, I think, attributed the death to exposure and overexertion: "His burros wandered away from camp in a storm, and after searching for them at least a day he [O'Neil] died with his head in a mudhole."

But O'Neil's sad tale didn't end there. According to a 1939 Southwestern National Monument report, the two prospectors who originally found and buried O'Neil ran out of tobacco while on a 2-week prospecting trip in the nearby Tule Desert. Remembering they'd buried O'Neil's tobacco with him, they returned to his grave and dug it up; according to the report, one "companion would have none of it, but my friend's hard blue eyes dared me to smile when he added, 'and, lad, that tobacco chawed just as good as if it had been in my pocket all them two weeks.'" And according to an article by Robert L. Thomas in the May 2, 1975, edition of *The Arizona Republic,* O'Neil's grave was desecrated by unknown parties: "O'Neil's bones and parts of his clothing—which survived the years of his internment because of the exceedingly dry climate—were found scattered beside the open grave."

Mile 45 to 49. West of O'Neil's Grave, things started getting real interesting for Pumpelly's 1915 Model T expedition. At the time, much of the trail was obliterated by sand, but nothing would turn Pumpelly back. In fact, he'd prepared for just such an emergency by carting along two pieces of chicken wire 30 feet long and 18 inches wide; in "Tin Lizzies and Iron Men," Harold O. Weight wrote: "When we got stuck, we just laid them out in front of the wheels and all hands would push and we'd get one car after another over." Today, this section remains a deep, sandy track; you would do well to carry at least a shovel and extra water.

The Ancient El Camino

Mile 49, Las Playas. The most formidable section of the ancient El Camino del Diablo was the 60-mile stretch of scorched desert between Agua Salada south of the border and Tule Tank to the north. Many early travelers knew Las Playas would hold water after heavy rains, and because this ephemeral water source offered them that hope, according to Kirk Bryan, "All the ancient routes from Sonoita to Yuma came through Las Playas."

During his July 1861 crossing of El Camino, Pumpelly and five companions tried to outride a dozen "cutthroats" they'd been told were trying to waylay them in Old Mexico. Pumpelly and his outfit fled north across the border, where he reported temperatures of 118–126 degrees Fahrenheit in the shade and 160 degrees in direct sunlight. According to Pumpelly, there was little hope of making the 30-hour ride to the Gila River alive unless they found water en route. While they were camped dry somewhere on the edge of Las Playas, it stormed during the night. Of that life-saving rain, Pumpelly wrote: "A broad sheet of water, only a few inches deep, covered the playa for miles before us, and banished from our minds all fear of suffering."

Mile 50, Pinta Sands and the Pinacate Lava Flow. Whether or not Las Playas held water often determined the fate of travelers trying to cross the Pinta Sands and Pinacate Lava flow in order to reach Tule Tank. Although not nearly as pronounced a sand sea as the neighboring Mohawk Sand Dunes, the drifting dunes of Pinta Sands, which encircle and overlap the brittle black crust of the Pinacate Lava Flow, produced yet another formidable obstacle for early travelers.

Mile 53.4, Nameers Grave. Nameer was yet another pilgrim who choked on canteen dust while trying to cross the relentless grind of the Pinta Sands and Pinacate Lava Flow. His headstone sits out in the middle of the lava flow like some strange intaglio and in bold letters reads: "1871, NAMEER." Whoever Nameer was, he was not alone. Fifty yards south of his headstone, at the base of a small rise, you can make out the 3-foot-long stone alignments of others who may have been in his party: There's an F, what appears to be an S, and an E-, or BT, overgrown with brush . . . and this collection of headstones is only the beginning, for the trail beyond is littered with graves.

Mile 65, Gravestone Pass. You can see three or four other graves near here if you get out of your vehicle and look around.

Mile 67.5, Stone Cross Grave.

Mile 69.3, BM 1,103 feet. The left fork is the route of the ancient El Camino, which, until Tule Well was dug, bee-lined straight for Tule Tank. Continue straight ahead to Tule Well, not to be confused with the tinaja called Tule Tank.

Mile 71.4, Tule Well. Like Papago Well, Tule Well was not a reality during the gold rush of the 1850s; anybody traveling El Camino at the time had to struggle another 3 miles down the trail to Tule Tank. According to Kirk Bryan, Tule Well was dug sometime before the Boundary Survey of 1893 arrived; the Boundary Survey reported that an enterprising Mexican who wanted to sell water to travelers on El Camino dug it. According to yet another account, this idea didn't sit well with folks about to die of dehydration, and the man was promptly shot dead.

Whether that incident can be substantiated is uncertain, but one fact remains. The foul-tasting, sulfur-laden water at Tule Well is legendary. Pumpelly wrote of it after his 1915 Model T expedition when a friend asked how he liked the Tule Well water.

"'Not much,'" Pumpelly answered.

"'Naturally,'" the friend said, "'for we found and left a man in it two years ago.'"

A former Border Patrol station, modern Tule Well now consists of a windmill made in Chicago, a 10,000-gallon water tank that reeks of rotten eggs, a one-room shack, and a stone Boy Scout memorial.

Mile 73.9, Tule Tank turnoff. Located in a narrow canyon near the base of the Tule Mountains, Tule Tank lacks the modern amenities of Tule Well, but it's a far more esthetic place to crawl out of the noon day heat than Tule Well. First reported by archaeologist Malcolm Rodgers, Tule Tank was a prehistoric Sand Papago encampment that later became a pivotal water stop for other thirst-ravaged travelers on El Camino. Unlike the deep tinajas in the region, however, Tule Tank is a shallow rock catchment, often filled with sand, and it didn't always slake the thirst of weary pilgrims. Those who pulled out handfuls of damp sand when they'd expected cool, spring-fed mountain water were forced to struggle toward Tinajas Altas another 17 miles down the trail. Needless to say, many, many did not make it.

Mile 79.2. The ancient El Camino branches off to left; continue straight.

Mile 80. El Camino crosses the eastern edge of an unnamed lava flow fanning out from the base of the unmistakable black-and-white landmark of 2,107-foot Tordillo Mountain.

Mile 80.8, Figure-of-8 turnoff. Park your vehicle and walk half a mile south of the trail to the strangest grave on El Camino. According to Capt. D. D. Gaillard's "Perils and Wonders of the True Desert," this 30-foot circle of rocks marked one of the "most pathetic cases of death from thirst" on the entire El Camino del Diablo. Gaillard wrote of a Mexican family struggling to make the last 9 miles into Tinajas Altas when its team of horses gave out. While unloading the wagon, the water container, a glass demijohn, fell and broke, sealing the fate of the entire family.

Standing at this grim headstone, you can see an arrow-straight line of rocks within this stone circle pointing in the general direction of Tinajas Altas. However, if you were new to desert travel, as many people traveling El Camino were, this arrow could have been your death knell. It points toward a steep granite drainage where, characteristically, tinajas should be found. But the life-saving waters of Tinajas Altas are in the first canyon due north of this precipitous canyon.

Mile 85.4. El Camino exits the Cabeza Prieta National Wildlife Refuge and enters the Western Half of the Barry M. Goldwater Range; called 2301 West, this section of the bombing range is administered by the Marine Corps Air Station, Yuma. From this point in the Lechuguilla Desert, the historic El Camino del Diablo is maintained as a modern Border Patrol "drag road" in order to track undocumented workers headed north to work in the United States. The Border Patrol's policy of apprehending honest men who struggle across this merciless desert in order to feed their families unsettles some people, including me, but to their credit, a small group of dedicated Border Patrol trackers based out of Tacna and Yuma have saved the lives of well over two hundred people who otherwise wouldn't have made it out of this desert alive. . . . And if you ever find yourself in deep trouble on the Devil's Highway, you'll pray there's a good Border Patrol tracker cutting your sign, because chances are your signal mirror will look like another silver tow target to the fighter jocks screaming overhead.

During his 1861 crossing of El Camino, Pumpelly saw the dark humor awaiting him that might have turned back a less stalwart desert traveler on this stretch. Envision this: It's the middle of July, a bright moon is beaming across the sweeping Lechuguilla Desert, and Pumpelly's expedition members have just escaped with their lives at Las Playas. As they approach Tinajas Altas, they suddenly find themselves riding down a "long avenue between rows of mummified cattle, horses, and sheep. . . . This weird avenue had been made by some travelers with a sense of humor, and with a fertile imagination which had not been deadened by thirst."

Mile 89.2. Left fork to Tinajas Altas.

Mile 91.1, Tinajas Altas. El Camino del Diablo may be the most infamous desert track in the Southwest, but Tinajas Altas is the most famous desert waterhole in the United States. Period. Through the millennia, desperate men have struggled on hands and knees to reach what remains to this day the most reliable natural water source found anywhere on the Barry M. Goldwater Range. But Tinajas Altas, or "high tanks," isn't a single waterhole; it's a series of huge granite cups stacked atop one another in a natural spillway. According to El Camino historian, writer, and adventurer Bill Broyles' exhaustive study "Fifty Years of Water Management in the Cabeza Prieta," Tinajas Altas consists of ten rock tanks, not seven as is most frequently reported; when brim full, Broyles estimates, these rock tanks can hold up to 21,491 gallons of water! Enough water to slake any man's thirst, you'd think – but they haven't always held that much. The lowest, most accessible pools have always been the first to evaporate in the searing summer heat, and anybody who found those tanks dry after struggling to reach Tinajas Altas had to climb up slick, steep granite to reach the "high tanks." Stories have been told of men wearing their fingers to the bones trying to make the precipitous climb, and it's anybody's guess how many people actually died trying to climb what would probably be rated an easy 5.3 by most well-hydrated rock climbers today. As late as 1917, Kirk Bryan reported, "The number of people who are supposed to have perished at this watering place is doubtless an exaggeration, but at least 65 graves can now be counted." But whether the number of deaths is closer to two thousand, as Pumpelly estimated, or four hundred, as the International Boundary Commission reported, one thing is certain: The death toll still is, as the Boundary Commission originally suggested, "a record probably without parallel in North America."

Nor has El Camino's death toll abated. Once vital to the Sand Papago, Tinajas Altas today remains an important water source for desert bighorn sheep. Ironically, no evidence or eyewitness accounts suggest that Mexican nationals use this historic waterhole on their heroic treks to reach Interstate 8 from this vicinity. Tragically, a modern death toll, estimated to be anywhere from seventy to three hundred people in the last decade, now adds to the long desperate history of travel along El Camino del Diablo.

Reverse Fork.   From Tinajas Altas back to El Camino del Diablo.

Mile 92.   Resume traveling north on El Camino along the base of the Tinajas Altas Mountains. Now comprising the 79,000-acre Tinajas Altas State Natural Area, this jagged desert sierra is considered a premiere example of a Basin and Range–type mountain range and has long been considered as a possible western addition to the Cabeza Prieta National Wildlife Refuge.

Mile 93.   Anza cutoff on the left (west). Turn off to Tinajas Altas Pass. Most travelers who made it to Tinajas Altas and pushed on to Yuma turned due north from Tinajas Altas and headed for the Gila River in the vicinity of modern-day Wellton; in doing so, they followed a well-trod route along the east slope of the Tinajas Altas and Gila Mountain ranges. But in 1774, Juan Bautista de Anza pioneered a bold new route through Tinajas Altas Pass across the waterless Yuma Desert. The most comprehensive, and perhaps important, single volume on this modern despoblado is Luke Air Force Base's *Natural Resources Management Plan;* according to this detailed study, de Anza's "party consisted of Fathers Garces and Juan Diaz, a guide and courier named Valdes, 20 volunteer soldiers, a runaway mission Indian, a Piman interpreter, a carpenter, five muleteers, and two of Anza's personal servants. Additionally, there was a pack train of 35 mule-loads and 65 cattle."

Foreshadowing the multifaceted demands currently placed on what some might like to see removed from military tenure and protected along the lines of a Despoblado National Park, the *Natural Resources Management Plan* added, "Although de Anza's party was larger than most that traveled the Camino, many expeditions used animals that relied on the grass and water encountered along the route. The natural resources of this arid region could not long survive heavy use of this sort, especially as most of the use was concentrated near the few well-known watering places." Currently you must obtain a special permit from the Marine Corps Air Station, Yuma, to retrace de Anza's route across the Davis Plain, because it parallels sensitive military testing areas. It has been nominated as the Juan Bautista de Anza Historic Trail.

Mile 93 to 100.   From Tinajas Altas Pass turnoff, continue north across the Lechuguilla Desert, which forms the broad desert valley between the Tinajas Altas and Gila Mountains, west, and the Copper Mountains and Baker Peaks, east. Although the desert seems to be vapid, offering nothing to the casual visitor, many hidden areas await further exploration.

Mile 100.   El Camino del Diablo sign post, left.

Mile 104.7.   Gate (sometimes locked). Get current instructions with your permit from Cabeza Prieta National Wildlife Refuge.

Mile 106.2.   Mohawk Canal.

Mile 107.1.   Interstate 8.

Mile 107.8. Southern Pacific Railroad Tracks and road to Wellton and then to Yuma. At Yuma, Pumpelly described the end of the first recorded traverse of El Camino del Diablo by automobile: "We made a sorry looking procession into a large and comfortable hotel. The sun had burned the skin off the back of my hands. The girls hid, behind thick veils. . . . We had left the golden desert, its painted mountains, its mysteries and dangers, but we already felt the call to return."

Travel Notes

•**Primary access.** Ajo and Wellton.

•**Average elevation.** 250 to 500 feet above sea level.

•**Mileage.** 107.8 miles, one way.

•**Traveling time.** 1½–2 days.

•**Suggested campsite.** Tule Well.

•**Water sources.** Carry your own water. The water from these sparse sources must be treated, but more importantly, Sonoran pronghorn (some believe), Desert bighorn, and other wildlife depend on it year-round.

Permanent water: Bates Well (pump needs to be turned on by caretaker); Papago Well (windmill needs to be unlocked by Game and Fish); Tule Well (tastes like rotten eggs).

Emergency water: Tule Tank and Tinajas Altas (important water sources for desert bighorn, so avoid if possible. Purify in emergency).

Seasonal/marginal water: Cuerda de Lena, San Cristobal Wash, Las Playas.

•**Emergencies.** When you get your permit from the Cabeza Prieta National Wildlife Refuge, you'll be required to fill out a detailed itinerary; if you don't deviate from it and you're late, the Marine's Rescue-1 helicopter or a Border Patrol tracker will probably reach you before Refuge personnel do.

•**What to bring.** In addition to 2 to 3 gallons of water per person per day and an emergency car survival kit, you might bring some of the things Pumpelly thought to include in 1918: "Our blankets were in canvas rolls lashed to the automobile hoods. Tins of gasoline, boxes of food and cooking utensils were strapped to the running boards, and canvas bags of water

hung on the sides of the cars. The food was bacon, cheese, bread, mar-
malade, canned beans, tea and sugar. And there was a frying pan, wooden
plates to be burned, and cups." And don't forget a roll of chicken wire.

•**Seasons.** . November through mid-April. Unless you're an experienced
and fit desert traveler, stay out of this desert between the end of April
and October.

•**Maps.** Ajo, Bates Well, Agua Dulce Mountains, Cabeza Prieta Peak,
Tule Mountain, O'Neil Hills, Isla Pinta, Sierra Arrida, Tinajas Altas, and
Wellton Hills (15-minute quadrangles).

•**Nearest supply points.** Ajo, Wellton, Tacna, Yuma.

•**Managing agencies.** Organ Pipe Cactus National Monument, Cabeza
Prieta National Wildlife Refuge, Luke Air Force Base, Marine Corps Air
Station, and Bureau of Land Management.

•**Backcountry information.** Permit and Military Hold Harmless agree-
ment required; contact: Cabeza Prieta National Wildlife Refuge, 1611
North Second, Ajo, AZ 85321; (602) 387-6483. (See Travel Notes for
Mohawk Sand Dunes entry for information regarding permits required
for backcountry travel.)

Off-road vehicle travel is not permitted anywhere.

Firewood is scarce and may not be collected within half a mile of El Camino
del Diablo; bring your own.

Camping is not permitted within half a mile of any waterhole.

•**Biotic communities.** Sonoran Desert scrub (lower Colorado and Arizona upland subdivisons).

Notes on Trekking

Traveling El Camino del Diablo has always been a question of math—and
endurance. Can you carry enough water to reach the next waterhole? And
what are you going to do if the waterhole is dry? Or what happens if you
go down somewhere in between those known waterholes?

The math for El Camino is simple enough: 17, 23, 31, 3, 24, and 32—
the mileages between known water sources. And the best season to make
the trek is unquestionably winter. However, as part of my ongoing field
research retracing prehistoric and historic trails in the Southwest, I was
inexplicably drawn to attempt a midsummer trek of El Camino del Di-

ablo in order to understand exactly why men like Garces fared so well where so many others perished. To make use of seasonal and ephemeral water sources between known water sources (as the Sand Papago undoubtedly had done), I specifically planned the trek to coincide with peak August monsoon weather, giving myself some marginal insurance that even the 1854 Texas Western Railroad survey hadn't had during its incredible journey along El Camino in the shadeless, searing month of June. To get as diverse and challenging a feel for El Camino del Diablo as was possible, I planned my route to link the Yuma Wagon Road, the ancient El Camino, and Juan Bautista de Anza's Route. As my departure date drew near, I learned that others had at least pondered the possibility of trekking El Camino midsummer. In the end, I joined with two men I felt were most likely to succeed and survive: the late David Roberson, a Border Patrol pilot and tracker; and Major Bruce Lohman, a Marine rescue helicopter pilot. Together, the three of us finished the trek.

From that unprecedented trek, I've compiled and included data on water requirements, because so much misinformation has been published concerning individual fluid requirements for desert travel and survival. I hope that this information will give you a practical base for gauging your own fluid requirements wherever you may travel in the desert. You should be aware of two other things in reviewing these figures. I was strongly opposed to traveling during the cooler nighttime hours, as many people advised. While walking through the desert at night for a few hours can be a wonderful experience, this was a prolonged, hot-weather endurance trek that would require key judgment calls along the way; if I disrupted my normal sleeping cycles by trying to walk at night for as many as 5 to 7 days, I knew I would further fatigue myself and cloud my judgment. Second, the profusion of aggressive sidewinders we encountered were difficult enough to see by day; they would have been all but impossible to see at night.

•Day 1, 17 Miles: Ajo to Bates Well. August 22, 1988
Water Carried: 3 gallons.
Water Consumed: 2½ gallons each.
Traveling Time: 7 hours, 6:00 to 10:40 A.M. and 12:30 to 2:40 P.M.
*Temperature: 106°F, with appalling humidity.
Permanent Water: Bates Well.
Standing Water: In washes between Highway 85 and Darby Wells, found but not used. (Numerous sand tanks, 2 to 5 gallons.)

•**Day 2, 23 Miles: Bates Well to Papago Wells. August 23**
Water Carried: 4 gallons.
Water Consumed: 3 gallons each.
Traveling Time: 9 hours, 6:00 to 11:30 A.M., 2:15 to 3:30 P.M., and
4:00 to 8:30 P.M.
Temperature: 106°F, with appalling humidity.
Permanent Water: Papago Wells.
Standing Water: San Cristobal Wash, found but not used. (Thigh deep,
100+ yards long.)

•**Day 3, 31 Miles: Papago Wells to Tule Well. August 24**
Water Carried: 5 gallons.
Water Consumed: 4 gallons each.
Traveling Time: 14 hours, 5:15 to 11:30 A.M., 3:30 to 8:00 P.M., and
9:30 P.M. to 1:00 A.M.
Temperature: 104°F, with appalling humidity.
Water Sources: Tule Well, not used.
Standing Water: On El Camino, 100 yards west of Nameer's Grave, found
but not used (approximately 3 gallons).

•**Day 4, 3 Miles: Tule Well to Tule Tank. August 25**
Water Carried: 5 gallons.
Water Consumed: 2 gallons each.
Traveling Time: 1 hour, 5:00 to 6:00 P.M.: scheduled day off.
Temperature: 106°F, with stifling humidity.
Water Sources: Tule Tank, not used.
Standing Water: none.

•**Day 5, 24 Miles: Tule Tank to Davis Plain, Via de Anza's Route
From Tinajas Altas. August 26**
Water Carried: 3 gallons from Tule Tank to Tinajas Altas; 6 gallons from
Tinajas Altas north.
Water Consumed: 5 gallons each.
Traveling Time: 9 hours and 45 minutes, 5:30 to 11:30 A.M., 5:15 to
9:00 P.M.
Temperature: 106-plus°F.
Permanent Water: Tinajas Altas.
Standing Water: None seen, though there were indications water might
be found in Coyote Wash.

• **Day 6, 32 Miles: de Anza's Route to El Camino Historical Marker.**
August 27
Water Carried: 5 gallons.
Water Consumed: 5 gallons each.
Traveling Time: 11 hours and 45 minutes, 4:50 to 11:45 A.M., 4:45 to
   9:30 P.M.
Temperature: 108-plus°F.
Permanent Water: Tinajas Altas.
Standing Water: None.
*(All temperatures based on Yuma recordings; most stretches consider-
ably hotter.)

The Ruby Road

Nogales-Arivaca Road, Coronado National Forest

Landform

The Ruby Road traverses the rugged 4,000-foot-high border country between
Nogales and Arivaca, via the southern end of the Tumacacori Mountains.
Originally thought to be one mountain range, the Tumacacori Mountains are, according to Kirk Bryan, "a complex group consisting of several
more or less independent units." East to west, those mountains—and
lowlands—include the 5,460-foot Pajarito Mountains, the 6,422-foot Atascosa Mountains, 4,183-foot Bear Valley, 5,370-foot Cobre Ridge, and
3,716-foot Arivaca Wash.

Historical Overview

In *Pumpelly's Arizona: 1860–1861*, the former Harvard professor–turned–
adventurer wrote of one night en route to Arivaca on the west end of
the Ruby Road: "To this grand landscape the brilliant light of the full moon
lent its enchanting power. . . . Not a sound, nor even a breath of air, broke
the silence of the night; and as I yielded to the influence of the scene,
I seemed to be a wanderer in dreamland." But any illusions Ralph Pumpelly had of being a "wanderer in dreamland" were dispelled long before
he ever reached the site of a grisly massacre near Arivaca. Wolves chewed
through his saddle while he lay dreaming about moon-dusted Arizona nights.
The following afternoon, a sandstorm knocked a loaded pistol to the ground.
The gun went off and the bullet tore through the thigh of its owner, a

Mr. J. Washburn; the hot ball of lead ripped around Washburn's pelvis and up his spine, where it mushroomed in his shoulder blade. The quick-thinking Pumpelly dispatched a Papago Indian to ride hell-for-leather for Tucson to fetch a doctor, while another companion, Col. Charles Debrille Poston, headed to Arivaca to get an ambulance. When the Papago returned from his 160-mile ride 2½ days later—with Washburn's horse practically dead—he brought a note telling the hapless adventurers to make an appointment: The doctor couldn't make it. Nobody knew what had happened to Col. Poston, who would later become "the father of Arizona."

Stranded somewhere in the middle of Papagueria, without provisions, Pumpelly and Washburn survived 126-degree temperatures by drinking milk that they bought from the Papago Indians. Realizing they had a seller's market, the enterprising Papagos doubled the price of milk for the luckless pair to two strings of beads per quart. When a one-man rescue team finally arrived from Arivaca 2 weeks later, the Mexican brought a note from Colonel Poston to explain his delay. Apparently the colonel and his guide had gotten lost trying to cross the Baboquivari Plain at night, and "after wandering about for three days without food or water, the guide became insane and strayed away toward the south." On the fifth day, Colonel Poston finally reached Arivaca, but he'd just about gone mad himself from the heat.

Temporarily fortified with grub and with Colonel Poston's hard-luck story, Pumpelly was still stuck in the middle of the desert with no way to safely move his wounded companion. By sheer coincidence, however, eleven Mexicans driving a team of oxen happened to be using the remote track Pumpelly was stranded on as a shortcut back to Mexico. Pumpelly quickly cut a deal, and for $5 the Mexicans agreed to take him and Washburn with them to Sáric, Sonora, where the women could fuss over Washburn's self-inflicted wounds. En route, however, the party literally became so deranged from hunger and lack of tobacco that Pumpelly was forced to stand guard over the oxen with a rifle for fear the party members would eat their only form of transportation. Not only did Pumpelly manage to spare the oxen, but he convinced the rest of the party to eat cactus till a second rescuer came with provisions and roll-your-own cigarettes. Wrote Pumpelly, "Thus ended one of the most awful episodes of my journey."

He thought.

When they finally got to Sáric, Pumpelly later wrote: " . . . the sympathies of the entire female population were immediately enlisted in behalf of Mr. Washburn. . . . " But Pumpelly must have felt left out because by the time Washburn recovered from his sharp-shooting episode, Pumpelly got sick; you'd think, fortuitously because he wrote he was " . . . the patient, in turn, of every lady in the village." No doubt, that raised the ire of some local hombres, because when Pumpelly headed back to Arivaca he said " . . . the men are mostly cut-throats, and the women angels. . . . " Still a hog's breath shy of Arivaca, Pumpelly was enlisted to help bury a Papago and a couple of Americans whom Apaches had reportedly done in. Later that same day he helped bury yet another murder victim, Richmond Jones, who'd been shot in the chest, speared in the side with two lances, and had had a pitchfork driven into his back.

When Pumpelly finally rode into Arivaca, or Aribac, as it was called on Padre Kino's map of Pimeria Alta in 1695, they found that John Poston (the colonel's brother) and several Germans working at the Heintzelman mine had been murdered in their sleep. In a fit of understatement, Pumpelly wrote, "The events of the past week, added to all that had gone on before, began to tell on my nerves . . . and [we] determined to leave the country by the nearest open route."

But the "wanderer in dreamland" was about to use a route on which hundreds of others had already perished. Pumpelly and Colonel Poston fled across El Camino del Diablo where, Pumpelly wrote, it was so hot "that to touch the black barrel of a gun, exposed to the direct rays of the sun, meant a blistered hand." And guns Pumpelly would need, because word on the dusty streets of Caborca, Sonora, was that twelve desperadoes were hot on his tail . . . and who knew how many of them were jealous husbands.

Directions

From Tucson, drive 55 miles south on I-19 to Exit 12, Highway 289, Ruby Road turnoff.

Road Log

Mile 0.   From I-19, drive west on paved Highway 289. Like many border routes in Arizona, the Ruby Road is also a well-worn smuggling route. (See Border Warning in the back of the book.) On April 20, 1989, an Arivaca man hauling $778,400 of "high grade buds" was apprehended by Santa Cruz County Sheriffs in conjunction with the U.S. Forest Service. They also seized semiautomatic weapons—an indication that you shouldn't tour the popular Ruby Road at night.

Mile 3.7.   On the left side of the road is a Coronado National Forest sign: MESQUITE CONTROL PROJECT. Among its more enlightening passages, it reads: "Mesquite has little or no value but competes with grass for food and water." Generations of Arizona Indians who have thrived on mesquite would no doubt disagree, as did Buster Bailey. In Charles Bowden's passionate defense of the Santa Catalina Mountains, *Frog Mountain Blues,* old-time Tucson cattleman Buster Bailey said, "These smart people want to poison the mesquite today. They don't want'm to live. If you're going to be an Arizonian, mesquite's been one of the most valuable things in the country since the year one. The Indians made just about everything they could eat out of that."

Mile 6.3, Calabasas Picnic area. On the left.

Mile 7. You get your first good view of the blocklike massif of the 6,422-foot-high Atascosa Mountains. According to the *New Revised Velazquez Spanish and English Dictionary, atasco* means "a barrier, obstruction," which makes you wonder which route the Spanish padres took around this impressive range. Near Mile 15, you can hike 3 miles up to the fire lookout and vista atop 6,422-foot Atascosa Peak, via USFS Trail No. 100.

Mile 9.5, Pena Blanca Lake turnoff. On the right; on the left, turn-off to Whiterock Campground. (The Spanish *pena blanca* translates to "white rock.")

According to scholar John P. Wilson, author of *Islands in the Desert: A History of the Uplands of Southeast Arizona,* the Pena Blanca Lake area served as a Civilian Conservation Corps (CCC) camp from 1935 to 1941, when Depression-era men were lured to the great outdoors to work on Forest Service projects such as building trails and fighting fires. But life at Camp Pena Blanca was not all biscuits and gravy; one camper was killed "when an apparent racial incident triggered a gang fight." Pena Blanca Lake itself became a reality in 1957, and now the 57-acre man-made reservoir hosts a resort and a convenience store. According to a June 4, 1989, Eyewitness News–4 television newscast by reporter Steve Daniels, eighteen people have drowned in this benign-looking lake. So beware!

Mile 10. Pavement ends and the fun begins. From this point on to Bear Valley 8 miles down USFS Road 39, the Ruby Road climbs, snakes, and contours the fluted drainages and ridges of the Atascosa Mountains much the way the backroad into Jerome does in Northern Arizona. (See entry for the Perkinsville Road.)

Mile 10.7. Castle Rock. On the left, the 300-foot-high tufa face of Castle Rock can be seen above Calabasas Canyon.

Mile 18.   Bear Valley Ranch turnoff on the left, private. As you'll see, Bear Valley is a whimsical hollow tucked away in a gentle land. Rolling hills carpeted with shaggy tufts of grama grass and dotted with Mexican blue oak form a delicate green-and-gold cyclorama west to the mouth of Sycamore Canyon. But this pastoral scene betrays Santa Cruz County's sinister past. Like much of the Southwest during the 1800s, this historic Arizona backwater suffered from ruthless attacks by renegade Apaches on the run from General Crook, and from desperadoes from both sides of the line who thought they were onto the legendary silver mine called Planchas La Plata, which reportedly consisted of "deposits of native silver, which yielded enormous revenues to the Spanish Government."

Mile 19.5.   Sycamore Canyon turnoff on the left, and USFS Road 218. Once a working cattle ranch run by former freightmen John "Yank" Bartlett and Henry "Hank" Hewitt, Hank and Yank Spring is now an undeveloped Forest Service picnic area and jumping-off spot for hikers heading down Sycamore Canyon. (See entry for Sycamore Canyon, Southern Arizona.) But it wasn't always such.

On April 28, 1886, the Bartlett Ranch was under siege by three hostile Indians. Johnny Bartlett's father had been wounded in the shoulder and a neighbor, John Shanahan, was in the throes of death; two horses were also shot. Shanahan's son, Phil, had skedaddled to warn his mother and sisters of the impending danger.

Ten-year-old Johnny and his father waited several hours for young Phil to return with his family, occasionally returning the volley of rifle fire with the three Apaches. When by nightfall they didn't show up, Johnny left for Oro Blanco. Said Johnny, "Father told me to pull off my boots and to crawl out without making a noise and to go to Oro Blanco and to tell the people that the Indians had been at the house and had wounded Mr. Shanahan." That's just what little Johnny did, and he later received an inscribed rifle from the U.S. government for his heroic midnight run.

So when you drive west from Sycamore Canyon, think about that 10-year-old boy running to Oro Blanco, barefoot, in the middle of the night, with Apaches howling in the woods. Better yet, walk or run a stretch of Johnny Bartlett's route yourself.

Mile 22.1.   USFS Road 109 turnoff, Corral Nuevo and Hells Gate.

Mile 24.   On the left, a sign points south toward 5,376-foot Montana Peak, named for a small mining settlement called Montana Camp located near present-day Ruby. The Montana Mine first showed signs of life in the 1880s, but it didn't really get cranked up till 1909.

When J. Ross Browne first blew through Arizona in 1864, the Ruby Road was just a figment of his imagination; Browne thought a road could be forged through the foothills of the Atascosa Mountains as a shortcut to Arivaca, though at considerable expense. The owners of the Montana Mine, who apparently thought along the same lines, put their money up to build it. According to Kirk Bryan, the road was "maintained in a passable condition for motor trucks as far as the Montana Mine." That was in 1917; it's unclear when the Ruby Road, or Oro Blanco Trail beyond, was first built, though in 1918 Col. H. B. Wharfield reported that the Tenth Calvary took the "Oro Blanco trail across the border country." By 1921, the Ruby Road was impassable, according to Bryan. You can thank J. Ross Browne that you can now drive through the same country that proved so threatening for the likes of Ralph Pumpelly and little Johnny Bartlett but that was so appealing to the cast of other characters who hooted and hollered, murdered and pillaged their way across the Tumacacori Mountains in the heyday of frontier Arizona.

Mile 25. The Ruby turnoff on the left, no admittance. In Ruby's boom years, two thousand people jammed into a mining camp that probably looked like most modern homeless shelters to work the rich veins of the Montana Mine. Today, however, Ruby is a ghost town, privately owned, with signs warning you to stay out. Ruby has never embraced visitors with open arms. According to *Ghost Towns of Arizona*, the Ruby store was knocked over for a second time in the summer of 1921; Frank and Myrtle Pearson were both murdered during the brutal robbery. The bandidos fled south, but they didn't exactly cover their tracks. A $5,000 bounty was put on each of their heads—mounted or unmounted. Almost a year later, Manuel Martinez and Placido Silvas were brought to justice after a deputy "overheard a bartender in a cantina in Sásabe, Sonora, trying to sell five gold teeth to a customer." The teeth had belonged to Myrtle Pearson.

Mile 27. Warsaw Canyon turnoff on the left and USFS Road 217. From this point on, the country opens up and you get your first glimpse of eagle-headed 7,734-foot Baboquivari Peak 25 miles to the northwest. (See entry for Baboquivari Peak.)

Mile 28.6. Oro Blanco once prided itself in being "a quiet little town, inhabited by a superior class of miners and workmen . . . opposed to sharps, tramps, and jumpers." The October 11, 1880, edition of the *Daily Arizona Citizen* also reported, "They are an intelligent class generally, and are determined to keep a model mining camp, free from loafers, rowdies, and reckless characters." One of Oro Blanco's most respected citizens was, according to *Ghost Towns in Arizona*, James A. Robinson, "the richest man in Arizona"; in 1899, Robinson and his Mexican wife lived on a mere $500 a year, while they continued to salt away $45,000 a year to the estimated $1.2 million stuffed in their mattress!

Mile 36.2. Junction with Tres Bellotas Road. Turn right.

Mile 36.6. Pavement and Arivaca. Come see for yourself why Pumpelly tried so hard to get to Arivaca, why in the 1700s, according to local historian Fred Noon, "Aribac was a 'visita' for the Padres of Quevavi Mission who administered to the Indians." Once a Pima Indian village, Arivaca is a charming ranch community nestled in the high desert grasslands along Arivaca Wash.

Return the way you came or, better yet, follow the Arivaca Road back to I-19 along the original route, which first linked Tucson with Arivaca.

Travel Notes

•**Primary access.**   Highway 289 and the Arivaca Road.

•**Elevation.**   Approximately 4,000 feet, average.

•**Mileage.**   37 miles from I-19 to Arivaca (dirt road for 27 miles; paved, 10 miles).

•**Traveling time.**   2 to 3 hours.

•**Suggested campsites.**   Many areas to choose from on Coronado National Forest lands.

•**Season.**   All year; avoid monsoon season.

•**Maps.**   Coronado National Forest Recreation Map/Tumacacori Mountains.

•**Nearest supply points.**   Tucson, Nogales, and Arivaca.

•**Managing agency.**   U.S. Forest Service.

•**Biotic communities.**   Oak woodland-grassland.

Couts' Trail

Duquesne Road, Nogales to Coronado National Memorial

Landform

The flip side of the Ruby Road, the Couts' Trail, begins in the Santa Cruz
River Valley and climbs over the 6,000-foot-high Patagonia Mountains
before descending into the lush San Rafael Valley 2,000 feet below; there,
this storybook track crosses the Santa Cruz River for a second time near
its headwaters, which emanate from the high country surrounding the San
Rafael De La Zanja land grant. From this historic Mexican cattle ranch,
the Couts' Trail continues east, first by winding in and out of the deep
arroyos draining the 6,000-foot-high Canelo Hills, then by crossing the
southern arm of the 9,466-foot-high Huachuca Mountains at 6,575-foot
Montezuma Pass, where it finally plunges into the San Pedro Valley to
the east.

Historical Overview

In *The Journal of Cave Johnson Couts: 1848–1849*, the 6-foot Tennessee
ridge runner and West Point graduate describes several incredulous near-
drownings during the U.S. Army's epic march from Monterey, Nuevo
Léon, Mexico, to Los Angeles. Camped somewhere on the west slope of
the Sierra Madre Occidental a day's ride south of territorial Arizona on
October 2, 1848, 1st Lt. Cave Johnson Couts and the First Dragoons were
caught in a late-night torrential downpour; in an hour's time, a whimsical
little creek reportedly turned into a life-threatening flood—though you
couldn't have guessed it from the First Dragoons' actions. Grossly ignorant
of the fact that flash floods were a peril to be reckoned with in the Southwest, the First Dragoons stayed bedded down near this roaring "gully washer"
until it literally swept the lot of them downstream: "At the dead hour of
midnight," wrote Couts, "the torrent rushed over the camp and the men
up to their waists just did get the company wagons out in time. One hospital
wagon with a sick man was carried off in the current—wagon dashed to
pieces, but the man succeeded in clinging to a tree which he caught hold
of until found next morning."

Between this wagon-rafting adventure, or Camp Inundation, as it was
later called, and Couts' own character-building swim across the Lower
Colorado River a month and a half later, the First Dragoons staggered
across the picturesque borderlands of southeast Arizona via a route roughly
parallel to the modern dirt road from Nogales to Coronado National Monu-

ment. Not that they planned it that way; it's just that the California-bound Dragoons were led by Maj. Lawrence P. Graham, who, throughout his command of the 6-month, 1,057-mile-long expedition, reportedly tried to drown his sorrows with drink after his wife ran out on him. Much of Couts' frank and colorful journal, edited by Henry F. Dobyns, describes how Major Graham's whiskey-fueled command decisions affected the welfare and morale of his troops. "Last evening I came into camp with the rear guard and found the Major, as usual, beastly drunk . . . but it would require pages everyday to mention the many disreputable occurances resulting from continued and incessant drunkenness." Not long after the Camp Inundation debacle, a besotted Major Graham ordered his troops to camp in the middle of a cactus patch when a perfect camping spot reportedly lay nearby. Coming off yet another bender, Major Graham apparently said to hell with Cookes Wagon Road: "We must have a Major Graham's wagon route!" Thereby, he blindly led his sober troops past Cookes' reliable route into a mountainous cul-de-sac where, Couts recounted, they "suddenly butted against an old he mountain almost impassable for man or beast."

The First Dragoons weren't the only early travelers who found themselves wandering aimlessly across this pleasant border country. John Bartlett, commissioner of the United States and Mexican Boundary Commission, spent 2 weeks in September of 1854 riding his men in circles through the verdant grassland and hill country surrounding the San Rafael Valley in hopes of finding a route to Santa Cruz, Sonora. From Bartlett's description, however, you'd have thought he was trying to handcut a swath through the Amazon rainforest rather than saunter through the relatively open country that proved such easy going for Kino's and Manje's repeated sojourns during the 1700s. Wrote Bartlett: "This defile was filled with giant cottonwoods, with an undergrowth of rank grass, weeds, and jungle, rising above our heads even when on horseback. Among them grew a vine, binding all together; so that it was impossible to force a passage through." As had happened to Major Graham and his First Dragoons, Bartlett and his crew had to be led down the natural corridor of the San Rafael Valley to the village of Santa Cruz by local Mexican guides who came to the rescue.

Not everybody had such problems trying to figure out where they were in southeastern Arizona, or how to get from here to there. On a chart called "Southern Arizona in the Late '70s," traced from an 1879 military map by Paul Riecker, you can see that many of the early trails and roads between Los Nogales (as Nogales was then called) and present-day Coronado National Memorial followed natural corridors formed by the broad valleys separating mountain ranges like the Atascosas, Santa Ritas, Patagonias, Canelo Hills, and Huachucas. Through these valleys traveled the Spanish padres, including Fray Marcos de Niza, who is credited with being the first European "tourist" to visit the area in 1539. But the first road known to climb away from these well-traveled valley routes was the track that led from Los Nogales to the old Mowry Mine in the Patagonia Mountains; Spaniards first worked it in 1769, which indicates just how old the first leg of the modern Couts' Trail may be. As mining, ranching, and lumbering interests grew, pieces of this route were presumably extended from the Mowry Mine east to Washington Camp and Lochiel, then further east to Sunnyside during the 1860s. Finally, in 1933, the Civilian Conservation Corps built the last section to Montezuma Pass. So, unlike the prehistoric El Camino del Diablo, which was essentially one long uninterrupted track across the southwest desert, the modern Couts' Trail became a reality only when it made economic sense to link together individual sections of a frequently rugged route that traveled east to west across the natural grain of the land.

Thus Graham and Bartlett each had a difficult time remaining oriented in a landscape that others have found so appealing because each traveled contrary to the proven routes of the padres, who followed the path of least resistance through the region's natural travel corridors.

But what Bartlett lacked in route-finding abilities (as a boundary surveyor, no less) and what Major Graham lacked in principles (Couts reported that Graham took a Mexican girl back to camp against her and her father's repeated protests) they tried to compensate for in their observations of an untamed land that once ran wild with now-extinct animals. Wrote Bartlett: "Around us grew the maguey, the yucca, and various kinds of cacti, together with small oaks; while beneath us, the valley spread out from six to eight miles in width, and some twelve to fifteen miles in length. . . . [It] was covered with the most luxuriant herbage and thickly studded with live oaks, not like a forest, but rather resembling a cultivated park."

As late as the 1850s, this "park" was still inhabited by the Sonoran grizzly, wild mustangs, and Mexican wolves. As if surveying the U.S.-Mexico border — without getting lost — weren't sporting enough for Bartlett's survey party, a couple of his men tried to ride down two Sonoran grizzly bears — but the bears outran their horses. And to supplement their rations, Graham's Dragoons reportedly fished and killed a black bear; panthers and lobo wolves were also shot, though it's not reported whether these predators actually made it into the stew pot or whether they were simply left to rot. Even Sylvester Mowry, who spent much of his time mining underground, couldn't help but notice the profusion of wildlife above ground:

"The whole country abounds with rabbits, quails, and wild turkeys. It is not a rare occurrence to meet droves of deer and antelopes numbering from twenty-five to thirty."

Today, the Sonoran grizzly is gone, though there are still rumors of an occasional lobo seen loping through the same chest-deep grass that the Mexican jaguar once prowled. Fortunately, we may not have seen the last of the great spotted cat—whose habitat once extended as far north as the Grand Canyon—in southeastern Arizona. According to several reliable sources, a lion hunter living in nearby Dos Cabezas killed a Mexican jaguar in the western foothills of the 8,354-foot-high Dos Cabezas Mountains in 1987. The poacher's wife was apparently so excited that she couldn't keep from yammering on the phone to all her friends about it. But when authorities went to investigate, the jaguar pelt was, strangely, nowhere to be found.

Directions

To reach the former stomping grounds of Cave Johnson Couts, the Sonoran grizzly, and the Mexican jaguar, drive south from Tucson on Interstate 19 63 miles to the Nogales turnoff (Exit 8). Continue south on Grand Avenue to the Patagonia Road, also known as Highway 82. Turn right, follow the overpass, and take Highway 82, the Patagonia-Sonoita Scenic Highway, 4 miles to the Duquesne Road. Turn right (east) and begin Tour.

Road Log

Mile 0 to 1.9.   Highway 82 to Cottonwood Tree Pass. From the junction of Highway 82 and the Duquesne Road, proceed through the Kino Springs golf course. Around Mile 1.9, the Couts' Trail winds along the Santa Cruz River, which flows—when it rains—all the way to the Gila River near Phoenix. (Phoenicians call the Gila River a "flood" when it flows.) Kino and Manje traipsed up and down this stretch of the Santa Cruz River circa 1700. They called it a river, which indicates that its flow was more reliable historically than it is now.

Mile 2.4.   Coronado National Forest boundary.

Mile 4.1.   The two-lane road you've been cruising along narrows to one lane, where it begins to earn its reputation as the Couts' Trail; at Mile 6.2, it crosses Sycamore Canyon, not to be confused with Sycamore Canyon in the Pajarito Wilderness along the Ruby Road west of Nogales, or with any of the other Sycamore creeks and canyons in Arizona.

Mile 8.4 to 11.2. The Couts' Trail winds its way up to 6,000-foot Ambush Pass near the summit ridge of the Patagonia Mountains, called the Santa Cruz Mountains in the 1850s. This is the same stretch of road that first linked Los Nogales with the Mowry Mine.

From Ambush Pass, you have a sweeping vista of the San Rafael Valley below, and of the Huachuca Mountains 25 miles to the east. The pyramid-shaped peak southeast of the Huachucas is 8,000-foot-high San Jose Peak across the border in Chihuahua, Mexico. Assuming it hasn't been shot out of the sky by drug smugglers, you should also be able to see one of the U.S. Customs' $18 million, 747-sized balloons hovering 10,000 feet above the landscape searching for modern contrabandistas. Those who believe the 7-ton aerostat serves as a deterrent to smugglers endearingly call it Fat Albert; critics, who credit it with few actual drug seizures, call it a White Elephant. Whatever you call it, you'll be able to see the radar-equipped, Pillsbury Doughboy-shaped balloon throughout the rest of your journey along the modern Couts' Trail.

From Ambush Pass, the Couts' Trail begins its descent into the San Rafael Valley, headwaters of the Santa Cruz River.

Mile 12.2, BM 5,509 feet. On your left (north) is the turnoff to USFS Road 49; from here, it's 9 miles to Harshaw and another 8 miles to Patagonia. To continue on the Couts' Trail, turn right on USFS Road 61 and head toward Washington Camp and Duquesne.

Before you turn off, however, take a moment to consider this: USFS Road 49 heads toward the famous Mowry silver mine, which was successfully worked by Sylvester Mowry during the 1860s; Mowry first rediscovered the Spanish silver mine in 1856, long after Apaches reportedly routed out its last tenants. But Mowry himself was something of a controversial figure in these parts, a Johnny Reb sympathizer, some said, and in the end he lost his mine because of it. In a book dedicated in part to those "killed by the Apaches in the struggle to redeem Arizona from barbarism," Mowry described his own arrest and subsequent internment in *Arizona and Sonora: The Geography, History, and Resources of the Silver Region of North America:* "In June, 1862, [I] was seized by a large armed force, under the orders of General J. H. Carleton, while in the legitimate pursuit of business, and retained as a political prisoner for nearly six months. The seizure was made upon a false, ridiculous, and malicious charge." Mowry was eventually cleared of all charges and set free from the dungeon then known as the Yuma Territorial Prison; however, he was forced to give up his successful mining operation, which at one time had employed three hundred men, after government troops "made away with nearly all the goods, wool, coal, arms, and stores at the mine."

Mile 12.4 to 12.9. On the right, turn off to Washington Camp and Duquesne. Ironically, troops were stationed at nearby Fort Buchanan to protect mining operations such as Mowry's and those that later flourished at Washington Camp and Duquesne during the 1880s. But if there ever was a hardship post, Fort Buchanan was probably it. According to scholar John P. Wilson's *Islands in the Desert*, the swamplike surroundings of Fort Buchanan turned it into a fever pit of malaria "wherein there are several stagnant pools, in which vast herds of swine may be seen constantly basking in the mud or rooting up the foetid and miasmatic soil of the adjacent quagmires."

Mile 13.6. Resume two-lane road.

Mile 16. Road crosses private land of San Rafael Cattle Company, an outfit that's been running cattle along the headwaters of the Santa Cruz River since the Mexican government granted land to Manuel Bustello in May 1825. The best report of just how lush this grassland once was came from John Bartlett when he surveyed the area more than 2 decades later—assuming, that is, you can believe that Bartlett knew which valley he was talking about after turning his own outing through the San Rafael Valley into a bushwhack; Bartlett estimated that some forty thousand cattle grazed in the nearby Babocomori and San Pedro River valleys.

Mile 17.5. Fray Marcos de Niza Monument. De Niza was one of the few early drifters through these parts who wasn't screaming about Apaches or looking for grazing lands; he had other things on his mind—like Cibola, for one. De Niza crossed the line near here on April 12, 1539, in search of seven lost cities of gold. But his black guide, a soldier of fortune named Estaban, was killed by Indians upon entering the first "city of gold." De Niza fled the area, now presumed to be the vicinity of Zuni, New Mexico, shortly afterward and barely made it back across the line with his life. With him, though, he brought the now-legendary tale of the Seven Cities of Cibola: "The cities were surrounded with walls, with their gates guarded, and were very wealthy, having silversmiths; and . . . the women wore strings of gold beads and the men girdles of gold and white woolen dresses."

When Francisco Vásquez de Coronado's expedition reached Cibola on July 7, 1540, to check out de Niza's incredible story, the men were not amused; wrote expedition member Pedro Castenada de Nagera: "When they saw the first village, which was Cibola, such were the curses that some hurled at Friar Marcos that I pray God may protect him from them. It is a little, crowded village, looking as if it had been crumpled all up together."

Mile 17.8.   On the right, turn off to Lochiel. Most everyone who ventured through these parts after Coronado talked about Apaches, especially pioneer Arizonan Mary Harrison Chalmers. Chalmers' family moved to Lochiel in the 1880s, when it was still called La Noria ("the well"). In a 1926 interview, Mary Chalmers told how Apaches had butchered cattle right on her family's place. Said Chalmers: "Night after night, we used to sit on our porch in the summer-time, and watch their signals. . . . We would see a signal first on one mountain then on another. They always signaled with fires." When the fireworks proved dull, Mary Chalmers hunted lions and bears: "I'll never forget when my brother Jim and I poisoned a lion. My, but we were proud that we had killed him." Apparently, life was never dull in Lochiel. There were always "necktie parties" to attend. It started with the rustlers from Texas who shot up the town – outlaws, Mary said, who "would steal from us then go over into Mexico and sell their loot. The citizens finally got them [and] hung a few of them up in Tombstone."

When you pull away from the dusty streets of Lochiel today and head east across the San Rafael Valley, think about what this feisty pioneer woman said before her death in 1931: "Life at that time was full of excitement. Always something to do; seems lively compared to the quiet of the present day."

Mile 20.   USGS Gauge Station. The Couts' Trail crosses the Santa Cruz River for a second time.

Mile 23.4.   Parker Canyon. William Parker was yet another early vagabond who got lost traveling east to west across the natural lay of this land during the mid-1800s. According to William C. Barnes, Parker was headed to the California goldfields but lost the main trail somewhere near here. However, once Parker made it to California, he salted away enough money to move his family from Missouri to Phoenix. But Phoenix was getting crowded even back then and Parker needed some breathing room: He wrote, "In 1881, the family moved to Parker Canyon to avoid the 'congestion' in poulation developing in Phoenix." Parker is reportedly buried in this canyon.

On the left, Road Junction 194, turn right (south) and stay on USFS Road 61.

Mile 28.2.   Bodie. The road crosses Blacktail Canyon, not to be confused with Blacktail Canyon in the Grand Canyon.

Mile 30.1.   On the left, Road Junction 227 to Parker Lake Recreation Area. Turn right (east/southeast).

Mile 30.7.   Sunnyside Canyon. The road crosses this canyon (with no bridge) before crossing Sundown Ranch and the Santa Cruz-Cochise county line and then climbing Campini Mesa.

Mile 33.2.   School Canyon. No bridge.

Mile 35.6.   On the left, USFS Road 48 to Parker Lake and Sunnyside. Turn right (southeast) and stay on USFS Road 61. According to Sierra Vista resident and historian Bob Dowling, Sunnyside supplied Duquesne and Washington Camp with lumber during the boom days of the 1850s.

Mile 36.4.   Sycamore Canyon. Not to be confused with any other Sycamore Canyon mentioned in this book. At this point, the Couts' Trail has climbed out of the sprawling grass-and-oak woodlands of the San Rafael Valley and begun to chug up toward Montezuma Pass.

Mile 44.4.   6,575-foot Montezuma Pass, Huachuca Mountains, Coronado National Memorial. As early as 1700, the Huachuca Mountains were called the Guachucas by Capt. Juan Mateo Manje, who may have named the range after a nearby Pima Indian village. By the 1850s, however, Sylvester Mowry was calling them both the Wachukas and the Sierra Espuela ("Mountain of Spurs"). As for Coronado, the "Knight of the Pueblos and Plains," however, he supposedly never set foot in the Guachucas but is believed to have followed the San Pedro River immediately to the east while on the historic wild-goose chase perpetrated by de Niza's hallucinations of Cibola.

Why dedicate a National Memorial to an explorer who only discovered a village of mud huts? According to a National Park placard at Montezuma Pass: "Coronado National Memorial, set aside to commemorate his historic march, symbolizes both the importance of the Hispanic-Mexican background in southwestern history and culture, and the close relationship existing between the Republic of Mexico and the United States." But according to a National Park memo, Mexico didn't want any part in establishing an International Memorial to Coronado when the bill was originally sponsored by Arizona Senator Carl Hayden in 1940, or when it was introduced again in 1947 and still later in 1975 under then-Governor Raul Castro: "Perhaps we 'gringos' should remember that the idea of celebrating the explorations of Coronado is a delicate and sensitive matter. For the Mexicans, the coming of Spanish Conquistadores signified plundering, pillaging, and the enslaving of thousands. Coronado and his followers were considered antagonists and adversaries, not heroes. . . . The Mexican government isn't very interested in establishing a comparable park and creating an International Memorial to a 'Conquistador.'" So much for the gringos' vision of hands across the border.

Whatever the original intent, it's a good thing Coronado National Memorial now protects the area. Established in 1952, the 4,976-acre memorial provides seasonal habitat for 140 different species of birds, challenging hiking trails that fan out from Montezuma Pass into the 9,466-foot-high, 20,190-acre Miller Peak Wilderness Area, and one of the most spectacular, unspoiled scenic overlooks in Arizona. Looking west from Montezuma Pass is akin to looking through a window into yesterday; there is nothing to spoil your vision of what it may have been like when the Sonoran grizzly, the Mexican jaguar, and the lobo wolf roamed that vast sea of grass and live oaks. On a good day, you can see beyond the Patagonia Mountains, or the Sierra Chihuahuilla as they were also known, all the way to Baboquivari Peak 80 miles west. Not many drive-ins still show that picture show.

From Montezuma Pass, begin your descent into Montezuma Canyon and Coronado National Memorial headquarters.

Mile 45 to 46.   Hairpin turns.

Mile 46.6.   Pavement.

Mile 47.8.   Visitor Center.

Mile 53.8.   Highway 92.

Travel Notes

•**Primary access.**   I-19 or Highway 92.

•**Elevation.**   Between 3,832 feet and 6,575 feet.

•**Mileage.**   53.8 miles (dirt road for 46.3 miles; paved, 7.5 miles).

•**Traveling time.**   4 hours.

•**Suggested campsites.**   Many undeveloped areas to choose from on Coronado National Forest lands.

•**Season.**   All year. However, be advised not to drive the Couts' Trail during wet weather; rain turns this track into putty!

•**Map.**   Coronado National Forest Recreation Map.

•**Nearest supply points.** Tucson, Nogales, and Sierra Vista.

•**Managing agency.** U.S. Forest Service and Coronado National Monument.

•**Backcountry information.** Permit not required.

•**Biotic communities.** Plains and desert grasslands, encinal and Mexican oak-pine woodland, juniper-pinyon woodland, and Chihuahuan Desert scrub.

Canyoneering

Sycamore Canyon

Pajarito Wilderness Area, Coronado National Forest

Landform

Not to be confused with northern Arizona's rugged, 35-mile-long Sycamore Canyon Wilderness, Sycamore Canyon "south" is a charming 9-mile-long drainage that cuts through the heart of the 7,420-acre Pajarito Wilderness. The headwaters of Sycamore Canyon are formed by the precipitous north slope of 6,422-foot Atascosa Peak, high point of the Atascosa Mountains; after draining across Bear Valley into northern Sonora at 3,500 feet, Sycamore Canyon becomes the Arroyo de los Alisos, or "creek of the alder trees."

Historical Overview

The map of "Pimeria Alta: 1687–1711," prepared by Kino high priest and historian Herbert Eugene Bolton, shows a single track wandering off the heavily beaten paths of the Spanish missionaries and crossing the Sierra del Pajarito; ostensibly, Padre Kino made the first recorded traverse of the Pajarito Mountains via Sycamore Canyon in January 1691 while on a short soul-saving expedition to San Cayetano del Tumacácori, known today as Tumacacori National Monument. According to John P. Wilson's *Islands in the Desert*, Padre Kino "proceeded probably by way of Sycamore Canyon and Bear Valley." Kino—pioneer missionary explorer, cartographer, and ranchman—isn't so clear about that in *Kino's Historical Memoir of Pimeria Alta*, however. Translated, edited, and annotated by Bolton, Kino vaguely

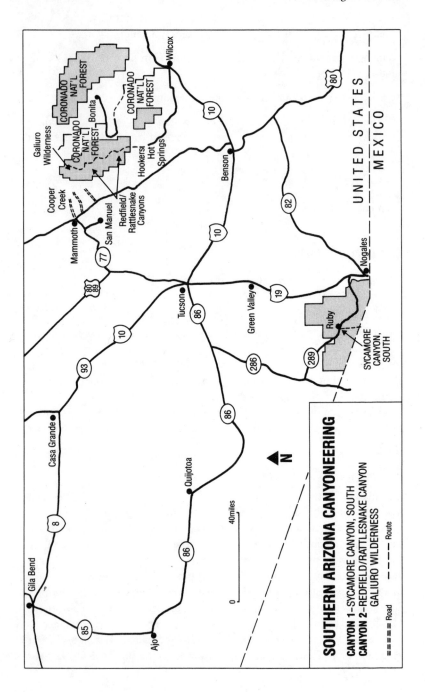

SOUTHERN ARIZONA CANYONEERING

CANYON 1–SYCAMORE CANYON, SOUTH
CANYON 2–REDFIELD/RATTLESNAKE CANYON
GALIURO WILDERNESS

==== Road   ----- Route

describes his route up Sycamore Canyon by noting: "Where upon we ascended to the Valley of Guebavi, a journey of about fifteen leagues . . . " A fortune-teller could read more into that than most historical sleuths would be willing to bet next year's grant money on; Kino could have taken any of a number of viable routes across the gentle mile-high Sierra del Pajaritos. But because it offers a dependable water source, historians might safely bet that Sycamore Canyon was Kino's route.

Eighty-three years later, Juan Bautista de Anza crossed the Sierra del Pajaritos, some think in the footsteps of Padre Kino. Anza, Padre Francisco Garces, and their men shivered for 2 nights after leaving the Arroyo de los Alisos; on Monday, January 10, 1774, Anza wrote: "At nine in the morning we set out toward the south-southwest, passing various ranges on our right and left, and having traveled about seven leagues we halted to pass the night at the site of Agua Escondida (Hidden Water). . . . Tuesday and Wednesday, the 11th and 12th, we remained at this place, because it had been raining and snowing incessantly since the night of the 10th." On January 13 the heavens parted and, according to Bolton's reading of Anza's diary in *Anza's California Expeditions* "As he [Anza] descended the southern slopes of the sierra a charming panorama met his gaze. . . . Shadowy ranges were outlined in the farther distance. In front lay the rolling plateau, cactus and mesquite covered, through which the Altar Valley made its way, sometimes above ground, sometimes below, to the sands of the California Sea."

The "sands of the California Sea" lay immediately to the south of hell-on-earth, where all the major players in the soul-saving trade had a chance to dance with the devil on El Camino del Diablo. Like Anza and Garces, Lieutenant Milcher of the Boundary Survey Expedition of 1855 first had to cross the Sierra de los Pajaritos before he got a crack at the Devil's Highway; also like Anza and Garces, he neglected to write a Totebook description of his exact route. But based on his report, you might assume that Lieutenant Milcher used Sycamore Canyon: "Following up one of the arroyos or gullies of this chain, we were soon locked in on all sides by high hills; the ravine through which we continued to wind for four miles became rocky, narrow, and difficult to pass, until we reached some small springs, 'Los Ojos de Alizos.'" As sketchy as Milcher's passage is, it does three things that Anza's and Kino's descriptions fail to do: It roughly describes the length and nature of Sycamore Canyon below the modern Ruby Road; it addresses the difficulties pack mules might face when negotiating slot pools in the upper end of Sycamore Canyon; and it at least matches by name Los Ojos de Alizos with the arroyo that Sycamore Canyon becomes when it pours over the Arizona-Sonora line. Whether Lieutenant Milcher, Anza, or Kino ever really tromped through Sycamore Canyon is still speculative; a systematic archaeological survey of the canyon has never been carried out. However, the Boundary Survey Expedition—and not the good padres—first named the mountains the Sierra de los Pajaritos; wrote Lieutenant Milcher: "Our trail led up a pretty little valley towards the west for eight miles, when we reached the base of the 'Sierra de los Pajaritos' (the Mountain of Little Birds)."

Another mystery concerning this alluring little canyon is whether Tuscoso Canyon and Sycamore Canyon are one in the same; modern topographical maps provide few clues, but if they are, then the Yaqui Indians used this natural corridor through the Pajaritos at the turn of the century to cross undetected from Mexico into the United States to work and to smuggle arms back into Mexico. According to a historical article, "A Fight with the Yaqui at Bear Valley," by Col. H. B. Wharfield, a group of Yaqui Indians fired on the Tenth Cavalry "on the afternoon of January 9, 1918 . . . because they had thought the Negro soldiers were Mexican troops." In a battle that Wharfield later described as "a courageous stand by a brave group of Indians," ten Yaqui Indians held off more than thirty troops from the Tenth Cavalry long enough for twenty other Yaquis to flee back into Sonora. When the ten remaining Yaquis were finally captured, they were lined up and ordered to put their hands atop their heads so they could be searched. "One kept his hands around his middle," wrote Wharfield. "Fearing he might have a knife to use on some trooper, I grabbed his hands and yanked them up. His stomach practically fell out." The Yaqui chief later died in a Nogales hospital from wounds suffered when his cartridge belt exploded; the nine surviving Yaquis were sentenced to 30 days in the Pima County jail. According to Wharfield's article, a sympathetic U.S. District Court Judge William H. Sawtelle believed his actions would ultimately prevent the Yaquis from being deported back to Mexico where they might face retributions by the Mexican government for another Yaqui group's misdeeds.

One early traveler who knew Sycamore Canyon better than most was biologist Leslie N. Gooding; according to the scientific paper "The Flora of Sycamore Canyon, Pajarito Mountains," "Gooding was the first biologist to recognize the scenic and biological values of the canyon. He made extensive plant collections in the area from 1935 into the 1950's." Among the 624 species of plants that Gooding identified is a rare fern, *Asplenium exiguum*, thought to be found only in the Himalayas and in parts of Mexico. Ultimately, Gooding's enthusiasm and dedication to studying the flora of this unique riparian habitat prodded the U.S. Forest Service into designating 545 acres of Sycamore Canyon as the Gooding Research Natural Area in 1970. In his own farsighted words, the late Gooding wrote: "Too frequently rare species of plants and animals as well as geological and archaeological remains are sacrificed in the name of progress, and what remains after a few years, are abandoned prospect holes, burned over forest areas and denuded landscapes. There is a place for industry, but there should also be certain spots where we may witness the works of nature unspoiled. . . . Sycamore Canyon is one of these spots."

Directions

From Tucson, drive 55 miles south on I-19 to Exit 12, State Route 289, the Ruby Road. Turn right and drive 19.5 miles west on the Ruby Road to the Sycamore Canyon trailhead near Hank and Yank Spring. (See entry for Ruby Road.)

Canyon Log

Mile 0 to 1. The Sycamore Canyon trail begins near the unprotected ruins of Hank and Yank Spring; a hundred yards south, the trail drops into the creek bed, where it's rimmed by 30-foot-high rhyolite cliffs; hillsides covered with deep grass and oak roll back from the canyon rim. The remains of a stone wall can be seen on the left (east) half a mile downstream. During the early 1970s, a drift fence apparently marked the northern boundary of the Gooding Research Natural Area. But that fence no longer exists and nothing prevents cattle from wandering into the heart of this pristine area now except their good sense and, failing that, a natural barrier of slot canyon pools a mile beyond.

Crooked Dick Rock marks the confluence of Tinaja Springs Canyon sluicing in from the west (right). A second spire on the south side of Tinaja Springs Canyon forms a postcard gateway into the mouth of this tributary canyon, named for the springs below 5,376-foot Montana Peak. A short walk below the mouth of Tinaja Springs Canyon, yet another finger-shaped spire erupts from the stream bed on the east (left); it looks as if it would make a fitting afternoon climb, though the rappel from that crumbly, 130-foot-high hairpin might raise the hair on the back of your neck. Lieutenant Milcher was one of the first to describe such geologic wonders in the area: "Powerful volcanic irruptions have at some earlier period of the world's history produced great disturbances in this part of the earth. Strata of limestone once horizontal, are now curved and bent by the force of action, and masses of igneous rocks have been upheaved through the fissures opened on the surface."

Mile 1 to 2.   The trail climbs out the east side of the creek bed and contours it 40 feet above; the stonework reinforcing the trail where it drops back into the creek bed suggests this detour has been around for some time. But unless Sycamore Canyon is "flashing"—in which case you might consider bodysurfing options—it's an unnecessary detour from the pleasant walk along this intermittent, perennial stream that provides habitat for both the Sonoran chub and the Tarahumara frog. The one large pool you'll encounter en route was undoubtedly a natural barrier for early range riders trying to herd beeves through this short, rugged canyon. But for someone on foot, this cowcatcher can be easily negotiated.

The slot pools are located in a narrow cleft of rock just above the confluence of Little Tinaja Springs Canyon; if you don't enjoy swimming with creepy-crawlies, the slot pools can be negotiated on the west with an easy boulder move. Below these slot pools you can forget the trail ever existed and just meander downstream. Below Little Tinaja Springs Canyon, yet another tributary canyon, called Black Tank Canyon, beckons further exploration on the east.

Mile 2 to 3.   About where Penasco Canyon slips in from the east, you leave the Gooding Natural Research Area; there's no drift fence on its southern boundary, either. With an attentive eye, you'll have the opportunity to observe the inimitable Arizona "slow elk" in action. If conditions are right, a select group from the bovine hierarchy may choose to accompany you on the remainder of your outing.

Two and a half miles out, about where Sycamore Canyon makes a dogleg turn south again, a bowl-shaped area on the north appears to offer a safe refuge and campsite above potential flash flood danger. Downstream from this camp, Ridge Canyon creeps in from the north; like Tinaja Springs Canyon and Little Tinaja Springs Canyon above, Ridge Canyon and Mule Canyon collectively drain the east slope of 4,500-foot-high Mule Ridge. Mule Ridge forms the geographical western boundary of Sycamore Canyon throughout much of its course.

Mile 3 to 4.   Willow Tank Canyon is the first of two parallel canyons that squeak in from the east; periodically, they drain the northwest flanks of 4,811-foot Manzanita Mountain. If you observe the northeast slope above this double confluence, you'll see totems of saguaro cacti standing along the broken dacite cliffs—a natural milepost heralding the Sonoran

Desert. Where Mule Canyon makes its debut on the north, ocotillo flail their spindly green arms out of a lush bedding of Mexican grasses on the hills above. Lieutenant Milcher wrote of the area's legendary mineral wealth and lush vegetation before it was annexed into the Gadsden Purchase: "'The Sierra de los Pajaritos' is said to form part of the Arizone mountains, reported to be the richest in Mexico. Many specimens of copper, gold and silver are found on the surface and they are no doubt rich in ore. The hills are covered with live-oak trees, and are overspread with a rich growth of grama grass."

Mile 4 to 5. About 4.5 miles out, near a small overhang on the west, an odd-looking mix of saguaro, prickly pear, oak, and pinyon can be seen. According to "Flora of Sycamore Canyon," "species with widely divergent geographical and ecological affinities grow close together."

Just before the canyon whips south again, an odd alignment of rocks could once be seen; from the way they were stacked, they appeared to mark a trailless route up a narrow depression. Fearing that they marked a drug cache along this historic smuggler's route, I remembered Wharfield's warning while traveling alone toward the border: "This is an uninhabited region, and an area reputed to be safe only when people traveled in pairs. Tales — all vague and unconfirmed — were common among the people of Ruby and Arivaca about mysterious disappearances in [this] border area."

Mile 5 to 6. Near the border, the fly-infested carcass of a 6-month-old calf lay gutted in the stream bed, its belly splayed open as if it had been cleaved with a long knife. In his book, *The Wolf in the Southwest*, David Brown may have provided a reasonable explanation for this sight: "There was one lobo down along the border near Ruby, that would invariably rip out the flank of a big calf, steer or yearling." While that may be sour news for stockmen under contract to deliver 7 jillion Bonus Jacks, it's exciting to think that a few wily Mexican gray wolves survived early Arizona's devastating eradication program brought about by those same stockmen.

A torn-down barbed-wire fence is all that marks the international boundary; a nearby sign advertises several Forest Service routes that smugglers can follow north through the Pajarito Wilderness to the Ruby Road: "BORDER TRAIL. Bear Valley, Summit Motorway, Tonto Canyon." It includes no translations for contrabandistas; this is Proposition 106 (Arizona's controversial mandatory English law) country. On the north, a small barbed-wire corral makes a fine holding pen for cattle rustlers working the Sonoran desert on both sides of the fence. The rugged hillsides surrounding this lonely corral are covered with mesquite, saguaro, ocotillo, and a plethora of grasses.

Mile 6. Sycamore Canyon turns south for the last time and enters Sonora, Mexico, where it becomes Arroyo de los Alisos. Near here in 1855, Lieutenant Milcher and his Boundary Commission laid out Border Monuments XVII and XIX; en route to them, Lieutenant Milcher wrote: "The trail for the first two [days] was almost over impassable mountains; massive rocks and steep precipices constantly impeded the progress of and turned the party out of its course, making the route circuitous as well as hazardous; rough ascents were surmounted, steep ravines followed down, and deep gullies passed; the mules actually had to be dragged along."

Travel Notes

• **Primary access.**   Ruby Road via Hank and Yank Spring.

• **Total elevation gain and loss.**   500-plus vertical feet each way.

• **Mileage.**   Approximately 12 miles round-trip.

• **Water source.**   Intermittent, flowing water in streambed.

• **Escape routes.**   Back the way you came.

• **Seasons.**   All year; however, avoid during summer monsoons and other periods of high runoff.

• **Maps.**   Ruby Quadrangle, Arizona-Sonora (7½-minute series).

• **Managing agency.**   Coronado National Forest, Nogales Ranger District.

• **Backcountry information.**   Permit not required. No camping or fires within Gooding Research Natural Area.

• **Biotic communities.**   Plains and desert grassland and encinal and Mexican oak-pine woodland.

Redfield and Rattlesnake Canyons

Galiuro Wilderness, Coronado National Forest

Landform

Twenty-five miles long and a dozen miles wide, the 7,633-foot-high Galiuro Mountains are a double chain of northwest-trending mountains cleaved lengthwise by Redfield Canyon on the south and Rattlesnake Canyon on the north. Now comprising a 76,317-acre wilderness area, these unforgivingly rugged mountains rear up out of the surrounding valleys for 3,000 to 4,000 feet, draining into Sulphur Springs Valley to the east, Aravaipa Canyon to the north, and the San Pedro River to the south and west.

Historical Overview

According to the eye-opening *Man and Wildlife in Arizona*, by Goode P. Davis, Jr., Kentucky trapper and frontiersman James Ohio Pattie "estimated that only 16 men out of 116 survived their first two years trapping in the Southwest." One incident Pattie describes in his telling and controversial book *The Personal Narrative of James O. Pattie* sheds remarkable light on the legendary hardships mountain men endured in quest of beaver pelts in Arizona; while traversing the Galiuro Mountains between March 31 and April 2, 1824, Pattie wrote:

> On the 31st, we reached the top of the mountain, and fed upon the last meat of our beavers. We met with no traces of game. . . . On the morning of the first of April, we commenced descending the mountain, from the side of which we could discern a plain before us, which, however, it required two severe days to reach . . . we had nothing to eat or drink. In descending from these icy mountains, we were surprised to find how warm it was on the plains. On reaching them I killed an antelope, of which we drank the warm blood; and however revolting the recital may be, to us it was refreshing, tasting like fresh milk.

That "fresh milk" sustained Pattie and his men until they finally found the next waterhole at noon the following day.

However, until Pattie traversed the Galiuros, presumably from east to west, few early explorers ventured into this remote—and still seldom visited—range. Coming from the south, as many early Spanish expeditions did, it was far easier to reach the Gila River to the north by following the San Pedro River along the west slope of the Galiuros, or by traversing Sulphur Springs Valley on its eastern flanks. Those who passed within the shadows of the Galiuros by way of San Pedro River, or via Eagle Pass between the Santa Teresa and Pinaleno Mountains, called the range everything from the Sierra del Arivaipa to the Sierra de San Calistro. According to *Arizona Place Names*, by William C. Barnes, the calistro name finally stuck, but not before it was anglicized tongue by tongue from "calitro," "calizo," and "caliuro" to its present name "Galiuro," which locals still like to pronounce "galureeze."

The Native Americans who ventured into the Galiuros after Pattie's 1824 traverse sometimes did so while on the run from military troopers who — if the My Lai–style massacre of eighty-five Indians in nearby Aravaipa Canyon in 1871 was any indication — thought it was great sport to murder defenseless women, children, and old men. According to a military document called "Where to Find Apaches: Southeastern Arizona, August 1870," "This range of mountains is very rough and affords splendid cover for Indians going north and south on their raids."

Two Apache women; for example, used the Galiuros for cover circa 1865 as they made a daring, 170-mile escape on foot. According to the 1931 recollections of Apache elder David Longstreet, published in Keith Basso's *Western Apache Raiding and Warfare,* Longstreet's mother and several other Apaches were shanghaied to Tucson after being captured by government troops during their bloody raid on the Apache encampment at the foot of the Santa Teresa Mountains. During the captors' victory-celebration dance in Tucson, Longstreet's mother and another woman vanished into the night. Said Longstreet: "They stayed in the Santa Catalinas that night and the next day traveled toward the Galiuro Mountains, making camp about halfway to them. The next day they got to the Galiuro Mountains. Here they saw some tracks, but they said, 'These tracks are of the Arivaipa Apaches and they are no good, so we will stay away from them.'" That they did, surviving on roasted mescal stalks until they rejoined their own people a week after fleeing Tucson. And when an officer later recognized Longstreet's mother from Tucson at Goodwin Springs, he was so impressed with her extraordinary escape that he "shook hands with her."

It wasn't until the "Apache problem" was brought to a head in the late 1800s — or, from the Indian's perspective, until they were cornered like dogs by government troops — that Anglo prospectors were lured into the Galiuros in hopes of carving out their own piece of the fledgling American dream. But the most famous (or infamous) prospectors who worked the hard, tangled, confused interior of the Galiuros didn't make the front pages of Arizona newspapers for hitting the mother lode; instead, they unearthed a nightmare that resulted in the largest manhunt in the history of Arizona.

The time was 1918. The United States was at war in Europe; some 20 million men would register for the draft under the Selective Service Act of 1917. Some called the Power boys slackers; others said their old man, Thomas Jefferson Power, didn't want them going off to fight somebody else's war; still others said the fight erupted because the local sheriff wanted the Powers' mine deep within the Galiuros. In a controversy that still rages in Graham County today, no one will probably ever know, as Sly Stallone once said, who "drew first blood": the sheriff's posse or the Power family. But other essential facts of the case are clear. A warrant was issued for the arrest of Tom and John Power for draft dodging. On the morning of February 10, 1918, four lawmen rode into the cold, snowy heart of the Galiuros to serve the warrant. Somebody opened fire; both sides claimed it was the other. Sixty seconds to 2 minutes later, three men (Sheriff McBride, Undersheriff Martin Kempton, and Deputy T. Kane Wooten) lay dead, while the senior Power lay in the throes of death.

Wounded in the shoot-out themselves, the Power boys dragged their father's body into the mine and, presumably with former calvary scout and paroled horse thief Tom Sisson leading the way, rode the dead men's horses out of the Galiuros, via Redington on the San Pedro River, and headed for Old Mexico. Before finally being captured just over the line in Chihuahua a month later, Sisson and the Power boys had, according to Border Patrol agent and border historian Dan R. Roberts, "eluded a thousand posse members and eight troops of the U.S. Calvary; in the process, they'd covered the last 170 miles of their exhausting twenty-seven day escape on foot, after abandoning their stolen mounts near the border in the Chiricahua Mountains."

Frontier justice was swift. The trio was tried, convicted, and nearly hanged on May 16. Tom Sisson died 29 years later in Florence Prison at the age of 87; the Power brothers were paroled after doing 40 years of hard time. Due to efforts spearheaded by Arizona's favorite son and author, Don Dedera, the brothers received a full pardon by Arizona Governor Jack Williams on January 25, 1969.

But the saga continues. In this remote Arizona mountain range, Graham County cattle rancher Eddie Lackner trapped and killed nine black bears during 1988 because he claimed they threatened his livestock—though no one has ever reported seeing a 250-pound Arizona black bear try to pull down 1,000 to 2,000 pounds of wild horned beef. Lackner's case was plea bargained in front of Pima County Justice of the Peace Jacque Felshaw, who, according to the August 2, 1988, edition of *The Arizona Republic*, slapped Lackner on the wrist with two years' probation, a suspended $274 fine, and "a program of range improvement."

Evidently Lackner took "range improvement" to mean killing any black bear and mountain lion still in the Galiuros. Less than 6 months later, he and a federal trapper killed seven mountain lions and another black bear on two of Lackner's government-subsidized grazing allotments. Incredibly, wildlife officials haven't thought to ask themselves, "If the Galiuros is such prime black bear and mountain lion habitat, maybe it's not such prime habitat for cows." In the February 17, 1989, edition of the *Tucson Citizen*, outdoor writer Bill Quimby wrote, "The Forest Service continues to blockade a historic road that formerly provided public access into Squaw Basin [in the Galiuros], the area where Lackner has admitted trapping the bears. . . . Coronado National Forest officials said the road was blockaded at Lackner's request." Lackner took full advantage of that enclosure; as of January 1990, he and predator-control agents had killed another thirteen mountain lions on his allotment according to Steven Johnson, guest columnist for the *Arizona Republic*. That's thirty bears and mountain lions to protect the seventy head of cattle that Lackner is still permitted to graze on 5,000 acres of public land in the Galiuro Mountains.

Directions

To reach the Galiuros will not be easy because no paved road goes near this isolated massif—which is the very reason you should go. You may even stumble onto a few lions and bears that have slipped past Lackner's dogs and traps.

Northern End. To reach the popular Rattlesnake Canyon Trail No. 96 into Power's Garden on the north end of the Galiuros, drive north from Wilcox on Fort Grant Road 33 miles to Bonita. Take Aravaipa Road 27 miles to the junction with Rattlesnake Canyon Road, USFS Road 96; turn left and follow USFS Road 96 11 miles to the trailhead at the top of Power's Hill. The 5-mile hike into Power's Garden gives a good introduction to canyoneering in the Galiuros. You might also consider exploring the length of Rattlesnake Canyon from the base of Power's Hill north to its confluence with Aravaipa Creek, via Turkey Creek Canyon, which was once a primary migration route for prehistoric Indians.

Southern End. To reach the southern end of the Galiuros, and the start of the canyon adventure described here, drive west from Wilcox on Cascabel Road 14 miles to Hooker Hot Springs Road; turn right (northwest) and follow this dirt road approximately 16 miles to Hooker Hot Springs, also called the Muleshoe Ranch. Road 691 leads to Jackson Cabin and the start of this trek, but at the time of this writing, access across Hot Springs Canyon was restricted. It's a rough, oil-pan–banging 4WD road approximately 15 miles long—so if vehicular access is restricted, or if your shuttle happens to be a low-slung pink Cadillac, plan at least an extra day to hoof it all the way to Jackson Cabin.

Canyon Log (all mileages approximate)

Hooker Hot Springs was named after pioneer Arizona beef contractor Henry C. Hooker, who ramrodded the nearby Sierra Bonita Ranch, the largest cattle outfit in Arizona during the 1800s, which supplied government troops with meat. According to notes on file by "Shaaf" at the University of Arizona's Special Collections Library, Hooker's Crooked H brand dates back to 1869 and "is considered the oldest continuously working brand in Arizona." Today the Arizona Nature Conservancy manages the historic adobe buildings at Hooker Hot Springs and the 55,000-acre Mule Shoe Ranch to protect the near-pristine habitat on the southern end of the Galiuros.

Mile 0 to 7.5.   Mule Shoe Ranch to Pride Ranch, via 4WD track. This stretch only gives you a taste of the wild ground awaiting you beyond. A paragraph in the September 1983 *Nature Conservancy Newsletter* underscores the area's ecological significance:

> Flowing through the canyon bottoms toward the San Pedro River, the spring-fed streams . . . support rich riparian communities dominated by sycamore, velvet ash, Fremont cottonwood, Gooding willow, and Arizona alder. Raptors such as black hawks, zone-tailed hawks, and gray hawks perch in cottonwoods along the stream banks, while golden eagles and peregrine falcons soar overhead . . . bighorn sheep [are sometimes seen] grazing stop the rimrock 2,500 feet above. At higher elevations mature stands of Arizona cypress and evergreen oak woodlands associated with juniper and ponderosa pine provide additional habitat for black bear, mountain lion, whitetail and mule deer, javelina, bobcat, coatimundi, and gray fox.

Mile 7.5 to 15.   Pride Ranch to Jackson Cabin, via 4WD track. Jackson Cabin, located above Redfield Canyon, is a good place to bed down for the night. Jackson was a little-known miner who punched a few glory holes in nearby Mitchell Canyon some time ago. According to John P. Wilson's *Islands in the Desert*, "Mineral samplings revealed variable but generally low values of silver and negligible percentages of gold and copper."

Mile 15 to 20.   Jackson Cabin to Negro Canyon, via Redfield Canyon Trail No. 289. The south fork of Negro Canyon Drains the northwest slope of 7,663-foot Bassett peak, high point of the Galiuro Mountains; according to *Arizona Place Names* author William C. Barnes, the peak was probably named after Bob Bassett, who ran cattle in the vicinity. But the real story behind Bassett Peak went down shortly after midnight on July

13, 1950; that's when an Air Force B-50 carrying ten crewmen and 8,000 gallons of fuel blew out a propeller at 13,000 feet. Somehow six crewmen managed to crawl out of the doomed B-50 through the nose landing gear before "zero-four-zero" exploded on impact on Bassett Peak, killing the four crewmen still trapped inside. Flames from the fire storm were reportedly seen 50 miles away in Tucson, and surviving crewmen recalled having to steer their parachutes away from the cataclysmic inferno. Fortunately, a local cowboy named Rocky Vindiola saw the flames and rode in the next morning to save the day.

Four decades later, Rocky was reunited with four of the surviving airmen on Bassett Peak, thanks to the extraordinary gumshoeing of Richard Johnson, who spent two years piecing together the still-classified military puzzle. According to one account in the May 11, 1986, edition of *The Arizona Republic*, by Nyle Leatham, "even after 36 years the file on the crash of this particular B-50 was still a national security secret. . . . Johnson guessed that this might have been a nuclear training flight. This later proved correct."

Mile 20 to 24.5.   Negro Canyon to Redfield-Rattlesnake Canyon Divide, via Redfield Canyon Trail No. 289. In *Frog Mountain Blues*, author Charles Bowden wrote: "There is a distance that must be crossed from this safe country where we now live to this other world, a place that looks hostile to us. That journey takes us to the wild ground that tugs at our memory and spooks us with its power." The entire length of Redfield Canyon from Jackson Cabin is just such a stretch of "wild ground"–but it becomes more so the closer you approach the Redfield-Rattlesnake Canyon Divide. Here you're halfway between hell and gone, midway between the San Pedro River a dozen miles to the west and Aravaipa Creek a dozen miles to the east. There are no simple solutions if you get into trouble, and nobody will come to your rescue–unless Rocky Vindiola's kin are still riding the range. But that's just what makes the Galiuros so enticing; they're genuine hardtack wilderness.

As far as the rest of the route is concerned, once the trail breaks out of Redfield Canyon and heads across Cedar Flat, it becomes less distinct; it frequently plays cat and mouse in dense stands of manzanita and pinyon juniper. But if you can visualize the Galiuros as a capital H, with you traveling from bottom to top via a canyon system linked by the crossbar of that H, you won't get snookered trying to find the Redfield-Rattlesnake Canyon Divide.

Mile 24.5 to 31.5. Redfield-Rattlesnake Canyon Divide to Power's Garden: 6,866-foot Keilberg Peak is less than a mile west and a thousand vertical feet above BM 5,889, which marks the pass you'll cross on the Redfield-Rattlesnake Canyon Divide. The peak is named after a Danish prospector who lived in the vicinity from 1875 to 1920.

Once you drop off the steep north side of the divide, you'll follow Rattlesnake Canyon Trail No. 96 all the way to Power's Garden. En route, you'll walk through fine stands of ponderosa pines clinging to the slopes near the Long Tom Mine, from which high-grade gold ore was extracted. About the time you reach Power's Mine, the trail becomes a washed out, hand-forged wagon track the Powers built in order to get to their "low-grade" gold mine in the early 1900s. According to *Shootout at Dawn*, by Tom Power with Tom Whitlach, John Power lived in the mine for some time after his release from prison and eventually removed the bones of his father, buried in the mine since the shoot-out, to a cemetery in Aravaipa Valley.

A mile and a half south of Power's Garden, 6,915-foot Grassy Ridge is to your left. *Arizona Republic* outdoor writer Bob Thomas reported finding an old-time wooden fire finder atop Grassy Ridge; horseback forest rangers had once used it to pinpoint fires during tinder-dry summer months. "The lookout 'tower' was a seat set in the crotch of a scrub oak about 6 feet off the ground," wrote Thomas.

Mile 31.5 to 36.6. Power's Garden to Power's Hill Trailhead, via Rattlesnake Canyon Trail No. 96. Today, the seemingly idyllic setting of Power's Garden belies the nature of the tragic gunfight that took place here more than 70 years ago. The Powers' chinked log cabin is still standing, backdropped by a verdant green meadow lined with ponderosas airbrushing the skies; this Western postcard scene is fleshed out with a corral, a pond, and a CCC–era ranger station that serves both as a line shack for cowboys working the gnarly upper slopes of Rattlesnake Canyon and as a refuge for hikers tromping into the heart of this range. But a brooding surrounds Power's Garden that's still difficult to pinpoint. On three separate occasions when I've traversed this range, it's never been sunny, there's usually been a damp chill in the air, and cacophonous thunder has always threatened. If ghosts still linger from that shoot-out in 1918, you will feel them here at Power's Garden.

Three miles north of Power's Garden, Rattlesnake Canyon and Trail No. 96 make a dogleg turn to the right (east). Look for cairns that mark the way through this flood-swept creek bottom to the base of Power's Hill—

or you might find yourself wandering aimlessly into Pipestem Canyon and over Fourmile Peak into Eddie Lackner's killing ground. Power's Hill is unimaginably steep; it's rocky; and it's not picturesque until you reach the top. It is, however, the one sure sign that you're leaving the stone-wild country of the Galiuro Wilderness.

Travel Notes

• **Primary access.** Power's Hill Trailhead, via Rattlesnake Canyon Road; and Mule Shoe Ranch, via Cascabel Road.

• **Total elevation gain and loss.** From Mule Shoe Ranch to the top of Power's Hill, approximately 3,000 vertical feet each way.

• **Mileage.** Approximately 37 to 40 miles point to point.

• **Water sources.** Intermittent stretches of Redfield and Rattlesnake canyons, with numerous seasonal springs en route.

• **Escape options.** Dial 1-800-ROCKY-VINDIOLA.

• **Seasons.** All year from Power's Hilltop to Power's Garden; otherwise spring and fall are best. Ovenlike temperatures in the Galiuro interior should discourage you from traversing the length of this canyon system midsummer, and old man winter deals his own interesting deck.

• **Maps.** Winchester Mountains, Redington, and Galiuro Mountains (15-minute topographical maps).

• **Managing agency.** Coronado National Forest.

• **Backcountry information.** Permit not required; limit campfires to streambeds.

• **Biotic communities.** Plains and desert grassland, encinal and Mexican oak woodland, interior chaparral, juniper-pinyon woodland, and montane conifer forest.

Trekking

Pinaleno Mountains

Coronado National Forest: peak ascent

Landform

At 10,720 feet above sea level, the Pinaleno Mountains are the third highest mountain range in the state; yet they encompass a 300-square-mile area and have the greatest vertical relief of any range in Arizona. Thirty-five miles long and 10 to 12 miles wide, the northwest-trending Pinalenos thrust up out of the neighboring San Simon and Sulphur Springs valleys for more than 7,000 vertical feet. Dramatically steep granite ridges like Eagle Rock, Marijilda, Deadman, and Trap frequently exceed 45 degrees. On the down side, perennial streams like Ash, Deadman, Grant, Marijilda, Moonshine, and Post drain into the Gila River to the northeast and Aravaipa Creek to the southwest. In short, no other mountain range in Arizona offers a more challenging and spectacular peak ascent than the Pinalenos — if you climb from the bottom.

Historical Overview

Some believe that 1st Lt. George M. Wheeler, of the U.S. Army Corps of Engineers, made the first recorded ascent of Mount Graham in 1872. In Volume III of the *Report upon Geographical and Geological Explorations and Surveys*, Lieutenant Wheeler vaguely describes his ascent: "Mount Graham I ascended from the northeast. . . . It is of imposing proportions, rising 6,000 feet from its eastern base (and nearly as much from its western) so abruptly that it is difficult of ascent."

But if the August 14, 1869, letter written by Capt. R. F. Bernard of the First Cavalry says what it suggests, then Lieutenant Wheeler may have been beaten to the punch; wrote Captain Bernard to his superior:

> Sir, I have the honor to report my return to camp [Bowie] after an absence of ten days, scouting in and around Mount Graham. The results of which are as follows . . . August 6th. Marched west along the base of the Mountain, crossing (4) streams with permanent water all running south. After travelling west about 7 miles, I turned north going up a very deep, long and narrow cañon, with a good sized stream of permanent water. crossed the mountain, camped on the headwaters of a stream running north. here is one of the finest Pine Forests I ever saw. the whole top and north side of this mountain is a magnificent Pine Forest. distance traveled about twenty (20) miles.

The following morning, Captain Bernard and thirty-three troops descended the opposite side of the Pinalenos and cut fresh Indian sign. As if traversing this towering range in 2 days weren't tiring enough, Bernard's men chased a band of Spanish-speaking Indians near the base of the mountains

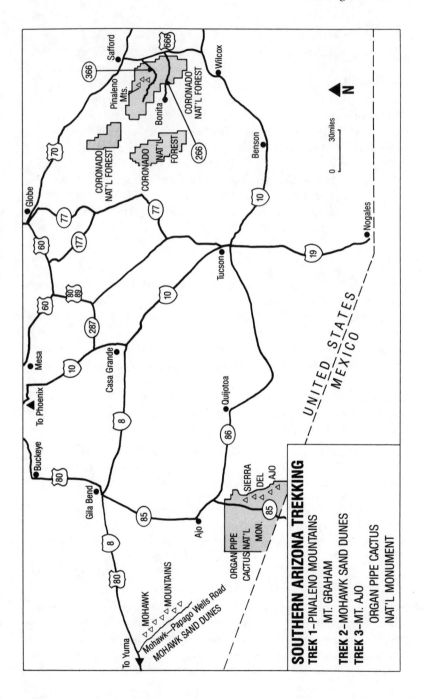

SOUTHERN ARIZONA TREKKING

TREK 1-PINALENO MOUNTAINS
MT. GRAHAM

TREK 2-MOHAWK SAND DUNES

TREK 3-MT. AJO
ORGAN PIPE CACTUS
NAT'L MONUMENT

and tried to strong-arm them into "abandoning their stock." Outnumbered two to one, the Indians bravely faced down the First Cavalry in a classic Mexican standoff.

Win, lose, or draw, Bernard's 1869 exploration may have been the first recorded ascent and traverse of the Pinalenos, though the region had been visited repeatedly by many earlier explorers who gave the range a variety of different names. According to John P. Wilson's *Islands in the Desert*, Gen. Fernandez de la Fuente first called the Pinalenos the Sierra de Santa Rosa in 1695. Two years later Juan Mateo Manje made the name even longer: Sierra de la Santa Rosa de la Florida. Both names were a mouthful and neither stuck. But when Lt. William H. Emory rode into Arizona in 1846, Indians told him the mountains were the "pinon lanos," or deer people, and Emory applied that name to the mountain the Mexicans had been calling the Sierra Bonita. Then, on October 28, 1846, Emory named the highest summit of the Pinalenos Mount Graham, though, according to *Arizona Place Names*, nobody knew for sure which Graham Emory named the peak after: Secretary of the Interior William H. Graham, First Dragoons Maj. Lawrence Pike Graham, or Boundary Survey member Col. James Duncan Graham.

This confusion didn't stop new settlers like Army wife Mary Banks Stacey from simply calling the Pinalenos "Mount Graham," which locals later shortened to "the Grahams." Nor did a bout with malaria stop Mrs. Stacey from accompanying her husband, Lt. Col. May Humphreys Stacey, on an arduous "camping trip" to the top of the Grahams on August 20, 1879. Ostensibly, the purpose of the trek was for Lieutenant Colonel Stacey's men to fell timber for nearby Camp Thomas. But when Mrs. Stacey later wrote to her mother about the outing, she was most excited about what could be seen from near the summit: "Last evening Col. Stacey and I walked up on one of the higher knolls near here and had a buano vista [good view]. We Could see for miles & miles of plains, valleys and strips of desert."

In 1886, Gen. Nelson A. Miles and his men built a heliograph station atop 10,022-foot Heliograph Peak; situated atop the Pinaleno's second highest summit, this heliograph station used mirrors to signal military troops of Indian movement in the valleys below. But the Heliograph Peak operation must not have been too successful, because the Army maintained an infirmary nearby on Hospital Flat—evidently to treat all the soldiers who missed the warning signals and were waylaid by Apaches.

Forerunners to Geronimo's men, the Cochise and Hohokam cultures first inhabited the fertile valleys at the foot of the Pinalenos some 10,000 years ago. Archaeologists believe they roamed the upper reaches of the

Pinalenos during the mild seasons to hunt and gather. But this delicate balancing act between man and nature was turned on its ear with the coming of the white man. In Robert J. Farrel's "Mount Graham and the Pinalenos," the *Arizona Highways Magazine* editor wrote: "By 1871 the Pinalenos belonged to the United States, and the 'Apache problem' belonged to Brigadier General George Crook: it was up to him to 'pacify' the hostiles. For months the skilled guerilla fighters led Crook's troops on grueling chases through hot desert valleys and the rugged mountains of southern Arizona, including the Pinalenos."

With the Army's hospital, heliograph station, and logging operation already in place on the summit crest of the Pinalenos, it was only a matter of time before prospectors swarmed over the mountain like starry-eyed maggots. But the Pinaleno's Precambrian granite and gneiss rarely yielded enough color to fill the average prospector's sorry, rotten teeth.

What the Pinalenos did offer was timber: more than 32 square miles of it above the 8,000-foot level. By the turn of the century, according to *Islands in the Desert*, "illegal sawmills . . . operated in every accessible canyon, so that very little timber could still be reached below 7,500 [feet]." Without roads to the high country, the most practical way to get the timber off the mountain was by flume. One undocumented story concerns a tow-headed lad who fell into a flume and slid all the way down the mountain, toward certain death, until a couple of quick-thinking mill workers caught him in a giant catcher's mitt fashioned from a mattress.

About the time commercial lumbering played out in the early 1920s, Safford residents began riding horseback up the mountain in quest of a summer haven from the appalling heat in the valley below. Word spread faster than the Pony Express, and before long the town fathers started promoting the idea of a road to the top of the mountain. When, in 1931, construction of the 32-mile-long Swift Trail was completed up Jacobson Canyon, reported to be a significant migration route for black bear and whitetail deer, the mountain's destiny was paved in stone. And it was only a matter of time before the next generation of opportunists arrived atop the Pinalenos; like the prospectors before them, the astronomy community also saw "gold in them thar' hills." But the scientists collided with environmentalists in a battle between telescopes and red squirrels, which, according to *Washington Post* columnist Colman McCarthy, involved "an unprecedented coalition of powers." Wrote McCarthy: "These range from Congress and the Smithsonian to Pope John Paul II. Throw in some academic powerhouses—the University of Arizona—plus Patton, Boggs, and Blow, of Washington, a lobbying titan, and this looms as the conservation battle of the decade. If the red squirrels last that long." Ultimately at stake, however, is the natural integrity of southern Arizona's highest mountain and modern man's right to destroy a rare Ice Age habitat on his own planet in order to study possible life forms on other planets. With the help of Arizona Congressman Morris K.

Udall, the University of Arizona had already established that precedent years earlier by erecting telescopes atop southern Arizona's other sky islands: 6,880-foot Kitt Peak in the Quinlin Mountains, 8,585-foot Mount Hopkins in the Santa Ritas, and the 9,157-foot summit of the Santa Catalinas. In "How the University Knocked Off Mount Graham," Charles Bowden wrote: "Udall himself at the dedication for Mt. Hopkins in 1973 had warned the astronomy community that this was their last mountain, that they had gobbled up enough." But when push came to shove a decade and a half later, Udall endorsed the University of Arizona's plans to erect more telescopes atop yet another southern Arizona summit. This time, they literally stole the crown jewels . . . without consulting the people of Arizona, including Udall's own conservation-minded constituents. As Udall admitted, according to Bowden's article, "'To short circuit the process Congress has established by law . . . is something I do not regard warmly.' And then he voted yes."

It's interesting to note that few people from either side of this long, controversial, still-raging battle have bothered to examine this magnificent mountain from bottom to top before attempting to determine its fate. Wherever you might stand on the issue, you're urged to climb this mountain. However, if you'd still prefer to drive within shouting distance of the summits of Mount Graham and Heliograph Peak, you can do so on the Swift Trail, Forest Highway 366 – but you should avoid that route during the late fall. When it came time for Arizona peak bagger extraordinaire Doug Kasian to climb the Pinalenos' three highest summits, Kasian drove to the top of the range and rounded up Heliograph Peak, Mount Graham, and 10,029-foot Webb Peak in an afternoon's romp. But "Karmic kickback" for not climbing the mountain from the bottom ambushed the mountaineer by nightfall and the ensuing snowstorm buried his small truck under a slab of fresh snow. Kasian and his fiancée were forced to bail off the west side of the mountain, descending by foot all the way to the Fort Grant Detention Center – 11 miles and 5,000 vertical feet below. Savage guard dogs hurled themselves at the cyclone fence that protected the tired couple as Kasian frantically tried to explain to armed guards patrolling the perimeter that his truck was stuck atop Mount Graham . . . and could they please use the phone. No stranger to Arctic winters, the Canadian-born Kasian returned to the Pinalenos a week later and, with the determination of a caged badger, spent 5 days burrowing his truck down off the mountain-top before the next winter snow buried it until spring. Kasian's epic — and ultimately successful — snow-shoveling expedition is a vivid warning to all prospective drive-in summiteers who visit the Pinalenos.

Directions

From Safford, follow the signs to the Mount Graham Golf Course. Take the dirt road paralleling the east side of the golf course south to a gate. This marks the Safford Water District Road; it turns into Frye Creek Road, which contours over to the foot of Trap Peak Ridge approximately 6 miles southwest. There's a pullout at the foot of Trap Peak Ridge near BM 4,606, and you can pinpoint the area by referring to your Mount Graham quadrangle and zeroing in on Section 8, T.8 S., R.25 E.

The Ridges Trek Log

Two major ridges lead directly to the summit of Mount Graham on its northeast side: Deadman Ridge and Trap Peak Ridge. Of the two, Trap Peak Ridge is far easier to climb; it's a straightforward ridgeline that you can hike from bottom to top, with only one minor obstacle en route. An ascent of Deadman Ridge is a far more serious mountaineering objective: It's longer, begins 1,000 feet lower, and requires challenging and time-consuming route-finding skills for the semitechnical difficulties and dense brush on its lower half.

Trap Peak Ridge Route

Mile 0 to 3. In *Explorations and Surveys*, Lt. George M. Wheeler wrote: "Standing near . . . the base of Mt. Graham, one can overlook the whole region. A splendid mirage makes its appearance on the southern horizons every clear morning in the form of a transmuting mountain-chain." From the foot of Trap Peak Ridge, you can see all the way up that "transmuting mountain-chain" to the summit of southern Arizona's premier sky island more than 6,000 vertical feet above — and it's no mirage.

From the foot of Trap Peak Ridge, meander up to the crest of the ridge-line, which is your ascent line. Other than a drift fence at the 5,400-foot level, there is little evidence that modern man has explored this magnificent ridgeline. Though it is undeniably steep in places, hiking Trap Peak Ridge is like a walk in the park when compared to climbing Deadman Ridge, which parallels Deadman Canyon immediately to the south. According to *Arizona Place Names*, "Graves of seven or eight men were found in this canyon c. 1870." No doubt the First Calvary had tried to muscle local Indians again into giving up their cattle; this time, the Indians named a canyon after them. With little scrambling to contend with on Trap Peak Ridge, there's plenty of time to save this timeline from desert grassland through oak-pine woodlands, ponderosa pine forest, mixed conifer forest, and, finally, spruce-fir forest on the summit. Prepared by the Maricopa Audubon Society, the "Biogeography of the High Peaks of the Pinalenos" is perhaps the single most important ecological overview of this range. According to this report, "Looking at the mountain range only as a series of isolated life-zones stacked on top of each other or an isolated 'sky-island' is to break apart the integrity of the Pinaleno ecosystem. The variety of vegetation condensed into one small mountain . . . is among the richest in western North America." Trap Peak Ridge is your stairway through this biological wonderland.

In the pinyon-juniper country below 8,106-foot Trap Peak, there is some brush to contend with—but nothing as debilitating as the precipitous jungle on the lower half of Deadman Ridge. Near Trap Peak, you should also see the first evidence of the Pinalenos' robust black bear population, estimated at 150 animals. According to the "Biogeography of . . . The Pinalenos," "the Pinalenos support the densest population of bear in the southwest with the smallest home ranges due, in part, to steep terrain permitting easy movement to multiple food sources. Bear scat at 10,500 feet has been seen with prickly pear seeds probably harvested at 3,500 feet."

Offering a 360-degree panorama, Trap Peak itself is the best place on Trap Peak Ridge for landscape photography: 80 miles north, you can easily pick out Arizona's second highest mountain range, 11,403-foot-high Mount Baldy, or Dzil Ligai ("White Mountain"), as traditional White Mountain Apaches know and revere it; the twin heads of 8,354-foot Dos Cabezas Peaks can be seen 30 miles south-southwest, backdropped by the rolling blue highlands of the 9,759-foot Chiricahua Mountains; and if you know exactly where to look—and if it's not vapor-locked under a blanket of Phoenix sludge—you can even make out 7,657-foot Four Peaks on the southern end of the Mazatzal Mountains a hundred miles northwest. It's worth waiting a few hours for "magic time," when late-afternoon light turns the tremendous ridges radiating from the summit of Mount Graham into a supernal mountain world. The only downside for photographers who lug their tripods and 4×5s up Trap Peak is that there's really no place there to set up a comfortable camp and wait for early-morning light. The view is inspiring enough, though, for dedicated professionals to consider curling up next to their cameras and bivouacking on this rocky perch to see what kind of mural early morning light might paint.

Mile 3 to 4.   An obvious, manzanita-choked notch on the west side of Trap Peak will lead you back down to Trap Peak Ridgeline, which, in turn, will lead you to its junction with Round-the Mountain Trail. The ridgeline on either side of this trail junction is covered with ponderosa pine and offers several level places for small parties to camp their first day up the mountain. This is also a good point to assess your progress and to decide whether you have the legs and enough water to climb another 3,000 vertical feet to the summit or whether you should descend the little-used Round-the-Mountain Trail into Deadman Canyon, water, and Trail No. 70 back to your vehicle for a leisurely second day.

Mile 4 to 6.   From Round-the-Mountain Trail, it's half a Grand Canyon depth to the summit of Mount Graham via the steep, heavily wooded, rocky upper half of Trap Peak Ridge; follow the crest of the ridgeline from Peak 8,030 to Peak 8,855 and then to Peak 9,930. At Peak 9,930 you'll have to get on the north side of the ridge crest to avoid the exposed, semi-technical difficulties of Mount Graham's northeast face.

The Summit

In the September 5, 1984, edition of the *Eastern Arizona Courier*, William R. Ridgeway excerpted a brief passage from Hyrum and Sarah Dall Weech's autobiography, *Our Pioneer Parents*; it described a September 1882 ascent of Mount Graham by Safford-area residents Hyrum Weech and John Campbell:

> By hard climbing, we went up on top of the mountain and found it to be a beautiful park of groves of pine timber, with open glades of grass and flowers. We camped for the night and found it quite cool to what it had been in the valley. We decided to explore the mountains and started out following the crest and came to the high peak.
>
> Here we found a small monument erected of loose stones and in this monument was a small can with the names of Lieut. Wheeler and party, government surveyors, who had been there 10 years prior to our visit. The government party had left notes on the elevation of the mountain, which they fixed at 10,500 feet.

This is the same unspoiled summit where ancient Indian shrines have been discovered; archaeologists believe these sites are associated with the Mogollon culture and date back to the year A.D. 1100, when the Pinalenos undoubtedly received their first ascent. These sacred shrines have been claimed by

New Mexico's Zuni Indian tribe, "believed to be descendants of the Mimbres culture that created the shrines."

This is also the same unspoiled summit on which the University of Arizona originally wanted to build its city of skyscraper-high telescopes. But, according to "Biogeography Of . . . The Pinalenos," "the high peaks forest of the Pinalenos is the southernmost development of a true subalpine forest (fir and spruce) in North America"—and thanks to the U.S. Forest Service's sensitive stewardship of this remarkable summit, no telescopes will top Mount Graham in the foreseeable future. Ancient Indian shrines, and the Pleistocene relic forest that surrounds them, will be left undisturbed.

The endangered red squirrel will also be left undisturbed, as will Mount Graham's superlative eastern vista. But as of this writing, the summit, frequently called High Peak by Safford residents, is temporarily off-limits to all comers. Here's why. In the deal that went down behind closed doors, the University of Arizona was granted permission to build the first of seven telescopes atop nearby Emerald Peak. Now 1,800 acres atop Mount Graham, down to the 10,000-foot countour level, sometimes called the Forbidden Zone, are closed to all sightseers, hikers, and climbers so that scientists can use it as a basis of comparison for studying the effect of building seven huge telescopes in the middle of that same red squirrel's prime habitat on nearby Emerald Peak. Unless you get special dispensation from the University of Arizona—and from the Vatican, which has reportedly dumped $2 million into the telescope kitty—you can't climb the highest mountain south of the Mogollon Rim from the bottom or, more popularly, from the nearby Columbine Ranger Station at the 9,500-foot level.

Life was simpler in the days of Lieutenant Wheeler, and when he climbed to the top of the neighboring 7,848-foot-high Pinal Mountains more than a century ago, he described a view comparable to that still seen from the eastern edge of Mount Graham today; in *Explorations and Surveys*, Lieutenant Wheeler wrote:

> To stand on the edge . . . upon a quiet day, and look off upon those wonderfully silent and arid plains, with their innumerable 'lost mountains' rising like precipitous islands from the sea, all bathed in most delicate tints, and lying death-like in the peculiar, intangible afternoon haze of this region, which seems to magnify distant details rather than subdue them, impresses one most deeply. The wonderful monotony seems uninclosable by an horizon; and one imagines the scene to continue on the same and have no end. Though the gulf and ocean are three hundred miles away, yet here is the continent's real southwestern border.

The Descent

To descend off the "continent's southwestern border," either head down the USFS road or follow the southern ridge of Mount Graham down to High Peak Cienaga. According to "Biogeography," High Peak Cienaga is one of three cienagas, or alpine meadowlands unique to southern Arizona, located atop the Pinalenos. Fill up your water jugs here; then continue following Trail No. 308 down Deadman Ridge until it forks. From here, the easiest option is to take Trail No. 325 back over to Trap Peak Ridge, descend the ridge to Round-the-Mountain Trail, and follow trail No. 70 down Deadman Canyon back to your vehicle.

Or you can descend Deadman Ridge. If this is your choice, continue down Trail No. 308 until it turns off into Gibson Creek; then continue picking your way down Deadman Ridge over and around Peak 9,420, Peak 8,835, and Peak 8,500. This section requires sound judgment and good route-finding skills, but you won't encounter any technical or exposed situations if you stay on route. The same applies to the stretch between Peak 8,500 and the junction with Round-the-Mountain Trail—a good place to camp if you're burning daylight on the descent.

From the junction of Deadman Ridge and Round-the-Mountain Trail, it's a straight shot down wonderfully wild Deadman Canyon via trail No. 90. The two 100-foot-high waterfalls near the lower end of Deadman Canyon on the south side also warrant a visit.

Travel Notes

• **Primary access.**   Safford, via Frye Creek Road.

• **Secondary access.**   Deadman Ridge, via Lebanon Reservoir No. 1 Road.

• **Elevation gain and loss.**   7,000-plus vertical feet each way.

• **Mileage.**   14 to 16 miles round-trip, depending on your line of descent.

• **Water sources.**   Deadman Creek and High Peak Cienega.

• **Seasonal water.**   Snow on the northern exposures of Trap Peak Ridge and Deadman Ridge, generally above their junction with Round-the-Mountain Trail.

• **Cache points.**   Round-the-Mountain Trail, where it crosses over Trap Peak Ridge or Deadman Ridge.

• **Escape routes**

   Trap Peak Ridge:
   1. Below Trap Peak, back the way you came.

2. Between Trap Peak and Peak 9,930, Trap Peak Ridge to Round-the-Mountain Trail to Deadman Canyon.

3. Between Peak 9,930 and Mount Graham, your call: In the summertime, Columbine Ranger Station might be your best option; in the wintertime, you would do better to descend Trap Peak Ridge to Round-the-Mountain trail to Deadman Canyon.

Deadman Ridge:
1. Between Peak 9,420 and Peak 8,835, you can descend directly into Deadman Canyon, with care.

2. Below Peak 8,500, follow Deadman Ridge to Round-the-Mountain Trail to Deadman Canyon.

•**Seasons.**   Fall and spring are ideal. It would be difficult in midsummer to carry enough water to climb Trap Peak Ridge, let alone Deadman Ridge. Winter months frequently bury the upper sections of both ridges under deep snow and ice, thereby offering southern Arizona's greatest mountaineering challenge.

•**Maps.**   Mount Graham and Thatcher quadrangles (both 7½ minute) and Coronado National Forest Recreation Map.

•**Nearest supply points.**   Safford and Thatcher.

•**Managing agencies.**   Coronado National Forest, University of Arizona, the Vatican.

•**Backcountry information.**   Permit not required. Check current status of climbing through the Forbidden Zone.

•**Biotic communities.**   Sonoran Desert scrub (Arizona upland subdivision), plains and desert grassland, encinal and Mexican oak-pine woodland, montane conifer forest, and spruce-alpine fir forest.

Mohawk Sand Dunes and Mohawk Mountains Dune Traverse

Landform
Eighteen miles long and 1 to 3 miles wide, the Mohawk Sand Dunes form Arizona's largest dune system; they parallel the west slope of the Mohawk Mountains, a double range of northwest-trending mountains 29 miles long. Bordered on the north by the Gila River and Interstate 8, the tail end of the Mohawk Sand Dunes dissipates in a pass between the northern and southern halves of the Mohawk Mountains called Rat Gap. At its highest

point, the granitic summit of 2,775-foot Mohawk Peak has a vertical relief of 2,000 feet above the Mohawk Sand Dunes, though a vertical relief of 1,500 feet is more common throughout the Mohawk Mountains, which drain into the Gila River via the San Cristobal and Mohawk valleys.

Historical Overview

As late as 1927, huge tracts of the Mohawk Sand Dunes and Mohawk Mountains were nothing but a blank spot on the 15 Minute Kim, AZ quadrangle. Roads like the Mohawk–Papago Well Road ended, as if gobbled up by a great white sandstorm; contour lines fell off the edge of the desert into . . . well . . . nothing; and a simple tag line warned all comers, if they'd bothered to pick up the map in the first place: "Unsurveyed Area." But that's just the kind of invitation a true desert rat looks for. One of the most literate to visit the area, Olga Wright Smith, wrote in her enchanting book, *Gold on the Desert:* "Purple veils of heat smoked over the vast reaches of the Lechuguilla Desert that stretched away from the Copper Mountains. White, transparent veils of heat rippled across the fiery sands." Smith came to know the southwestern Arizona desert well; she spent a year prospecting the Copper Mountains with her husband Cap and his father "Old" Cap Smith in the 1930s. But they didn't venture near the Mohawk Sand Dunes.

No one did, except for the ancient Sand Papago, or No-Villagers, who wandered the harsh Yuma, Tule, and Lechuguilla deserts as late as the 1700s. But this desert proved too hostile even for the intrepid Sand Papago, who marched into extinction after spending centuries eking out a hard-scrabble existence in one of the driest and most forbidding desert regions in North America. Evidence of their desperate nomadic existence can still be seen throughout the vast Barry M. Goldwater Range, including on the Mohawk Sand Dunes.

Blown up against the steep, western flanks of the Mohawk Mountains, the Mohawk Sand Dunes created a formidable barrier for most early travelers. Like the Sierra Estrellas a hundred miles northeast, however, this potential death trap was simply avoided by all but the most recent desert travelers. Situated 10 miles south of the Gila River, the Mohawk Sand Dunes weren't an obstacle that had to be dealt with the way the Pinta Sands had to be faced on El Camino del Diablo immediately to the south. Nor did this sand trap hold the promise of wild game or gold. Most prospectors heading to the California goldfields during the 1850s traveled either by way of the Gila River or down the corridor of death along the Mexican border that became known as the Devil's Highway.

The handful of prospectors who stayed behind focused their diggings in the area's twenty-three basin-and-range–type mountain ranges that now occupy the Barry M. Goldwater Range. Those who narrowed their search down to the Mohawk Mountains generally based out of Mohawk Station. According to a 1933 Arizona Bureau of Mines bulletin, "The sole population of the Mohawk Mountains centers around Mohawk station . . . because the mountains themselves contain no wells and almost no rock tanks or waterholes." While the indefatigable Kirk Bryan did note a rock tank on the east slope of the Mohawk Mountains, and one on the west slope near Glynns Falls, these waterholes were marginal at best. So any early traveler venturing into the Mohawks had to have a good reason to do so and had to haul his own water to boot – usually from the Gila River or Mohawk Station. (The three existing waterholes in the Mohawk Mountains today are water catchments constructed by the Arizona Game and Fish Department for the Desert bighorn sheep.)

Located in a gap on the north end of the Mohawk Mountains 75 miles from Yuma, Mohawk Station was a pivotal stop on the Butterfield Overland Stage Route during the late 1800s. According to the letters of John F. Crampton, "The old man John Killbright committed suicide at Mohawk – took poison and jumped in the well. Next day the stage driver let the stage coach run away and the leaders [horses] ran into the well. That was o.k. We had to dig another well [anyway]."

The two most active mines in the Mohawk Mountains proved slim pickings. The Red Cross Mine, located on the east slope of the Mohawk Mountains 5.5 miles south of Mohawk Station, was owned by George W. Norton, a onetime bridge builder, farmer, and politician. But according to the Arizona Bureau of Mines, that mine produced only $10,000 worth of silver ore in 1910. Located 6 miles south of Mohawk Station on the west slope of the Mohawks, the Tasvaci (or Victoria) Prospect yielded even less gold. Today, little remains of man's early efforts to carve a niche in this hard country.

Those who reaped the biggest cash bounty, though, may have been the moonshiners who operated stills on the east slope of the Mohawk Mountains in the San Cristobal Valley. Remnants of their bootleg operations can still be seen. But perhaps the strangest sign of those times is the intaglio-sized name of AMALIA S. MYERS etched in the black malpais between the Mohawk Mountains and the Mohawk Sand Dunes. No record has been found as to who Amalia S. Myers was or why she might have delved so deeply into her water cache to scrape her name 30 feet across a desert where water has always been the greatest treasure of all.

What has survived the ravages of heat and man's faint marks upon this land are the Mohawk Sand Dunes and the Mohawk Mountains, which now comprise an 85,000-acre state natural area. Few modern adventure travelers have visited this seldom-explored area on foot; most who have were headed north from Mexico during the last decade. Skulls of those who succumbed to the waterless, 50- to 75-mile-long treks from the Mexican border to the farms north of Interstate 8 can still be seen staring up from the blowholes of this great dune and serve as a haunting reminder of what the American desert—and immigration policy—is on its most brutal terms. Obviously, it's best to avoid this desert during the summer.

In winter, though, during those clear, spring-warm days, there is no finer desert to explore on foot. In the 1976 Mojave-Sonoran natural Region Study, it was called "the best major reserve of unspoiled desert in the Southwest." In large part, that's because much of the Arizona desert south of the Gila River, east of the Colorado River, and west of State Route 85—all the way to the U.S.-Mexico border—is now part of the Barry M. Goldwater Range. While some view military stewardship as a two-edged sword, others feel that status as a bombing range protects this immense desert from development, mining, off-road-vehicle use, and heavy visitor use. Generally, no more than a thousand registered users visit the area each year—and that's the very appeal to the true desert rat. "Keep them out of the Cabeza . . . send them to Organ Pipe," I was told by one desert rat.

Directions

From Gila Bend, drive west on Interstate 8 86 miles to Tacna; from Yuma, drive 50 miles east on Interstate 8 to Tacna. From Tacna, drive south over the interstate overpass. Turn left (east) immediately and follow the dirt road parallel to Interstate 8. At Mile 6 the road passes the unmarked turnoff for the Tule Wells Road. At Mile 8, it crosses the north end of the Mohawk Sand Dunes, a good place to jump out if you just want to poke around the north end of the dunes.

If you want to traverse the dunes, though, continue east. At Mile 9, take the right fork. The road turns south 10.6 miles out from Tacna; at Mile 11, take another fork to the right. There's been some confusion among desert afficionados and Border patrol trackers about the Papago Wells Road; some call the Tule Well Road, which parallels the west side of the Mohawk Sand Dunes, the Papago Wells Road. According to Kirk Bryan and the Mohawk Mountains SW 7½ Minute quadrangle, the Mohawk–Papago Wells Road skirts the east side of the Mohawk Sand Dunes. This is the road you'll take to reach the south end of the dunes; it's a bumpy though enthralling ride because it follows the natural corridor formed by the serrated crest of the Mohawk Mountains and the Mohawk Sand Dunes. Twenty-four miles out from Tacna (NW ¼ of Section 29, T.10 S. R.13 W. on the Mohawk Mountains SW quadrangle) you'll pass the turnoff to Game Tanks; 50 yards beyond will be a turnoff to the right. This is the cutoff to the Tule Wells Road; by following this sandy track for a mile you'll get into the middle of the Mohawk Sand Dunes, where you can begin your traverse.

Trek Log

Mile 0 to 4. A prominent eastern rim can be followed across the length of the Mohawk Sand Dunes, but to gain the foot of this sand ridge you'll need to wander in a general northwest direction for the first 3 miles. The first mile out, you can key off of a large silver dart, or tow target, embedded in the sand like a giant arrowhead. Ths tow target, and hundreds of others concentrated in the San Cristobal Valley to the east, are used by military pilots to simulate fighting enemy aircraft. However, few tow targets can be seen in the Mohawk Sand Dunes and the Mohawk Mountains because they lie within the buffer zone, which divides the Marines' 2301 western half of the Barry M. Goldwater Range from Luke Air Force Base's 2301 eastern half.

If for some reason you fail to see this 15-foot-high tow dart glinting in the sun, you can key off of 1,366-foot Baker Peaks, or use a compass. But if you need a compass in this desert, you probably shouldn't be wandering around in this despoblado (uninhabited land) to begin with. You can clearly see wherever you want to go, though distances frequently appear deceptively close.

Mile 4 to 10. At about Mile 4, you'll pick up the east rim of the dunes, which you can easily follow to your shuttle vehicle on the north end of the dunes. The best way to stay oriented on this traverse is to key off of nipple-shaped Mohawk Peak North while following the rim of the dunes. The high point of the Mohawk Mountains, though, is 2,775-foot Mohawk Peak, which will be on your right (to the east); it towers above Glynns Falls, a series of rock tanks that, according to William C. Barnes, "seldom hold enough water to form falls." So don't count on Glynns Falls as an emergency water source.

Mile 10 to 12. At about Mile 10, you can see a playa, or dry lake, at the eastern foot of the dunes. This ephemeral water source has been identified as an archaeological site by Arizona State Museum: on the edge of the Mohawk Playa, archaeologists discovered a stone awl, among other artifacts, and some calcified bones indicating that ancient Indians like the Sand Papago used this area during favorable wet weather.

The Mohawk Playa is also a good place to measure your progress across the dunes and to decide whether or not you'll need to camp out before reaching your shuttle vehicle. If you're thinking about building a campfire, though, there are two good reasons not to. First, the prominent forms of vegetation in the dunes are bur sage, Mormon tea, creosote, and big galleta grass, so there is no firewood to speak of. And second, the corridor between the Mohawk Sand Dunes and the Mohawk Mountains is sometimes used by drug runners who make use of several remote airstrips on the western periphery of Mexico's Pinacate Protected Zone; they're known to fly this corridor at night without lights, reportedly with night-vision goggles, and unless you'd like to share your tortillas and beans with Uzi-packing desperadoes, it's best to keep your own lights turned off as well.

Mile 12 to 16. At about Mile 12, or Elevation Point 607, you'll have one last chance to gaze southeast along the crest of the dunes all the way to Rat Gap 20 miles away. According to the Luke Air Force Range's landmark *Natural Resources Management Plan*, the Mohawk Sand Dunes "are composed of semi-stabalized, wind-blown sand . . . derived from Colorado River delta sediment." From the middle of the Mohawk Sand Dunes, though, it's difficult to imagine that a piece of the Grand Canyon was blown into the heart of this despoblado. If you haven't done so already, take time to explore the blowholes of this sand sea, where you may see remnants from the ancient Sand Papago, or the abandoned, sun-cracked plastic water jugs of more recent desert nomads. Fortunately, there is little evidence of all-terrain-cycle or off-road-vehicle use in the Mohawk Sand dunes; the occasional vehicle tracks you'll see are usually those left years earlier by Border Patrol trackers trying to save the lives of heat-ravaged Mexican citizens trekking north.

To reach the northeast end of the dunes, continue keying off of Mohawk Peak North. Head for Peak 853 on the border of Sections 26 and 25, T.8 S. R.15 W. on your Mohawk quadrangle, and you'll be out of the dunes.

Shuttle vehicle. A good place to park your shuttle vehicle is near the base of Peak 853. Aim your rearview mirrors southwest so you can see the late-afternoon sun glinting off of them when you come off the northeast end of the dunes.

Travel Notes

- **Primary access.** Tacna, via Mohawk–Papago Wells Road.

- **Elevation gain and loss.** Approximately 500 vertical feet each way.

- **Mileage.** Approximately 16 miles each way.

- **Water sources.** No perennial water en route. Emergency water can generally be found in a sheep guzzler known by three different names: Mohawk Catchment No. 2, Game Tanks, or Agua de Banado; it's located in the SE ¼ Section 16, T.10 S. R.13 W. on your Mohawk Mountains SE quadrangle. Seasonal water may be found in the Mohawk Playa for a short period after winter rains and summer monsoons.

- **Cache points.** Not applicable.

- **Escape routes.** Game Tanks, or Interstate 8, whichever is closest. You may be able to signal military or Border Patrol pilots with a mirror if they don't mistake your flashes for the sun flickering off a silver tow target.

- **Seasons.** Late fall through early spring. Walking the dunes after a winter rain is like strolling along the beach after the tide goes out; midsummer, it could become a death slog.

- **Maps.** Mohawk, Mohawk SE, Mohawk Mountains SW, and Mohawk Mountains NW (all 7½-minute quadrangles); and AJO (1 × 2 Degree, Scale of 1:250,000).

- **Biotic community.** Sonoran Desert scrub (lower Colorado subdivision).

- **Nearest supply points.** Gila Bend, Tacna, and Yuma.

- **Managing agency.** Barry M. Goldwater Range.

- **Backcountry information.** Permit required.
    The Mohawk Sand Dunes and Mountains are located on 2301 West-half of the Barry M. Goldwater Range. Contact Fleet Liaison Office, S-3 Department, Marine Corps Air Station, Yuma, AZ 85364; (602) 726-3558.
    To explore the country east of the Mohawk Sand Dunes and Mountains on 2301 East-half of the Range, contact Department of the Air Force, Headquarters 832D Combat Support Group (TAC), Luke Air Force Base, AZ 85309; (602) 856-7653.
    You'll be sent a Visitor Information Kit; once you review the Explosive Safety Awareness Handout, you'll be required to sign a Hold Harmless Agreement.

Once you receive your military permit to visit the Range, you should also contact the U.S. Border Patrol, Tacna Station, P.O. Box 70, Tacna, AZ 85352; (602) 785-9364. Let them know that you have a permit to be in the area, what your vehicle looks like, the size of your party, what kind of shoes you're wearing, and your itinerary. If you get into trouble, they should be able to find you – if the Marines haven't already bailed you out.

Sierra del Ajo

Ajo Range, Organ Pipe Cactus National Monument: peak ascents

Landform

Seventeen miles long and 7 miles wide, the 4,812-foot-high Sierra del Ajo is a north-trending fault-block mountain range that rises abruptly out of the surrounding desert bajadas for more than 3,000 vertical feet; these sweeping, cactus-covered lowlands include the Valley of the Ajo to the northwest, the Sonoyta Valley to the southwest, and the Bajarita and La Quituni valleys to the east. The Sierra del Ajo is elongated on the south by a 2,921-foot-high border-hopping subsidiary range, called the Sierra de Santa Rosa, and is crowned on its northern end by a 3,634-foot-high grotesque pyramid of clastic rock, called Montezuma's Head.

Historical Overview

During his 1980 archaeological survey of the Ajo Crest, Michael G. Mallouf located and recorded fifty-one archaeological sites, which, he reported, represented the late prehistoric or early Papago period. What had to be a physically arduous survey to conduct substantiates the fact that the aboriginal Papago, Tohono O'Odham, had climbed to the top of Mount Ajo long before Dr. William T. Hornaday first saw the range on November 7, 1907, during a monthlong bio-geographical expedition to the Pinacate region in Mexico's El Gran Desierto. In his classic account of that adventure, *Campfires on Desert and Lava,* Hornaday wrote: "Early in the afternoon we reached the gap between the Gunsight Mountains on the north and the Ajo Mountains (please pronounce it Ah'ho) on the south. . . . A terminal ridge . . . comes down from the Ajo Mountains; and on beyond that looms up a remarkable peak that is called Montezuma's Head. . . . Naturally, this peak is a conspicuous landmark for desert travelers, but particularly for those in the Ajo Valley."

From the trailhead in Tucson, the Hornaday expedition had first skirted the northern end of the Sierra del Ajo via the old Tucson-Yuma Road before turning south on the historic Sonoyta Road, which took them along the western flanks of the range to Sonoyta, Sonora. But the Hornaday Expedition wasn't the only one to journey within the shadows of the Sierra del Ajo. Originating 100 miles south of the border at Caborca, Sonora, the ancient El Camino del Diablo turned west at Sonoyta near the southern end of the range; yet another historic route traveled north through the Quijotoa Valley on the east slope of the Sierra del Ajo. According to Luke Air Force Base's *Resource Management Plan,* "This route was used extensively by the Spanish when they traveled north from Mexico to settlements along the Gila River. . . . Fathers Kino and Sedelmayr and Pedro Fages all used this route during the 1700s. It usually began at one of the missions in northern Mexico and headed north into what is now the Papago Indian Reservation, through the Quijotoa Valley and between the Saucedas and the Sand Tanks [mountains]."

A widely published and respected historian and geographer, the late Ronald L. Ives, retraced the route of Lt. Col. Pedro Fages' 1781 expedition, which covered 980 miles in 106 days. Fages' circuitous route not only looped Organ Pipe Cactus National Monument but completely encircled the entire 4,100-square-mile hidden quarter now occupied by the Barry M. Goldwater Range. After passing through the late-afternoon shadow wall of the Sierra del Ajo on October 4, Fages wrote: "We set out after dinner, in order to shorten the [next] day's march and be able to reach water. . . . After going eight leagues to the north through good pasturage, we halted on some plains abounding in it. There was no water." After traveling north through the pass between the Sauceda and Sand Tank mountains 4 days later, Fages wrote: "We set out at midnight, continuing our northward march over very broken and stony ground—especially bad were the three leagues lying in a small pass with several ravines. . . . Then we continued our journey in order to reach water."

If the brief passages from Fages' diary address anything it's the problem associated with trying to visit someplace on the scale of, and as dry as, Organ Pipe Cactus National Monument: a 514-square-mile desert sanctuary completely surrounded by the sparsely populated modern despoblado of two countries and one Indian nation. It can't all be taken in in a day, or even a week. Maybe a month. So if you really want to see this desert, you have two choices: by vehicle or on foot. But as enticing as the 53-mile Puerto Blanco and 21-mile Ajo Mountain Loop drives are for early-morning and late-afternoon tours, a drive is a drive—and no true desert wanderer ever felt the power, the loneliness, the empty beauty of the desert from the saddle of his pickup truck. In *The Wilderness of Desert Bighorns and Seri Indians,* the mountain-climbing Charles Sheldon wrote, "I am alone again, an outlaw . . . near the route of the insurrectos. The moon is nearly full; the mountains are mysterious. The wind has begun to roar." You have to go on foot to get that feeling. But keep in mind: Except for a dozen or so miles of trail, all hiking in Organ Pipe is cross-country, and Fages has already provided some historic insight into what crossing vast stretches of rocky open ground in search of water is like.

Once known as Santa Rosa Peak, Mount Ajo is, at 4,812 feet, the highest mountain in Organ Pipe. It has the vertical relief of "a two thousand-foot mountain, a steep face, and a serrated top," in the words of Indiana-born and New York City-bred desert rat William T. Hornaday. And where better to survey this ancient land form than from the prehistoric perch of the aboriginal Papago?

Directions

From the Visitor Center at Organ Pipe Cactus National Monument, take Ajo Mountain Drive to Milepost 16, the Estes Canyon Picnic Area. Park here.

Trek Log (all mileage approximate)

Mile 0 to 2.   Via the Bull Pasture Trail. If you have problems following one of the only maintained trails in all of Organ Pipe Cactus National Monument, hire a local guide. But be careful in these parts, lest you run into trouble with La Migra (the Border Patrol). The Hornaday Expedition's Mexican guide, Charlie Foster, knew the desert's unmarked trails and waterholes extremely well, perhaps because he was something of an early-day *coyote,* or smuggler, having "successfully, albeit illegally, piloted several hundred Chinamen across the desert."

The Bull Pasture Trail switchbacks up 1,000 vertical feet in 2 miles from the Estes Canyon Picnic Area to the hikers' register at trail's end. From there, take some time to eyeball and consider the cross-country route from the register to the Ajo Crest; it's farther than it looks. It's *always* farther than it looks. So if you have any doubts about the rigors and peculiarities of rugged, cross-country desert trekking, venture out on some of Organ Pipe's less demanding cross-country treks highlighted at the end of this section. On February 3, 1971, a P.E. instructor from the University of New Mexico named Carol Turner went for a hike into Bull Pasture and

Adventurer Randy Mulkey traverses the crest of the Sierra del Ajo which forms the natural border between the Tohono O'Odham Indian lands to the east (background) and Organ Pipe Cactus National Monument to the west. Photo by John Annerino.

disappeared; in *Cactus Country,* the late Edward Abbey wrote: "At the height of the search [for her] a total of 130 men were involved . . . including Papago trackers, a United States Air Force helicopter, the Ajo town police, the border patrol, the county Sheriff's department and the entire volunteer search and rescue team of Pima County." Carol Turner was never found.

Mile 2 to 3.   From trail's end, you can follow an incipient track down into the first drainage to the east, the site of several tinajas and a spring. These waterholes were valuable to early *caballeros* (Mexican cowboys), who reportedly called them *Tinaja de los Toros,* "Watering Tanks of the Bulls." Kirk Bryan, however, was the first to note that water existed here; most likely because of that, a trail or route traversed the rugged Sierra del Ajo from west to east. Wrote Bryan: "A trail also goes northwest by way of Bull Pasture, a small but permanent spring, across the Ajo Mountains to Cochibo." Cochibo is a Tohono O'Odham Indian Village on the far eastern side of the mountain, and Bryan's discovery suggests that aboriginal Papago had worked out a demanding yet defined route across the imposing Sierra del Ajo from the vicinity of the Quijotoa Valley to the Sonoyta Valley long before the first white man ever laid eyes on the range. This route was also used between 1915 and 1917 by Villistas who found Bull Pasture an ideal hideout "to escape from their revolutionary adversaries." In his excellent *Historic Resource Study of Organ Pipe*, Jerome A. Greene wrote: "In one instance a [National] guard unit went up to Bull Pasture only to find its Mexican occupants had escaped over the sides of the basin by using ropes."

While it's worthy to note the location of these tinajas, you shouldn't drink from them except in a dire emergency; deer and bighorn sheep rely on them during Organ Pipe's prolonged hot dry spells. In the past, Organ Pipe officials have temporarily closed the trail to Bull Pasture to prevent people from frightening the area's small relic whitetail deer population during the sweltering month of June.

In the parched desert country of Organ Pipe, and in the bone-dry despoblado surrounding it, water is literally measured by the mouthful. Several important papers fill some of the gaps left by Kirk Bryan's otherwise life-saving *Routes to Desert Water Places in Papago Country*. Bill Boyle's *Fifty Years of Water Management in the Cabeza Prieta* is an up-to-date inventory of the Kabeza Prieta National Wildlife Refuge and surrounding region's "surface water, [which] constitutes a rare but crucial commodity in this extremely arid region of the Sonoran Desert"; those water sources include wells, tanks, troughs, tinajas, springs, seeps, playas, and charcos (mudholes). For the prehistoric Hohokam and Sand Papago, as well as for roving bands of Desert bighorn and fearless Mexican nationals who cross this vast desert in search of work, many of the waterholes described in Broyle's important survey have sustained life in the southwest region of Arizona for thousands of years.

So have many of the tinajas described in Bryan Brown and Roy Johnson's "The Distribution of Bedrock Depressions (Tinajas) as Sources of Surface Water in Organ Pipe Cactus National Monument," which telescoped in on the monument's fifty known tinajas. In the 329,199-acre national monument, that still only tallies up to one small, scum-covered waterhole for every 10 square miles, and these can be difficult to reach even if you know where to look for them.

Ronald L. Ives took the whole business of desert waterholes a step further when he looked at "Kiss Tanks"; in his eye-opening paper by that same name, Ives wrote:

Recently, another source of drinking water has become known to white men. This, called a 'kiss tank,' from the customary mode of drinking from it, was apparently known to the Indian inhabitants of the region since the time 'when God was a little boy.' Kiss tanks are very small pools of water, found in small depressions in very large rock surfaces, usually in deep canyons, where they are sheltered from the sun. Most of them, at any given time, contain from a few ounces to a few pints of water. They are replenished, on clear nights, by dew condensation and collection.

Yet, in spite of the size and variety of the Sonoran Desert's water sources, people continue to die of thirst there, simply because they don't first take the time to learn where prehistoric man's "convenient stores" are located.

From Tinajas de los Toros, the route heads cross-country east-northeast over a small ridge and then crosses an alluvial flank covered with clusters of bear grass and a profusion of gangly ocotillo. This is no doubt Los Portreritos, or "Little Pastures," one of the flattest pieces of ground this high up on the western slope of the Ajo Range. If observant, you'll also see a circular alignment of rocks, approximately 8 feet in diameter, a sleeping circle reminiscent of those used by the ancient Serrano Indians. These circles remain scattered over the desert pavement in Anza Borrego State Park and elsewhere throughout the California desert to the west. But according to Mallouf's "Archaeological Survey of the Ajo Crest," twelve of the thirty-three sleeping circles recorded in the Sierra del Ajo were found at the 3,800-foot level, more than 2,000 feet above the neighboring bajadas where they are normally found. From that perspective, it's strange to see one this high up in the Ajos. Mallouf believes these sleeping circles and other rock shelters on the Ajo Crest were used by aboriginal Papago as temporary camps for hunting deer and bighorn sheep and collecting food such as saguaro fruit.

From Little Pastures, you can take a closer look at two principal routes that will lead you through broken ground to the Ajo Crest without taking you through exposed territory: facing east, you will see what appears to be the easier, though longer, of the two routes leading around the north side of an odd-looking cluster of conical turrets of volcanic tuft; the more direct route heads northeast up a series of interconnecting gullies and chutes to the crest proper. Whichever route you choose, you'll be able to safely gain the Ajo Crest within an hour or so if you don't climb up anything you can easily scramble down.

Mile 3 to 4-plus.   The Ajo Crest is the demarcation line between the Organ Pipe Cactus National Monument to the west and the Tohono O'Odham Reservation to the east. West of here, three deserts converge and overlap in Organ Pipe Cactus National Monument: the Upland Arizona Succulent Desert, the Central Gulf Coast Phase of the Sonoran Desert, and the California Microphyll Desert. Because of this unique biological setting, Organ Pipe was selected in 1976 as one of twenty U.S. Biosphere Reserves that are part of a global network of natural habitats "representing all of the recognized reserves of the world."

From the Ajo Crest, you'll also see both the present and ancestral lands of the Papago Indians, what early travelers called Papagueria. East of the Sierra del Ajo are the reservation lands of the Tohono O'Odham, which, loosely translated, means "desert people who have emerged from the earth." This 2.8-million-acre Indian nation stretches as far east as Tucson at the foot of the Santa Catalinas, north to the Gila River, and south to the U.S.-Mexico border; it once stretched as far south as the Magdelena River in Sonora.

Traditional Pima and Papago occupants adapted to this sprawling desert region in one of two principal ways. According to Volume 10 of *Handbook of North American Indians*, the One-Villagers (Pima) lived near permanent water such as the Gila River, while the Two-Villagers (Papago) traveled between summer field villages and winter mountain wells like those found in the 7,734-foot Baboquivari Mountains. The No-Villagers (Sand Papago), on the other hand, were believed to be divided into two subgroups. The Pinacateños roamed the desolate volcanic region of the 3,904-foot Sierra del Pinacate and the endless sand sea of El Gran Desierto southwest of the Sierra del Ajo in what's now the frontier of northern Sonora; among their food items were sand roots (often this parasitic tuber was their only source of moisture) and sometimes even sea lions hunted in the Gulf of California. The Areneños, on the other hand, roamed the vast, waterless domain immediately west of the Sierra del Ajo along El Camino del Diablo, similarly subsisting on the most rudimentary of foodstuffs. It's not known whether members of the No-Villagers or of the Two-Villagers first climbed the Sierra del Ajo.

As you pick your way along the summit crest of Sierra del Ajo, you'll come to the false summit of Peak 10. After you've pieced together an abrupt series of ledges on the southeast corner of Peak 10 to its summit, Mount Ajo will still be half a mile away.

The downside of day hiking to the summit of any major desert peak is that you can't watch the sun set and still comfortably reverse your route in the dark; therefore, you might consider an overnight trek to Mount Ajo. Once the luminous glow of the setting sun enshrouds the crest of the Sierra del Ajo, it will cast a 15-mile-wide shadow wall east across

Papagueria, and in those fleeting moments you'll be able to grasp the big picture of this immense desert frontier: To the southeast, a small band of fleet-footed Papago Indians periodically ran several hundred miles to the Gulf of California on their visionary salt pilgrimages; to the south and west, the indefatigable Padre Kino forged El Camino del Diablo across the harshest stretch of what was once known as Pimeria Alta; and to the southwest, scientists and naturalists like Charles Sheldon, William Hornaday, and Carl Lumholtz explored on foot and horseback what today remains a largely unexplored desert region. In their journals, each wrote in his own way about the essence of what Hornaday meant when he wrote in *Campfires on Desert and Lava:* "You will note with profound surprise that these Arizona deserts are not barren and desolate wastes, but literally teeming with plant and tree life." But, Hornaday advised, "Go with an open mind; for the voices of these arid wastes are entitled to a hearing. If you cannot endure a certain amount of thirst, heat, fatigue and hunger without getting cross with Nature, it is best to stay at home."

Travel Notes

•**Primary access.**   Estes Canyon Picnic Area at Milepost 16 on Ajo Mountain Drive.

•**Total elevation gain and loss.**   2,500-plus feet each way.

•**Mileage.**   Approximately 9 miles round-trip.

•**Water sources.**   No perennial water sources en route; emergency water may be found seasonally in tinajas scattered throughout Bull Pasture east of the Bull Pasture Trail.

•**Cache points.**   Bull Pasture, but save the tinaja water for the sheep and cache your own additional water here for the return trek.

•**Escape routes.**   Back down the line of your ascent to Ajo Mountain Drive, which park rangers and tourists patrol regularly; if you get in trouble and bail off the Indian side of the mountain, it could be days before you reach help—if you ever do.

•**Seasons.**   Late fall through early spring. Summer has proven deadly in this desert region.

•**Maps.**   Organ Pipe Cactus National Monument topographical map (1:62,500), available at Visitor Center.

• **Nearest supply points.** Sells, Ajo, Why, and Lukeville, Arizona; and Sonoita, Mexico.

• **Managing agency.** Organ Pipe Cactus National Monument, Route 1, P.O. Box 100, Ajo, AZ 85321; (602) 387-6849.

• **Backcountry information.** Permit required for all overnight hiking; campfires not permitted. Dogs—even wolf hybrids—not permitted in the backcountry.

• **Biotic communities.** Sonoran Desert scrub (lower Colorado and Arizona upland subdivisions).

Other Hikes and Treks

Except for the Bull Pasture-Estes Canyon Loop and several nature trails, only the old, abandoned mine roads provide hiking without cross-country travel in Organ Pipe Cactus National Monument. Several enjoyable walks or runs avoid the more heavily driven roads: Three fine examples come immediately to mind: the 4.25 mile-long Senita Basin Road through a forest of organ pipe cactus at the foot of the 3,145-foot Puerto Blanco Mountains; the 23-mile-long smuggler's route along the West Boundary Jeep Trail from the prehistoric Sand Papago encampment of Quitobaquito Springs to Mile 23 on the Yuma Wagon Road leg of El Camino del Diablo; and the 5-mile-long border-hugging Camino de las Republicas from Highway 85 east to the historic setting of Dos Lomitas Ranch at Blankenship Well.

If you've come to Organ Pipe to hike, the biggest attraction will be the peak ascents you can make of its isolated volcanic summits. According to the National Park Service, registers are maintained on Diaz Peak, Diaz Spire, Kino Peak, Pinkley Peak, Tillotson Peak, and Twin Peaks, as well as on Mount Ajo. Each of these peak ascents, however, involves cross-country travel and scrambling on loose, sometimes dangerously crumbly rock. If you are familiar with this kind of desert travel, you would do well to climb peaks like Twin Peaks, Pinkley Peak, and Tillotson Peak before attempting more difficult treks on Mount Ajo and Kino Peak.

Paloverde Trail

Location

Pick up the trail adjacent to the Visitor Center parking lot or outside the campground; it connects the two.

Description

This is a pleasant 1.5-mile stroll through ocotillo, paloverde, mesquite, creosote, saguaro, and staghorn and teddy-bear cholla, providing fine views of Twin Peaks.

Degree of difficulty

The Paloverde Trail makes a good morning or evening walk, particularly during the spring wildflower season. No water en route; three benches for rest stops.

Twin Peaks

Location

West end of Residential Loop, adjacent to the Visitor Center; or select a route from the group campground.

Description

According to the Park Service, 2,615-foot Twin Peaks is the most frequently climbed summit in Organ Pipe because of its accessibility and good views. From the Residential Loop, head east cross-country to the saddle. From the saddle, scramble up to the notch, traverse beneath the southeast slope, and head toward the east summit. The west summit and register is a stone's throw away.

Degree of difficulty

No trail, loose footing, crumbly rock. No water en route. Many routes to the summit. Good views. Approximately 900-foot elevation gain; 1 mile, one way. Allow 1½ hours minimum.

Pinkley Peak

Location

Milepost 4 on Puerto Blanco Drive.

Description

From Milepost 4, head due west across the bajada through saguaro, organ pipe, ocotillo, and teddy-bear cholla on the south side of the main wash draining the east face of 3,145-foot Pinkley Peak. Follow this drainage to its head, then cross over and follow a ramp of volcanic tufa to a small saddle. From this saddle, pick your way up to the base of a small fin located in the highest saddle. Skirt the base of this fin on its north side, then continue zigzagging up. When it seems like you've cliffed-out, use your best judgment ahead. Some scrambling will be involved, but if you've pieced together the correct route, you won't be exposed. Once atop the east summit, proceed along a knife-edge ridge to the west summit and register. (If you're caught on this peak during foul weather, there's a cave to hole up in between the east and west summits.) You'll find excellent views of Mount Ajo and the Sierra del Pinacate in Mexico.

Degree of difficulty

Like most peak ascents in Organ Pipe, Pinkley Peak requires a rudimentary knowledge of cross-country travel and route finding. The highest summit in the Puerto Blanco Mountains, it's a good stepping-stone between Twin Peaks and Mount Ajo. Pinkley Peak has no trail, loose footing, garbage rock, and no water en route; it's named after Frank Pinkley, former superintendent of Southwestern National Monuments. Approximately 1,200-foot elevation gain and 1.5-plus miles one way. Allow a minimum of 2 hours round-trip from Milepost 4.

Tillotson Peak

Location
Milepost 10, Ajo Mountain Drive.

Description
From Milepost 10, head west cross-country toward Peak 2,832. On the north side of Peak 2,832, follow a ridge of golden tufa to the south summit of 3,374-foot Tillotson Peak, named after former National Park Service Director Minor L. Tillotson. From south summit, it's a 5- to 10-minute boulder hop along the serrated ridge to the register at the true summit.

Degree of difficulty
No trail, loose footing, and lots of cholla on the upper slopes of this peak. No water en route; best to make this trek during the wintertime and not during warm weather. Approximately 1,000-foot elevation gain and 2 miles one way. Allow a minimum of 2 hours round-trip from Milepost 10.

Quitobaquito Nature Trail

Location

Milepost 20 on Puerto Blanco Drive.

Description

Together with the Paloverde Nature Trail, this short, well-marked trail within earshot of Mexico's Highway 2 is an excellent introduction to Organ Pipe's rich flora and fauna. More than 150 species of birds have been identified at this prehistoric oasis and Sand Papago encampment, which doubles as a popular swimming hole for Mexican children who hop the border fence to frolic in its soothing waters.

Climbing

Baboquivari Peak

Baboquivari Mountains, Tohono O'Odham Indian Reservation: peak ascent, rock climb

Landform

Thirty miles long and 5 to 10 miles wide, the 7,734-foot-high Baboquivari Mountains erupt out of the fertile Altar Valley to the east and the high desert of Baboquivari Valley to the west; they are bordered on the south by the 4,701-foot-high, border-crossing Pozo Verde Mountains, and on the north by the Coyote and the Quinlan mountains. Named after James Quinlan, who operated a stage station at the foot of the mountains in 1884, the 6,880-foot-high Quinlan Mountains serve as the northern terminus of the Baboquivari Mountains. You could argue that the 6,529-foot Coyote Mountains are also a mountain range unto themselves, but these granite, dome-covered mountains are, as Bryan suggested, merely "an eastern extension of the Quinlan Mountains, which form the north end of the Baboquivari Mountains." At 7,734 feet, the north-trending Baboquivari Mountains are the highest mountains on the 2.8-million-square-acre Tohono O'Odham Reservation, as well as the longest. What sets the Baboquivari Mountains apart from Arizona's 192 other mountain ranges, however, is the 1,000-foot-high pyramid of porphyritic felsite that crowns its serpentine 6,000-foot-high ridge crest.

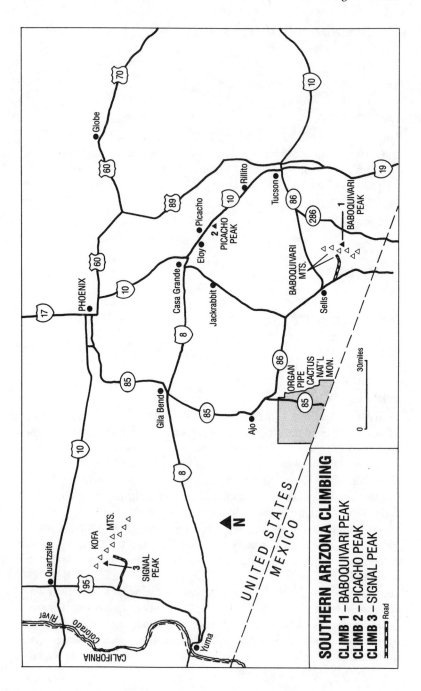

SOUTHERN ARIZONA CLIMBING

CLIMB 1 – BABOQUIVARI PEAK
CLIMB 2 – PICACHO PEAK
CLIMB 3 – SIGNAL PEAK

Road

ried and took his young bride on a honeymoon flight over "Old Babs." According to a 1953 newspaper account of that flight:

> Mrs. Forbes, after her look at her new husband's idea of recreation, commented:
> "Robert, I don't think I'll ever let you climb Baboquivari again."
> Said the doctor, "We'll see. We'll see."

Indeed, it's a domestic scene that's played out in climbers' households throughout the world. But Forbes never got to make that seventh ascent. What he did do was leave behind a legacy that's been followed by successive generations of Tucsonians who, like Forbes, have fallen under Baboquivari's spell; some, who now also consider this sacred mountain the center of their universe, have reportedly climbed the Forbes/Montoya route twenty times!

Directions

There are two standard approaches to Baboquivari Peak: The Riggs Ranch area provides the most direct access from Tucson via the east slope and Highway 286, while the longer, more scenic Tohono O'Odham side provides access via the west slope. Included here are directions and trail descriptions for the less-traveled Tohono O'Odham approach. From Tucson, drive west on Highway 86 to Sells, tribal headquarters for the Tohono O'Odham Indians. Drive south from Sells on the blacktop 10 miles to a sign marking the turnoff to the Baboquivari Campground. Turn left and follow the dirt road 12 miles to the campground.

Baboquivari Campground.   Near the entrance to the campground is a one-room house staffed by a Tohono O'Odham ranger. Pick up your permit here; it costs $3 for the night. If the Ranger feels like talking to you, he may point out the cave where I'toi dwells; then he may tell you how most traditional Tohono O'Odham feel: that the archaeological remains excavated from I'toi's cave belong back on Indian lands, not in the artifact-clogged basement of some white man's museum. Traditional Native Americans don't embrace the "science" of archaeology with the same enthusiasm that most anglos do. Said Pewnee Indian attorney Walter Echo-Hawk in the April 1991 issue of *Outside:* "If you desecrate a white grave, you wind up in prison. But desecrate an Indian grave and you get a Ph.D." The large stone house next to the campground was built in 1934 under the auspices of the CCC's Indian Service. Incredibly, you can rent either half of the stone house for an additional $3 a night, and individual fireplaces warm both sides. Bring your own firewood.

The Approach

Summit trail. In 1934, the CCC built a trail to the summit of Baboquivari, where they maintained a fire lookout. While it's no longer possible to hike to the summit, you can still follow that steep, well-marked trail to the foot of the Great Ramp, a huge diagonal slash across Baboquivari's west face. New hand-painted "Summit Trail" signs lead out of the campground up 2,600 vertical feet in 4 miles to west ridge below Baboquivari Peak. There are several outstanding places to camp in the saddle on the west ridge around the 6,400-foot level. Early morning or late afternoon, the view from this camp is exceptional; you can see *represos* shimmering in the distance. Douglas first wrote about them in 1951: [Near] the top I kept looking for represos which cattlemen on both sides of the international boundary have built for their stock. These are ponds dammed up or dug out in drainage areas to catch the runoffs of water. . . . Now in the lowering sun I began to spot them—dozens of tiny blue hazes, looking like sapphires set in a vast, green fabric."

From this ridge-top campsite, you can also see the Great Ramp. The Summit Trail leads to the foot of the Great Ramp, where you can begin climbing the Standard Route or link up with the Southeast Arête. If you've come to climb the Spring Route, you're on the wrong side of the mountain. (See For Hardmen Only, following, in this section.)

The Standard Route (Grade II, Class 4)

The Great Ramp. From the foot of the Great Ramp, scramble up to the base of Baboquivari's west face. The Great Ramp lies at a 45-degree angle, but you shouldn't have any problems scampering to the top of it as long as you follow the steep gully formed by the Ramp and the west face. At one time, the CCC's Depression-era stairway offered pedestrian access up the Great Ramp that even a gun moll could climb. But as early as March 1950 Justice Douglas found the wooden stairway "in dangerous disrepair." So uncoil your rope. If you're observant, the nonmaintained Summit Trail will lead you from the top of the Great Ramp through the shrub oak around the northwest side of Baboquivari until the trail dead-ends in a cul-de-sac. Here you'll face the most famous pitch on "Old Babs."

The Cliff-Hanger Pitch. The Standard Route joins the Forbes-Montoya Route at the foot of the 80-foot Cliff-Hanger Pitch, which, for more than a century, has been the crux of this climb. It was here that Forbes employed his remarkable bat hook in 1898. In 1934, the CCC simplified matters by building a stairway up this pitch; when Justice Douglas climbed the peak in 1950, he noted "the structure sways at every touch. But I partly employed this evil structure, using it to steady myself as I managed to throw my weight to the iron posts." With the stairway now gone, you may also find yourself employing the Douglas technique, because the crux of this pitch is an unprotected, lichen-covered 5.6 move to the first old stairway anchor. From there, easier face climbing leads to the Rappel Tree and the end of the pitch. For ladder lovers, though, this pitch takes on an even more menacing tone when, midwinter, it's covered with glare ice and the claw marks of skilled desert climbers who have managed to retreat using only their raw, partially frozen, bloody fingertips as ice climbing tools.

Nor is ice the only hazard on this dastardly pitch. When El Camino del Diablo veteran Glenton Sykes climbed Baboquivari in the 1930s, he thought he was going to be swept off this pitch to his death; in "Rumblings in Baboquivari," Sykes wrote: "We had climbed perhaps 50 feet, when, without any previous warning, there began a rumbling and crackling sound . . . like the rolling and tumbling of huge masses of rock. We expected at any instant to be buried beneath several thousand tons of falling rock . . . [but] never so much as a single chip fell." In the 1937 account of his ascent, Sykes attributed these strange rumblings to the intermittent heating and cooling of large masses of rock. This was the first time this geological phenomenon had been reported on Baboquivari.

To the top. Assuming you survive this pitch, turn right at the Rappel Tree and scramble up a broken ledge through the brush to a huge chockstone marked by an old ladder hanger. Surmount the chockstone and continue up the rock-strewn gulley to the base of the wall. Turn left (east) and follow the Summit Trail and your instincts to the top.

The Southeast Arête (Grade III, 5.6)

If you enjoyed the book or the movie *Gorillas in the Mist,* chances are you'll enjoy tree whacking on the Southeast Arête; if not, you'd better stay home and watch love blossom from the burning Amazon rainforest in *The Emerald Forest* video. The Southeast Arête was first climbed on March 31, 1957, by Jerry Robertson, Don Morris, Rick Tidrick, Tom Hale, and Dave Ganci. The Arizona lads must have stumbled onto something good, because some of America's premier rock stars of the day— including Yvon Chouinard, T. M. Herbert, and John Harlan and his wife Mara—quickly repeated the ascent.

Southwest author Dave Ganci was a member of the first ascent party which climbed Baboquivari Peak's S.E. Arête on March 31, 1957; pictured here over three decades later, Ganci stares up at the last pitch of the S.E. Arête, backdropped by the Altar Valley to the East. Photo by John Annerino.

Approach. From the foot of the Great Ramp, turn right (east) and follow a faint climber's trail through the brush along the base of the wall until you reach the Southeast Arête. On this stretch, you may find yourself employing another Douglas technique; wrote Douglas: "The last few hundred yards were steep going through brush that overhangs the trail and makes one stoop ape-like to clear it." If the Douglas technique doesn't help you find the Southeast Arête – a "ridge to those who are uncultured mountaineers," as the first ascent party graciously pointed out – you probably won't find your way *up* it.

The climb. Originally climbed in eleven pitches, the Southeast Arête is now done in seven or eight pitches. The key to this enjoyable and spectacular route is to follow the path of least resistance. Once atop the Southeast Arête, you need to rappel, or downclimb, into the notch separating the Southeast Arête from the summit cap before continuing to the top.

For Hard Men Only

After Glenton Sykes made his 1930s fact-finding expedition to Baboquivari, he described the range as "The Matterhorn of the Southwest" – with good reason. Until members of the Grand Canyon Commando Alliance climbed Tooth Rock near Lee's Ferry over a 4-day period in February 1977, Baboquivari sported Arizona's only Grade VI multiday rock climb. Rated Grade VI, 5.9, A-4, the Spring Route ascends Baboquivari's largely overhanging east face. Colorado climbers Bill Forrest and George Hurley were the first to climb it in April 1968. However, Joanna McComb and Dan Jones made the first successful probe up the east face in October 1966 via Don's Crack (Grade III, 5.8); Dave Baker, Mike McEwen, and Marty Woerner later free climbed this "huge, prominent crack" in July 1971. Baker and McEwen returned in April 1973 to pull down Humungous Woosey (Grade IV, 5.9) near the northeast corner. Lately, there's been talk of another new line on Baboquivari, respectfully called I'toi; it ascends the intimidating east face between the Spring Route and Humungous Woosey. But the last-known line to fall on the mountain was Time Lost, or the South Face Direct (Grade IV, 5.9); Robert Anderson, Clay Sanford, and Steve Sanford climbed it in January 1978 and reported it as "sustained and serious due to numerous runouts on poor or non-existent protection."

If you really are a hardman, hump your gear straight up from Riggs Ranch to Lion's Ledge below the east face to climb any of these routes.

The Summit

However you reach the bald, 7,734-foot summit of Baboquivari, you're in for a surprise once you get there; this is one of southern Arizona's premier summit views, rivaling the 360-degree panorama from the summit of 9,453-foot Mount Wrightson. To the east lie the Altar Valley, the Old Pueblo of Tucson, and the 8,000- and 9,000-foot-high ramparts of the Rincon and Santa Catalina mountains. North is telescope-covered Kitt Peak—the best evidence against the University of Arizona's cluttering yet another magnificent southern Arizona summit like Mount Graham or Emerald Peak with telescopes. But the views to the south and the west are best appreciated from Baboquivari's summit.

Looking south. Forty-one years before Forbes built his famous bonfire, the 1857 Crabb Filibustering Expedition survived El Camino del Diablo and passed within the shadow of Baboquivari en route to Caborca, a few miles south of Altar, Sonora. The group couldn't have timed its expedition more poorly. The general consensus among *Mexicanas* at the time was that they'd gotten the short end of the stick when the 1853 Gadsden Purchase deal went down. So after the motley Crabb Expedition arrived on April 1 hoping to explore investment opportunities in what remained

Baboquivari Peak. Photo by John Annerino.

of northern Sonora . . . suffice it to say their remains were literally fed to the village pigs. In his book *Crabb's Filibustering Expedition,* Robert H. Forbes reported that 16-year-old Charles Evans was the lone survivor of the ninety-odd men who made up the disastrous Crabb Expedition. Evans reported that a Mexican man led him to a large earthenware jar he kept in his small house, and "He put his hand in and immediately drew out Mr. Crabb's head, holding it by the hair. . . . He laughed and asked me if I knew who it belonged to."

Looking west. At one time, the vast ancestral lands of the Tohono O'Odham stretched as far west as you can see from the summit of Baboquivari — and beyond: west all the way to the Colorado River, and south from the Gila River to the Gulf of California. When Douglas reached the summit, he hoped to see the Gulf waters as well. He couldn't, but his vivid summit description of Papagueria still rings true today:

> Sugar loaves, camel backs, cones and spires — these were the shapes of the pieces of mountains . . . the Peaks and ridges that dot the Mexican desert below. . . . This March day they were deep purple in the haze that hung on the horizon. As this haze lifted along the skyline a new peak or range would suddenly come into view. It was indeed a scene of fantasy as if mirages of imaginary mountains came and went. The Gulf of California lay less than 100 air miles away. But I could not get even a glimpse of its sparkling, blue water.

Papagueria below. According to Donald M. Blair's "Pima and Papago Social Organization," the Papago had three ways of adapting to their expansive domain: The One-Villagers lived near permanent water; the Two-Villagers traveled between "summer field villages and winter mountains wells"; and the No-Villagers roamed the harshest and furthest reaches of their world. About the mid-1800s, though, the Papago began fearing the same atrocities that befell the Crabb Expedition and they fortified themselves in defense villages. They feared not the Mexicans but hostile Apaches, who were making bold raids into their territory. Life changed. Their world got smaller.

That was then; today the vast sea of desert you see from the summit of Baboquivari has gotten even smaller for the Tohono O'Odham. But now it's the U.S. Air Force they fear. According to an article written by Enric Volante for the November 23, 1986, edition of *The Arizona Daily Star,* "more than 41,000 sorties were flown over the reservation last year," much to the dismay of the Tohono O'Odham, who consider military flights over their sovereign nation illegal. In 1979 the Defense Department disagreed and issued a waiver allowing "pilots to fly at supersonic speeds over the reservation at altitudes as low as 10,000 feet." Windows were shattered, walls were cracked, and the tribe's spiritual strength was sapped. As one tribal elder reported to Volante: "When the boom goes off . . . It takes part of my life away." The Tohono O'Odham filed suit. The issue has not been resolved. Their world has become even smaller. Their peace remains shattered.

In the meantime, you can still take comfort in the words of former Supreme Court Justice William O. Douglas: "From the summit, the land runs to the horizon in every direction. This is the land to possess and embrace. It is land to command as far as the eye can see. Here is the ultimate."

And so it remains today.

Descent

For all routes, return via the Standard Route

Travel Notes

• **Primary access.**   Sells, via Baboquivari Campground.

• **Elevation gain and loss.**   Approximately 4,000 feet one way.

• **Mileage.**   Approximately 5 miles one way.

• **Water sources.**   No perennial water en route. Seasonal water on Lion's Ledge beneath east face.

• **Cache points.**   West Ridge camp.

• **Escape routes.**   Back the way you came, or via Riggs Ranch.

• **Seasons.**   Fall and Spring. Winter can be icy on the Cliff-Hanger Pitch, and summer can be a trifle warm.

• **Maps.**   Baboquivari Peak (7½-minute quadrangle).

• **Nearest supply points.**   Sells and Tucson.

• **Managing agency.**   Tohono O'Odham Tribe.

• **Backcountry information.**   Permit required.

• **Biotic communities.**   Sonoran Desert scrub (Arizona upland division), plains and desert grassland, and encinal and Mexican oak-pine woodland.

Picacho Peak

Picacho Peak State Park

Landform

Rising 1,500 vertical feet out of the surrounding "Ninety-Mile Desert," 3,374-foot Picacho Peak is an isolated volcanic peak midway between the Gila River to the north and the Old Pueblo of Tucson to the south. Estimated to be some 22 million years old, Picacho Peak drains into the Santa Cruz River on the southwest and is separated from the main massif of the 4,500-foot-high Picacho Mountains by McClellan Wash, or Picacho Pass, on the northeast.

Historical Overview

Picacho Peak has long been touted as the site of Arizona's only Civil War battle. Called the "Battle of Picacho Pass," it took place on April 15, 1862, and went down in a thicket at the foot of Picacho Peak—the kind of place you thrash around in for half an hour if you ever lose a trail in the desert. According to Capt. William Perry Calloway, "the first fire from the enemy [Johnny Rebs] emptied four saddles"; three Yanks from the California Volunteers were also blown away in a desperate battle that lasted an hour and a half.

In a separate and unrelated incident involving yet another group of sharp-shooting California Volunteers, an unnamed corporal was marched before a firing squad comprised of his own men for protesting the arrest of his sergeant. The first two volleys reportedly missed, as did the third, but a ball from the third round ricocheted off the ground and ripped through the corporal's heart. According to the February 2, 1863, edition of the *Sacramento Union*, the carnage didn't end there: "Whilst firing at him, they killed a Mexican and a woman, and wounded another; and also killed a soldier belonging to Company A . . . The Mexican who was killed was on top of a church on the opposite side of the Plaza." All this took place at Apache Pass, sometimes called Puerto del Dado (Pass of the Dead).

But long before the deadeye California Volunteers and the Johnny Rebs last drew blood on Arizona soil, Picacho Peak was a noted landmark for early travelers crossing what some called the Ninety-Mile Desert and others knew as "a jornada of seventy miles." (A *jornada* is, loosely, that section of a desert journey without water.)

As early as October 29, 1775, Spanish missionary Francisco Garces first saw Picacho Peak en route to the Gila River: "We approached Rancheria Quitoac, inhabited at times by the Papagos, and halted near a picacho which the Indians call the Cerro de Tacca." According to turn-of-the-century historian Elliot Coues, who translated Garces' official diary into two volumes titled *On the Trail of the Spanish Pioneer, tacca* might have been related to the Pima Indian word *ta-kju,* which he thought meant "iron." Coues didn't say what iron had to do with a peak others would soon call *Picacho* (meaning "peak") Peak, or peak peak.

Garces and Juan Bautista de Anza had both been using the same route along the Santa Cruz River that Padre Kino had used years earlier; however, neither mentioned using the tinajas near the base of Picacho Peak later described in Lieutenant Milcher's *Report* on the 1857 Boundary Survey: "From Gila [River] to Tucson . . . is a second jornada, seventy miles in extent. Near the middle of it you pass a detached sierra called 'Picacho,' or peak, an upheaval of volcanic rocks. Tinajas are here found which remain filled with water for short periods after the rainy season."

It is not commonly known whether the Ninety-Mile Desert had a death toll comparable to that of the treacherous El Camino del Diablo 100 miles to the southwest, or even to that of the Forty-Mile Desert that crossed the small despoblado between the Pima villages and the Gila River 50 miles to the northwest. But a brief passage in J. Ross Browne's *A Tour Through Arizona — 1864* notes "emigrant parties suffered much in crossing this inhospitable desert." Browne was no doubt referring to wagon trains that crossed the Ninety-Mile Desert en route to the Gila River before 1857; that's when the Butterfield Overland Mail Route dug wells and operated Picacho Station just north of Picacho Peak.

Whether one traveled by foot, horseback, or stage coach, few natural mileposts broke up the dreary monotony of the Ninety-Mile Desert for early travelers better than Picacho Peak, a stark monument of lava that could easily be seen for 45 miles in either direction. Even today, many commuters would agree with Browne's description of the stretch between Phoenix and Tucson, a vapid drone of Sonoran Desert hacked here and there by tasteless interstate pit stops and backdropped by a burgeoning agricultural greenbelt: "A journey across the Ninety-Mile Desert prepares the jaded and dust-covered traveler to enjoy all the luxuries of civilization which an ardent imagination may lead him to expect in the metropolis of Arizona. The Picacho . . . presents a prominent and picturesque landmark from both points."

Other than documentation of the construction of the CCC Trail to the summit of Picacho Peak in 1933, there is no record of who climbed the peak first. Petroglyphs abound in the area around the base of the adjacent Picacho Mountains, however, indicating that some nimble-footed Hohokam may have climbed the peak some 1500 years ago. Few Arizona summits tantalize more people than this craggy finger of rock astride Interstate 10, called the "gateway to your soul" by one early Arizona historian. Park rangers estimate that anywhere from six thousand to ten thousand people climb the peak each year.

Directions

To reach Picacho Peak State Park, take Interstate 10 50 miles north of Tucson, or 70 miles south of Phoenix, to the well-marked turnoff at the foot of Picacho Peak.

The Hunter Trail Log

Named after Confederate Capt. Sherod Hunter, the Hunter Trail was constructed by Explorer Scout Troop Post 922 from 1972 to 1973; it links up with—and eventually replaces—the lower half of the original CCC trail. According to information furnished by Park Ranger Cindy Swing, the CCC trail was constructed up the backside of Picacho Peak in order to maintain a 50-foot beacon authorized by the Civil Aeronautics Authority "to aid pilots in navigation . . . [and to light] the aerial highways until 1965." The Hunter Trail was designated a National Recreation Trail in 1974 and today remains the most popular and accessible route to the summit of Picacho Peak.

Mile 0 to 1. The Hunter Trailhead is located on the southwest corner of the Park's Barrett Loop, near the Saguaro Ramada. From the trailhead, you can see the first mile of this steep, rocky, well-marked trail. Frequent trail signs and steel-cable handrails pull you up through the paloverde, creosote, ocotillo, and saguaro over the eastern headwall to the main saddle between Picacho Peak and 3,161-foot-high Bugler Peak. From this saddle, you'll get your first view of the serpentine Santa Cruz River below, which Kino, Anza, and Garces followed more than 2 centuries ago. Even the First Dragoons stomped beneath Picacho Peak en route from Monterey, Nuevo Léon, Mexico, to Los Angeles; and in his 1848–1849 journal Cave Johnson Couts provides one of the best descriptions of what the waterholes at Picacho Peak meant for thirsty travelers: "On the 28th marching at 8 made 22 miles to Picacho, from Charco de las Yumas, where we found small pools of water, very bad and muddy, but made out to water our animals, this saved hundreds though have lost about 25 all told since leaving Tucion [*sic*]. On 25th night of 25th and 26th it rained a great deal. Yet this was the only water found between Tucion and the Gila. What a kind Providence!"

Mile 1 to 2.   Beyond this saddle, the second mile of the Hunter Trail earns its reputation as one of Arizona's classic cable climbs—something you're more likely to encounter in the crowded Italian Dolomites than on a historic escarpment in frontier Arizona. The Hunter Trail drops several hundred vertical feet down along the base of a headwall and is protected with cable railings and railroad-tie wooden steps. After the trail bottoms out near the junction with the original CCC trail, it climbs abruptly, contouring and switchbacking its way toward the summit of Picacho Peak. En route, it takes on the feel more of a jungle gym or of *Raiders of the Lost Ark* than of an actual climb or trek. And you begin to wonder whether an unemployed bridge contractor had his fingers in this pie as switchbacks of steel cables, wire-mesh-enclosed catwalks, and gangplanks lead you to the summit.

Summit View

Unfortunately, there's a disturbing vision associated with climbing to the summit of any Arizona peak this close to civilization—and Picacho Peak is no exception. On the one hand, you'll immediately be swept away by the titillating wonders of a sprawling desert that fans out toward peaks and mountain ranges that, on a clear winter day, you can identify for 100 miles in every direction; on the other, you'll be confronted with the distorted vision eastern developers continue to wreak upon Arizona's magnificent land. In the August 24, 1986, edition of *The Arizona Daily Star*, Ed Severson wrote: "In a way, when you stand on top of Picacho, you see less and less of what you go up to find." Suffice it to say, the scars beneath Picacho Peak are permanent.

   It is interesting to note not only what was built near Picacho Peak, but exactly where things were built. For example, Interstate 10 follows Picacho Pass along a historic route—as do many of the nation's highways and interstates. However, as an Associated Press article titled "Great Gash in Earth Appears Near Picacho, Reason Is Unknown," reported in the September 15, 1927, evening edition of *The Tucson Citizen*, "A great gash in the earth . . . has appeared three miles east of Picacho on the Tucson-Casa

Grande highway. . . . Fayette A. Jones, geologist . . . who inspected the unusual fissure yesterday, expressed a belief that it was caused by an earth movement . . . induced by tension variation due to internal adjustment in the Rock Formation on the Picacho Peaks." Twenty-two years later, almost to the week, another newspaper headline read: "Huge Earth Separation in Picacho Peak Area Reported by Scientist." As of this writing, it's been 40 years since that last headline, and no one knows when the next earth tremor or 100-year flood will pry this giant earth crack open again and split the sternum of Interstate 10.

Nor does anyone know when the Central Arizona Project (CAP) 2 miles north might spill Colorado River water over the sprawling Ninety-Mile Desert like a ruptured artery. The CAP canal was gouged right across the western flanks of the 6,400-acre Wilderness Study Area, which archaeologists have identified as having "an amazingly large and complex assemblage of petroglyph sites." According to Henry D. Wallace and James P. Holmlund in *Petroglyphs of the Picacho Mountains*, "Over 4,100 separate designs have now been recorded in the area, making it only one of a handful of such concentrations in the state." You begin to wonder if Arizona might not have been better served had the CAP been tunneled under this amazing site—or had it been funneled down the Great Gash all the way to parched Tucson—or, at the very least, had this remarkable area been preserved as a natural interpretive park to be enjoyed by future generations of Arizonans and tourists long after the CAP has been sucked dry.

In every direction from the summit of Picacho, you're confronted with the dichotomy between ancestral desertland and the progress we've trundled upon it. Perhaps it's best to look beyond these modern scars to see how Arizona once looked, so we can envision how the future could look if we decide to maintain the natural integrity of what we still have. Granted, there are no simple solutions, but life is not as simple as it was when all man had to worry about was making it to the next waterhole alive—and not whether he could, or should, try to divert the entire waterhole for himself.

It wasn't that long ago when J. Ross Browne saw a vision where hundreds of happy campers now hunker down in the comforts of an RV resort gouged into the very flanks of Picacho Peak: "An isolated mountain in the distance seemed at first view to rise abruptly out of a lake of silver, the shores of which were alive with water-fowl of brilliant and beautiful plumage. As we journeyed toward it the lake disappeared and the mountain changed to a frowning fortress, symmetrical in all its parts—a perfect model of architectural beauty. Still nearing it, the ramparts and battlements melted into a dreamy haze. . . ."

Travel Notes

- **Primary access.** Via Hunter Trail; secondary access via CCC Trail.

- **Elevation gain and loss.** 1,370 vertical feet each way.

- **Mileage.** Approximately 2 miles one way.

- **Water sources.** No permanent water en route.

- **Cache point.** Saddle between Bugler and Picacho peaks.

- **Escape routes.** Back the way you came.

- **Seasons.** Fall through spring.

- **Map.** Newman Peak (7½-minute quadrangle).

- **Nearest supply points.** Tucson, Casa Grande, and Phoenix.

- **Managing agency.** Arizona State Parks.

- **Backcountry information.** Permit not required.

- **Biotic communities.** Sonoran Desert scrub.

Note: Picacho Peak is included under the Climbing section because, without the iron mongery, it would *be* just a desert rock climb.

Signal Peak

Kofa Mountains, Kofa National Wildlife Refuge: peak ascents, via climbing and trekking

Landform

Seen from nearby Highway 95, the 4,877-foot-high Kofa Mountains appear to be comprised of a single monolithic buttress that erupted out of the La Posa Plain a fiery millenia ago; in reality, however, the unmistakable blocklike massif called Signal Peak serves as the Kofa's western front, and it guards a cauldron of seemingly impassable cliffs, deep-grooved gorges, box canyons, and jagged volcanic pinnacles characteristic throughout the 200-square-mile range. Rising more than 3,000 vertical feet on its most dramatic western side, the northwest-trending Kofa Mountains comprise the most rugged and spectacular terrain in the entire 663,700-acre Kofa National Wildlife Refuge.

Historical Overview

What are you doing hiking?
Are you broke?

One miner to another
Kofa Mountains, circa 1890

Historically located in the heart of the 10,000-square-mile despoblado formed north of the Gila River, east of the Lower Colorado River, south of the Bill Williams River, and west of the Hassayampa River, the Kofa Mountains were bypassed by all the early Spanish explorers—including Kino, de Anza, Garces, and Juan de Oñate. Virtually all the boundary surveyors and stagecoach lines gave the Kofas a wide berth as well. Even dangerous immigrant trails like El Camino del Diablo, which went right to the core of bad country, skirted the Kofas 100 miles to the south, as did the heavily used Gila Trail only 50 miles south and the routes that followed the 35th parallel more than 100 miles to the north. In short, nobody ventured into the Kofas—except for stalwart desert Indians like the Tolkapaya (Western Yavapai) and perhaps the Yuma-area Quechan.

. . . And prospectors. The earliest recorded explorations into the Kofa Mountains were by gold seekers during the 1890s; according to more than one account, prospectors originally named the Kofas the S.H. Mountains after a favored outhouse, and that's how the range originally appeared on the earliest maps of the region. One of the most arduous treks to the S.H. Mountains was made by William Keiser in the 1890s; he trekked 116 miles from Blaisdell to the Cornish-run King of Arizona mine, via Mohawk Station, to look for work. Wrote Keiser:

> The train slackened speed at Blaisdell, ten miles out, and a Wells Fargo agent poking a double-barreled sawed-off shotgun into my ribs said, "Get off! Get off!"
>
> I "got" and . . . I still had seventy miles to go and it looked like a long, long hike; so I started counting the ties. About three in the morning I was beginning to get pretty weary. I ran across two other fellows at a water tank. "You fellows counting the ties, too?" They said they were headed for the mines—ten day miners, broke. . . . So we plodded along. By eight a.m. we still had about forty miles to go. The sun came up and we only made about three miles an hour. We would rest under a culvert. Got water from another railroad tank and were thankful when the sun went down. After dark we could see a light ahead, but it never seemed to get any closer. We made guesses, and about ten o'clock caught up with it; a lantern hanging on a switch.

In Keiser's colorful memoir of mining in the Kofas, he also reports how the King of Arizona mine was originally discovered. That passage also sheds some light on the fact that ancient Indian trails penetrated these rugged mountains long before the "Cousin Jacks" (Cornish miners) started hacking and blasting their way into its southern ramparts. Now on file at the Yuma County History Society, Keiser's diary said: "An old Indian trail went over the mountain and going up this trail he [Charlie Eichelberger] discovered a small cave, an overhanging rock where evidence showed that the Indians cooked there. He sat down under the shade as it was fairly warm. Where the smoke covered the wall he noticed some bright yellow spots—gold." Eichelberger and the unnamed Yuma businessman who grubstaked him sold the find in 1897 for $250,000; it became known as the King of Arizona mine, and because some of the womanfolk were none too pleased with the name S.H. Mountains, it was later changed to Kofa Mountains.

The Indian trail that Eichelberger followed to the mother lode could have been a hunting trail that led into the Kofas' prime desert bighorn country; or it could have been a spur trail that led to several tinajas in the area. The Kofa Wilderness Summary reports that "one of the principal Quechan trade and war party routes crossed the Kofa Game Refuge." But whether any of these trails actually originated with the Quechan is suspect. Both bands of the Western Yavapai—the Haka-whatapa ("red-water people") and the Hakehlapa ("people of the running water")—also crossed the area. Whichever Indians used the region's trails, however, they generally stuck to the flat, desert pavement, where travel was relatively fast and easy—except when they were drawn into the Kofas' rugged interior in quest of food or water. If you're observant, as Eichelberger was, you too can find remnants of these antipodean tracks.

But whether or not you find those ancient footpaths, the Kofas remain the domain of the desert bighorn sheep, and the few trails you encounter will most likely be the faint tracks of desert bighorns where they bound from ledge to ledge and make their way from one tinaja to the next. Except for man, who's allowed to "harvest" a handful of these magnificent animals each year, the Kofas' estimated eight hundred desert bighorn have few natural predators in this Wildlife Refuge. The U.S. Fish and Wildlife Service, the Youth Conservation Corps, and the Arizona Desert Bighorn Sheep Society have improved the Kofas' marginal water sources and browse, consequently making the Wildlife Refuge "the main source for Bighorn sheep re-population efforts in the Southwest," according to a February 12, 1984, *Arizona Republic* article written by Phyllis Gillespie. If you're patient and quiet and know how to cut their sign, you'll have excellent opportunities to observe Desert bighorn in their natural habitat.

Ruth Mendenhall, her husband John, *Desert Magazine* editor Randall Henderson, and his son Rand were the first known people to use Desert bighorn sheep trails to climb the forbidding west face of Kofa Mountain, known today as Signal Peak, in 1941. In "Up the West Face of Kofa Mountain," Ruth Mendenhall wrote: "The dim path beneath the great yellow walls led cleverly among rocks and shrubs. Here, on the unclimbed, barren west face of Kofa Mountain, we were following the trail of mountain goats . . . where the goats [desert bighorn] could go, surely we with modern rock climbing methods could go up as well." While this was the first recorded ascent, Western Yavapai Indians or prospectors no doubt reached the summit of Signal Peak long before the Mendenhall-Henderson ascent; nontechnical ascents can be made by trekking up Indian or Ten Ewe canyons on the mountain's northeast side. (See descriptions near the end of this section.) But the 1941 Mendenhall-Henderson ascent is significant because it was the first time that modern man had explored this far corner of the western Arizona desert solely for the adventure of standing on a remote summit and not in quest of gold.

Directions

From Quartzite, drive south on Highway 95 20 miles to the Palm Canyon Road; turn left and drive another 7 miles to the mouth of Palm Canyon. Park at the road's end.

Trail Log

Mile 0 to 1.   Via Palm Canyon Trail. Nowhere else in Arizona do people drive so far to hike so short a trail as they do for the mile-long Palm Canyon Trail; they travel 90 miles from Yuma, 150 miles from Phoenix, and 300 miles from Tucson by the shortest routes. What makes this trail so alluring—and so important—is the fact that it's the only place in Arizona where native palms, *Washingtonia arizonica*, grow in their natural habitat. At last count, an estimated forty-two native palms grew in the precipitous tributary drainages above the floor of Palm Canyon, where they were sheltered from backcountry arsonists who torched the most magnificent and accessible of the species years ago.

From road's end, hike approximately 1 mile to the upper east end of this popular trail; this makes a good turnaround point for a morning or afternoon stroll.

From a climber's perspective, Palm Canyon forms the most natural line of ascent from the bajadas fanning out from the base of Signal Peak to its barren rock summit; Ruth Mendenhall realized this when she described Palm Canyon as the "tremendous gap in the west face of Kofa, which splits the mountain from skyline to desert floor in one precipice-walled V." It's strange, then, that the Mendenhall-Henderson party traversed out of this direct line near the end of the Palm Canyon Trail and, according to the published photo of their meandering route, wandered north; perhaps they were hoping to follow a desert bighorn trail all the way to the summit. Wrote Mendenhall: "It seemed incredible that a hoofed animal could surmount these rocks, but the goats' path was marked unmistakably by their small black oval droppings. Cautious climbing was now essential, lest a careless step dislodge rocks stuck precariously in dirt banks, and send them rattling down on those below."

West Face Route

(*Advisory:* Beyond the Palm Canyon Trail, the route up the west face is short, steep, and enjoyable. But it demands solid route-finding abilities and at least a rudimentary knowledge of rock climbing. One of the most important considerations for the remainder of this spectacular route is to physically mark—or make mental notes of—its key sections for the descent: Specifically, note where to reverse Pitches 1 through 4 and how to get back into the head of Palm Canyon. Several look-alike canyons radiate off the west face of Signal Peak, and you will end up cliffed-out, or dangling off the end of your rope, if you pick the wrong one.)

Mile 1 to 2-plus. About the time the Palm Canyon Trail fades, you'll start scrambling up the brush-covered drainage above; as the drainage narrows, it becomes choked with large boulders. Your objective is to attain a broad bench, or plateau, rimming the head of Palm Canyon near the 4,200-foot level. Up to this point, the route does not involve rock climbing; if you *are* climbing, you're off route.

Once atop this plateaulike bench, below what Mendenhall described as "tremendous, castle-crowned cliffs. In a great golden amphitheater well up the canyon . . . ," continue angling east-southeast into the uppermost arm of Palm Canyon. Traces of a faint trail lead up through brush-covered talus and low-angle rock along the bottom of a drainage that dead-ends at the base of a short, steep headwall. Skilled rock climbers can easily negotiate this section with a rope and a minimum of hardware. To stay on the "dog route," however, backtrack down the drainage a short distance until you come to a narrow passage between an overhang on your right (east) and a Toyota-sized boulder on your left; approximately 50 feet north will be a low-angle chute with a horn at the top of it.

Rope Up Here.

•**Pitch #1.** Scramble up this chute to the obvious horn (5.3); the horn serves as a rope anchor when you rappel or downclimb this section on the descent.

•**Pitch #2.** Easy scrambling above the horn leads to an easy rock rib left (west) of a natural depression until you reach a seemingly blank face.

•**Pitch #3.** Traverse right across this unprotected face (5.6ish) 40 feet into a gully; scramble up this easy gully to the base of a short headwall.

•**Pitch #4.** With the heat off, continue using your intuitive route-finding skills to scramble up an interconnecting gully, which will bring you out on a spectacular ridgeline. You can eyeball your way to easier ground and the summit of Signal Peak from this ridgeline.

Summit Views

At 4,877 feet, Signal Peak is the highest mountain in southwestern Arizona (from the Colorado River east to Highway 85, and from Interstate 10 south to the U.S.-Mexico border). As such, it offers outstanding views of the western Arizona desert and, beyond its natural boundary formed by the lazy silver ribbon of the Lower Colorado River, west across California's Mojave Desert. At one time, you could see 10,800-foot-high Mount San Jacinto looming above Palm Springs 160 miles west-northwest and the mountain ranges of upper Baja California Norte 140 miles southwest. What often mars that incredible visibility today is the smog rolling in over the Lower Colorado River. Arizonans love to lay the blame on gas-guzzling Los Angelinos, but in truth the dreck from Phoenix frequently converges with that of Los Angeles near the Arizona-California state line. Still, the view from Signal Peak can be exceptional—especially on a clear winter day.

Of the summit view, Ruth Mendenhall wrote: "Almost 3,000 feet beneath, the wonderful openness of the desert stretched smoothly off in every direction to a skyline ring of mountains. Kofa's northern pinnacles, which had looked so important that morning, had diminished to a far line of lowly needles. Small black buttes, possibly ancient volcanoes, studded the near desert. Eastward an impressive sea of sharp peaks churned up like waves. To the west an elbow of the Colorado River bent into view." Except for the periodic waves of dense smog over the region, Mendenhall's description still rings true more than half a century later.

That's why you journey to a remote range like the Kofas: to see life as it still exists out here in the far reaches of the Tolkapaya's breathtaking ancestral lands. Even today this desert beckons modern man to cross it on foot simply for the adventure of self-discovery. In the summit register was an account of a young California man, Steve Tabo, who had set out across the desert on foot. According to his brief log, dated June 25, 1981, he'd left Moro Bay, California on November 20, 1980. It was 110 in the valleys, he wrote, when he crossed the southern end of the Mojave Desert to climb Signal Peak from the west. From the Kofas, he was headed east; he wasn't sure how far. "Destination: Continental Divide (or Rio Grande?)" Whether he made it as far east as the Rio Grande, or whether he packed it in along the way somewhere, there's little doubt his tracks across the outback found journey's end—wherever he chose that to be.

Travel Notes

•**Primary access.**   Via Palm Canyon.

•**Secondary access.**   Via Indian and Ten Ewe canyons.

•**Elevation gain and loss.**   2,700 vertical feet each way.

•**Mileage.**   Approximately 2 miles one way.

•**Water sources.**   No perennial water en route; tinajas are scarce and difficult to find, and kiss tanks can only be found seasonally. So drive a water truck to the trailhead.

•**Cache point.**   At the bottom of Pitch #1.

•**Escape routes.**   While challenging, the three routes up Signal Peak described here are not dangerous, but any time you're in the backcountry it's imperative you know your escape options—especially in someplace as remote as the Kofa Mountains.

> *Between pitches 1 and 4:* It's probably best to descend Palm Canyon. Prescott College periodically conducts mountain rescue training in the area, attesting to the viability of the route as a corridor for successful mountain rescues on foot.

> *Near the summit:* Signal military pilots who conduct training flights in the area. Military helicopter pilots, like those in the Marine Corps Air Station's Rescue-1, can find suitable landing zones on the summit ridge

or use a skyhook to extract an injured party from some sections of the west face route.

Lower reaches of Indian and Ten Ewe canyons: Back the way you came.

• **Seasons.** Late fall through early spring; unless you're a coyote, a mad dog, or an Englishman, don't mess around out here in the summertime.

• **Maps.** Livingston Hills (15-minute quadrangle).

• **Nearest supply points.** Quartzite, Yuma, and Blythe.

• **Managing agency.** U.S. Fish and Wildlife, Kofa National Wildlife Refuge, P.O. Box 6290, Yuma, AZ 85364; (602) 783-7861.

• **Backcountry information.** Permit not required. Firewood is scarce.

• **Biotic communities.** Sonoran Desert scrub (lower Colorado subdivision and Arizona upland subdivision).

Indian and Ten Ewe Canyons

For nonclimbers, the easiest route to the summit of Signal Peak is up Indian Canyon—though this trek still involves a knowledge of route finding and cross-country desert mountain travel.

Directions

From State Route 95, drive 4 miles east on the Palm Canyon Road to the first road intersecting from the left (north). Take this jeep trail north approximately 1.5 miles to a second road intersecting from the east. This track is the Kofa Queen Canyon Road; follow it approximately 7 miles to the foot of Indian and Ten Ewe canyons. (Refer to your Livingston Hills quadrangle on the drive in.) The last 3 miles of the Kofa Queen Canyon Road follow the creek bottom—so if you're there after a good rain, you'll either need a 4WD or have to hoof it the rest of the way in.

Trek Log

Indian Canyon. If you found the mouth of Indian and Ten Ewe canyons, you shouldn't have much difficulty following the 2-mile route 2,300 vertical feet up Indian Canyon to the summit of Signal Peak. Indian Canyon is easier to hike than Ten Ewe Canyon, and it's more direct; some remnant markings point the way, and cairns mark key sections. When ascending Indian Canyon, stay on the left (east) side of the drainage to avoid the drop-off formed by its headwaters. Near the north side of 4,600-plus-foot Ten Ewe Mountain, turn right (west) and head toward a Gibraltar-shaped buttress; from the base of this buttress, follow the obvious drainage to the summit ridge of Signal Peak.

Ten Ewe Canyon.   Once you have hiked up Indian Canyon, you may want to explore the more challenging and circuitous 2.5-mile Ten Ewe Canyon approach to Signal Peak. About 20 minutes up Ten Ewe Canyon, you'd have to scramble up some fairly steep falls about 30 feet high; this is the key to this trek. Once you've negotiated this section, stay on the right (west) side of the drainage until you reach the saddle on the southeast side of Ten Ewe Mountain. It will take 30 to 45 minutes of concerted effort to contour the base of the mountain on its southwest side in order to gain the summit ridge on the west. Trek up the ridge, past the radio tower, to the summit of Signal Peak.

Central Arizona

Car Tours

Apache Trail

Tonto National Forest, Phoenix to Roosevelt Lake

Landform

Nearly 50 miles long, the Apache Trail parallels the prehistoric course of the Salt River drainage through the rugged divide formed by the 7,645-foot southern end of the Mazatzal Mountains and the northern brink of the Superstition Mountains. But where the wild Salt River once surged beyond its confluence with Tonto Creek west to the foot of 5,057-foot Superstition Mountain, a chain of man-made reservoirs has stilled the heartbeats of this great river and of the ancient people who traveled along it in order to breathe life into the modern pueblo "that rose from its ashes" near the Salt's confluence with the Gila River.

Historical Overview

Formerly called both the Tonto Trail and the Yavapai Trail for the Tonto Apache and Yavapai Indians who first used it, the Apache Trail has an early history that closely parallels that of the Salt River corridor, which

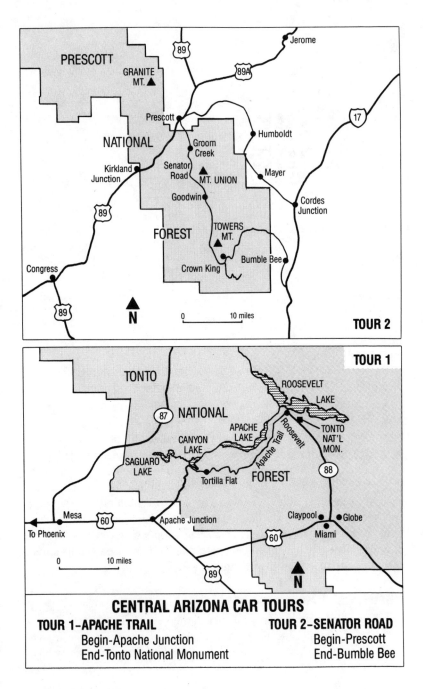

CENTRAL ARIZONA CAR TOURS

TOUR 1–APACHE TRAIL
Begin-Apache Junction
End-Tonto National Monument

TOUR 2–SENATOR ROAD
Begin-Prescott
End-Bumble Bee

it follows. (See entry for Upper Salt River.) Mountain men like Kit Carson and James Ohio Pattie undoubtedly traveled portions of the Apache Trail while trapping beaver up the length of the Salt River in the late 1820s, but Fray Marcos de Niza may have been the first non-Indian to travel here as early as 1540; Adolph F. Bandelier's 1890 bare-bones description of de Niza's route seems to place the early adventurer squarely on the Apache Trail: "The portion of the Lower Rio Salado [Salt River] between the Tempe Delta on the west and the upper Salt River Valley on the east is almost impassable. The mountains on both sides, the Superstition Range and the Mas-a-sar [likely the Mazatzals], are rugged, forbidding, and very scantily watered." To this day, that description remains accurate.

But even before the Spaniards and mountain men traversed this foreboding Sonoran Desert passage, the Coyotero Apaches traveled the trail from their White Mountain Villages to raid the Pima Indians 100 hard miles west in the Salt River Valley. According to Robert M. Brock, in *History of Tortilla Flat*, "The trail was used not only by the Coyotero, but also by the Tonto Apache for similar reasons, and perhaps, by the Salado Indians, an ancient tribe from the Roosevelt, Arizona area as far back as 900 A.D. It is believed by some that the latter traded pottery, jewelry and implements for food to another ancient tribe, the Hohokam, who irrigated and farmed southern Arizona deserts raising corn, beans and squash."

Because of the Native Americans' steadfast oral tradition, no known written Indian account exists to describe the ceremonies they may have performed, the discoveries they might have made, or the difficulties they may have faced while following the Apache Trail. One of the best accounts of the Apaches' use of the trail was written by George Wharton James in 1917; in *Arizona: The Wonderland*, he wrote:

> It is almost impossible for the ordinary mind to conceive that a horse, carrying a human being, can perform such feats as were the every-day experiences of these Bedouins of the American deserts. . . . The landscape they rode over, trampled under their horses' feet, was befitting their own nature. It was wild, rugged, desolate, awe-inspiring, weird, mountain-surrounded, different. It was distinctly Arizonan and Apachean. Nothing could tame it, subdue it, bring it under control, gentle it.

Nothing could tame it until 1905, that is, when construction began on Roosevelt Dam, the pivotal reclamation project that shaped the future of Phoenix and the Valley of the Sun. When finally completed by Italian stone masons in 1911, Roosevelt Dam was the highest masonry dam in the world; it was more than 300 feet high and 1,100 feet wide, cost $5.46

million, had a watershed of 6,000 square miles, and created a lake more than 30 miles long. Ironically, the Apaches themselves helped make this engineering marvel possible. Using picks and shovels, they chiseled out a 50-mile-long road atop their ancient track, which allowed twenty-mule teams to haul men, supplies, and equipment to the dam site from Mesa. According to James, the Apaches told Louis C. Hill, supervising engineer of the U.S. Reclamation Service: "Tell us what you want us to do; show us how to do it; then leave us alone. We need neither bosses nor spotters. We'll do our work faithfully and well." In a little more than a year, four hundred Apaches had done just that.

Once roughrider-turned-president Theodore Roosevelt had dedicated Roosevelt Dam in 1911, motorists soon realized that one of the most spectacular and historic roads in Arizona had also been created. Wrote James:

> Where the Apache used to ride in wild abandon the automobile now races, and my lady, in her silks and satins, venturing from the . . . ultra-civilized avenues of Eastern and Southern cities, looks out in wonderment and surprise, often in enthusiasm and delight, over scenery her eyes have never before contemplated. Here is the Arizona rarified atmosphere, translucent, pellucid, clarified beyond anything elsewhere on earth . . . here are the desert and mountain colors found only in the lands of magic enchantment.

Directions

From Phoenix, drive west to Apache Junction and begin at the intersection formed by Highway 60 and State Route 88.

Road Log

Begin. In 1941 you could still bed down in a U.S. Forest Service campground for free, and during that year the Tonto National Forest produced a series of road logs for tourists interested in using the CCC-built campgrounds while motoring central Arizona's backcountry. One edition, *Motor Trip No. 2: Phoenix and Payson and Pine and Pleasant Valley*, describes one of Phoenix's premier sights during its cow-town days, before the first post office was established in Apache Junction in 1950: "The trip through urban and suburban Phoenix, Arizona's State Capital, with a population of 65,414, takes you past many a fine institution, among them being Tovrea's Packing Plant that processes much of the beef raised on the range country covered by this trip." It is no longer possible to take a guided tour of that historic meat-packing plant; instead, a long line of fast-food establishments offer imported beef from Argentina as you travel through modern Phoenix, Tempe, and Mesa to Apache Junction.

Mile 0 to 3.5. From Apache Junction, paved State Route 88 contours the western front of Superstition Mountain. Next to the Grand Canyon, this is Arizona's most famous postcard scene; it's also Arizona's most legendary mountain. Perhaps no other quote describes the irresistible lure of this mountain and 160,000-acre Sonoran Desert wilderness it guards better than that of Pedro de Castenada, circa 1545: "Granted that they did not find the riches of which they had been told: they did find the next best thing—a place in which to search for them." But treasure, and the fifty-one people who died under the spell of the Lost Dutchman's Gold reported to be hidden here (see entry for Weaver's Needle), are only part of the history of the "Killer Mountains."

As far as the Pima Indians were concerned, Superstition Mountain was *Kakatak Tamai,* "Crooked-Top Mountain." One of their ancient songs describes traversing the mountain's crest between sunup and sundown:

> From Superstition Mountain rose the Eagle
> From the sluggish-moving Gila rose the Hawk
> There I am going; there I am going
> There I am running; there I am running
> The shadow of the Crooked Mountain

At Mile 3.5, the Mountain View pullout on the right provides an excellent view up Siphon Draw to the 5,024-foot north summit of Superstition Mountain; Siphon Draw is the normal descent route for trekkers who embark on the airy ridgeline traverse from the mountain's southern end, via Carney Springs Campground and the West Boulder Trail.

Mile 3.5 to 5.5. Along this 2-mile stretch, you'll pass the turnoff for the Mining Camp Restaurant, where you'll find the best slab of beef in Lost Dutchman country; Goldfield, a boom-to-bust ghost town established in 1893; Lost Dutchman State Park, a 300-acre park dedicated to the legend and the Sonoran Desert from which it emanated; and, during the wintertime, makeshift camps cradling hundreds of homeless people drawn from the cold, cavernous cities of the East by the warm Arizona sun.

Mile 5.5. First Water Trailhead turnoff on the right, via USFS Road 78. A popular 11-mile hike through the Superstition Wilderness leaves First Water Trailhead via Dutchman's Trail 2.6 miles from the Apache Trail and connects with the Peralta Canyon Trail; between these two points, the trail system meanders through the hoodoo rock country of Weaver's

Needle before exiting Peralta Canyon via the most heavily used trailhead in the Superstition Wilderness.

Mile 7.7. "Needle Vista" turnoff on the right. One of the only views you'll get of this 4,535-foot-high Arizona landmark from the Apache Trail. (For the history and climber's route, see entry for Weaver's Needle.)

Mile 8. "Whiskey Road" turnoff on the left. Not to be confused with Prescott's historic Whiskey Row. According to Apache Trail historian Robert M. Brock, the Hiram Walker Company buried a case of Canadian Club Whiskey in this vicinity as part of a promotional campaign. After the company advertised clues in national magazines, Larry Hedrick finally found the redeye in 1978. His was probably the only treasure ever found in these fabled mountains in modern times.

Mile 12. Apache Gap. In the 4 miles between Whiskey Road and Apache Gap, the Apache Trail weaves through a molten cluster of globs, knobs, and baubles of volcanic rock; early morning and late afternoon light provide striking color images of these rock formations, or you can capture the scenic view of 7,645-foot Four Peaks over Canyon Lake immediately to the north.

Mile 12.3. Canyon Lake Vista. Overlooking Canyon Lake mountain reservoir and the river it buried, this scenic viewpoint also provides a mournful glimpse into Arizona's tragic and bloody past. The time was December 1872: Under the orders of Gen. George Crook, government troops were trying to rout out the last of the tireless Apache warriors when three detachments of the Fifth Cavalry cornered a hundred Indians in a cave high above the Salt River. With Maj. William Brown and Lt. John G. Bourke leading and Apache Indian scout and turncoat Natanje guiding, the carnage was swift and almost complete. Wrote Lieutenant Bourke:

> The noise was frightful; the destruction sickening. Our volleys were still directed against the inner faces of the cave and the roof and the Apaches seemed to realize that their only safety lay in crouching close to the great stone heap in front, but even this precarious shelter was now taken away; the air was filled with bounding, plunging fragments of stone, breaking into thousands of pieces with other thousands behind, crashing down with the momentum gained in the descent of hundreds of feet. No human voice could be heard in such a cyclone of wrath.

In all, some seventy-six men, women, and children were reportedly massacred by gunfire or pulverized by boulders rolled into the cave from high above; only eighteen Indians escaped with their lives. Although the victims were originally thought to be Apache, recent archaeological evidence suggests that they were Yavapai. Skeleton Cave, discovered in 1906 by cowboy Jeff Adams, is now being studied as an official historic site. According to Prescott's Sharlot Hall Museum *Gazette*, Norm Tessman, curator of collections, with the assistance of archaeologist Alan Ferg, hopes to identify the tribe of the victims and to establish "a memorial, a reminder of a dark time in our state's history, and a monument to the people who died there."

Mile 12.5 to 17.6. The road crosses First Water Creek and Boulder Creek while winding around Canyon Lake.

Mile 17.6, Tortilla Flat. This way station for stagebound tourists en route to see the highest masonry dam in the world is named for a nearby rock formation. In the *History of Tortilla Flat*, Robert M. Brock reported that novelist John Steinbeck thought enough of the name to use it as a title for his 1935 novel. According to Brock, the fact "that Tortilla Creek crossed the [Apache] trail—offering dependable water, shade, and cover—has made this a natural stopping place on the trail for perhaps a thousand years or more." Because of its proximity to Phoenix, and because the Apache Trail strings together a series of spectacular man-made reservoirs (Saguaro, Canyon, Apache, and Roosevelt), Tortilla Flat remains a popular way station for modern travelers.

Mile 21.9. Horse Mesa Road turnoff on the left, via USFS Road 80. Experienced hikers can sometimes obtain special permission from the Salt River Project to cross the Horse Mesa Dam in order to gain access to the southern flanks of the 53,500-acre Four Peaks Wilderness—and one of the densest black bear populations in Arizona—via the Painted Cliffs and Alder Trail.

Mile 22.8. End pavement. Where the fun really begins.

Mile 23.5. J.F. Trail turnoff on the right, via USFS Road 213. By following the J.F. Trail No. 106 9 miles south to the J.F. Ranch, it's possible to traverse the seldom-explored eastern end of the Superstition Wilderness from north to south. Among the highlights there are: 6,056-foot-high Iron Mountain, high point of the Superstition Wilderness Area; the Pueblo-style cliff dwellings of Angel Springs, located near the junction of Rodgers Canyon Trail and Frog Tanks Trail; and the canyon-crawling car tour through Hewitt Canyon on USFS Road 172 to the southern trailhead near the J.F. Ranch.

Mile 24.4.   Fish Creek Overlook. The 1.5-mile plunge into Fish Creek Canyon is one of the steepest and most exciting 2WD vehicle descents in Arizona. Fish Creek Hill is like a graded avalanche; when stagecoach drivers approached its top and during the early 1900s, they fired three shots into the air to warn everyone to get the hell out of the way. After driving up the hill circa 1916, George Warton James wrote: "After leaving Fish Creek Station we come to the real thrilling portion of the road. . . . From a distance our car must look like a fly on a wall, and though we go up on 'high' [gear], we crawl. The rocks are wild, rugged, impressive, grand; the canyon below, threaded with a silver stream, and made bright with many rustling leaves. We breathe easier when the summit is reached."

Mile 26.   Fish Creek Canyon bridge. Fall through spring, the refreshing pools of water in Fish Creek Canyon provide seasonal estivation sites for Valley residents who like to wear little more than T-shirts boasting, "Yeah, but it's a dry heat!" The scramble and hike up this rugged, boulder-choked canyon is probably the most breathtaking in the Superstitions. Once you've gained the headwaters of Fish Creek Canyon near Lost Dutch Spring, you can traverse the western half of the wilderness area on any of a variety of trails to reach the Peralta Trailhead on its southern end.

Mile 26.8.   Old Fish Creek Lodge Site, used by tourists during the heyday of the Roosevelt Dam.

Mile 29.9.   Reavis Ranch turnoff on the right. Perhaps the most colorful historic site in the Superstition Mountains, Reavis Ranch can be reached by driving 3 miles south on USFS Road 212 to Reavis Ranch Trail No. 109. No one, except possibly the Pima Indians, and the Apache Indians who reportedly feared these mountains, knew the Superstitions better than Reavis, "the hermit of the Superstitions." Reavis lived at a small ranch cleaved into the side of a canyon during the late 1800s, and during the 22 years he cultivated his 15 acres, he made $30,000. In short, Reavis made more money farming a hard patch of ground in these storied mountains than anyone ever did prospecting them. Vegetables like potatoes fetched him 8 cents a pound, and he sold them by the burro load to the nearby Silver King Mine. In one season alone he pocketed $5,000, which, in 1890s territorial Arizona, was akin to growing the mother lode in your backyard.

But whether it was because Reavis was such a cunning hunter between plantings or because his appearance kept them at bay, Indians were said to give him a wide berth. The August 2, 1894, edition of *The Arizona Daily Star* painted a vivid portrait of the man and his life:

Living among the lonely fastness of the mountains of Pinal county, in a canyon with walls thousands of feet high, to which there is but one entrance, is a hermit, as secluded and as content as is any of that mysterious world-renowned class of men of any period, ancient or modern. His hut is one of the most inaccessible in the world. Fifteen miles away is the nearest wagon road, and for that distance the climb is a hard and perilous mountain trail. . . . Reavis is the name of this strange character. Old, he is, as all hermits are, dressed in rags. He wears his clothes until they go almost to shreds. His hairy breast he disdains to cover, and his shirt is open in the front to his belt. His hair is white and hangs down his breast, and his beard is long and wavy and venerable. He is well informed, keeping alive to the topics of the day, and knowing more of this busy world of ours than many in the midst of it.

Evidently the wealth Reavis made and undoubtedly stashed somewhere near his ranch may have been his undoing; his decomposed body was found 2 years after the article was published, and no one knows who murdered him. (See Weavers Needle entry.)

Mile 36.6 to 47.8. The Apache Trail winds along Apache Lake, the highest masonry dam in the world, and the lake behind it before ending at the turnoff to Tonto National Monument.

To return to Apache Junction. Either reverse the tour, or continue 30 miles on State Route 88 to Globe-Miami, then 70 miles to Apache Junction via Highway 60/70.

Travel Notes

• **Primary access.** Apache Junction or Globe-Miami.

• **Elevations.** 1,719 feet at Apache Junction; 3,053 feet at Fish Creek Hill; 2,235 feet in Fish Creek Canyon; and 2,400 feet at Roosevelt.

• **Mileage.** 47.8 miles (dirt road for 21.1 miles; paved, 26.7 miles).

• **Seasons.** All year; summer is crowded and hot, but "it's a dry heat."

• **Nearest supply points.** Apache Junction, Roosevelt, and Globe-Miami.

• **Maps.** Tonto National Forest Recreation Map.

• **Biotic communities.** Sonoran Desert scrub (Arizona upland subdivision) and interior chaparral.

Senator Road

Prescott National Forest, Prescott to Bumblebee.

Lanaiorm

Forty miles long and nearly 25 miles wide, the 7,979-foot-high Bradshaw Mountains are among the most rugged mountain ranges in central Arizona. Bordered on the east by the Agua Fria River and on the west by the Hassayampa River, the rocky, saguar-covered southern flanks of the Bradshaw massif climb abruptly out of the Sonoran Desert near the 2,000-foot level on its southern end and reaches its high point atop ponderosa pine–covered Mount Union near its northern end. Closely following a historic wagon road along the crest of the Bradshaws, the modern Senator Road still provides an exhilarating tour of what was once considered an impenetrable mountain range.

Historical Overview

The earliest people to inhabit the Bradshaw Mountains were believed to be the southeastern band of Yavapai Indians, called the Kewevkapaya, between A.D. 1100 and A.D. 1600. No one knows whether the Yavapai were descendants of the Sinagua, inhabitants of the Coconino Plateau country to the north, or migrants to the area related to the Yuman-speaking tribes of the Lower Colorado River. What *is* certain is that they were unique among desert-dwelling Indians of the Southwest in that they readily adapted to the environmental extremes of the Bradshaw Mountains. According to Volume 10 of *The Handbook of North American Indians*, the vast ancestral land of the Yavapai "includes Sonoran desert, mountain, and transition zone environments of which the transition itself is a highly varied topographic and climatic region. . . . This extensive and comparatively rich land base provided the mobile hunter and gatherers with a steady and varied food supply of plants and animals."

The first known non-Indian traverse of the Bradshaws took place in May 1863. Led by legendary mountain man and guide Joseph Reddeford Walker, thirty-odd prospectors concluded their roundabout, 2-year, 2,000-mile journey from Keyesville, California, by following the Hassayampa River to its headwaters in the heart of the Bradshaw Mountains. Written by expedition member Daniel Ellis Conner and published posthumously in *Joseph Reddeford Walker and the Arizona Adventure*, Conner's account accurately depicts the same difficulties modern canyoneers would face if they attempted to follow Walker's route out of the lower Sonoran Desert from the vicinity of Wickenburg today:

> The creek was a narrow gorge-like canyon that could not be traced with any degree of certainty as to its general course, and wound its way amongst the mountains apparently down deep beneath the general

level . . . of the country. Numerous obstacles in its bed, such as falls, accumulated boulders, etc. over which it was impossible to take the mules, frequently turned us out of its banks, where our route would become either up or down continuously. . . . On one occasion in descending one of those steep hillsides, the crupper of Captain Walker's saddle gave way and tossed him over the mule's head down the hill, where he landed upon his shoulders into a bunch of prickly bear bushes.

A 6-foot, 200-pound Tennesseean, Walker escaped without injury and several days later led his weary men out of the searing desert heat to the forested crest of the Bradshaws. Of their camp somewhere between the headwaters of Hassayampa Creek—what they called "the Haviamp"—and Wolf Creek, Connor wrote: "We considered our long journey at an end, for we were at last in the unexplored regions of central Arizona, the place of our destination, and located in the finest and largest woodland country by far to be found within the extensive limits of the whole territory." This unexplored region abounded with deer, and that evening expedition member George Lount volunteered to hunt down supper. Not 300 yards from camp, he came upon a fresh lion kill and hauled the bloody carcass back to camp. Wrote Conner: "Not having heard the report of his gun, some one asked how he got the deer and he replied that he had run it down and killed it with his knife."

The rich lodes of silver and gold that the Walker party discovered along Hassayampa and Lynx creeks led to the first mining districts in the Bradshaws. But no single strike was richer than the one found by the Weaver Expedition on Rich Hill in the nearby Weaver Mountains a year earlier. Depending who's telling the story, Abraham Harlow Peeples and his party gathered between $4,000 and $7,000 in gold nuggets before breakfast. Six months later, that strike became one of the richest placer finds in Arizona history.

The discoveries made by the Weaver and Walker parties caused a stampede of gold seekers, thousands of them descending on the Bradshaws in hopes of staking claims in the mother lode. "Glory holes" were punched into every nook and cranny throughout the range, and mining camps sprung up to support those diggings; for the most part, those camps and settlements received supplies via the wagon road that led southward out of Prescott, Arizona's territorial capitol. But it's hard to pin down exactly when that wagon road was first built. Unnamed until the turn of the century, when S. O. Fredericks named it after his Senator Mine, the wagon road appears on the 1882 Reconnaissance Map of Prescott (a 15-minute topographical map). No doubt each section of the road had its origins with the next mining settlement, penetrating deeper into the Bradshaws southward from Prescott. By 1882 — if not sooner — the wagon road linked Prescott and adjacent Fort Whipple with settlements strung across the length of the Bradshaws, like Hassayampa, Bueno, Alexandra, Meesville, and, finally, Tip-Top, where it plunged off the southern end of the range and linked up with the Black Canyon Road to Phoenix.

As late as the 1940s, long after the last glory hole played out, at least one family was still riding horseback across the Bradshaws out of necessity. Bud Brown and his wife Isabelle were building a summer camp in Groom Creek, based on "western traditions and wholesome values . . . gained only through intimate participation in life in the country." Their Friendly Pines Camp needed horses — and lots of them — and at the time, the only cheap, practical method of transporting horses from Phoenix to Prescott was to ride them 100 rugged miles across the Bradshaws. So the Browns and their two young daughters, Beebee and Nancy, would ride to Phoenix to pick up anywhere from fifteen to forty head of horses and drive them back across the Bradshaws. According to Bud Brown, crossing the Bradshaws was the easy part; even during June it was relatively cool as long as they stayed up high, and when they dropped off the southern end, they would hold up for the night at New River Station. Then, as Bud Brown said, "I'd get up at three o'clock in the morning, feed the horses, start breakfast, and by four we'd broken camp and were on the desert . . . and we'd trot those horses just as hard as we could until the sun came up. And boy when it did, it was like somebody just turned on the blow torches. So we'd slow down to a walk across that desert, flat, abandoned, open desert all the way to north Central Avenue [in Phoenix]."

But even before the Brown family made its first 2½-day horseback ride across the Bradshaws, travel writer George Wharton James was extolling the virtues of the area in his book *Arizona: The Wonderland*. The mountain community of Prescott would become a popular place to live for the same reason Friendly Pines Camp became internationally renowned: its friendly people, mild climate, scenic mountains, healthy, pine-sweet air, and "wholesome values based on Western traditions." James wrote: "Prescott, too, is wonderfully favored in its scenic roads. There is not one city in a thousand in the United States that has its advantages in this regard. . . . Merely to mention the localities . . . quickens the heart to glorious reminiscences of canyon and forest, mountain peak and thrilling ravine, divides and crests, with outlooks of incomparable beauty, sublimity, and grandeur." To this day, Prescott offers the highest concentration of scenic backcountry roads in the state — and the all-time classic among them is the Senator Road. Drive it, ride it, run it, or walk it — but take it!

Directions

From the historic Courthouse Plaza in downtown Prescott, drive east on Gurley Street to Mount Vernon Street; turn right and begin tour.

Road Log

Mile 0 to 5.6. Prescott to Groom Creek. Some folks say the Bradshaws don't begin until you reach Groom Creek, a onetime stage stop and mining settlement 5 miles up Senator Road. But if a fellow wanted to split hairs, he could say those mountains actually begin right there next to the old post office . . . about where they giddy-up past the graveyard for the old Senator Drive-in to form a remuda of 7,000-foot-high peaks like Spruce, Davis, Union, Tritle, and Maverick.

That's just the short of it, though. This cirque of pine-clad peaks—once called the Silver Range—forms the headwaters for three main creeks, the mainstay of Prescott for as far back as anyone cares to remember, Lynx Creek pours its heart out into Lynx Lake, 5 miles below the mining camp turned summer haven of Walker; Hassayampa River trundles down off the west slope of the Bradshaws to Wickenburg before it evaporates into the hot sand and creosote bush flats west of Phoenix; and Groom Creek cascades off Spruce Mountain during the spring thaw, providing the well spring for the historic colony that has thrived around it since it first changed its name from Oakdale back in 1901.

En route to Groom Creek, a pullout on the right at Mile .7 provides a fine overlook of Prescott at sunset; Mile 3.4 marks the turnoff for the Goldwater Lake Recreation Area: and Mile 4.9, on the left, marks the Spruce Mountain Road turnoff (USFS Road 52A) to the Spruce Mountain Lookout. According to writer Rosemary Holusha, this stretch of the Senator Road was "once part of the Prescott and Lynx Creek toll road, where a charge of $1.50 was made for a wagon and 25 cents for a horse and rider."

Mile 5.6. Groom Creek Store. This is a good place to whet your whistle, grab a bite to eat, and catch up on the local gossip. According to *Arizona Place Names,* Groom Creek was officially established on August 19, 1901, and took its name from Col. Bob Groom, a Kentucky transplant who had his fingers in everything from prospecting and surveying to territorial legislating.

Mile 6. On the left is the historic Groom Creek School and a nature trail for disabled individuals.

Mile 6.3. Spruce Mountain Trail begins on the left and takes you 3 miles to the 7,693-foot summit of Spruce Mountain, mistakenly named for spruce trees once thought to grow near its summit; though it was later discovered that they were Douglas fir. Whether you drive up the Spruce Mountain Road or hike up the Spruce Mountain Trail, this misnamed summit makes a worthwhile detour, with views that rank it with nearby Mount Union. From the summit of Spruce Mountain, you can see the 12,633-foot-high San Francisco Peaks 75 miles northeast, the 7,903-foot-high Mazatzal Mountains 60 miles southeast, beyond the 6,574-foot-high Weaver Mountains 25 miles west, and too many other landforms to name here. Bring a good map.

Mile 6.3 to 11.4. Spruce Mountain Trailhead to Senator Mine. En route to the hulking remains of the Senator Mine 5 miles up the road, the pavement ends at Mile 7.3 and the turnoff to Upper and Lower Wolf Creek Campgrounds veers off immediately to the right via USFS Road 97; at Mile 9.7, this twisting mountain road narrows, so use caution. Native desert pigs, called javelina, frequently cross Senator Road along this stretch; apparently, they've extended their range from the Sonoran Desert up into the Mountain Transition Life Zone and can now be seen tromping through midwinter snows above the 7,000-foot level. If you're running on foot up the Senator, don't be surprised if one of those nearsighted, tusked critters chases you up a pine tree.

On the right, at Mile 11.4, you'll see the remains of the Senator Mine, which reportedly produced $530,000 in gold during the 1860s.

Mile 11.4 to 12.1. Senator Mine to Walker Road Junction. This narrow stretch of the Senator Road, literally gouged into the side of the mountain, parallels and then crosses Hassayampa Creek before passing the remains of the old Senator post office. Once you reach the junction of the Walker Road (USFS Road 197), it's less than a mile via the Walker Road to Hassayampa Lake, the prettiest mountain lake in Arizona.

Mile 12.1 to 13.7. Walker Road Junction to Mount Union Pass. To continue on the Senator Road, turn right at the Walker Road junction and climb up the switchbacks to Mount Union Pass; this 7,196-foot-high pass lies at the head of Crook Canyon between Mount Tritle and Mount Union. The 2.5-mile detour up Mount Union is probably the most breathtaking side trip off the northern half of the Senator Road.

According to *Arizona Place Names*, Charles Debrille Poston was known as the "Father of Arizona because it was due largely to his efforts that the territory of Arizona was created by act of President Abraham Lincoln." In Pauline Henson's history of Prescott, called *Founding a Wilderness Capital,* she reprinted Poston's 1800s description:

> From its summit, I obtained the grandest view that I have ever seen, and the grandest that I shall ever see again. To the southeast, near the Pimo Villages, we could see the Massasal [likely the Mazatzal Mountains], to the southwest, some seventy-five miles, the Pen-hatch-a-pet; to the east, the San Francisco or Verde river with its tributaries; and way beyond them the mountains in Apache country where to go is death.
>
> On the north, the grandest mountain range of the Territory, Mount Whipple [San Francisco Mountains], looming 12,000 feet above the level of the sea; and away to the west, Bill Williams Mountain, and the mountains near the Colorado River and Fort Mojave. The little mountains were scattered all around like the waves of the sea after a hard storm. On the northeast we could see a stream called the Agua Frio, making its way to the Verde, shining in the sunlight like a thread of silver . . .
>
> We had a grand time climbing these mountains, eating venison, and drinking the delicious mountain water, sleeping on the ground, and arising in the morning more refreshed than those who have slept on beds of down.

Henson speculates that Poston most likely obtained this grand view from the summit of Mount Union. No other summit in the Bradshaws offers the kind of far-reaching, 360-degree panorama that Mount Union does.

Mile 13.7 to Mile 18.1. Mount Union Pass to Palace Station. There are two points of no return along the 68-mile Senator Road, and weather, road conditions, your vehicle, and your driving skills will determine whether you should push beyond these two points. The first is at Mile 8.3; Yavapai County snow plows do not maintain the road beyond this point in winter. The second is immediately below Mount Union Pass, on its south side. The drop into Crook Canyon is a long and steep one, and if the road is icy, as it frequently is midwinter, or if it appears that a summer monsoon is about to hammer the area, as they frequently do, turn back. If the weather is fair and the road is dry, enjoy the plunge down Crook Canyon to Palace Station.

The Forest Service's wooden sign in front of Palace Station sums up the history of this territorial cabin: "This cabin was built in 1874 by the Spruce Family and is one of the oldest structures in Arizona. It served as a stage station on the Senator Trail from Prescott to Phoenix until 1910 and is now used by the U.S. Forest Service as a private residence. Stay out." However, if for some reason you have an emergency midway between Prescott and Crown King, Palace Station is your best bet for help.

Mile 22. Goodwin and Road Junction 67. If you need to cut this tour short, go 10 miles to Mayer, located on Highway 69, via USFS Road 67; from Mayer, circle back to Prescott or head down the hill to Phoenix. Officially established in 1896, the mining town of Goodwin died in the 1940s along with the dreams of destitute gold seekers.

Not far from Goodwin — it's difficult to nail down the exact site — the small mining settlement of Bueno thrived during the 1880s. In *Ghost Towns of Arizona*, authors James and Barbara Sherman wrote: "The early, dangerous years of the 1860s passed, and by the 1880s Bueno, no longer hampered by Indians, was an active settlement. Two mills were in operation, gold and silver were shipped, mail arrived semi-weekly, and stages ran between Bueno and Prescott. The population of 250 people supported a general store, meat market, and school, and had in residence a lawyer and a justice of the peace." Thoroughly researched and appended with maps, *Ghost Towns of Arizona* is an invaluable resource for backcountry motorists.

Mile 22 to 31.3. From Goodwin to Towers Creek, the Senator Road threads its way through the Bradshaws' dense chaparral country, becoming one of the windiest mountain roads anywhere. It roller-coasters in and out, up and down every little nameless creek draining the western flanks of Towers Mountain. As long as you have this one-lane track to yourself, hang on and enjoy the wild ride. But if you have a road whale lumbering through the mountains ahead of you, or a fifteen-vehicle caravan of four wheelers, you'll wish you had never pulled out of the driveway — so avoid the Senator Road during crowded summer weekends.

Mile 31.3 to 38.6. From Towers Creek, the Senator Road climbs out of the hot, dry chaparral country back into the cool ponderosa pine forest that crowns the southern crest of the Bradshaws.

Officially established in 1874, Bradshaw City was home to an estimated 5,000 people during the brief, wild decade when it flourished with the nearby gold and silver Tiger Mine. The February 4, 1871, *Weekly Arizona Miner* summed up the character of the bustling mining camp: "A settlement started there known as Bradshaw City, where for many months there were many saloons and dance halls in full blast, but there were no churches." According to *Ghost Towns of Arizona*, the saddle train from Prescott took 2½ days to reach Bradshaw City at the time.

Mile 40. USFS Road Junction 259 and 52. The Senator Road (Road 52) forks at this junction. If you have time, follow Road 52 along the southern crest of the Bradshaws at least as far south as Horsethief Basin Recreation Area; this approximates the route of the old Senator Trail. Better yet, if you want the most breathtaking view of the central Arizona desert, pick your way south to the horse camp called Coal Camp Spring. From there, hike up an old fire road to a cluster of granite boulders called South Fort, which marks the highest point on the southern end of the Bradshaws; for adventurers used to camping on airy perches, this old Indian encampment is the most exciting place to bivouac in the entire range. But if you're going to camp at South Fort, you need two charts: one for the stars and the other for the landforms. While you're gazing into the horizon, try to imagine what it was like for Bud and Isabelle Brown and their two 8-year-old daughters to drive a herd of horses across the desert below; South Fort marked the area where that hardy Arizona family plunged off the southern end of the Bradshaws to ride hell-for-leather to Phoenix.

To reach Crown King and complete the tour to Bumblebee from this junction, turn left onto Road 259 and drive a rocky half a mile to the turnoff to Crown King via Road 259A.

Mile 40.5. Crown King. Officially established on June 28, 1888, the mining settlement of Crown King lured a different type of miner than did nearby Bradshaw City. According to *Ghost Towns of Arizona*, Crown King "was quiet, clean, and orderly. The company did not tolerate drunkenness in their employees, therefore, a more respectable type of man was attracted to the camp." At the time, pack trains hauled the precious ore to Prescott for $21.50 a ton; by 1904, the Crown King branch of the Bradshaw Mountain Railway replaced the pack trains. But for more than one reason, that branch was called the impossible railroad. For one thing, the railroad builders were not exactly teetotalers; according to a *Daily Phoenix Herald* account, "The consumption of beer in the camps of railway builders is enormous. . . . At Bismarck I saw an entire freight train of 30 cars laden with bottled beer from a Chicago Brewery, bound for the nearest town at the end of the track. The chief engineer of construction reported to me that an average of one bottle per tie laid was consumed, and that the tie and the beer cost the same: 50 cents." But drinking among the three hundred–man work force wasn't the only problem railroad management faced; according to Tosh Plumlee's article, "Arizona's Impossible Railroad," published in *Arizona Highways Magazine,* "blasting a cut for the approach to the #2 tunnel, exposed a massive body of gold and copper over 400 feet long and 12 feet wide. It took only a short time for half the work force to abandon the road bed and begin digging ore for themselves." By the time the Crown King branch of the Bradshaw Mountain Railroad was finally completed in May 1904, ten corkscrew switchbacks had been blasted up the east face of the Bradshaws along Poland Creek in order to reach the mine.

Still a ghost town in 1954, the 6,000-foot-high mountain hamlet of Crown King today boasts of having Arizona's only working one-room schoolhouse. Many of the students are children of Prescott National Forest employees who now reside in Crown King. Other residents include folks who run Crown King's general store, saloon, and restaurant, which cater to the needs of thousands of heat-ravaged Phoenicians who make their annual summer pilgrimage to this cool mountain retreat.

Mile 40 to 53.8. From Crown King to Cleator, you will essentially follow the historic bed of the Crown King branch of the Bradshaw Mountain Railroad, quickly switchbacking your way down 3,000 feet from the ponderosa pine forest to the Sonoran Desert. En route, you will pass through no less than eleven road gouges, wind around four genuine hairpin turns, and cross four one-lane bridges. Pull over at Mile 43 and take in the magnificent vista of Hells Hole, Horsethief Canyon, and rugged Poland Creek, which forms the northern border of the 29,770-acre Castle Creek Wilderness.

Mile 53.8. Cleator. Officially established as Turkey Creek in 1869, Cleator took its current name when James P. Cleator bought this territorial mining camp in 1925. According to *Arizona Place Names*, when the ghost town was once again offered for sale in 1949, "It consisted of twenty houses, a grocery, service station, saloon, and water works, and had about sixty residents." Today you can sometimes buy a soda when the old store is open.

Mile 57.6. Junction. You can end the tour here by looping back toward Prescott via Road 259, to the left, and going 11 miles to Mayer, located on Highway 89. To continue to Bumble Bee and Phoenix, go straight ahead.

Mile 63.1. Bumblebee. This former mining camp takes its name from a group of unlucky prospectors who were swarmed by bumblebees when they tried to bag some free honey from the nearby creek in 1863.

Mile 63 to 68. From Bumblebee, it's a straight shot to Interstate 17 and the end of this tour.

Travel Notes

•**Primary access.** Prescott and Bumblebee.

•**Secondary access.** Via Mayer.

•**Distance.** 68 miles (paved road for 7 miles; dirt, 61 miles).

•**Elevations.** 5,200 feet at Prescott; 7,196 feet at Mount Union Pass; 5,399 feet at Towers Creek; 5,984 feet at Crown King; 2,523 feet at Bumblebee.

•**Seasons.** Dry weather of fall is best; summer can be hot and crowded. August monsoons and winter snows can turn this into more of an adventure than you bargained for.

•**Nearest supply points.** Prescott, Crown King, and Mayer.

•**Emergencies.** There's a telephone in Crown King, and one at the Sunset Point Rest Area on I-17; also, if the Palace Station rangers are home, you may be able to get help by using their Forest Service radio.

•**Map.** Prescott National Forest Recreation Area.

•**Managing agency.** Prescott National Forest.

•**Biotic communities.** Interior chaparral, montane conifer forest, plains and desert grassland, and Sonoran Desert scrub (Arizona upland subdivision).

River Expeditions

Upper Salt River

Salt River Canyon to Roosevelt Lake: whitewater rafting

Landform

The headwaters of the Salt River emanate from the forested slopes of 11,420-foot Mount Baldy, the fourth highest summit in Arizona; also known as *dzil ligai* ("white mountain"), Mount Baldy is the sacred mountain of the White River Apache and the high point of eastern Arizona's White Mountains. En route to the unquenchable green lawns of Phoenix some 200 miles downstream, the main stem of the Salt River is formed by the White and Black rivers; from Mount Baldy to the sprawling Valley of the Sun, the Salt River descends more than 10,000 vertical feet and drains an estimated 2,500 square miles. The most famous leg of the Salt River, however, is the 52-mile-long stretch that boils down Salt River Canyon at Highway 60 and empties into Roosevelt Lake near the foot of the 7,748-foot Sierra Anchas at the Globe-Young Highway; this wild stretch of the Upper Salt descends an average of 25 feet per mile (the average for the Colorado River in the Grand Canyon is only 8 feet per mile); it has more than two dozen rapids, which have challenged early travelers since Coronado's men first called it Rio de las Balsas ("River of Rafts") in 1540.

Historical Overview

It's difficult to pinpoint exactly when the Upper Salt River was first run, but from the name Coronado's men bestowed upon it, we can surmise that they built reed rafts to ford it so they could continue their quest for the fabled Seven Cities of Cibola. In an 1890 Cambridge historical paper, Adolph F. Bandelier wrote of the difficulties Coronado's Fray Marcos de Niza might have faced in traversing the rugged country surrounding the Upper Salt:

> The portion of the Lower Rio Salado [Salt River] between the Tempe Delta on the west and Upper Salt River Valley on the east is almost impassable. The mountains on both sides, the Superstition Range and the Mas-a-sar [likely the Mazatzal Mountains], are rugged, forbidding and very scantly watered. Beyond the junction of the Arroyo Pinal the headwaters of the Salt River are extremely difficult to traverse; and had he [Fray Marcos] turned northward, avoiding the Sierra Ancha, in order to get into Tonto Basin, months would have been required to reach either Zuni or Moqui from the Gila.

That puts Coronado's men somewhere on the Upper Salt River circa May 9, 1540. Sample Gila River Basin cubic feet per second (cfs) charts for the years 1970 through 1980 indicate that those early boatmen might have encountered water as low as 121 cfs or as high as 10,300 cfs; to put those numbers in perspective, you can wade across the Salt River in many places at 121 cfs, but 4,000 cfs is considered a wild ride in a modern neopreme raft—let alone in a flimsy reed raft.

The next Spanish explorer to lay eyes on the Salt River was probably the dauntless Padre Kino, who called it a salty river (Rio Salado), on March 2, 1699. During his fifth *entrada* (journey) through "Unknown Arizona

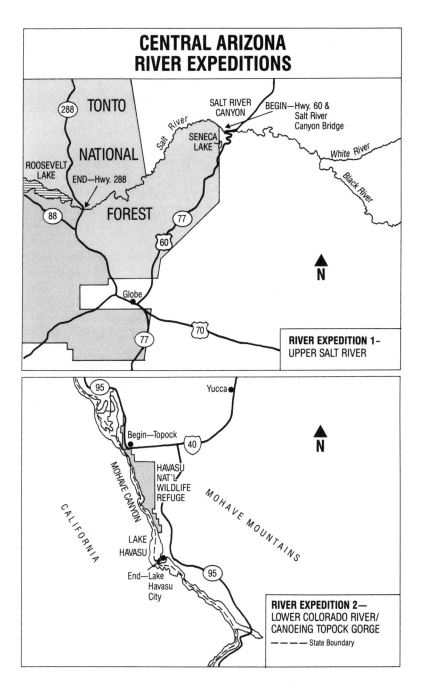

CENTRAL ARIZONA
RIVER EXPEDITIONS

288 TONTO

SALT RIVER
CANYON

BEGIN—Hwy. 60 &
Salt River
Canyon Bridge

Salt River

SENECA
LAKE

White River

NATIONAL

Black River

ROOSEVELT
LAKE

END—Hwy. 288

88

FOREST

77

60

N

Globe

77

70

RIVER EXPEDITION 1–
UPPER SALT RIVER

95

Yucca

N

Begin—Topock

40

MOHAVE CANYON

HAVASU
NAT'L
WILDLIFE
REFUGE

MOHAVE MOUNTAINS

CALIFORNIA

LAKE
HAVASU

End—Lake
Havasu
City

95

RIVER EXPEDITION 2—
LOWER COLORADO RIVER/
CANOEING TOPOCK GORGE
– – – – State Boundary

and Sonora," Kino covered 950 miles in 35 days following a route out of northern Sonora across the treacherous El Camino del Diablo to the Colorado River near Yuma; there he turned northeast along the Gila River and followed the Jornada de las Estrellas ("the day's journey of the stars") across the Forty Mile Desert to the foot of the Sierra Estrellas. In *Luz de Tierra Incognita*, Capt. Juan Mateo Manje wrote: "Traveling east and climbing to the top of a small mountain, which the [Indian] guides pointed out to us, we could plainly see the Verde River which takes rise in the land of the Apaches, running northeast to southeast, with a grove of trees along its banks. It is joined by another salty river, running from east to west, and the two merging together flow into this Rio Grande River [Gila]." Whether Kino and Manje actually climbed one of the higher peaks of the Sierra Estrellas (See entry for Montezuma Peak), as W. Early Merrill suggests in his *One Hundred Footprints on Forgotten Trails*, is suspect; crossing the Forty Mile Desert from the Gila River east to the Pima Villages would have put Kino near the southern end of the Sierra Estrellas, from which he could have seen the confluence of the Salt and Verde rivers from either Sacaton Butte, or from the lowly southern end of the Estrellas. What is known is that Kino saw the Valley of the Sun and the dependable conduit of the Rio Salado that would turn this area into Arizona's own Los Angeles 300 years later.

Trapper James Ohio Pattie became the first non-Indian to travel the length of the Upper Salt in 1826, though he most likely followed its rugged course on foot and on horseback. But Pattie's diary provides few clues as to the difficulties he and a party of French trappers encountered on their mid-winter journey; because the White Mountains are usually buried in deep snow, February runoff is generally very low, and Pattie and his company might have had easy going and enjoyed balmy temperatures. However, if it rained on the snowpack, they could have been trapping up and down a snowmelt like that in February 1980 that peaked at 41,200 cfs. In modern rafting terms, that's virtually unrunnable by all but the most seasoned "hair boaters." Wrote Pattie:

> In the morning of the 1st of February, we begin to ascend Black [Salt] River. We found it to abound with beavers. It is a most beautiful stream, bounded on each side with high and rich bottoms. We traveled up this stream to the point where it forks in the mountains; that is to say about 80 miles from its mouth. Here our company divided, a part ascending one fork, and a part the other. The left fork [Verde River] heads due north, and the right fork [Salt River] north east. It was my lot to ascend the latter. It heads in mountains covered with snow, near the head of

the left hand fork of the San Francisco [the White River, some think].
On the 16th, we all met again at the junction of the forks.

If Pattie and his men started from the confluence of the Salt and Verde
and trapped all the way to the White River, they would have covered
more than 300 miles along a slippery, boulder-strewn river course in 2
weeks. Evidently the beaver were plentiful then, because 3 years later famed
scout Kit Carson trapped there as well.

The only historic account of anyone actually trying to raft or float anything down the Upper Salt River was in 1873; according to *Guide to the
Geology of the Salt River Canyon Region, Arizona*, edited by Claudia Stone
and Judith P. Jenney, that's when Charles T. Hayden tried to float timber, harvested from the Sierra Anchas, down to the Valley of the Sun.
"Upon exploring the upper reaches of the canyon and floating a few logs
down the river, Hayden realized that many 'box canyons' would break
up the lumber long before it reached its destination, and thus the enter-
prise was abandoned."

Since it was first named the Rio de las Balsas in 1540, the Salt River
has been called the Rio Compuesto ("put together river," for the confluence
of the Salt and the Verde), the Rio de la Asuncion ("Assumption"), and
other names. Perhaps the most interesting name is the Papago-Pima "Onk
Akimel" (*onk* meaning "salty" and *akimel* meaning "river"). Whatever you
call it, as long as the 60-mile-long course remains undammed it will continue to offer much the same wild water and country that challenged the
region's earliest travelers.

Directions

To get to the put-in, drive north from Globe 35 miles on Highway 60
to the Salt River Canyon Bridge. You can put in below the bridge on
the river's north side (the Whiteriver Apache side) via the Cibecue Creek
Road, or above the bridge on the south side (San Carlos Apache side).
The River Log starts at the latter.

To get to the take-out, drive north from Claypool 15 miles on Highway 88; turn north and take State Route 288 6 miles to the bridge across
the Salt. The take-out is located below the bridge on river right. *You must not
miss this take-out!* Unsuspecting rafters have drowned while trapped in the
deadly, recycling falls produced by a small diversion dam immediately below it.

Allow 2½ to 3 hours to shuttle vehicles between the put-in and the
take-out before and after this 4-day river trip.

River Log

Mile 60 (river miles counted downstream from the put-in). You'll find a small parking lot and campground at the put-in immediately above the Salt River Canyon Bridge, on the south side of the river.

Indian Rapid is the first rapid below the put-in and above the bridge; during peak runoff—and the prime river-running season—of March and April, it exudes the Upper Salt's true character: It is undammed, and thus untamed, and as boatmen you need to adapt to its daily and seasonal fluctuations as it churns down the terra incognita of Salt River Canyon to Roosevelt Lake.

Indian Rapid is also about where the Arizona Game and Fish Department wanted to release a deadly fish toxin called rotenone in hopes of suffocating twenty-five thousand catfish along a 52-mile stretch of the Upper Salt. According to *The Arizona Daily Star*, public outcry was so great that the plan will not be considered anytime in the near future. (See entry for Mount Bangs.)

Boatwoman Sandra Howe rows her raft toward the takeout, after a wild, four-day whitewater raft expedition down the Upper Salt River. Photo by John Annerino.

Mile 59.9, Salt River Canyon Bridge. Actor Robert De Niro swam the Upper Salt immediately below this bridge while playing a tenacious bounty hunter in the 1989 feature film *Midnight Run.*

Mile 59.7. At Island Rapid, also called Mule Hoof Falls, the river splits around a gravel bar during low water.

Mile 59 to 57. Mule Hoof Bend. In the parlance of geologists, Mule Hoof Bend is "an entrenched meander loop."

Mile 58.2. Maytag Rapid.

Mile 58.5. Cienega Creek. The silver white tailings of the Chrysolite Asbestos Mine can be seen high above on river left; according to *Guide to the Geology of the Salt River Canyon Region, Arizona,* edited by Claudia Stone and Judith P. Jenney, Charles Newton first discovered asbestos here in 1872.

Mile 58.1. Grunman Rapid, also called Reforma Rapid.

Mile 57.6. Motha Rock, also called Sleeper Rapid, after a cocky bronze river god who fell asleep at the oars and flipped on this exposed rock.

Mile 57.1. Overboard Rapid, also called Eagles Nest Rapid. According to the Tonto National Forest, the Upper Salt provides habitat for two pairs of endangered bald eagles: "The 11 known active nesting pairs found on the Salt and Verde Rivers are the only known desert nesting bald eagles in the world."

Mile 57 to 53. Coyote Canyon to Cibecue Creek. Once you emerge from Mule Hoof Bend, the river lets up long enough for you to take in the splendid riparian community, the dichotomy of the Mountain Transition Zone and the Lower Sonoran Desert Zone, which this river and its narrow, basalt-filled channel divide. On the south side of the river, lush mountain grasses surround dark green clusters of pinyon and juniper; on the north side, yucca and prickly pear grow among brittlebush and crown of thorns.

Mile 53.7. Exhibition Rapid, also called Winnebago Falls, undoubtedly in honor of some snowbird who thought he could drive his road whale across the river at this point.

Mile 53. Cibecue Creek. One of the principal tributaries of the Upper Salt, Cibecue Creek is the normal take-out for the half-day run from the Salt River Canyon Bridge; it's difficult to drive the Cibecue Creek Road beyond this point when the creek is running strong. According to *Arizona Place Names,* military troops retreated down Cibecue Creek from above when overwhelmed by Coyotero Apaches in 1881; today, increasing numbers of canyoneers explore this precipitous tributary canyon from below.

Mile 53 to 49.3.   Cibecue Creek to the Salt Banks.

Mile 52.9.   Cibecue Rapid. In Apache, *cibicu* means "reddish bottom land."

Mile 52.2.   Sluicebox Rapid, also called Threeway Rapid. Boatman and geology instructor Mike Young considers Threeway Rapid "the most unique gravel bar on the Salt, because the river has cut three separate channels through it, rather than just one."

Mile 50.8.   Mescal Rapid.

Mile 49.3.   Salt Banks. These billowing white mushrooms of chloride are located on river right. According to *Guide to the Geology of the Salt River Canyon Region, Arizona,* "In the 1870s . . . dissolved solids (mostly sodium) were being added to the Salt River from the Salt Banks at the rate of 140 tons a day, or 50,000 tons per year." Hence Kino's name, Rio Salado. This was the same vast deposit of table salt that King S. Woolsey began mining in 1878. An article in the September 21, 1878, edition of *The Salt River Herald* described Woolsey's mining operation: "From Wash Jacobs, who has just returned from the Salt Works 120 miles east of Phoenix, we learn that the work of getting the salt has commenced. Sixteen vats 50 feet square have been finished and water is run to a depth of 18 inches. By the time the last vat has received sufficient water, the first one has evaporated and the salt is removed. Thus it is seen that none of the salt stream is wasted."

Mile 49.3 to 48.4.   Salt Banks to Walnut Canyon.

Mile 49.1.   Ledges Rapid, also called Regal Falls.

Mile 48.5.   Tomato Juice Rapid.

Mile 48.4.   Walnut Canyon. When it's flowing, Walnut Creek is undoubtedly the prettiest cascade on the Upper Salt. During the uranium rush of the 1950s, Tomato Juice Mine operated near the confluence of Walnut and Regal canyons, a quarter-mile above the falls—but, like the old Salt Works, it has ceased operations. Today the streaming bridal veil of Walnut Creek remains a must-stop on the river.

Mile 47.3. Rock Creek Ruins. A short, steep hike through towering stands of saguaro will bring you to these ancient ruins, built at the base of an overhanging cliff and inhabited by the Hohokam circa A.D. 1000. In the April 1981 Wild and Scenic River Environmental Impact Study for the Upper Salt, the Tonto National Forest pronounced: "Based on available information, the area does not have 'outstandingly remarkable' historic or cultural value. . . . No significant historical events or physical remains of events are known." Rio de las Balsas, Cibecue Creek, and the Salt Banks notwithstanding, these spectacular cliff dwellings easily rival the heavily visited Anasazi granaries above Nankoweap Delta in the Grand Canyon; whoever inhabited them located these eminent dwellings so that the view from them would take in the bold sweep of mesas and mountains both upstream and down. And as you look back upstream, you can't help but wonder how many more "unremarkable" ruins are scattered along the Rock Creek monocline and elsewhere throughout Salt River Canyon.

Like the ancient Hohokam, the Western Apache reportedly engaged in subsistence farming throughout most of the Salt River and Gila river watersheds.

Mile 46.1. Rat Trap Rapid, also known as Fiasco Falls, is a gnarly little rapid at the head of a narrow gorge in the ruin granite; actually, according to Mike Young, it's "monzonite . . . characterized by rounded boulders, highlighted with pink feldspar crystals." Floating through this riverine passageway, you get the feeling that you're in old Arizona. It's old in the sense that few but the hardiest had ever seen this country before whitewater rafting became popular, and old in the geologic sense. Don Livingston of the University of Arizona has done research "that shows there are younger precambrian rocks . . . that are equivalent in age to the missing formation at the Great Uncomformity at the Grand Canyon. The Salt is one of the very few locations where this formation is exposed." How old? Seven hundred and fifty million to 1.2 billion years old!

Mile 41.8. Gleason Flat. The land opens up as you enter the cow and pasture country of Gleason Flat, and the river slows. You'll have the opportunity to see great blue herons take flight from the upper branches of enormous cottonwood trees along this stretch, their long, graceful wings flapping in slow motion above the lazy draft of the river. This is the calm before the storm that awaits you a dozen miles downstream.

Mile 38.1 to 37.7. Eye-of-the-Needle to Black Rock Rapid. As the river turns south from Gleason Flat and coils through the Redmond Formation, the current picks up steam and slams you through Eye-of-the-Needle (also known as Watergate Falls), then drops you like a stone in Black Rock Rapid (sometimes called Ambush Falls). You can avoid having a bad day at Black Rock by scouting from river right.

Mile 28.3. Quartzite Falls, "the ultimate portage." If you've seen German filmmaker Werner Herzog's monumental *Fitzcaraldo,* featuring the Sisyphean task of hauling a 320-ton steamboat over a rugged jungle isthmus separating two tributaries of the Amazon River, you have a pretty good idea what the portage at Quartzite Falls is like.

"If you miss the pull-in, you're going to run the falls." It's a line that plays like a cassette on auto-wind in the minds of most boatmen as they head downriver through Upper and Lower Corral Rapids and the river section called the Maze. You can hear the falls long before you see them. The cacophony reverberating off the brooding canyon walls is enough to put the fear of God into you.

Few have run Quartzite successfully. Grand Canyon outfitter Rob Elliott was the first known person to take a paddleboat through; he stationed someone with a throw bag on river left to make a life-saving toss to ensure that his paddleboat wouldn't be vacuumed back into Quartzite's deadly reversal. Hair-boater extraordinaire Brad Dimock, who has kayaked Paria Canyon and was one of the first to kayak the Little Colorado River Gorge, has twice kayaked Quartzite: once at 800 cfs, the other time at 4,000 cfs. Of those runs, Dimock said: "I tried it twice and got through, so I never have to try it again."

Before you begin your half-day portage, you must have a look at Quartzite. Really it's a double falls, and the speed and power of the river is accentuated by the constriction of the river channel and the abrupt drop it makes over the White Ledges Quartzite Formation. The first fall is a smooth, steep tongue that looks reasonable enough taken by itself. But it pours over a 7-foot-high river-wide shelf, ending in a toilet-bowl reversal, a North Shore–sized hydraulic that has stripped oar boats of their gear and passengers before spitting the lucky ones out. When you look at Quartzite, try to imagine it with 117,000 cfs (the upper Salt's all-time high) roaring over it as in March 1941.

Mile 28.2. Corkscrew Rapid. Once you're safely beyond the wrath of Quartzite, set up immediately to run Corkscrew, also called Jump-Off Falls. At high water (4,000 to 7,000 cfs), a large lateral wave avalanches off a slick wall on river right, and you have to take it head on to avoid spinning out and flipping. If the wave breaks over you, you'll be completely swamped, and if your crew can't bail fast enough, you'll pinball off one wall into another in this serpentine fissure gouged in the Redmond Formation.

Mile 24.2 to 15.8.   Cherry Creek to Coon Creek. Entering from river right at Mile 24.2, Cherry Creek was named for the cherry trees planted here at the turn of the century. At Mile 22.5, the river loops around Horseshoe Bend before winding down at Redmond Flat near Mile 17.4.

Mile 8.1.   Highway 288 Bridge and take-out. By the time you reach the take-out immediately below the bridge on river right, you'll be wondering, as Mike Young did, "what it would have been like to run the Salt all the way . . . down the Gila to the Colorado, all the way to the Gulf?" That might have been possible before Phoenix—fed by the four mountain reservoirs that now sustain it—virtually erupted from the Valle del Sol ("Valley of the Sun"). After you've rafted this wild river for 4 days, the Upper Salt will leave its mark on you, and you're sure to wonder what it would have been like to keep going. A passage from Hermann Hesse's *Siddhartha* says it best: "It is as I thought; the river has spoken to you. It is friendly to you, too; it speaks to you. That is good, very good."

Travel Notes

• **Primary access.**   Salt River Canyon Bridge.

• **Secondary access.**   Put in and take out via Cibecue Creek.

• **Elevation.**   At put-in: 3,420 feet; at take-out: 2,196 feet.

• **Elevation loss.**   1,234 vertical feet.

• **Mileage.**   52 miles from Salt River Canyon Bridge to Highway 288 Bridge.

• **Escape routes.**   In the event of an emergency, the most practical escape route is via the Cibecue Creek Road, which parallels the north side of the Upper Salt from the Salt River Canyon Bridge as far as the Salt Banks at Mile 49.3; however, it may be impossible to drive beyond Cibecue Creek at Mile 53 when it is running.

Below the Salt Banks, several remote Forest Service jeep trails provide access to the Salt (refer to Tonto National Forest map for complete details):

–USFS Roads 473 and 473A take you within hiking distance of Walnut Canyon (Mile 48.4) via Highway 77.

–USFS Roads 303 and 303A reach the river at Gleason Flat (Mile 41) via Highway 77.

–USFS Road 219 reaches the river at Horseshoe Bend (Mile 21.5) via Highway 288.

• **Seasons.** Late winter through spring; call the Salt River Project recording at (602) 236-5929 for daily flows into Salt River Canyon and Roosevelt Lake.

• **Maps and guides.** Tonto National Forest recreation map; "A River Runner's Guide to the Salt River," by Dana Hollister (write Salt River Guide, c/o Dana Hollister, P.O. Box 56784, Phoenix, AZ 85079); *Guide to the Geology of Salt River Canyon Region, Arizona* (write Department of Geosciences, The University of Arizona, Tucson, AZ 85721).

• **Backcountry information.** If you put in on the San Carlos Indian Reservation side (south side of the river, above the Salt River Canyon Bridge) or on the White River Apache side (north side of the river, below the bridge), you will have to pay a nominal fee for a permit to run the Upper Salt. Indian rangers will most likely approach you and expect you to pay for the permit before you put in the river. While the Upper Salt also flows through U.S. Forest Service land, at the present time permits are not required there. For the Forest Service's information sheet on running the Upper Salt, write Tonto National Forest, 2324 East McDowell Road, Phoenix, AZ 85010.

• **Biotic communities.** Juniper-pinyon woodland, interior chaparral, and Sonoran Desert scrub (Arizona upland subdivision and lower Colorado subdivision).

Topock Gorge

Lower Colorado River, Havasu National Wildlife Refuge: canoeing

Landform

Extending from Black Canyon on its northern end southward to tidewater on the Gulf of California, the 550-mile-long stretch of the Lower Colorado River drops only 600 vertical feet; yet it serves as the natural dividing line between Arizona and California and, south of the U.S.-Mexico border, between Sonora, Mexico, and Baja California Norte. Tamed by Hoover and Glen Canyon dams, and further subdued by Davis, Parker, and Laguna dams, little remains of this prehistoric waterway's original lush riparian habitat first used by the region's ancestral inhabitants. Currently masquerading behind the gaudy veil of tourist traps, gambling casinos, motorboat marinas, and—if you can believe it—the London Bridge, the lower leg of the once-mighty Colorado River has channeled through a sprawling agricultural greenbelt that chokes the life out of it long before it trickles down to water-hungry farmers south of the U.S.-Mexico border—or even before it reaches the Colorado River Delta, where the Grand Canyon empties into the Sea of Cortez.

One of the few remnant stretches of the Lower Colorado River that does still exist is the 14-mile leg that winds its way through Havasu National Wildlife Refuge. Called Mojave Canyon in the heyday of early exploration, Topock Gorge offers modern adventurers one of the only opportunities to see the land and boat the river much as the Mojave Indians did when they first plied its peaceful waters on small reed boats.

Historical Overview

The first descent of the Lower Colorado River was probably made by the Mojave, the Quechan, or the Cocopa Indians—all Yuman-speaking tribes that inhabited the area at least as early as 1540. That's when Melchior Diaz first called the Colorado River the Rio Tizon, "firebrand river." A passage in *Obregon's History of Sixteenth Century Explorations in Western America* explains the name: "They called this great river the Tizon because the natives cross it, in spite of its width, on great rafts of agave. On this day they cross paddling with their feet and carrying a lighted torch in their hands in order to keep fire on both sides." Ostensibly, the firebrands were used to ward off the chill of winter and the mosquitoes of summer.

The best eyewitness account of the Mojave's balsa rafts comes from Baldwin Möllhausen, a writer and naturalist with the 1857–1858 Ives Expedition. Assigned by the War Department to survey the head of steamboat navigation from the Gulf of California, the Ives Expedition steamed out of the Colorado River Delta on December 31, 1857. While ferrying across the river in an inflatable canvas boat—perhaps the first inflatable used anywhere on the Colorado River—on February 25, Möllhausen wrote, "As the sun rose higher and warmed the atmosphere the Indians came streaming by hundreds towards us; and the river swarmed with brown swimmers. . . . Some of them came floating down on little rafts made of bundles of rushes (the only species of craft I ever saw among inhabitants of the Colorado valley), and landed on the island on the eastern shore."

Long recognized as prodigious runners who could cover 100 miles a day on their trading expeditions to the Pacific Ocean and back, the Mojave were equally adept at swimming, which may seem incongruous for desert dwellers who inhabited one of the harshest deserts in North America; then, perhaps, the Mojave were simply the Southwest's first biathletes and natural masters of two environments. Möllhausen was justifiably impressed by their swimming prowess, particularly that of a young mother:

> A young woman . . . had very quietly and innocently disencumbered herself of her petticoat in our presence, and folding it up laid her baby upon it in a little flat but strongly made basket, and with her under one arm, a little thing of about four years old held by the hand, and two elder children of seven or eight following her, had taken to the water, and giving a glance backward occasionally at the two youngsters, who were romping and splashing about as they followed in the track she made on the surface of the water, I watched them as they landed on the small island, walked quickly across it, and then plunged into the river again on the other side. It was a pretty family picture.

It wasn't until the end of John Wesley Powell's first expedition through the Grand Canyon in 1869 that the first non-Indians boated all the way down the Colorado River from its headwaters to the Sea of Cortez. Powell officially concluded his expedition at the mouth of the Rio Virgen (now under Lake Mead), but four of his men continued downstream in order to continue with the river survey begun by the Ives Expedition in 1857. Consisting of Andy Hall, Jack Sumner, Billy Hawkins, and Sgt. George Bradley, the party split up near Fort Mojave "after taking on some snake medicine." Hawkins and Bradley were last reported seen near Ehrenberg, 315 miles below the Rio Virgen. But Hall and Sumner went all the way to tidewater, another 282 miles below Ehrenberg. Of that slow, meandering stretch, Sumner wrote:

> From there we rowed down through the dismal mud flats of the lower Colorado and camped on an island. Pulling out from our island camp, we dropped past the squaws and wikiups of the Cocopas, and about noon came to tidewater at the head of the Gulf of California. Not wishing to locate a ranch here, we stayed only two hours. . . . I believe Hall and I are the only men that ever navigated the Green and Colorado rivers for so long a distance—from Green River Station, Wyoming, to tidewater at the head of the Gulf of California.

Sumner and Hall were probably also the first men to make a sail out of a wagon sheet in order to ride the winds back upstream to Fort Yuma.

The most famous descent of the Colorado River from Green River, Utah, to the Gulf of California, however, was begun on September 8, 1911, by Emery and Ellsworth Kolb, who hoped to make the first motion picture of their own epic voyage through the canyons of the Colorado. (See entry for Colorado River.) The Kolb brothers reached Needles on January 12, 1912, but it wasn't until May 1913 that Ellsworth, traveling without Emery, finished the final leg of the river below Needles for his book, *Through the Grand Canyon From Wyoming to Mexico*. Ellsworth hadn't wanted to go alone, but nobody he knew in Needles would go with him; in fact, everyone tried to talk him out of the voyage. Wrote Ellsworth:

> One would have thought from the stories with which I was regaled, that the rapids of the Grand Canyon were below Needles, and as far as going to the Gulf, it was suicide. I was told of outlaws along the border, of the firearms and opium smugglers, who shot first and questioned afterward, and of the insurrectos of Lower California. The river had no real outlet to the ocean, they said, since the break into the Salton Sea, but spread over a cane-break, thirty miles or more in width. Many people had gone into those swamps and never returned, whether lost in the jungles or killed by the Cocopah Indians, no one knew. They simply disappeared. It was all very alluring.

Directions

To get to the put-in at Topock Bay, drive 21 miles north on Highway 95 from Lake Havasu City to Interstate 40; take I-40 10 miles west to the Highway 95 Exit at Topock. You can put in at Topock Golden Shores Marina.

To get to the take-out at Castle Rock Bay, drive 5.5 miles north on Highway 95 from Lake Havasu City to the Castle Rock Bay Road turnoff. Take the Castle Rock Bay Road to the parking area on the east side of Castle Rock. The bay is located several hundred yards west.

Allow 45 minutes to shuttle vehicles before and after this 1-day canoe trip.

River Log

(river miles counted downstream from the put-in)

Mile 42. Topock Bay. As soon as you paddle through the still waters of Topock Bay, the slow, steady current of the Colorado River will carry you beneath three distinct bridges. The first, built in 1943 to replace the 1880s-era wooden trestle 10 miles upstream, is a railroad bridge still used by the Atchison, Topeka, and Santa Fe Railroads. The second is Interstate 40. And the third, Old Trails Bridge, used during the heyday of Route 66, now supports three natural gas pipelines that carry gas from West Texas and New Mexico to Southern California.

Mystic Maze-Mojave Trade Route. Immediately below the Old Trails Bridge, on river right, the remains of the Mojave Indians' ancient running maze can still be seen cordoned off behind a U.S. Fish and Wildlife fence, west of the Pacific Gas and Electric plant. As early as 1776, Padre Francisco Garces followed sections of an Indian trade route that stretched from the Pacific Ocean across the stark Mojave Desert, through the mesa and high country of northern Arizona to the Zuni pueblos in New Mexico. It was along this desolate 1,100-mile track that Indians like the Mojave, Walapai, Havasupai, and Hopi traveled to each other's distant villages to trade seashells, deer and bighorn sheep skins, woven goods, and pottery, some of the tribes acting as middlemen for others, the Mojave running 100 miles a day. Before and after their epic runs to the coast and back, the Mojave would run through a football-field–sized maze, which had been scraped into the desert pavement, in hopes of escaping evil spirits. In *The North American Indian*, Indian photographer Edward Curtis wrote, "The Mojave Indian nearby have utilized the area . . . as a maze into which to lure and escape evil spirits, for it is believed that by running in and out through one of these immense labyrinths one haunted with dread may bewilder the spirits occasioning it, and thus elude them."

Mile 39.   Gaging Station. On river left, about 50 feet above the river, are two white wooden crosses that face the setting sun. According to Stan Jones' "Boating and Exploring Map to Lake Havasu Country," "On April 5, 1987, a group of boaters floating down the river were horrified to see a small airplane fly low between high walls of the narrow gorge and collide with the cable [crossing the river]. The plane was severed and its parts and two passengers spilled into the stream." The small, discreet memorial overlooking the river honors the pilot, Rocky Tolman, and his passenger, Douglas Casper.

Mile 39 also marks one of the narrowest portals through Mojave Canyon, once dreaded by steamboat captains who had to navigate the pinched-out river channel in sluggish, unwieldy paddle wheelers. In his *Report upon the Colorado River of the West,* Ives was able to record the magic of the moment even as his expedition lumbered and groaned through the head of Mojave Canyon on February 9, 1858, some 400 miles above tidewater: "The waning day found us still threading the windings of this wonderful defile, and the approach of twilight enhanced the wild romance of the scenery. The bright colors faded and blended into a uniform dark gray. The rocks assumed dim and exaggerated shapes, and seemed to flit like giant spectres in pursuit and retreat along the shadowy vista. A solemn stillness reigned in the darkening avenue, broken only by the splash of the paddles or the cry of a solitary heron."

Mile 38. The Needles. Undoubtedly, one of the most enchanting aspects of canoeing the Lower Colorado River is making the lazy approach to The Needles, a cluster of three jagged spires of volcanic rock on the northwest end of the Mojave Mountains. Lieutenant Amiel W. Whipple named The Needles in 1854; according to Byrd Granger's *Arizona's Names*, the Mojave called them Huqueamp avi ("where the battle took place") after the mythological battle in which "the god-son Mastambo killed the sea serpent."

But if The Needles have formed a scenic milepost for nearly every river runner that has passed them, you couldn't tell it from the writing of Ellsworth Kolb. He took little notice of the spectacular formation clawing out of the landscape near river's edge, either because the heat was getting to him or because he was struggling with tricky river currents. In *Through the Grand Canyon from Wyoming to Mexico,* Kolb wrote: "By the time I had reached the spire-like mountainous rocks a few miles below the bridge, which gave the town of Needles its name, the sun was well up and I was beginning to learn what desert heat was . . . Here, the stream which spread a mile wide above, had choked down to two hundred feet; small violent whirlpools formed at abrupt turns in this so-called canyon and the water tore from side to side."

Below The Needles, the 5,100-foot-high Mojave Mountains form the rugged eastern skyline of Topock Gorge on Arizona's side of the Havasu National Wildlife Refuge. Some three hundred species of birds inhabit this 45,000-acre sanctuary dedicated to preserving this unique desert marshland. The birds include great blue herons, golden eagles, snowy egrets, and Canadian geese, to name a few. Arizona's "everglades" also provide habitat for wildlife, sans 'gators, as diverse as otter, muskrat, javelina, and desert bighorn sheep.

Mile 37. Topock Gorge. Pulpit Rock, on river left, marks the entrance to Topock Gorge, and shortly thereafter the river careens around the 90-degree turn called Devil's Elbow, a name that probably dates back to territorial Arizona and early travelers like Martha Summerhayes.

When young, ebullient Army wife Martha Summerhayes accompanied her husband to the Arizona frontier in the summer of 1874, the two sailed from San Francisco, around the Baja Peninsula, and up the Gulf to Point Isabel on the Colorado River Delta. There Martha and her husband, Lt. Jack Summerhayes, boarded the steamboat *Cocopab* for the next leg of their journey to Fort Mojave. But for all practical purposes, the *Cocopah* was a frontier version of the dilapidated swamp-prowler made famous by Humphrey Bogart and Katharine Hepburn in *The African Queen;* it chugged upstream against the current on low water in the middle of August "towing a barge loaded with soldiers." Twenty-three days later, the *Cocopah* finally reached Fort Yuma, a mere 157 miles upstream!

Boarding another steamer, called the *Gila*, the newlyweds pressed on to Fort Mojave, another 300 miles upstream. But steerage on the *Gila* wasn't anymore comfortable than it had been on the *Cocopah*. It was the end of August, but it was still miserably hot and the scenery was so intolerably dreary that the 11-day river journey dragged on interminably. It wasn't until the *Gila* steamed through Topock Gorge on September 3 that life on-board briefly sparked—only for a moment, because the oppressive heat prevailed, as it always does in the Arizona desert from June until the middle of October. Wrote Summerhayes: "We passed through great cañons and the scenery was grand enough; but one cannot enjoy scenery with the mercury ranging from 107 to 122 [Fahrenheit] in the shade. The grandeur was quite lost upon us all, and we suffocated by the scorching heat radiating from those massive walls of rocks between which we puffed and clattered along."

With a river experience like that, it's easy to understand how somebody could have named the dogleg turn through Topock Gorge Devil's Elbow.

Mile 36.5. Floodwater Sand Dunes. Immediately below Topock Gorge proper, on river left, is the finest gathering of sand dunes on this stretch of the Lower Colorado River; the half-mile hike to the top is a memorable side trip. From the dunes' crest, you can look north and see the broad, creosote-covered flood channel that the river has used during historic floods. In Philip L. Fradkin's *A River No More*, the author quotes: "Unharnessed it tore through deserts, flooded fields, and ravaged villages. It drained the water from the mountains and the plains, rushed it through sun-baked thirsty lands and dumped it into the Pacific Ocean—a treasure lost forever." Standing atop these dunes, it's easy to imagine the great red river boiling through this floodwater passage, carrying entire cottonwood trees and slowly depositing the tons of silt and sand that created these untracked dunes.

Mile 34. Beaver Inlet. As you paddle through Mojave Canyon, look for the small natural arches that periodically wink from these burnt cliffs like the scaly eye of a giant reptile. And take time to explore the intriguing rock coves and inlets along both sides of the river; it's in the hidden recesses that you're most likely to see a fat Arizona beaver paddling silently through the still, shimmering waters of this desert marshland. You only have to read a passage or two from *The Personal Narrative of James Ohio Pattie* to understand why the sight of a beaver in these parts is such a rare and rewarding experience. After first building canoes in which to float down the Lower Colorado River, the legendary mountain man noted his party's remarkable success at trapping beaver. "We started on the 9th [December, 1857], floating with the current, which bore us downward at the rate of four miles an hour. . . . We floated about 30 miles, and in the evening encamped in the midst of beavers. We set 40 traps, and in the morning of the 10th caught 36 beavers, an excellent night's hunt. We concluded from this encouraging commencement, to travel slowly, and in the hunters' phrase, trap the river clear; that is, take all that could be allured to come to bait."

Frontier Arizona hadn't always been so kind to these pioneer canoeists; in fact, only a month earlier, Pattie and his party had literally been reduced to eating crow just to reach the "red river." Wrote Pattie:

> We commenced an early march on the 6th [December], and were obliged to move slowly, as we were barefooted [they wore out their moccasins], and the mountains rough and steep. . . . On the 8th, our provisions were entirely exhausted, and so having nothing to eat, we felt less the need of water. Our destitute and forlorn condition goaded us on. . . . On the morning of the 13th, we killed a raven, which we cooked for seven men. It was unsavory flesh in itself, and would hardly have afforded a meal for one hungry man. The miserable condition of our company may be imagined, when seven hungry men, who had not eaten a full meal for ten days, were all obliged to breakfast on this nauseous bird.

Their situation quickly grew worse; that evening they killed and ate a buzzard. After hardships like those, it's no wonder they wanted to "trap the river clear"; besides, beaver were bringing $15 a pelt at the time.

Mile 35. The Chemehuevi Mountains. This broad range of mountains on the California side of the river takes its name from the Chemehuevi Indians; unlike the Mojave, Quechan, and Cocopa, who have lived along the Lower Colorado River since before the first Spanish entradas, the Chemehuevi have only recently extended their range to include the Lower Colorado River. According to Kenneth M. Stewart's chapter on the Mojave in Volume 10 of *Handbook of North American Indians*, "The Mohave . . . in the nineteenth century . . . allowed the Chemehuevi, migratory desert Indians, to infiltrate and farm along the river in what is now known as the

Chemehuevi Valley." According to Carobeth Laird's eloquent ethnography, *The Chemehuevi*, the Mojave called the Chemehuevi "lizard eaters," while the Chemehuevi, equally revolted by the Mojave's diet, called them "fish eaters." Like their symbiotic neighbors, the Chemehuevi were awesome runners; they periodically ran from their villages near the river to the southern end of Death Valley, among other places, to hunt desert bighorn. They sang territorial hunting songs en route to their ancient hunting grounds, a type of oral map that told them through which valleys to run, at which mountains to turn, and where the all-too-precious tinajas were located. Laird also reports that the Chemehuevi runners carried their water in the rumen of a bighorn sheep (a sort of bota bag), which could also be boiled and eaten as an emergency ration during their two-hundred-mile-long runs.

As one paddles along the base of the Chemehuevi Mountains today, thoughts turn to what the twentieth century has done to the Indians' traditional way of life. Married to her principal informant, the late great Chemehuevi runner George Laird, Carobeth Laird wrote: "No more moccasin feet tread silently upon hardpacked trails whispering tcawa, tcawa, tcawa . . . a whole mode of perception is lost, forgotten, never to be regained. Even if the native people increased and prospered, their thought has so departed from the old ways, that there would be no eyes to see desert, mountains, and River as they were once seen."

Mile 34. Picture Rock. One place where the old ways can still be seen is at Hum-Me-Chomp, "the rock where the river once churned to make this place inaccessible to the living," on river left. Only the Mojave themselves can describe the importance of this stirring petroglyph site, as written on a sign near the river's edge:

> We are the Aha-Makaav, Mojave Nation, People of the Colorado River. The beautiful land graced before you in all its natural splendor and grandeur is a sacred and holy place to the Aha-Makaav. Since the beginning of time traditional songs and narrations have passed to succeeding generations. This sacred site is one that brings joy, awe, gratitude, and utmost respect to the living as well as the spirits of our departed. The petroglyphs (rock writings) before you indicate this and tell our story. . . . Peace is found in the quiet, tall pillars of the high cliffs. Listen to the songs that the winds bring around Hum-Me-Chomp. A reminder that this is sacred ground.

Mile 32 to 28. The river sweeps around Blankenship Bend and drifts silently toward Castle Rock Bay at Mile 28.

Travel Notes

• **Primary access.** Put in at Topock Bay, Arizona, or Park Moabi, California; take out at Castle Rock Bay, Arizona.

• **Elevation.** Put in at 505 feet; take out at 480 feet.

• **Elevation loss.** 25 vertical feet.

• **Mileage.** 14 miles, Topock Bay to Castle Rock Bay.

• **Escape routes.** Remote jeep trails reach the river at several points en route; however, you'd probably do better flagging down a motorboat or using a signal mirror to flash an airplane while still floating toward the take-out.

• **Seasons.** The most idyllic time is during the spring-warm days of January and February, when most of the motorboats and attendant crowds are still dry-docked. Spring can be crowded and noisy; summer is insufferably hot—and crowded. Take your chances in the fall.

• **Maps and guides.** Lake Havasu and Lake Mojave Recreation Guide by Aquamaps, Inc.; Stan Jones' Boating and Exploring Map of Lake Havasu.

• **Backcountry information.** Day trips only; fires and overnight camping are not permitted.

• **Managing agency.** Havasu National Wildlife Refuge, P.O. Box A, 1406 Bailey Avenue, Needles, CA 92363; (714) 326-3853.

• **Canoe outfitters.** Lake Havasu–based Bob Mann's Canoe Trips has been outfitting canoe trips in Topock Gorge and elsewhere along the Lower Colorado River for 18 years. Offering reasonable rates for dependable services, Bob Mann rents canoes, paddles, vests, and so on, and also provides shuttle services to the put-in and take-out for parties of up to twenty-four people. For further information, write Bob Mann's Canoe Trips, P.O. Box 784, 3079 Marlin, Lake Havasu City, AZ 86403; (602) 855-4406.

• **Biotic communities.** Mojave desert scrub.

Canyoneering

Sycamore Canyon

Coconino Plateau: day hike and end-to-end trek.

Landform

According to *Arizona's Names*, there are no less than seventy-four Sycamore canyons, basins, creeks, mesas, points, rims, springs, and tanks in Arizona alone. But of all the geographical features named after the Arizona sycamore tree, none is more rugged or beautiful than northern Arizona's Sycamore Canyon. Twenty-five miles long and up to 7 miles wide, this deep chasm gouged its way from the base of the 12,633-foot San Francisco Mountains through the southwestern brink of the Mogollon Rim, a 200-mile-long escarpment that forms the southern edge of the 7,000-foot-high Coconino Plateau. Sometimes viewed as a miniature Grand Canyon because of its geologic similarity, much of the 55,937-acre Sycamore Canyon Wilderness still offers modern canyoneers the same primeval beauty and conditions that existed when the ancient, cliff-dwelling Sinagua last prowled its wild depths.

Historical Overview

The first descent – or ascent – of Sycamore Canyon was undoubtedly made by the Sinagua circa A.D. 600; they inhabited the vicinity of the San Francisco Mountains – and many of the canyons that eroded through the Mogollon Rim – until sometime before this spectacular precipice was named in honor of Don Juan Ignacio de Mogollon, "mogey-own," the governor of New Mexico, circa 1712. While archaeological evidence indicates that these prehistoric canyoneers were sophisticated masons, George Wharton James, in 1917, was one of the first to actually view and describe their Sycamore Canyon cliff dwellings; in *Arizona: The Wonderland*, James wrote: "In the walls of this canyon hundreds of cliff-dwellings may be seen and on some of the salient points are buildings that appear to be fortresses. . . . Some of the dwellings have been excavated and arrow points, spearheads, stone-axes, ropes made of the fibre of the bear grass, or amole, sandals, ears of corn . . . have been collected."

Antonio de Espejo may have seen the Sinagua – or Yavapai – near the lower end of Sycamore Canyon during the 16th century. According to a 1930 paper by Dr. Harold S. Colton, titled "A Brief Survey of the Early Expeditions into Northern Arizona," Espejo's was the first recorded expedition by white man in the San Francisco Mountain region. Espejo's nine-man expedition reportedly left Zuni, New Mexico, and headed into northern Arizona expressly to find the silver rumored to be near present-day Jerome. The journal of expedition member Diego Perez de Luxan paints a vivid picture of the difficulties the expedition encountered, as well as the dis-

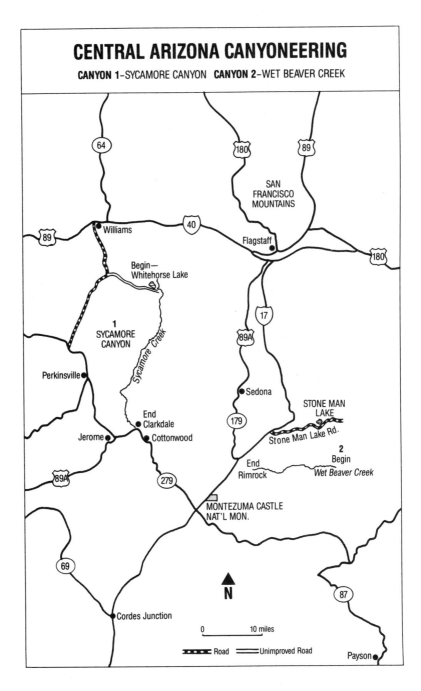

CENTRAL ARIZONA CANYONEERING

CANYON 1-SYCAMORE CANYON **CANYON 2**-WET BEAVER CREEK

coveries they made while traversing Sycamore Canyon—if in fact they descended Sycamore Canyon and not Wet Beaver Creek, as some believe. (See entry for Wet Beaver Creek.) In *Expedition into New Mexico by Antonio de Espejo: 1582–1583*, Luxan wrote:

> We left this place [Flagstaff] on the fifth of the month [May] and traveled seven leagues through a very broken and rough mountain with bad roads and very dangerous in an enemy country. We descended a slope so steep and dangerous that a mule belonging to Captain Antonio de Espejo fell down and was dashed to pieces. We went down by a ravine so bad and craggy that we descended with difficulty to a fine large river which runs from northwest to southeast. At this place this river is surrounded by an abundance of grapevines, many walnut and other trees. It is a warm land in which there are parrots. . . . This river we named El Rio de Las Parras [The river of the Grapevines].

Luxan's journal was translated and annotated by Ph.D.s George P. Hammond and Agapito Rey, whose footnote and "Map of the Region Traversed by the Espejo Party" has the expedition crossing Las Parras [Sycamore Creek] before reaching Rio de Las Reyes [Verde River]. While Espejo's prospecting venture was a bust, the expedition was befriended by maize-growing Indians who gave members "metals in addition to food as a sign of peace." One can only imagine what it'd be like to see a tribe of modern Sinagua still living peacefully in Sycamore Canyon—Havasupai-style—among hand-tilled plots of corn and wild parrots.

Probably Gen. W. J. Palmer wished he'd seen only parrots when he struggled down Sycamore Canyon in 1867. Assigned by the Kansas Pacific Railroad Company to find the best route for a southern railway to the Pacific Coast, Palmer and his men were on their way back to the Colorado Chiquito (Little Colorado River) from Val de Chino (Chino Valley) when they were ambushed by "Apaches" somewhere in the cold, rugged depths of Sycamore. Whether the raiding party was truly Apache, or whether Palmer mistakenly called them that, as many early travelers did when they came face to face with unfriendly Indians in the Arizona territory, is uncertain. Whatever the case, Palmer's encounter with Sycamore Canyon Indians was not the congenial reception that Espejo had enjoyed near the confluence of the Verde River 300 years earlier. In his seven-volume, turn-of-the-century *History of Arizona*, historian Thomas Edwin Farish reprinted Palmer's account of his Sycamore Canyon adventure. Wrote Palmer:

> [The canyon bottom] was strewn with fragments of red sandstone from the size of a church to that of a pebble, over which we dragged our

footsore animals very slowly. We had made some eight miles when, as it seemed, at the roughest part of the whole way, where nature had made a sort of waste closet at random for all the shapeless blocks and sharp-cornered masses of rocks and washed out boulders . . . we suddenly heard a shot from the brink of the canyon at our rear, and the dreaded war-whoop burst upon us. Then we looked up to the right and left, ahead and to the rear; but the walls seemed everywhere as tall as a church-steeple, with scarcely a foot hold from top to base. They had looked high before, and the chasm narrow, but now it seemed as though we were looking up from the bottom of a tin mine, and no bucket to draw us up by. Soon the shots were repeated, and the yells were followed by showers of arrows.

Incredibly, Palmer decided to engage the Indians from the expedition's vulnerable position on the floor of Sycamore Canyon, so he ordered six men to climb up "an almost vertical wall of sandstone" on the west side while he led another small party up Sycamore's east wall. Even more incredibly, no one was injured during the attack or the ascent. Of their hair-raising climb, Palmer wrote:

How we got up, God knows; I only remember hearing a volley from below, shots from above, Indian yells on all sides, the grating roar of tumbling boulders as they fell, and the confused echoing of calls and shots from the canyon. Exhausted, out of breath, and wet with perspiration, boots nearly torn off, and hands cut and bleeding, I sat down on the summit and looked around. Across the narrow chasm I saw the other scaling party. Everything was quiet as death, the Indians had disappeared — melting away as suddenly and mysteriously as they had first appeared.

Not everyone encountered such difficulties in Sycamore Canyon; some, like travel writer George Wharton James, envisioned it as even more fantastic than the Grand Canyon 65 miles to the north. Wrote James: "In Sycamore Canyon alone — a miniature Grand Canyon — with narrow walls two thousand feet high, [the] colors are even more striking than [in] the great gorge itself." Fortunately, James' prediction that a resort would be developed in Sycamore Canyon has not come true. Yet.

No doubt, senior canyoneer Raymond Weece might have dreamt about a resort — or some kind of comfort — the week he spent in Sycamore Canyon on the verge of death in 1971; at the time, the 64-year-old Weece admitted he was arthritic. Yet Sycamore Canyon beckoned to him, perhaps because of the healing effect of the wilderness, or because of its solitude. Whatever the reason, Weece had been exploring the rugged canyon during solitary, week-long backpacking trips for 2 years without incident. Then one warm day he had his wife drop him off near the rim with the explicit instructions not to pick him up until the following Sunday. What ensued was a life-or-death struggle to survive the deadly bite of a rattlesnake far from the remotest possibility of help. In an *Outdoor Arizona Magazine* account of his inspiring tale, Weece wrote: "I had made about five miles from the pass down to the bottom of the canyon when I came upon a big rock in the middle of the trail. I threw my left leg over intending to slide across and my foot hit a sleeping rattlesnake which, so rudely awakened, promptly bit me on the leg just above my boot top."

While Weece steeled himself to treat the painful bite with the equally painful cut-and-suck method (a now-controversial and potentially dangerous method for treating snake-bite victims), he undoubtedly saved his own life with his determination to stay calm and stay put. Except for short crawls to gather precious firewood and water, he hunkered down in a lonely bivouac until the monstrous swelling in his leg started to subside and his body had slowly absorbed most of the rattlesnake's corrosive, muscle-and-blood–digesting hemotoxin. When Weece finally crawled and hobbled out of Sycamore Canyon a week later, he wrote: "The diary? I can't make any sense out of most of it but that week has a recorded eight days. Two of them a very feverish Wednesday. After about three months, my leg healed over but I have a very black ring there that I'll carry from now on. Strangely enough, my arthritis seems to be improving steadily since that snake bite but I sure wouldn't recommend it as a cure."

Of men like Weece, and of Sycamore's allure, James wrote: "Of course the self-dependent have been camping there already for years, and few spots in Arizona are more historically romantic, ruggedly wild, [and] grandly picturesque."

Directions

To get to the upper end, drive south on 4th Street from the intersection of Bill Williams and 4th Street in Williams; follow this street as it turns into USFS Road 173, the Perkinsville Road (see entry for Perkinsville Road); 7.6 miles south of Williams you'll come to the Whitehorse Lake turnoff. From here it's another 10 miles via USFS Roads 110 and 109 to this popular summer recreation area at the headwaters of Sycamore Canyon Wilderness Area.

To get to the lower end, drive 10 miles north from Clarkdale on USFS Road 131 to the Packard Trailhead.

Canyon Log

Begin. From a geological standpoint, trekking the length of Sycamore Canyon is similar to hiking to the bottom of the Grand Canyon; you'll descend through four of the principal formations encountered along many of the Grand Canyon's rim-to-river trails: Kaibab Limestone, Toroweap Formation, Supai Formation, and Redwall Limestone. What's more tantalizing is the fact that few other canyons in the state offer canyoneers the unique opportunity to cross the threshold between the Colorado Plateau Province to the northeast and the Basin and Range Province to the southwest; this rugged, 2- to 3-day trek will take you from the ponderosa pine forest, which rims the head of Sycamore Canyon, through the Transition Zone, and along the canyon's verdant riparian habitat until it merges with the confluence of the Verde River, where it enters the Sonoran Desert. What makes this canyon adventure even more interesting is that it's virtually trailless until you reach the lower end; consequently, many of the conditions faced by General W. J. Palmer and company in 1867 still challenge canyoneers today. Wrote Palmer: "We [were] . . . faint from hunger and fatigue, having come nearly twenty miles on foot, up and down canyons and steep ravines, climbing through mountain passes and stumbling over the rocky bed of the streams—equivalent to at least sixty miles, as we thought, on level road." Such difficulties don't deter an estimated one thousand canyoneers from exploring Sycamore Canyon each year (though usually from the more accessible southern end).

Mile 0 to 1. Whitehorse Lake to Sycamore Canyon. At the time of this writing, no trail led into the head of Sycamore Canyon; so you'll have to prowl around the rim of the canyon a few hundred yards east of Whitehorse Lake to find the normal descent line. Look for one of two minor drainages that provide relatively easy access into the bed of Sycamore via a short, exposed downclimb usually protected by an old sling nailed into place by a piton. (Bring a 20-foot piece of rope just in case some hungry cougar has gnawed off this sling.) General Palmer's description of Sycamore Canyon still captures the essence of the Whitehorse Lake approach more than a century later: "If 'unexpectedness' be one of the elements of romantic grandeur in scenery, this gulf of brown and grey rock has high claims for pre-eminence in this respect, with its precipitous sides, 500 feet deep, and apparently so narrow that it is first difficult to appreciate fully the hard fact that, before you can continue your march, it is absolutely necessary to descend to the very bottom."

Canyoneers Randy Mulkey (front) and Bob Farrell wade through thigh-deep water near the beginning of a three-day trek down the length of Sycamore Canyon. Photo by John Annerino.

Once you've reached the bottom of this tributary arm (a good turnaround point for a day hike from Whitehorse Lake), you'll have to trek about a mile downstream to reach the main stem of Sycamore Canyon; from there, it's all downhill to the Verde River—so to speak. The clincher is this: While Sycamore Canyon receives an average of 20 inches of precipitation a year, its streambed is so porous that most of the runoff seeps underground; consequently, its stones and boulders aren't cemented into place like those of its neighbors, the West Fork of Oak Creek and Wet Beaver Creek. So use caution in hopping from one boulder to the next, all the way to the Rio de las Reyes.

Mile 5. Geronimo Spring. In addition to the loose nature of Sycamore's streambed, your other principal concern is water. According to the Geological Survey Bulletin *Mineral Resources of Sycamore Canyon,* only a handful of perennial springs exist along the streambed. The first you'll encounter is Geronimo Spring, located a short hop up Little Lo Spring Canyon, which enters from the left (northeast). Tank up here, because if the thermometer's tickling the century mark and you can't find any of Sycamore's widely spaced tinajas, you'll be hallucinating by the time you reach Parson's Springs 17 miles downstream.

Mile 13. Taylor Cabin. One of the next logical places to look for water is at Taylor Cabin; when George Wharton James wrote about Sycamore Canyon's Indian ruins, he also reported: "On nearly all the rocky shelves where the cliff-dwellings are found, rock pockets for holding of water for a few days can be found." Evidently, when the original homesteaders upgraded Taylor Caves to the status of a line shack, they had the same idea as the ancient Sinagua, because several deep tinajas can be found in the streambed near this historic site. According to the National Register of Historic Places Inventory-Nomination Form, John and Ben Taylor first used the original cave dwellings at the Taylor Cabin site circa 1885; that's when the territorial cowboys hung a door on one of the caves and called it home so they could use the area as a winter range for their livestock. The Taylors reportedly ran cattle in Sycamore Canyon until 1904, but the Taylor Cabin wasn't actually built until 1931, when the Cross D and Windmill ranches, along with the Johnson Cattle Company, chipped in to hire local stone mason Oscar N. Despain to build the present cabin. Named in honor of John and Ben Taylor, Taylor Cabin is a popular Sycamore Canyon destination for an overnight hike from Whitehorse Lake; it can also be reached from Turkey Butte via USFS Road 538B, which provides access to Buck Ridge and the Taylor Cabin Trail.

Mile 15. Sycamore Canyon at large. General Palmer, who camped about 10 miles above the confluence of the Verde River, shed some insight on the difficulties modern canyoneers will also face if, for instance, they're out of water, or if another emergency arises and they try to hike through Sycamore Canyon at night:

> That night's march up the canyon, over broken rocks and through the tangled thickets, was worse, if anything, than the attack. Every pebble in the darkness was magnified to a boulder, and every boulder seemed as large as a house; fording the rapid stream twenty times, we shivered with cold and wet. . . . Near midnight, we halted under some sheltering rock, and concluded to take some sleep; but the guides protested against having a fire, saying the Indians would detect and shoot into it. To sleep without one, however, was impossible. At last I concluded that it was better to die from an Indian arrow than to freeze to death in the darkness.

Mile 18. Cave dwellers, prehistoric to Stone Age. Throughout its long history, Sycamore Canyon has been inhabited by a diversity of cave dwellers unheard of in the region's other deep gorges. Foremost of these were the ancient Sinagua, who mastered the environment far better than most white strangers, who stumbled around in the black, wretched night, not knowing if they were struggling up canyon or down. Author Stewart Aitchison wrote briefly of a Mormon family who "fled persecution in Flagstaff . . . [and] for three years . . . lived in a nearby cave and raised some horses and cattle." Most recently were the flower children of the 1960s who, until the federal government ferreted them out, tried to eke out a new life during a tumultuous decade by inhabiting many of the caves near Sycamore's lower end.

Mile 21 to 25. Parson Springs to South Trailhead. According to *Mineral Resources of Sycamore Canyon*, perennial springs like Parsons and Summers, 2 miles downstream, discharge 4,550 to 5,125 gallons of water a minute into the lower end of Sycamore Canyon during the driest months of July and August; that accounts for the vast popularity of this section of the canyon. Ironically, few people who visit this streambed paradise realize that they're frolicking in the vicinity of the legendary Geronimo Mine. Imagine, for instance, running 250 to 300 miles across southeastern Arizona to reach the confluence of Sycamore Canyon and the Verde River. That's what Geronimo reportedly did to work "a gold deposit found and worked by Spanish explorers." So if by the time you reach the Southern Trailhead your legs and feet feel a bit sore, think about running back home to Phoenix or Tucson before you could cash in your own lode of tales mined from the depths of El Rio de las Parras.

Travel Notes

•**Primary access.** Whitehorse Lake and South Trailhead.

•**Elevation.**   6,600 feet at Whitehorse Lake; 3,600 feet at Verde River.

•**Elevation loss.**   3,000 vertical feet.

•**Mileage.**   Approximately 25 miles end to end.

•**Water sources.**   Geronimo Spring, Dorsey Spring, Parsons Spring, and Summers Spring. Seasonal tinajas at Taylor Cabin and elsewhere throughout the canyon.

•**Escape routes.**   Whitehorse Lake or South Trailhead—whichever is closest.

•**Seasons.**   Spring and fall; summer can be murderously hot and dry in the lower end, and wintertime can be snowy and cold in the upper end.

•**Maps.**   South Kaibab and Coconino National Forest Recreation Maps; also, Bill Williams Mountain (15 minute) and Sycamore Point, Loy Butte, Sycamore Basin, and Clarkdale (7½ minute).

•**Nearest supply points.**   Williams, Flagstaff, and Clarkdale.

•**Managing agency.**   Coconino, South Kaibab, and Prescott national forests.

•**Backcountry information.**   Permits not required.

•**Biotic communities.**   Plains and desert grassland, montane conifer forest, interior chaparral, and juniper-pinyon woodland.

Wet Beaver Creek

Mogollon Rim: day hike and end-to-end trek/swim.

Landform

Formed on the southern flanks of 7,301-foot-high Apache Maid Mountain and on the west slope of 7,571-foot-high Buck Mountain, Wet Beaver Creek drains an area nearly 250 square miles. En route to its confluence with the Verde River more than 30 miles downstream, Wet Beaver Creek descends more than 5,000 vertical feet as it chisels its way through the western escarpment of the Mogollon Rim. Perennial flows for Beaver Creek, as it was called during the 1800s, average 30 cfs, while peak flows reached a historic high of 7,670 cfs during September 1970. A principal tributary of the Verde River, the main canyon system formed by Wet Beaver Creek is a narrow labyrinth approximately 14 miles long; it forms the heart of 6,700-acre Wet Beaver Creek Wilderness.

Historical Overview

Like Sycamore Canyon 25 miles northwest, Wet Beaver Creek lies within the ancestral lands of the Sinagua culture, and archaeologists are still investigating evidence of the Indians' prehistoric occupation near the mouth of Wet Beaver Creek on 4,123-foot-high Sacred Mountain. Dating back to A.D. 1300, the Sacred Mountain pueblo is unique because of its ball court, partially lined with rock, and its extensive prehistoric fields and irrigation systems. Thus situated on the lower end of Wet Beaver Creek, the sophisticated, maize-growing Sinagua had ample opportunity to roam the rugged tributary canyon to hunt and gather supplementary food and were probably the first to trek—and swim—the length of Wet Beaver Creek, long before the Wipukpaya (northeastern Yavapai Indians) roamed the region.

In May of 1582, Antonio de Espejo and nine men left the Hopi Indian villages of northeastern Arizona to explore the mines rumored to be in the vicinity of modern-day Jerome. While most historians agree on the approximate location of these mines, a controversy still exists as to whether the expedition descended the Mogollon Rim to the Verde River via Sycamore Canyon or traveled along the rim and streambed of Wet Beaver Creek. In *Expedition into New Mexico Made by Antonio de Espejo: 1582–1583*, authors Agapito Rey and George P. Hammond take a broad view of the topography that expedition member Diego Perez de Luxan describes and conclude that what he calls El Rio de las Parras "was perhaps Sycamore Creek." (See entry for Sycamore Canyon.) In *Notes upon the Routes of Espejo and Farfan to the Mines in the Sixteenth Century*, on the other hand, author Katherine Bartlett uses Luxan's diary to examine Espejo's possible route from one geographical feature to the next, and suggests it may have followed an old Hopi Indian route from the Hopi villages to the Verde River via El Rio de las Parras, "which could be Beaver Creek."

While both factions agree that the El Rio de los Reyes, which Luxan later describes, is unquestionably the Verde River, Hammond and Rey believe that Espejo crossed the Mogollon Rim and headed south to the Verde from the vicinity of Flagstaff, while Bartlett thinks Espejo could have traversed the Mogollon Rim further to the east from either Mormon Lake or Chavez Pass. Bartlett presents evidence that would lead one to agree that Espejo's route did indeed follow the course of Wet Beaver Creek—if it weren't for the fact that Luxan described El Rio de las Parras as "a fine large river which runs from northwest to southeast" (Wet Beaver Creek flows from northeast to southwest). If, as Bartlett suggests, Espejo's "directions appear to be wrong" and he really meant northeast to southwest, then one is inclined to side with Bartlett. Still troubling, however, is Luxan's description of the canyon: "We descended a ravine so bad and craggy that we descended with difficulty to a fine river." His brief passage accurately describes the arduous nature of trekking the length of both Sycamore Canyon and Wet Beaver Creek to the Verde River, but it doesn't mention any of the two-dozen-odd plunge pools that must be negotiated in the heart of Wet Beaver Creek. That glaring omission, and the fact that the south-trending Sycamore Canyon more closely aligns with Luxan's directions, leads one to agree with Hammond and Rey.

If it's difficult to believe that the Espejo Expedition could have descended the narrow and rocky, plunge-pool–choked Wet Beaver Creek on mule or horseback, you need only examine the uncompromising terrain and daunting environmental conditions that other early Arizona adventurers had ridden through and endured in quest of untold wealth: along 60-mile-long Kanab Creek, for one (see entry for Kanab Canyon), or along El Camino del Diablo, for another. Several historians have written of men riding horseback down the Mogollon Rim's gorgeous, seemingly impenetrable canyons. In *Al Sieber*, Chief of Scouts Dan L. Thrapp summarized Gen. George Crook's successful Apache campaign in the region of Camp Verde: "By this time [April 6, 1873] the various commands, or at least most of them, had congregated at Verde, coming in one after another, riding down the white stone benches in long, swinging columns, working their way up the Verde or down it, down Beaver Creek, which joins the Verde right at camp, down West Clear Creek or Oak Creek." Or look at John Gregory Bourke's now-classic *On the Border with Crook*:

> At Camp Verde, we found assembled nearly all of Crook's command, and a dirtier, greasier, more uncouth-looking set of officers and men it would be hard to encounter anywhere. Dust, soot, rain, and grime had made their impress upon the canvas suits which each had donned, and with their hair uncut for months and beards growing with straggling growth all over the face, there was not one of the party who would venture to pose as an Adonis; but all were happy, because the campaign had resulted in the unconditional surrender of the Apaches.

Not all early travelers who ventured across the western end of the Mogollon Rim, sometimes called "the divide," trekked through the rugged canyons of West Clear Creek, Sycamore Canyon, and Wet Beaver Creek; some, like Army wife Martha Summerhayes, braved the hardships of frontier Arizona by traveling from one remote military outpost to the next in a horse-drawn military ambulance. Of all the vivid memories Summerhayes describes in *Vanished Arizona*, none is more colorful than that of her adventure along the Stoneman Lake Road. A military wagon route, the Stoneman Lake Road paralleled the edge of the Mogollon Rim above Wet Beaver Creek and hooked up with the General Crook Trail to link Fort Verde with Camp Apache in the White Mountains. Named after George Stoneman, the Stoneman Lake Road first appeared on an 1871 map prepared under 1st Lt. George M. Wheeler, Corps of Engineers, for his "Preliminary Report Concerning Explorations and Surveys: Principally in Nevada and Arizona." En route to Stoneman Lake along this rugged wagon road on May Day, 1875, Summerhayes wrote:

> In the course of the day, we had pased a sort of sign-board, with the rudely written description, 'Camp Starvation,' and we had heard from Mr. Bailey the story of the tragic misfortunes at this very place of the well-known Hitchcock family of Arizona. The road was lined with dry bones, and skulls of oxen, white and bleached in the sun, lying on the bare rocks. Indeed, at every stage of the road we had seen evidences of hard travel, exhausted cattle, anxious teamsters, hunger and thirst, despair, starvation, and death.

Incredibly, what Summerhayes remembered most was that Stoneman Lake was "the most beautiful spot" she had ever seen in Arizona.

Beyond Stoneman Lake to the west, however, was the difficult, dangerous, 4,000-foot plunge that Stoneman Lake Road made along the rim of Wet Beaver Creek off the western escarpment of the Mogollon Rim to Fort Verde. Of that adrenaline-fueled descent the following afternoon, Summerhayes wrote: "At four o'clock we crossed the 'divide,' and clattered down a road so near the edge of a precipice that I was frightened beyond everything: my senses nearly left me. Down and around, this way and that, near the edge, then back again, swaying, swerving, pitching, the gravel clattering over the precipice, the six mules trotting their fastest, we reached the bottom and the driver pulled up his team. 'Beaver Springs!' said he, impressively loosening up the breaks." When she asked the teamster why he'd driven so fast, Summerhayes was told: "'Had to, ma'am, or we'd a'gone over the edge.'"

Directions

Mouth of Wet Beaver Creek/Beaver Creek Ranger Station is the popular and frequently crowded lower end of Wet Beaver Creek. If you want to day hike, start here. From the junction of Interstate 17 and Highway 179, the Sedona Interchange, turn right on USFS Road 618 and drive just over 2 miles to the ranger station. The trailhead for Bell Trail No. 13 is located on the east end of the parking lot above the ranger station.

Head of Wet Beaver Creek at Waldroup Canyon provides access to the creek's pristine, seldom-traveled upper end. From the Sedona Interchange, drive north on Interstate 17 7 miles to Exit 306, the Stoneman Lake turnoff; turn right and take paved USFS Road 213 6.5 miles along the same route that Martha Summerhayes once traveled to USFS Road 229. Turn right on Road 229 and drive 5 miles south to Road 620; turn right on Road 620 and drive 2 miles to Road 620E. Follow road 620E half a mile to a spur road simply marked 9288; walk or drive this 4WD road 1 mile down to Waldroup Place Tank. This stock tank is at the head of Waldroup Canyon and marks the beginning of this canyon adventure. (Refer to your Apache Maid Mountain quadrangle on the drive in.)

Canyon Log

Begin. As at Sycamore Canyon, when you traverse the length of Wet Beaver Creek you'll cross the divide between the Colorado Plateau Province to the northeast and the Basin and Range Province to the southwest; in doing so, you'll journey from a verdant ponderosa pine forest to the Sonoran Desert and descend through four principal geological formations: basalt, Kaibab Limestone, Toroweap Formation, and Coconino Sandstone. For the most part, however, that's where the similarities between these two Mogollon Rim canyons end. Whereas Sycamore Canyon is virtually a dry, boulder-strewn streambed until you reach its lower end, Wet Beaver Creek is a backcountry swimmer's dream; no fewer than twenty-five plunge pools (from 25 to 75 yards across) must be negotiated between the headwater springs near the mouth of Waldroup Canyon and Bell Crossing 8-plus miles below—not including those that require only wading. How efficiently you swim and float your pack across these enticing, cool plunge pools will largely determine the time required to descend the length of Wet Beaver Creek. Allow 1½ to 3 days for this unforgettable canyon adventure; bring adequate flotation for you and your pack; and, most importantly, know how to identify poison ivy.

Mile 0 to 1.5. Waldroup Place Tank to main stem of Wet Beaver Creek. According to *Arizona Place Names*, there are several stories behind the naming of Apache Maid Mountain, all three centered around a young Apache girl who was "adopted" by government troops or immigrant travelers during the late 1800s. Located on the southern flanks of this storied mountain, Waldroup Canyon is a 1.5-mile-long tributary drainage that forms the gateway into the upper end of Wet Beaver Creek. From Waldroup Place Tank, head due south along a dry, shallow creek bed to the head of Waldroup Canyon, marked by a U.S. Forest Service Wilderness Boundary sign east of hill 6,188. Once in Waldroup Canyon, avoid or climb down seven boulder drops to reach Wet Beaver Creek 1,000 vertical feet below. You can safely negotiate all of them if you bring along a 50-foot piece of climbing rope with which to belay members of your party.

- **Drop 1, approximately 30 feet.** Avoid this drop by following the rimrock 50 yards to the right (west).

- **Drop 2, approximately 20 feet.** Climb down, or avoid by moving 20 yards to the right.

- **Drop 3, approximately 30 feet.** Where the canyon turns west, avoid by moving 20 yards to the right.

- **Drop 4, approximately 30 feet.** Where the canyon turns south, climb down on the left via solid but exposed boulder moves; lower your packs and belay your horse down with rope. From here, you can see Wet Beaver Creek for the first time.

- **Drop 5, three broken ramps.** Easily negotiate this one without rope by staying left.

- **Drop 6, in white limestone.** Find the trail on the right and a rock shelter in the vicinity.

- **Drop 7, approximately 30 feet.** This is a two-part drop through a natural slot.

Allow 1½ hours for a party of three people and one hybrid wolf to descend Waldroup Canyon.

Mile 1.5 to 10. Mouth of Waldroup Canyon to Bell Crossing. This is where the fun begins . . . and doesn't let up until you reach Bell Crossing. To describe this incredible route plunge pool by plunge pool would eliminate the real adventure of exploring this riparian wilderness for the first time. Some paradises you need to discover for yourself, and this is one of them. You might, however, be interested in how Wet Beaver Creek might have been seen 100 years ago. In *Argonaut Tales: Stories of the Gold Seekers and the Indian Scouts of Early Arizona*, author Edmund Wells wrote:

> Taking the back trail of the Indians he followed it in the direction whence they came, and on reaching the . . . mountain . . . he got a distant view of the green-foliaged Beaver Creek as it wound its way among the hills and low mountains. . . . Avoiding all trails and places on the creek favorable to Apache ambuscade, Pauline [Weaver] kept well up the mountain slopes from which elevation he held in view the course of the winding creek along which the main Indian trail ran. At the same time he was sheltered by the heavy growth of chaparral and occasional clusters of cedar and juniper trees.
>
> Night found him continuing his direction, guided by the stars, thinking that by night travel he might catch the light of burning fires marking the camp of either white or red men. His way led him into a canyon running down from the rim of the mountain he was rounding. Deciding to stay there the remainder of the night, he took shelter in a cluster of oak brush lying in under a cliff of rock. After refreshing himself from his jerked meat and canteen of water, he spent the time until morning smoking and sleeping.

Mile 10 to 14.   Bell Crossing to Beaver Creek ranger station trailhead. A heavily used 2-mile trail takes you to a secondary dirt road, and in another 2 miles drops you're at the trailhead.

Travel Notes

• **Primary access.**   Beaver Creek Ranger Station and Waldroup Canyon.

• **Elevation.**   6,100 feet at Waldroup Place Tank; 3,800 feet at Beaver Creek Ranger Station.

• **Elevation loss.**   2,500 vertical feet.

• **Mileage.**   14-plus miles end to end.

• **Water sources.**   Bring a snorkel!

• **Escape routes.**   Waldroup Place Tank or Beaver Creek Ranger Station — whichever is closest; also acquaint yourself with the remote USFS jeep trails above Wet Beaver Creek. Due to the nature of Mogollon Rim Canyons — including Sycamore Canyon — you should also be prepared to

signal overflying aircraft, or go out to the ranger station to direct in a rescue helicopter. Yuma is a long flight away, but the Marine Corps Air Station's Resue-1 is unquestionably the best Arizona-based airbourne rescue
team to extract an injured hiker from a deep, water-choked fissure like
the upper end of Wet Beaver Creek.

•**Seasons.** Warm – even hot – dry periods of May, June, and September
are best. Avoid this canyon during summer monsoon weather. Late fall
through early spring can be dangerously cold if you don't have a dry suit
or an inflatable kayak. You can enjoy the 4-mile trail from Beaver Creek
Ranger Station to Bell Crossing all year.

•**Maps.** Coconino National Forest Recreation Map; and Apache Maid
Mount and Casner Butte (both 7½-minute quadrangles).

•**Nearest supply points.** Campe Verde, Sedona, and Flagstaff.

•**Managing agency.** Coconino National Forest.

•**Backcountry information.** Permit not required, but check with ranger
station for current weather information and stream flow.

•**Biotic communities.** Montane conifer forests, juniper-pinyon woodland, and Sonoran Desert scrub (Arizona upland subdivision).

Trekking

McDowell Mountains

McDowell Mountain Regional Park: peak ascent and ridge traverse

Landform

Rising more than 2,000 vertical feet out of nearby Paradise Valley, the
4,067-foot-high McDowell Mountains form a 12-mile-long massif of rugged
3,000- to 4,000-foot-high peaks that drain into the Verde River to the
east and the Salt River to the south. This dwindling, northwest-trending
range has been pinched in on four sides by explosive growth and development. Fortunately, however, this wild and verdant Sonoran Desert mountain
range still offers respite from the frantic pulse of the valley below.

Historical Overview

In *Vanished Arizona: 1870–1900,* Martha Summerhayes wrote: "As we wound our way through this deep, dark cañon . . . I remembered the things I had heard of ambush and murder. . . . The night fell in black shadows down between those high mountain walls, the chollas . . . took on a ghastly hue. They grew nearly as tall as a man, and on each branch were great excrescences which looked like people's heads, in the vague light which fell upon them. They nodded to us, and it made me shudder; they seemed to be something human."

What most often washes out when you try to mine a little color in the McDowell Mountains is the military fort first located in 1865 above the confluence of the Salt and Verde rivers. Little else is known about the late human history of the McDowell Mountains. For the most part, this isolated desert range was overshadowed by nearby ranges such as the Superstition Mountains immediately to the southeast and the Bradshaw Mountains to the northwest: Both promised gold, though the auriferous Bradshaws were better at delivering on the bet than the windy, blood-curdling tales being blown out of the Lost Dutchman's stomping grounds.

According to a 1963 historical survey of McDowell Mountain Regional Park by the Arizona Historical Foundation, the McDowells had just enough minerals "to tempt and taunt man, but not sufficient to pay for powder and caps they used in blasting." Named after Gen. Irwin McDowell, this rugged, virtually waterless range was also situated too high above the Verde River to be irrigated and didn't receive enough rain for growing crops. In short, the McDowells didn't offer prospectors or settlers any of the big-ticket items normally associated with the West. Nor were they situated along any major routes of travel; the only historic trail to cross them was a section of the Stoneman Road, which contoured around the mountains' northern end and reportedly served as a secondary supply route connecting McDowell to Fort Whipple in Prescott during the late 1860s.

So few people actually ventured into the McDowell Mountains. About the only ones who did were cowboys who ran cattle on their lower slopes. Outfits like Hinds and Hooker were "contracted to supply Fort McDowell with its beef needs during the 1870s . . . [and] Stock Raising was the only dependable occupation . . . in the . . . region after bootlegging lost its lure," according to the 1963 survey. A century later, cattle ranchers discovered—as they had elsewhere throughout the West—that they might do better by selling out to land speculators than by trying to support one cow on 350

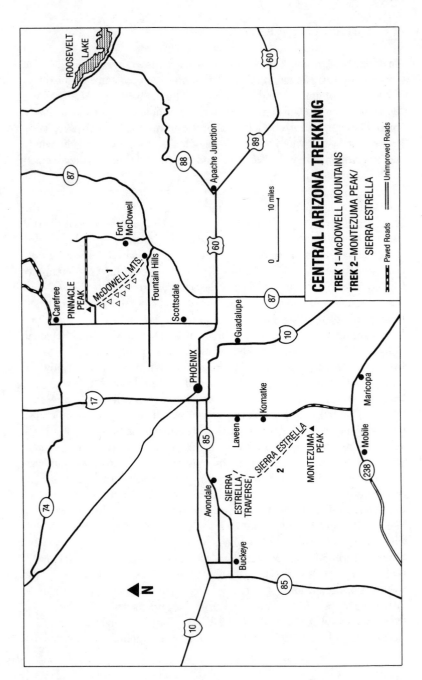

CENTRAL ARIZONA TREKKING

TREK 1 – McDOWELL MOUNTAINS

TREK 2 – MONTEZUMA PEAK/
SIERRA ESTRELLA

--- Paved Roads   ▬▬ Unimproved Roads

10 miles
0

N

acres of Sonoran Desert scrub. Ironically, some of those same speculators now "rent" cattle to graze on this desert land for the tax incentives
associated with land appraised as ranch land rather than real estate.
Prehistorically, the McDowell Mountains comprised only a small portion of the ancestral lands occupied by the Kewevkapaya, or southeastern
Yavapai Indians; together, the southeastern Yavapai, northeastern Yavapai,
and western Yavapai inhabited an estimated 20,000 square miles. What
made the Yavapai unique, though, was not only the size of their ancestral
lands but the diversity of their natural habitat. According to E. W. Gifford's
Northeastern and Western Yavapai, "They were not confined to a single ecological area . . . but ranged over a wide variety of territory . . . from blistering desert to shady mountain streams, from lower Austral life zone to
Canadian life zone."

Unfortunately, the Yavapai's ancestral lands comprised the heart of central Arizona's prime real estate. Sigrid Kerha and Patricia S. Mariella re-
count what remains the Yavapai's worst nightmare (next to the Skeleton
Cave massacre) in *The Fort McDowell Yavapai: A Case of Long-term Resistance
to Relocation*. During the winter of 1875, fourteen hundred Yavapais were
forced to walk 160 miles from Camp Verde to the San Carlos Apache
Indian Reservation "through some of the toughest territory in the
West. . . . sick and old people were mercilessly left on the way to die . . . exhausted people were forced to cross a high running river that swept many
away to their death. Food provisions were spoiled and people became ill.
Stragglers were physically punished; the mutilation of some of the survivors gave testimony to such physical punishment." No doubt the Yavapai
have their own descriptions for General Dudley, the Bureau of Indian Affairs
agent who refused to give Gen. George Crook wagons for the Yavapai's
forced relocation. "They are Indians. Let the beggars walk," Dudley told
Crook.

Forerunners of the Yavapai, the Hohokam were originally thought to
use the land now comprising McDowell Mountain Regional Park between
A.D. 1100 and A.D. 1145. Of the five archaeological sites originally discovered in this 17,000-acre county park, archaeologists believed several
represented "temporary camps of people who came to the area to hunt,
gather, and collect stone" for making tools. However, when the survey
was submitted in 1963, archaeologists were literally scratching the surface
in the McDowell Mountains; it wasn't until September 1987 that they
finally hit pay dirt.

That's when the Pinnacle Peak Land Company began to develop a 70-
acre parcel of a 640-acre planned community in Scottsdale, in the pass

between the north end of the McDowells and Troon Mountain. Whoever was wielding the backhoe that day couldn't help noticing that he was scooping out buckets of prehistory. Developer and company president Jerry Nelson knew that Pinnacle Peak was onto something big, too. In a news release sent out to the local media, he said, "This village is part of Hohokam history and it would be a crime to lose it. As a developer, I have an obligation to preserve the integrity of the desert as well as the historical treasures it may hold." Nelson called an immediate halt to development in the vicinity and, in a rare move that would become an image maker's dream, his company sponsored Arizona State University's anthropology department for excavation of the site.

In an overview of the spring 1988 excavations at the site, archaeologist and dig director Patricia A. Gillman wrote "the site has an abundance of special artifacts that would stand out at any site." Among those finds was an extremely rare copper bell, one of only fifty discovered in the entire history of Southwestern archaeology, according to Dr. Charles Redman, director of ASU's Department of Anthropology. Gillman was right on the mark when she wrote, "In terms of amounts and kinds of artifacts alone, the site merits preservation." But, according to one unconfirmed report by a source who spoke on the condition of anonymity, the excavation may have discovered more than that. In addition to the wealth of artifacts from twenty-five trash mounds and eighteen pit structures dating from A.D. 300 to A.D. 1150, a sacred Indian burial site may have been unearthed.

How much of Scottsdale's oldest subdivision will be preserved will ultimately fall on the shoulders of Jerry Nelson and the Pinnacle Peak Land Company. Thus far, Nelson has had the courage and the foresight to do what most Arizona developers wouldn't consider doing: Preserve an irreplaceable piece of our cultural heritage.

Directions

In Scottsdale, from the junction of Scottsdale Road and Shea Boulevard, drive west on Shea Boulevard 16 miles to Gilbert Road. Turn left (north) and drive a quarter-mile to a turnoff on your right. This road winds through a new development to the base of a brown water tank. (At the time of this writing, public access to the south end of the McDowells was somewhat restrictive. If this approach now crosses private property, you'll either have to secure permission from the owner or try your own approach directly north from Shea Boulevard. Begin your traverse on the southernmost end of the McDowell crest in T.3 N., R.6 E., Section 18, on your Sawik Mountain quadrangle.

Trek Log

Mile 0 to 1.5. Peak 2,507 to Peak 3,080. Gain the southern end of the McDowell crest in Section 18 and use Peak 2,507 as your guide to attain this skyline crest and Peak 3,080. Beyond Peak 3,080, follow the McDowell crest all the way to the northern terminus of the range. It's a straightforward ridge traverse that involves a minimum of scrambling, though you'll trek approximately 13 miles and climb and descend a vertical mile in each direction before you complete it. If you're out for a day hike, any of the peaks en route to Thompson Peak offer good vistas and turnaround points.

The McDowell Crest Traverse departs from the vicinity of the 1914 Joseph Morgan homestead. According to the 1963 historical survey of McDowell Mountain Regional Park, "In 1909 the original Homestead Act of 1862 . . . had provided for the settlement on 160 acres of land." At the time, homesteads in and around the McDowell Mountains were presumably claimed for farming or for running cattle. But Morgan's reason for choosing to homestead the steep, southernmost end of the McDowells undoubtedly had more to do with uncovering a ledge of gold than with raising king cotton or Arizona "slow elk," also known as cows.

Mile 1.5 to 2.5. Peak 3,080 to Peak 3,060. The prospects directly below Peak 3,060 in Section 7 date back to 1918 when claims were filed in what was then known as the Dixie Mining District. Magnificent stands of saguaro cover the southern end of the McDowells near these prospects, sometimes swaying in the wind like weaving sentinels. Their days have been numbered, though, by Arizona's growing ranks of cactus rustlers and developers. But every once in a while, nature calls in its own markers: Not far from here an erstwhile target shooter was using a shotgun to blow away a saguaro cactus, limb by precious limb, when the mutilated saguaro fell on the young lad and promptly killed him.

Mile 2.5 to 3.5. Peak 3,060 to Peak 3,804. If you're wondering what the sprawl directly to the east is, it's Fountain Hills. In the early 1970s, Arizona was so starved for growth that the chamber of commerce realized it needed to hire a couple of fast-talking used-car salesmen to lure people from back East. Now, thanks to their sales genius, the London Bridge has been reassembled block by block on the banks of the Colorado River 160 miles to the west of the McDowell crest, and the "highest fountain in the world" spews out of the desert floor for 560 feet a few miles to the east.

Mile 3.5 to 5. Twin Peaks. You'll need to negotiate Peak 3,804 and Peak 3,702 before tackling Thompson Peak.

Mile 5 to 6.5. The steepest descent and ascent on the entire McDowell crest lie in the 1.5-mile stretch between Thompson Peak and McDowell Peak. Not even William C. Barnes, author of *Arizona Place Names*, could find out who Thompson was, or why this prominent 3,980-foot peak was named after him or her; Barnes does note, however, that the name has been used since 1910. Before the proliferation of radio antennas and microwave dishes in the 1970s, Thompson Peak was a spectacular place to camp during a 1½-day trek along the McDowell crest; then, only a single generator-powered radio relay used by the sheriff's department rose from atop an otherwise bald summit, and to escape the screaming whine of that tireless generator you had only to camp in the noise buffer on the flanks below the peak. It was a reasonable trade-off for being able to watch a full winter moon shine over the snow-covered 7,657-foot Four Peaks 25 miles to the east.

Today, however, Thompson Peak is more the full-blown radio facility that the McDowell Peak quadrangle claims it to be than any summit you'd want to camp on. If you do want to camp, slide off the steep north side of Thompson Peak and slalom through the cholla forest to the first un-named saddle at 3,300 feet.

A mile and a half due east from Saddle 3,300, you'll see the Dixie Mine, a small copper mine dating back to the turn of the century. Pickings here were slim then, and according to the 1963 McDowell Mountain histori-cal survey, the Dixie Mining District didn't even "warrant recording on the list of Arizona Mining Districts by the U.S. Bureau of Mines." From a survival standpoint, however, the water trickling out of the Dixie Mine's open tunnel could be construed as a last-ditch water source: A clandestine desert survival program that occasionally trains U.S. Special Forces teams in McDowell Mountain Regional Park has reportedly used the Dixie Mine as an emergency water source during summer months without short-term ill effects. Since the source is a mine tunnel, however, consider it only in an emergency.

Mile 6.5 to 8.5. McDowell Peak to Peak 3,949. The crest between these two peaks is your last major obstacle on this traverse; use care in eyeballing the best routes into and out of the saddle 1,000 vertical feet below McDowell Peak. En route, you should be able to pick out the drainage to the west; it feeds Mountain Spring, the site of an early silver mine. At one time, Mountain Spring was called Frazier Spring for Francis Frazier, who sold the Mountain Spring and Silver Leaf Lode mining claims in the Dixie Mining District to E. O. Brown in 1918. Soldiers from Camp

MacDowell also detoured south off the Stoneman Road to water up at Mountain Spring as early as 1870. (See Mile 10 to 12-plus.)

Mile 8.5 to 10. Peak 3,949 to Peak 3,941, via Tom's Thumb. A rock climber's playground, Tom's Thumb is the most striking feature on the northern end of the McDowells; use this Stonehenge-shaped monolith to key off of as you romp through jumbles of granite slabs and boulders to the ridge on its northwest side. From the base of Tom's Thumb, follow this main ridge northwest until you reach an unnamed saddle in the SW ¼ section of Section 14; from Saddle 3,500, continue following the ridgeline to Peak 3,941.

Mile 10 to 12-plus. From atop Peak 3,941 you can see several prominent landmarks. Of historical interest, Rock Knob can be seen 2 miles to the northeast, and 3,054-foot Fraesfield Mountain can be seen 4 miles north-northwest. On the 1878 military map prepared for R. J. Hinton's *Handbook of Arizona,* the Stoneman Road is clearly marked. According to the McDowell Mountain historical survey, Stoneman Road traversed the desert valley between Rock Knob and Fraesfield Mountain to Cave Creek around 1869, with a secondary trail branching off to Mountain Spring. You can eyeball most of that wagon route from Peak 3,941, as well.

Where wagon wheels once churned across this lush Sonoran Desert, however, golf balls now roll. Three and a half miles northwest of Peak 3,941, the unmistakable granite finger of 3,100-foot-high Pinnacle Peak pokes at the heavens. But the cactus-studded bajadas of that once-pristine Arizona landmark have been buried under a fuji green carpet of manicured golf courses and stylishly tacky Gunite-sprayed-over-chicken-wire adobe-type homes. Martha Summerhayes may have foreseen the death of this great desert more than a century ago when she wrote:

> Sometimes I hear the still voices of the Desert: they seem to be calling me through the echoes of the Past. I hear, in fancy, the wheels of an ambulance [military wagon] crunching the small broken stones of the malpais. . . . I hear the rattle of the ivory rings on the harness of a six-mule team . . . I see my white tent, so inviting after a long day's journey. But how vain these fancies! Railroad and automobile have annihilated distance, the army life of those years is past and gone, and Arizona, as we knew it, has vanished from the face of the earth.

Unless we preserve what remains of the McDowell Mountains, yet another corner of native Arizona will vanish from the face of the earth.

Mile 12-plus to 13-plus. From Peak 3,941, pick your way along the McDowell crest to Peak 3,755; the unnamed saddle immediately below Peak 3,755 is your descent route. Drop off the north side of Saddle 3,500 and follow this drainage until you meet an east-west drainage on the south side of an unnamed 3,100-foot-high butte. Follow this drainage west for approximately half a mile, or until you see Peak 2,910 on the south side of 3,519-foot-high Troon Mountain: a detached, blocklike massif covered with granite boulders, slabs, and pinnacles. Pinnacle Peak Village is located in the pass between Peak 2,910 and Troon Mountain, and as you come down off the north side of the McDowells you can clearly see why archaeologist Patricia Gillman wrote that the village's "location near both the Verde River Valley to the east and the Phoenix Basin to the southwest suggests its possible role as a trading center between two valleys."

Exit for a car shuttle at BM 2,371 on the corner of Pinnacle Peak Road. To get there, take the paved road through Troon Village.

Travel Notes

• **Primary access.**   On the southern end, Shea Boulevard and Gilbert Road; on the northern end, Pinnacle Peak Road, via Troon Village; for the east slope, McDowell Mountain Regional Park.

• **Elevation gain and loss.**   Point to point: Gain – 5,230-plus vertical feet; loss – 5,530 vertical feet.

• **Mileage.**   Point to point: 13 to 14 miles.

• **Water sources.**   No perennial or seasonal water sources en route; emergency water in season may be found at Dixie Mine, Mountain Spring, and the Windmill in the NE ¼ section of Section 25, T.4 N., R.5 E. on your McDowell Peak quadrangle.

• **Cache points.**   None on this point to point.

• **Escape routes.**   Thompson Peak Road, the Mountain Spring jeep trail, Tom's Thumb rock climber's road.

• **Seasons.**   Late fall through early spring; summertime is nasty and hot, so you'd do well to emulate the Yavapai's ancestral roamings by heading for either the Bradshaws or Four Peaks.

• **Maps.**   Sawik Mountain and McDowell Peak quadrangles (7½ minute).

• **Nearest supply points.**   Scottsdale and Phoenix.

• **Managing agency.**   McDowell Mountain Regional Park.

• **Backcountry information.**   Permit not required.

• **Biotic communities.**   Sonoran Desert scrub (Arizona upland subdivision).

Sierra Estrella Mountains

Sierra Estrella Mountains: peak ascent and mountain traverse

Landform

Twenty-five miles long and 3 miles wide, the 4,512-foot-high Sierra Estrella Mountains form a formidable wall of desert peaks that erupt out
of the Sonoran Desert floor for more than 3,000 vertical feet. Seen from
nearby Phoenix, the northwest-trending Sierra Estrella Mountains look
like a peripheral extension of the 2,720-foot-high South Mountains;
topographically, they are not. Waterman Wash courses through Rainbow
Valley and drains the Sierra Estrellas on the southwest, while Santa Cruz
Wash drains the range immediately to the northeast. Near the confluence
of Santa Cruz Wash and the Gila River, the Gila River wraps itself from
east to west around the northern terminus of this great range. Ending just
as abruptly on its southern end, the Sierra Estrellas are flanked there by
2,948-foot-high Sevenmile Mountain, the 2,121-foot-high Palo Verde
Mountains, and the lone sacred hummock of Pima Butte.

Historical Overview

As early as 1925, explorer and hydrologist Kirk Bryan recognized the sublime stature of the Sierra Estrellas in his USGS water-supply paper "Routes
to Desert Watering Places in Papago Country." Wrote Bryan: "Much of
the topography and scenery is as rugged, wild, and grand as any found
in the United States or Alaska." Bryan was as qualified as anyone to make
that statement. In 1917, he was assigned by the USGS to survey "the driest, hottest, and least explored part of the desert region . . . in southeastern
California and southwestern Arizona." Of the 60,000 square miles surveyed for the report, the Sierra Estrellas ("Star Mountains") were among
the few mountain ranges in which Bryan failed to locate any tinajas or
perennial water sources. Most early explorers simply avoided the Sierra
de San Joseph de Cumars, as they were called by Padre Francisco Garces
in 1775; even the dauntless Padre Eusebio Francisco Kino skirted the
southernmost flanks as early as 1699.

   The Pima and Maricopa Indians, who lived, farmed, and fought hostile
Yuman and Mojave Indians within the shadows of the mountain, which

they called *kamatuk,* had little reason to climb its jagged upper reaches. According to anthropologists, the Pima and Maricopa subsisted on flood-water agriculture and a digging-stick economy, and they could ill-afford the time to successfully hunt the Estrellas' desert bighorn sheep as the Papago did in similar desert ranges further to the south. As one Pima chief explained to anthropologist Frank Russell, "Sheep were game fit only for the Papagos, who had no fields to look after."

Recent archaeological evidence, however, suggests that the Hohokam, forerunners of the Pima and Maricopa, explored the imposing summit crest of the Sierra Estrellas for just that reason: to hunt sheep. According to *Petroglyphs of the Southern Sierra Estrella* by Donald Weaver and Bettina Rosenberg, two petroglyph sites are located "at prominent waterholes along trails leading from the base of the mountain to the summit." Petroglyph sites have long been associated with ancient Native Americans' utilization of an area, whether for hunting and gathering, trading, or farming.

More recently, in Volume 10 of *Handbook of North American Indians,* Henry O. Harwell and Marsha C. S. Kelly reported in *Maricopa* that the Maricopa Indians revered the Sierra Estrellas for their mystery and majesty and that "younger men, finding special routes into the higher and less accessible reaches of the Estrellas, returned to report fresh springs, mountain sheep, and treasure stashed by outlaws."

Both enlightening and vague, these two reports comprise virtually all accounts of early exploration in the Sierra Estrellas. Most men simply avoided them—and most still do. Considering their proximity to downtown Phoenix, that's incomprehensible. Those who do make the effort to explore the range on its terms find one of the most rugged, unspoiled desert mountain ranges anywhere in the Southwest.

Directions

Northern End, for day hiking: Enter via Sierra Estrella Regional Park off Southern and Dysart roads.

Southern End, for Peak Ascents and Traverse: Enter from U.S. 80 and 51st Avenue in Phoenix, drive south on 51st Avenue 10 miles to the village of Komatke, and then another 2 miles south to the Santa Cruz turnoff. Turn right on the Santa Cruz Road and follow it across the Gila River 3 miles to the settlement of Santa Cruz. From Santa Cruz, follow the main road south along the eastern flanks of the Sierra Estrellas 8 miles to a secondary road junction at BM 1,257. (Refer to T.3 S., R.2 E., Section 27, on your Montezuma Peak quadrangle.) Turn right at the east end of the prominent ridgeline radiating down from Montezuma's Head and drive or walk a quarter-mile northwest of BM 1,865 into Montezuma's Head Canyon. This marks the start. (Refer to the Laveen and Montezuma Peak quadrangles on the drive in.)

About the Petroglyphs

The area near Montezuma's Head Canyon has, according to some sources, the densest concentration of petroglyphs in Arizona. An array of designs depicting mountain sheep and stick-figure men adorn granite slabs and boulders throughout the area, as do panels of serpents, suns, and other amazing figures. But what must have been a sacred area for ancient Native Americans has not been protected and is now being destroyed by a new subspecies breeding rampantly in the state, *Cretin arizonica.* One particularly elegant panel has been spray painted with "P & R PAVING '83," and "TONY HOWARD 7-5-17," while gun-wielding artisans have riddled this irreplaceable rock-art site with flying lead. The matter needs to be resolved and the area protected for future generations to enjoy, so Native Americans and archaeologists can interpret this priceless rock art for all. Take your time to explore these petroglyphs; you may be the last generation to have the opportunity.

Trek Log

(all mileages approximate)

Mile 0 to 2.   Montezuma's Head Canyon to Hidden Valley. According to *Petroglyphs of the Southern Sierra Estrella,* an ancient Hohokam-Pima Indian Trail leads up Montezuma's Head Canyon to a tinaja near the head of the canyon, and beyond that to a rock shelter near the 2,411-foot summit of Montezuma's Head. But locating and following this ancient track through jumbles of black granite boulders will take some time. Whether you want to day hike up to Hidden Valley or spend the night atop 4,300-foot-high Montezuma Peak South, piece together the ancient trail as follows: From Montezuma's Head Canyon, gain the ridgeline paralleling it on its north side and follow this ridgeline to the unnamed saddle immediately below (north of) Peak 2,911. Much of this first mile involves scrambling, which is made even more interesting by the profusion of cholla, ocotillo, and Spanish daggers. But this subsidiary ridgeline is characteristic of the terrain throughout this range and is the key to gaining the skyline crest of the Sierra Estrella Mountains on this route.

From this unnamed saddle at 2,800 feet, continue following this ridgeline northwest to Saddle 2,834, then thread the pass between Peak 3,092 and Peak 3,025 to Hidden Valley, sometimes called Surprising Valley because you don't expect to find a flat piece of ground anywhere near the serrated crest of the Sierra Estrella. This basin, and other smaller ones like it, were farmed prehistorically, but according to archaeologists they produced relatively small total yields of food. Hidden Valley makes a good turnaround point for a day's outing, or an excellent place to camp for an overnighter.

Mile 2 to 6. Hidden Valley to Montezuma Peak. Head northwest across Hidden Valley for about half a mile, then turn north and climb Peak 3,293. En route, you may discover the remains of an old plane wreck, or the borehole caps and chains left behind by helicopter geologists. According to the Arizona Bureau of Geology and Mineral Technology's "Reconnaissance Geology of the Crest of the Sierra Estrella, Central Arizona," the Gila River Indians gave permission to the Arizona Bureau of Geology to make a daylong "helicopter-assisted field reconnaissance of the crest" on June 27, 1984. This report substantiates, among other things, that modern man had traversed the Sierra Estrella crest on foot before—at least in part.

From Peak 3,293, head for BM 3,051, which, for all practical purposes, signifies the start of the Sierra Estrella crest. Follow the crest northwest to Montezuma Peak, via Peak 2,883. The antenna-topped 4,300-foot-high summit of Montezuma Peak South makes an excellent turnaround point for trekkers interested in climbing this remote peak via its challenging southern crest, or its bald summit offers a more comfortable place to camp than does the nearby rocky summit cap of Montezuma Peak proper.

The Summit View

To the west. As twilight torches your perch a luminous pink, you'll be able to look out over the cool, lavender Forty Mile Desert far below. In *Lt. Emory Reports,* edited by Ross Calvin, Lt. W. H. Emory wrote: "The mirage . . . now began to distort the distant mountains which everywhere bounded the horizon into fantastic shapes." Lieutenant Emory was describing the notorious Forty Mile Desert he crossed on November 13 and 14, 1846, which now lies at your feet; it's bordered on the east by the steep, western flanks of the Estrellas and on the west by the meandering Gila River. The most discernible physical relief you'll notice in that purple sea of desert is a long, narrow, low-lying black range called Sevenmile Mountain. Paralleling Sevenmile immediately to the west is Watermelon Wash, which, in the setting sun, looks like an undulating serpent slithering across the landscape. Juan Bautista de Anza was forced to lay over there on November 5, 1775, when *two* women in his party were reportedly " . . . taken with violent child-bearing pains."

Further to the west, you can make out a smattering of desert hills, the 3,272-foot-high Maricopa Mountains; distance and aridity notwithstanding, the pass through the Maricopas was the last physical obstacle anyone trying to follow in the bold footsteps of Padre Kino across the Forty Mile Desert would encounter—but most went willingly, from the pilgrims and argonauts en route to the California goldfields to the hard-driving stagemen of the Butterfield Overland Mail. They followed the route Kino had forged 150 years earlier because it was the only proven shortcut on this stretch of the Gila Trail, cutting off the 60-mile loop that the Gila River takes from the Pima villages around the northern end of the Sierra Estrellas to present-day Gila Bend. But the hardships many of those early travelers endured became legendary, and the waterless trek across the Forty Mile Desert became known as the *Jornada de las Estrellas*, "the day's journey of the stars."

The Spanish padres, and the thousands of eager pioneers who later followed, weren't the only ones to cross that vast desertscape in hopes of reaching the Colorado River via either the Jornada de las Estrellas, the Gila Trail, or El Camino del Diablo. In *Maricopa*, Harwell and Kelly wrote: "Beyond this horizon, trail networks linked the middle and lower Gila [River] overland to Halchidoma and Mojave country on the Colorado. The connections were very old—perhaps predating Yuman people—and brought trade goods from the Gulf [of California] and Pacific coasts. On the week-long journey to the [Colorado River] delta country, for instance, Maricopas obtained the Pai-pai's *u.v.sax* (rotten tobacco) through the Cocopa." Imagine running—or walking—300 miles across the desert for a carton of cigarettes!

The Traverse

By the time you reach the summit of Montezuma Peak South you will know whether or not you want to tackle the Sierra Estrellas' magnificent summit crest. Only you can make that call. What lies beyond this point is the most spectacular—and difficult—mountain traverse in Arizona—a standing wave of ridges stacked up behind one another like a series of tsunamis about to break over its knife-edged crest. Next to some areas below the North Rim of the Grand Canyon, this ridgeline comprises the most rugged—and awesome—terrain in Arizona; traversing it requires constant judgment in route finding. In *Routes to Desert Watering Places in Papago Country*, Kirk Bryan wrote: "Climbing this range is arduous work and many of the slopes can be ascended by a pedestrian only with the greatest of difficulty." So if you have any doubts, save this adventure for another time.

Mile 6 to 10. Montezuma Peak to Butterfly Mountain. Northwest of Montezuma Peak, the summit crest between Peak 4,029 and 4,119-foot-high Butterfly Mountain comprises a large section of the proposed 18,830-acre Sierra Estrella Wilderness; this stretch also made up Traverse No. 2 of the 1984 Geological Recon, surveyed by Englishman J. E. Spencer. But to piece together this leg, you'll have to link together Peak 3,920 with Peak 3,815, Peak 3,804, and the unnamed crest peaks between . . . and by the time you reach Butterfly Mountain, you'll come to grips with the unrelenting nature of the Sierra Estrella crest and learn how best to read the ridgeline: whether to parallel it on one side or the other or to follow the top of the crest itself.

From Peak 3,930 you can clearly see the summit wings of Butterfly Mountain; derived from the Spanish word *mariposa*, Butterfly Mountain is a flying double buttress of Precambrian granite. It has become the preferred haunt of a small band of climbers who must relish the steep, thigh-burning hump directly up the east slope of the Sierra Estrellas. According to *Petroglyphs of the Southern Sierra Estrella*, a second ancient Hohokam-Pima trail climbed up to the crest of the Sierra Estrellas from the west side and, like the Montezuma's Head Canyon route, led to a tinaja. This giant cup of water is reported to be located in the upper arm of the canyon draining Butterfly Mountain on its southwest side. But be aware that even Kirk Bryan missed it. If you find it, it could be the one pivotal water source you could rely on in this upheaved desert.

While contouring the north side of Butterfly Mountain, you'll see maidenhair ferns growing near its base, which indicates a seasonal trickle of water, or seep—if Arizona isn't experiencing a drought. The boojum tree from Baja can also be found in this area, as can remnant stands of juniper.

As you continue north from the Summit Wings, the natural tendency is to get sucked out into easier ground near BM 3,567. This is a false summit, though. Continue grappling around the base of the Summit Wings to gain the 3,700-foot saddle on its west side.

Mile 11 to 12. Butterfly Mountain to Montezuma Sleeping. If you're looking for a place to bed down midway between Butterfly Mountain and 4,000-foot-high Montezuma Sleeping, consider Peak 3,695. If you gaze into the sea of lights of nighttime Phoenix from this peak, it will seem as though you could reach out and grab a handful of those toy skyscrapers. In fact, though, it would be another full day—or more—before you could actually drink from the water fountains gurgling at the foot of those skyscrapers.

From Peak 3,695, it's a direct shot to Montezuma Sleeping via Peak 3,426.

Mile 13 to 16. Montezuma Sleeping to Montezuma Peak North. The terrain actually lets up along this stretch of the Sierra Estrella crest, but if you're running low on water, don't consider bailing off the mountain's west side. The only trail leading to water in the Sierra Estrellas, aside from the ancient Hohokam tracks, is the Santa Cruz Road—and that's on the east side of the range.

At 3,400-foot Gravesite Pass, in a low saddle a quarter-mile south of Peak 3,873, near Mile 15, is an unmarked grave, a body-length, rectangular mound outlined by stones. One can only speculate who's buried here—but perhaps the clues can be found in *Maricopa*. Wrote Harwell and Kelly: "Miners, they say, still keep the unwary at a distance with rifle fire."

From Gravesite Pass, 4,512-foot-high Montezuma Peak North presents a tempting challenge, though a resistible one if you're running low on water or if you don't look forward to climbing up to yet another godforsaken radio tower. You would do better to continue looking for the remnant herd of Desert bighorn still inhabiting this range.

Mile 16 to 18. Montezuma Peak to Pack Saddle Pass. Looking up at the western flanks of Montezuma Peak, you can see why it served as one of the mythological cornerstones for the Maricopa's ancestral lands, bordered on the west by the Sierra Estrellas, on the east by South Mountains, and on the south by Pima Butte. In *Maricopa*, Harwell and Kelly wrote:

> The northwestern flanks of the Sierra Estrella are dominated by a peak called 'berdache mountain' in Maricopa, recalling epithets hurled by opposing bands of Yuman warriors taunting each other to skirmish. On the Salt River Range [South Mountains] to the east Coyote wiped his paw after eating the heart of Chipas, the culture hero plucked from the funeral pyre at the Colorado River. The core of Maricopa land, at least since the early nineteenth century, was . . . in the Gila Valley circumscribed by these three landmarks [also including Pima Butte] and a fourth, called 'water divider,' an outlier of the Sierra Estrella just west of the Gila-Salt confluence.

From Peak 4,232 at the foot of berdache mountain, follow the crest northwest along the western edge of Maricopa land to Peak 3,655, which points to water divider. At Peak 3,655, you can drop off the northeast side of the crest and angle over to the route of the Pack Saddle Pass Trail, or continue down this ragged crest to 2,400-foot-high Pack Saddle Pass directly below Peak 2,918. Once at Pack Saddle Pass, determine whether you have enough water to finish traversing the northern terminus of this great range into Estrella Mountain Regional Park. If you've been caught by a rising thermometer and you're out of water, your only option will be to bail off the crest or pass and go for the Gila.

Mile 18 to 23. Pack Saddle Pass to the Gila River. Located in the NE ¼ of Section 1 (T.2 S., R.1 W.) on your Avondale SE quadrangle, Pack Saddle Pass once provided the only direct link between Rainbow Valley and the Gila River Valley on the opposite side of this mountain barrier. This little-known seldom-used route was rediscovered in the early 1950s by pioneer Arizonan Ben Humphreys; in the 1952 *Arizona Days and Way* article "Pack Saddle Pass," writer Ida Smith quoted Humphreys on the history of the route: "Pack Saddle Pass was a portion of the first road from Yuma to Fort Whipple in the early days, going through Gila Bend and later, Phoenix. It was at first a horse trail so I have been told, and then a wagon, or more likely, a buckboard road. . . . But where it emerged from the mountains to go through Rainbow Valley it has been erased in the numerous crossroads of later times."

Much of the route has been erased below Pack Saddle Pass on its eastern side as well, so use your judgment in heading off the pass into the canyon below. From Pack Saddle Pass, you'll trek northeast some 5 miles down the canyon and across the bajadas to the Gila River greenbelt via the Pack Saddle Pass Trail. Since the Pack Saddle Pass Trail was the only trail to cross the Estrellas in historic times, en route to the Gila you might consider the plight of those who didn't use this mountain cutoff, or follow the loop of the Gila River, but instead attempted the Jornada de las Estrellas. In *The Gila Trail*, Benjamin Butler Harris describes his crossing of the Forty Mile Desert in 1848:

> We resumed our pilgrimage, taking advantage of night travel over the forty-five mile desert stretch, the road over which was a cord cutting off the [60-mile-long] elbow made by Gila Bend. At twenty-four miles we camped without water amid a grove of giant cactus—*larrea mexicana latera* [creosote]—with sage growing among them. Tormented all night with an intense headache, and being worse at daylight, I went forward alone to get shade where road and river met again, twenty miles ahead. Reaching the river, where there was much fresh Indian sign, wracked to madness by pain, I had sanity enough to water my mule.

When you finally crawl through the jungle of tammies (tamarisk) choking the last precious drops of water from the trickling mudhole, the once-mighty Gila River, you'll emerge from one of Arizona's greatest mountain ranges. When you do, "walk in beauty," as Arizona's Indians wisely advise.

Mile 23 to 26. Gila River to the corner of 85th Avenue and Dobbins. From BM 962 in the Gila River, follow a jeep trail 2 miles north to BM 966; turn right and walk the last mile east to the corner of 85th Avenue and Dobbins. If you're willing to share your adventure with one of the local Pima or Maricopa Indians en route, you might get a drink from the garden hose you've been dreaming about for the last 24 hours—or you might hear something about the mountains, like what Bernard Donohue said on April 29, 1986: "Nobody's ever been up there before. Those mountains are a mystery to everyone." That's exactly why you should explore them. One million Phoenicians still don't know they exist.

Travel Notes

•**Primary access.**   Southern end, via Montezuma's Head; northern end, via Sierra Estrella Mountain Regional Park.

•**Elevation gain and loss,** point to point:

> *Peak ascent/Montezuma's Head:*
> Gain—4,056 vertical feet.
> Loss—1,044 vertical feet.
> *Traverse/Sierra Estrella Crest:*
> Gain—8,936 vertical feet.
> Loss—9,461 vertical feet.

•**Mileage,** point to point:

> *Montezuma's Head:* Approximately 6 miles.
> *Sierra Estrella crest:* Approximately 25 miles, though you'll probably cover 30 miles to do 25.

•**Water sources.**   No perennial water en route. Water might be found seasonally on the north side of Butterfly Mountain.

•**Cache points.**   For Montezuma's Head, use Hidden Valley and BM 3,051.

•**Escape routes.**   Don't consider bailing off the west side of the mountain; nobody is out there to help you. If you don't have any luck using your signal mirror with one of the sail planes that frequently soar above the crest, consider the following options:

> *Peak Ascent:* Beneath Hidden Valley, retrace your line of ascent. Follow Hidden Valley to Montezuma Peak South and head for the Santa Cruz Road via the east slope.

Traverse: From Montezuma Peak South, go east to Butterfly Mountain and then head for the Santa Cruz Road via the east slope. Or, from Butterfly Mountain, go north to Pack Saddle Pass, again on the east slope.

•**Seasons.**   Late fall through early spring; *stay out of this range during hot weather.*

•**Maps.**   Montezuma Peak, Mobile NE, Avondale SE, and Laveen quadrangles (7½ minute).

•**Nearest supply points.**   Komatke and Phoenix.

•**Managing agencies.**   Gila River Indian Reservation, Bureau of Land Management, and Maricopa County Parks.

•**Backcountry information.**   Check with Gila River Indian Reservation for up-to-date permit information. Firewood is scarce to nonexistent on the summit crest.

•**Biotic communities.**   Sonoran Desert scrub (Arizona upland subdivision and lower Colorado subdivision).

Climbing

Weaver's Needle

Superstition Mountains: peak ascent

Landform

Bordered on the west by the single, blocklike massif of 5,057-foot-high Superstition Mountain and on the east by 6,056-foot-high Iron Mountain, 4,553-foot-high Weaver's Needle pokes its way out of a standing eruption of mountains, bluffs, ridges, and canyons that drain into the Salt River reservoir system to the north and the Gila River to the south. Totaling some 300 square miles, the rugged desert topography encircling Weaver's Needle has long been described as "look-alike" and confusing; in reality, if you follow the natural lay of the land, travel and orientation are comparatively easy in the Superstitions—especially if you stay within sight of the striking landmark reportedly named for territorial scout Pauline Weaver.

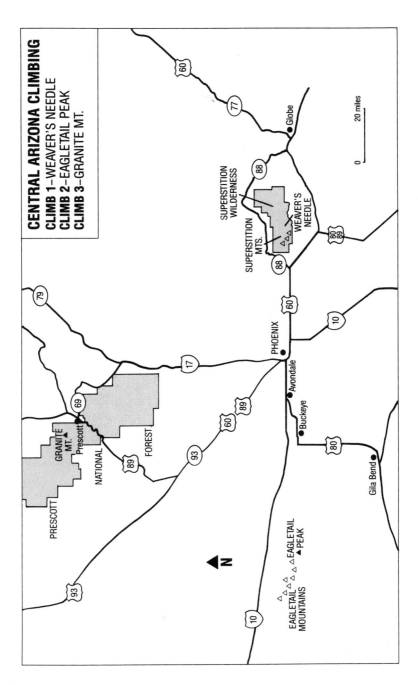

CENTRAL ARIZONA CLIMBING
CLIMB 1 – WEAVER'S NEEDLE
CLIMB 2 – EAGLETAIL PEAK
CLIMB 3 – GRANITE MT.

Historical Overview

In "The Other World of the Superstitions," Bernice McGee wrote that the body of E. M. Reavis, who was murdered after going over the Reavis Divide, was found on April 20, 1896. "His dogs and horses remained near his decomposed body. Some say he was partly eaten by wolves and coyotes." If the description of the Superstition hermit sounds like an account straight out of Old West, that's because it is. No legend of lost gold has fired the imagination more than that of the fabled "Lost Dutchman's Gold Mine." Whether the mine was really a mine or, as some historians believe, a cache of Spanish gold hidden deep within the dark recesses of these mountains no one really knows. One thing is certain, though: Strip away the fancy and you're still faced with the fact that no fewer than fifty-one people have died in the Superstition Mountains since the turn of the century, and that doesn't include lost hikers. Many of the deaths have been gruesome, unsolved murders believed to be directly related to the tireless search for the Lost Dutchman's Gold, and few of the killers have ever been brought to justice. Yet, to this day, the carnage seems to breed upon itself, and ironically this "local color" continues to lure people into the "Killer Mountains."

Few people have seen the Superstitions, or Sierra de La Spuma ("Mountains of Foam") for what they really are: a 160,000-acre Sonoran Desert wilderness comprised of some of the most unique hiking and climbing country in the Southwest. For most, an overnight trip into the Superstitions remains a dare and harkens back to campfire tales told at summer camp. As the August 15, 1896, edition of *The Winslow Mail* reported, under the headline "A Ghostly Inspiration – An Uncanny Spot in Arizona": "The most terrible things told are the swinging stones that turn out from the walls of the canyon and crush the passerby . . . trees that reach out their branches and entangle all who come near them . . . wild animals by the thousands come right out of the solid rocks. Fishes with legs come from the lakes and drown all within their reach. Fire and smoke and horrible groans and howls fill the air on all sides." To this day, few people leave these haunted mountains without some story of their own to tell.

The most famous story of all was told by the white-bearded Dutchman himself, Jacob Waltz, when on October 25, 1891, he uttered his last words from his Phoenix deathbed: "There's a great stone face looking up at my mine. If you pass three red hills you've gone too far. The rays of the setting sun shine upon my gold. Climb above my mine and you can see Weaver's Needle." Most subsequent searches for the "Dutchman's gold" – and many of its related murders—have taken place within the shadows of this famous Arizona landmark.

It's anybody's guess who first climbed the "Finger of God." One published account tells of climbing Weaver's Needle during the 1950s, though an agile Apache, Pima, or Maricopa Indian probably climbed its summit hundreds of years earlier. A column in the Thursday, August 10, 1893, *Oasis* sheds some light on how the region's earliest visitors went *into* Superstition Mountain; based on the tale of a Pima Indian chief, the article said: "Montezuma was a great chief and ruler over thousands of souls, the inhabitants of very large cities . . . populating the extensive plains of this country. Fearing then a great calamity was about to befall him and his people, he caused them to assemble on the plains adjacent to the [Superstition] mountain and then with his magic wand, he caused an opening to be made in the side of the mountain, into which he and his people went. Then the stone gateway was closed and to this day Montezuma and his people dwell within the center of the rugged old mountain."

Most early *Anglos* looked upon Weaver's Needle as their only compass point in their quest to find the Lost Dutchman's Gold; it was not something to climb. In fact, most saw it in the same light that writers like Robert Joseph Allen still view it: "A strange, phallic finger of smooth, black basalt rock, Weaver's Needle emerges perpendicularly from the plateau and towers hundreds of feet into the air. Incredibly deep crevices, sheer cliffs, and ravines choked with catclaw, prickly pear, paloverde, saguaro, and ocotillo guard its base."

Indeed, who would dare try to climb such a ghastly fissure of rock—especially after warnings like those published in *A Ghostly Inspiration* "Don't go unless your nerves are strong"?

Directions

From Apache Junction, drive east on U.S. 60 8 miles to the Peralta Road. Turn left and drive another 8 miles to the Peralta Canyon trailhead. En route, you'll see that the desert bajadas fanning out from the periphery of the Superstitions are finally recovering from the heyday of the Silver King Mine; between 1875 and 1900, a 5-square-mile area was reportedly denuded of firewood by Cornish miners to fuel the Silver King operation to the east. Those same Cornish miners may also have been the first Anglo "backpackers" in the Superstition region; they used to hoof it 20 miles across the desert to Globe on Friday nights to drink away pay day, then walk the whole thing off en route back to the Silver King on Sundays.

Trail Log

Mile 1 to 2.25.   Peralta Trailhead to Fremont Saddle. The hike up Peralta Canyon to Fremont Saddle is one of the most popular spring day hikes in the Phoenix area. Once you start up this well-used trail, you'll see why. Along the short stretch of canyon are some of the most spectacular rock formations in the Superstitions. At one time a native herd of Desert bighorn also thrived in the Superstitions' craggy terrain, but that was before the last of them ended up in a prospector's skillet circa 1850.

Mile 2.25 to 3.   Fremont Saddle to Piñon Camp area. For those who just want to hike up and look at Weaver's Needle, there's no better vista than from 3,766-foot-high Fremont Saddle. Seen from here, the Needle is an imposing piece of rock. Steel your nerves and push on to Piñon Camp, where you first see what awed sightseers standing atop Fremont Saddle can't see: that Weaver's Needle is actually two needles, split from base to summit by a steep gully. Located approximately half a mile north of Fremont Saddle, Piñon Camp used to be a great campsite before the area was stripped of firewood and the camp's stately ponderosa pine trees were hacked by tomahawk-wielding campers determined to prove that green wood *does* burn. The area still makes a good camp if you want to bed down after the walk-in and climb the Needle early the next morning in order to make it back out to your vehicle the same day. Another wide spot in the Peralta Trail a quarter- to a half-mile north of Piñon Camp provides a more direct line of ascent up to the base of Weaver's Needle.

The area around the base of Weaver's Needle has always figured prominently in the quest for the Dutchman's Gold. On November 11, 1958, the long-standing feud between prospectors Ed Piper and Celeste Jones finally came to a head on the Needle's slopes; claiming self-defense, Ed Piper shot and killed Robert St. Marie, a bodyguard from Jones' rival camp who also had mining claims on Weaver's Needle.

The Approach

The Killer Talus Slope, South.   Veteran Grand Canyon climbers like George Bain call the talus slope beneath Zoroaster Temple the Killer Talus Slope for its abrupt, calf-burning steepness. (See entry for Brahma and Zoroaster Temples.) Bain should have named it the Killer Talus Slope North, because the Killer Talus Slope South is located at the foot of Weaver's Needle.

From your camp in Peralta Canyon, head up the Killer Talus Slope South to the foot of the obvious gully that splits the Needle on its west side.

Once at the foot of the gully, continue scrambling up several sections of conglomerate rock to the bottom of the first pitch. In the early 1970s there were sections of old wooden ladders on these lower rock steps dating back to the days of Celeste Jones, but no doubt they now sit proudly above someone's fireplace.

Pitch 1. Is marked by a tubular pipe drilled into the rock 20 feet above the start of the pitch; two other pipes offer the best protection on the grungy rock leading up to the huge chockstone above. Turn the chockstone on the right (5.6) and belay from several belay bolts. If you're carrying a pack, or if you're gripped about the poor protection this crumbly volcanic plug offers, spelunk your way beneath the chockstone.

Pitch 2. From the Notch, scramble up a 15-foot-high rock step on your left (north). The canyon you see far below to your east is Needle Canyon.

Pitch 3. Head north up a long, steep gully broken by a series of rock steps. This gully leads to the base of a headwall immediately below the summit; turn left (west) and continue along the base to the west end.

Pitch 4. Offers the easiest and most exposed climbing on this route. But it's also the most dangerous, simply because there isn't a good place at the bottom of the pitch to put in a natural bombproof belay anchor— short of drilling a bolt, and nobody has thought that necessary. That may have been the reason why two Arizona climbers plummeted to their deaths, roped together, from this very pitch more than a decade ago. But theirs were not the first deaths here. (See Summit View, following.)

Climb a short ramp diagonally left, then straight up an obvious crack with jug-sized holds to a horn near the top of Pitch 4; if this hollow-sounding horn unnerves you for a belay anchor, back up your belay on two rappel bolts 50 feet north.

Summit View

On March 26, 1963, opera singer turned prospector Celeste Jones hired mining engineer Vance Bacon to climb to the top of Weaver's Needle to assay its mineral wealth. Jones believed the mother lode was located inside the Needle, through a hidden entrance or the like. (Bacon's tubular rods are those craftily drilled and hammered into the porous rock on Pitch 1.) Shortly after reaching the summit of the Needle, Bacon "fell off, screaming all the way to his death on the jagged rocks below." At least one historian believes that another of Jones' men may have pushed him because he was willing to tell Jones that her mining claim on the Needle was worthless.

Today the incredible 360-degree panorama from the summit of Weaver's Needle is often obstructed by smog from Phoenix 35 miles to the west; by smelter emissions from the Globe-Miami mining region 30 miles east; and by smelter emissions from the Hayden-Winklemen-San Manuel copper belt extending 70 miles to the south—so bring a good Arizona map to help guide you through the vast clyclorama radiating outward from the "Finger of God." . . . Even on the Superstitions' worst days, you can see, and sometimes hear, how the Killer Mountains earned their foreboding reputation. An 1893 quote from *The Oasis* read: "When heavy winds blow against the south and east sides of the mountain, the terrified listener hears the most piercing and heart-rending and unearthly shrieks and howlings and . . . soul piercing sounds proceeding from out the caves and caverns, inaccessible crevices of the mountain." When you start hearing these "unearthly shrieks and howlings" from Weaver's Needle, you'll know it's time to rap off.

Descent
From the summit, rappel from two bolts over the headwall. Retrace the gully back to the notch and rappel off the chockstone all the way down Pitch 1.

Travel Notes
- **Suggested gear.** A helmet, 2 150-foot ropes, slings, small- to medium-sized nuts, and a tweezer for removing cactus spines.

- **Primary access.** Peralta Canyon trailhead.

- **Secondary access.** Via Needle Canyon and First Water.

- **Elevation gain and loss.** 3,400 vertical feet each way.

- **Mileage.** Approximately 8 miles round-trip.

- **Water sources.** No perennial water en route; seasonal tinajas in Peralta and East Boulder canyons.

- **Escape routes.** Back the way you came.

- **Seasons.** Late fall through early spring are best. Avoid Weaver's Needle on busy spring weekends when inexperienced climbers gripped on Pitch 1 can turn this classic summit into a nightmare of waiting and when entire divisions of Boy Scouts can turn the walk-out into an adolescent paramilitary maneuver. In the summertime, a handful of die-hard legend hunters skulk around, but for most it's best to avoid this rattlesnake-infested inferno.

• **Nearest supply points.** Apache Junction and Globe.

• **Managing agencies.** U.S. Forest Service.

• **Backcountry information.** Permit not required; firewood scarce.

• **Biotic communities.** Sonoran Desert scrub (Arizona upland subdivision) and interior chaparral.

Eagletail Mountains

Eagletail Mountains: peak ascent, via trekking or rock climbing

Landform

Of the six major mountain ranges that occupy the desert outback west of Phoenix within the Gila River–Centennial Wash–Colorado River triangle, one stands out as a classic desert landform: the 3,300-foot-high Eagletail Mountains gnash their way out of the Harquahala Plain like a double row of igneous wolf teeth. Twenty miles long and up to 4 miles wide, the northwest-trending Eagletail Mountains rise up out of the Harquahala Plain for more than 2,000 vertical feet; 2,874-foot-high Courthouse Rock marks the 1,800-foot-high saddle that severs the Eagletails about midway; and three free-standing "feathers" on the southeastern end of the range offer trekkers and climbers peak ascents of three cloud-piercing pinnacles.

Historical Overview

Located in the same 10,000-square-mile despoblado as the Kofa Mountains (see entry for Signal Peak), the Eagletails were bypassed by the same Spanish explorers, mountain men, and immigrant trails that avoided the Kofas. As in the Kofas 40 miles to the west, however, the only known people to venture into the Eagletails were the Tolkapaya (western Yavapai); known as the Haka-Whatapa, the nomadic western band of Tolkapaya hunted deer and desert bighorn, gathered wild plants such as saguaro fruit, prickly pear, and mesquite beans, and made use of extensive trade networks. In *Deceptive Desolation: Prehistory of the Sonoran Desert in West Central Arizona*, Connie L. Stone reports that antelope living in the Harquahala Valley at the time "were spurned [by the Haka-Whatapa] because they 'ate toads.' Fish and waterfowl were also avoided. [But] the river Yumans played practical jokes on the Yavapai by feeding them ground fish bones mixed in with cornmeal mush." In her 1986 Cultural Resource Survey for the Bureau of Land Management, Stone also reported that "the Western Yavapai stored food in pots placed in caves. It was understood that visitors could help themselves. . . . The diversity and dispersed location of seasonally available resources required a great deal of mobility, often over long distances." Undoubtedly, the Haka-Whatapa could have easily climbed the northern satellite summit of Eagletail Peak to hunt the desert bighorn frequently seen in the area, as there are several tinajas and caves en route to these lofty hunting grounds. But the first recorded ascent of Eagletail Peak's highest summit is still in question.

In *The Lower Gila River Region, Arizona,* Clyde P. Ross was one of the first to describe Eagletail Peak; Ross' "Water-Supply Paper-498" formed the northern quadrant of what Kirk Bryan was already surveying south of the Gila River. Together Bryan's Papago Country and Ross' Lower Gila River region reports comprised the eastern half of the monumental 60,000-square-mile USGS water survey, which also included the bleak Salton Sea and Mojave Desert regions west of the Lower Colorado River. Of the summit area of Eagletail Peak, Ross wrote: "The range takes its name from a similar but even higher peak, near its east [southeastern] end, whose summit is broken into three points and has a fancied resemblance to an eagle's tail sticking straight up in the air. . . . This peak is reported to have been scaled, truly a worthwhile bit of mountain climbing."

Historical details are scarce, at best, and it's not known whether the peak scaling Ross alludes to involved scrambling up the nontechnical, northern satellite summit below the North Feather or whether someone actually succeeded in climbing any of the Feathers before the first recorded ascent in the 1970s. The North Feather was first climbed in 1976 by an Arizona-based group called the Kachina Members who used direct-aid (artificial-climbing) techniques to reach the summit; it was climbed free in 1977 by Arizona climbers Larry Trieber, Bruce Grubbs, and Chris Beal. The Trieber-Grubbs-Beal trio also made the first recorded ascents of the Middle and the South Feathers during that same year. Gold may have driven some fever-struck prospector up the South Feather to assay its mineral wealth earlier in the century; rated 5.0, it's the easiest of the Feathers to climb, and easier than Weaver's Needle 110 miles due east. According to the February 19, 1908, edition of the *Arizona Sentinel,*

> Will Copson, who formerly resided in Phoenix, and Gab Lopez came to town Saturday with some very fine gold ore. . . . Large pieces weighing

thirty to forty pounds are liberally sprinkled with coarse gold, and some of the smaller picked specimens are almost dazzling. The strike is about eighty miles from here [at Wickenburg] in the southeast end of the Eagle Tail Mountains. . . . The find was made by Lopez, who found a rich piece of float while on a prospecting trip in the Eagle Tails. Following up the dry wash in which he picked up the piece of float he came upon the ledge, which promises to make himself and his partner rich men. The property is in northern Yuma county and many prospectors have been attracted there by news of the rich strike.

Who knows whether or not one of the "Eagle Tails" above the Copson-Lopez strike looked like a giant gold bar to some whiskey-soaked prospector; at $190 a ton, it wouldn't have taken much to make one think about climbing up and dynamiting one of those Tails back down into camp.

Directions

From Phoenix, drive 65 miles west in I-10 to Exit 81, the Salome Road–Harquahala Road turnoff. Turn south onto the Harquahala Road and drive 5.6 miles to the Courthouse Road. Turn right (west) on the Courthouse Road and drive 7 miles to the junction of the Gas Pipeline Road. Turn left (southeast) onto the Gas Pipeline Road and drive just under 2 miles to an unmarked gate and fence on the right (south); this turnoff is a few hundred yards west of a branch arm of the Central Arizona Project canal. Once through the gate, drive south on this fenceline road 1.2 miles to a second gate on the right. (The construction of the new branch arm of the CAP has drastically altered the original approach to Eagletail Peak. This pivotal turnoff is in the NE ¼ of Section 14, T.1 N, R.10 W. on your Eagletail Mountain quadrangle.) Beyond this gate, drive through a junkyard. (That's right: Where better to put a junkyard than at the foot of this spectacular desert mountain range?) From there, drive 1.9 miles to a three-way fork. Take the middle fork 1.1 miles west to a fine primitive campsite overlooking a deep wash below the road, located approximately .5 mile south of 2,241-foot-high Granite Mountain.

Trek Log

Begin (all mileages approximate). The northern satellite peak of Eagletail Peak is only a few feet lower than the North Feather and thus offers a superb nontechnical objective for a day hike or overnighter. However, the Eagletails are comprised of some of the loosest and most crumbly desert rock (tuff and lava) in the region, so the approach still requires care. There are no perennial water sources en route, nor are there any trails—so be prepared for the rigors and hazards of exposed, cross-country desert travel.

Mile 0 to 1.   Deep Wash Camp to Sheep Trail. Cross the deep wash immediately below (south of) your camp and head southwest across the bajada toward the lowest, most prominent V-notch incising this end of the Eagletail crest. While traveling across the desert pavement capping this bajada, you may notice several circular stone alignments; not to be confused with sleeping circles, these may date as far back as 1500 B.C. when they served as the foundations of hunting blinds for ancient Hohokam or Patayan cultures who hunted in the Eagletails long before the Haka-Whatapa.

Mile 1 to 1.5.   Sheep trail to V-notch. At the foot of the Eagletail's northeastern flank is a steep, rocky scramble up a braided network of Desert bighorn sheep trails to the V-notch splitting the Eagletail Crest. En route, you may encounter the sun-bleached bones of desert bighorn, which use this route to reach the tinajas near the V-notch; these shallow water basins are the only tinajas on this end of this austere range, and the sheep rely on them—so don't camp near the V-notch or use these water sources except in an emergency.

Mile 1.5 to 2.5.   V-notch to Eagletail Saddle. From the V-notch, eyeball your route southeast along this steep, precipitous leg of the Eagletail crest to Eagletail Saddle; the key to crossing this airy stretch is to parallel the west side of the Eagletail crest just below the crest itself. Once atop the crest's high point you'll be able to eyeball your way down to the prominent saddle immediately below Eagletail Peak on its north side. This is 2,400-plus-foot-high Eagletail Saddle.

Mile 2.5 to 3.   Eagletail Saddle to Eagletail Peak. Located directly above the rock climbers' approach to Eagletail Peak, the small depression of Eagletail Saddle is the flattest and widest place to camp this high up on the Eagletail crest. It's also a good place to cache extra water and gear.

From Eagletail Saddle, the cross-country route up to Eagletail Peak is steep, straightforward, and nontechnical. It offers an excellent opportunity to photograph Desert bighorn in their wild desert habitat, so keep your eyes peeled.

The Feathers

Once at the base of the North Feather, trekkers can scramble up its northern satellite peak, or rock climbers can scale any of the three Feathers.

If you're interested only in climbing the highest Feather, you want the North Feather, or Eagletail Peak. But if you want to stand on the most exciting summit in the wind, you want the South Feather.

North Feather.   The most accessible of the three Feathers, the North Feather, has the longest and steepest pitch: 90 feet of 5.6. The route begins on the north corner of the North Feather above a large boulder with a belay bolt in it. An interesting move will gain the ledge 25 feet above; from this ledge, climb up the exposed, hollow-sounding, slick cracks to the grungy belay ledge just below the summit. Two bolts below the summit on its east side serve as your anchors for the 90-foot rappel.

Middle and South Feathers.   The approach to the Middle and South Feathers is more dangerous than the climb up either. From the base of the North Feather, descend a steep, loose gully southeast into an obvious notch between the North and Middle Feathers. Zigzag and scramble up a series of exposed, unprotected ledges to the summit ridge that links the Middle and South Feathers.

The route up the Middle Feather begins on its east side; it's a 50-foot face-and-crack climb (5.5) leading to a single belay and (rappel) bolt. You may find standing on the summit more challenging than the actual climb.

The route up the South Feather begins on its northeast side. An easy (5.0) 60-foot-long chimney leads to a single belay (and rappel) bolt. Standing on the very tip of the South Feather also presents an interesting challenge for those who succumb to the temptation.

The Summit View

As from many high desert peaks, the views from the summit Feathers of Eagletail Peak are superb 360-degree panoramas, though you may find it more relaxing to absorb the incredible vista from Satellite Peak.

To the west, somewhere in the heart of the Eagletails, is a remote spring that escaped even Clyde P. Ross's unusually thorough water survey. This spring is one of the only perennial water sources that ancient man used for more than 2,000 years in this virtually waterless range. Archaeologists are only now beginning to understand the significance of it and the extensive petroglyph site surrounding it. According to a registration form prepared for the National Register of Historic Places by archaeologist Connie L. Stone, "no known western desert sites, except for the larger Painted Rocks and Sears Point sites adjacent to the lower Gila River, match the substantial and visually impressive nature of the Eagletail site." Evidence discovered by archaeologists like Stone suggests that ancient man was forced to travel long distances across the western Arizona desert as early as 1500 B.C. in order to utilize the region's marginal food and water sources.

To the east, you'll see the rich agricultural lands of the Harquahala Valley, a striking dichotomy to the dry, rugged Eagletail interior to the west. According to Frank Norris' "Lessons in Despair," the federal government opened the Harquahala Valley to homesteading in 1925 specifically for World War I veterans who had fallen victim to mustard-gas poisoning. Because of the heat and dryness of the lower Sonoran Desert, the Harquahala Plain area was thought to be ideal for men suffering from respiratory illness. But nobody considered the area's abysmal lack of water, an average of 6 inches of rain or less per year. Consequently, by 1945 the drought-stricken Harquahala Valley had, according to Norris, become "a paragon of bleakness" for many who had come to homestead it.

Looking out over the lush Harquahala Valley today, however, you'll see that modern irrigation has changed all that. Lush fields of deep cotton now thrive where only the creosote bush once grew. Unfortunately for the U.S. farmers and Mexican migrant laborers who have wrested the Harquahala Plain from that "paragon of bleakness," it's only a matter of time before their rural farming community—and others like it elsewhere throughout western Arizona—will become water ranches for the artificial greenbelts and desert lakes now demanded by Phoenix and Scottsdale.

In his astounding *Cadillac Desert: The American West and Its Disappearing Water,* author Marc Reisner wrote: "To *really* experience the desert you have to march right into its white bowl of sky and shape-contouring heat with your mind on your canteen as if it were your last. . . . You have to imagine what it'd be like to drink blood from a lizard or, in the grip of dimentia, claw bare-handed through sand and rock for the vistigal moisture beneath a dry wash."

Gazing west out across the Haka-Whatapa's endless ancestral lands from high atop Eagletail Peak, you can easily see that it will only be a matter of time before modern man claws bare-handed through the desert again. And he won't be able to say he hadn't been warned.

Travel Notes

•**Suggested equipment.**   A helmet, two 150-foot ropes, slings, and small to medium-sized nuts.

•**Primary access.**   Via the V-notch from Granite Mountain Wash.

•**Total elevation gain and loss.**   1,800 vertical feet each way.

•**Mileage.** Approximately 6 miles round-trip.

•**Water.** No perennial water en route. Water can be found seasonally in V-notch tinajas, but it should be used only in emergency and otherwise left undisturbed for desert bighorn.

•**Cache points.** V-notch and Eagletail Saddle.

•**Escape routes.** Back the way you came via V-notch. Mountain rescue teams considering a litter rappel (stretcher) off of Eagletail Saddle as an alternative to making a carry along the Eagletail crest to V-notch should take into account that travel from the foot of Eagletail Saddle to your vehicle will be across the natural grain of the country.

•**Seasons.** Late fall through early spring.

•**Maps.** Eagletail Mountains and Cortez Peak quadrangles (15 minute).

•**Nearest supply points.** Harquahala Valley Store, Tonopah, and Phoenix.

•**Managing agency.** Bureau of Land Management.

•**Backcountry information.** Permit not required; firewood scarce.

•**Biotic communities.** Sonoran Desert scrub (lower Colorado subdivision and Arizona upland subdivision).

Granite Mountain

Granite Mountain Wilderness: hiking and rock climbing

Landform

Rising more than 2,000 vertical feet from base to summit, 7,626-foot-high Granite Mountain forms what looks like the northern terminus of the 7,180-foot-high Sierra Prietas ("black mountains"); in fact, on the 1882 Reconnaissance Map of Prescott, it was called Granite Peak and lumped together with the Sierra Prietas. In reality, however, Granite Mountain is a lone mountain comprising approximately 12 square miles; it is characterized by huge granite boulders and slabs and by a 500-foot-high southwest face of sweeping granite. Densely wooded with pinyon juniper and ponderosa pine, Granite Mountain is bordered on the north and east by the sprawling ranchlands of Williamson Valley, on the west by drainages of Skull Valley and Strickland washes, and on the northwest by the 7,272-foot-high Santa Maria Mountains.

Historical Overview

Granite Mountain's vivid early history was buried under the avalanche of newspaper accounts and books devoted to mineral discoveries in the nearby Bradshaw Mountains during the 1860s and to the day-to-day hubbub of the territorial capital (Prescott) and its military post of Fort Whipple. Established on Granite Creek shortly after the Walker party struck pay dirt (see entry for Senator Road), both Prescott and Fort Whipple grew out of the mile-high cul-de-sac formed by Granite Dells, Glassford Hill, the Bradshaw Mountains, the Sierra Prietas, and Granite Mountain. Taking a back seat to Prescott's founding landmark of 6,514-foot-high Thumb Butte, Granite Mountain sat within the transportation triangle formed by the Iron Springs leg of the Prescott-to-Phoenix stage route, the Aitchison Topeka and Santa Fe Railroad, and the Williamson Valley Road. Other than the "Apaches," and the Indian scouts who tracked them, few people had reason to visit what amounted to a natural fortress. The sketchy early accounts of those visits that do exist provide few clues as to what the Indians and their white adversaries experienced while traveling through Granite Mountain's rugged domain of rock and brush. In *Al Sieber: Chief of Scouts*, historian Dan L. Thrapp wrote of one long day famed Indian tracker Al Sieber and his men spent riding back and forth across central Arizona looking for Indian sign:

> On the fifteenth [of December, 1873], Schuyler moved south a mile to a tributary of Sycamore Creek, followed it downstream a short distance, then crossed over to Badger Creek, and sent Jose with some Indians to scout Granite Mountain and Sieber five miles down Badger Creek, but neither found anything. That was the story of Arizona scouting in this period: scores of miles of the most backbreaking work, and if any sign at all was uncovered, you were lucky, so elusive was the enemy. It was discouraging.

If cutting sign on hard rock in the vicinity of Granite Mountain was discouraging for Indian scouts like Sieber (who, according to Thrapp, "took part in more Indian fights than Daniel Boone, Jim Bridger, and Kit Carson together"), actually finding an Indian in someplace like Granite Mountain was next to impossible. Indians on the run from bloodthirsty troops knew this and took advantage of the area's granite strongholds, hiding in nearby Granite Dells. In *Argonaut Tales: Stories of the Gold Seekers and the Indian Scouts of Early Arizona*, Edmund Wells wrote:

> Rice, comin' up, pulled an arrer from one of the steers and discovered from the feathers and the marks it were a Apache-Mohave arrer. So

he made up his mind that the Indians was Apache-Mohaves and would at once git back to their country, and in going' there would go through the Point of Rocks [Granite Dells] and Granit Mountain. . . . Now you know, Captain, them rocks is some rocks. They cover several miles in acres, and tiny valleys, with streams of water running' through 'em. Some of the rocks and boulders as big as houses are scattered around and there are reefs and cliffs of rocks as big as young hills. Oak and cedar trees and brush grow in these little valleys and over the boulders and from the cracks and crevices of the cliffs, affordin' powerful places for Injuns to hide and put up a strong fight. Then agin, you know this Point of Rocks is the main crossin' place for the Apaches between the north and south sections of the country. The Walapais and other northern Injuns when goin' south to visit and trade with the southern Injuns pass thru Granit Mountain and the rollin' hills covered with timber and brush, to the Point of Rocks, and then thru the Rocks to the mountains to the south [most likely the Bradshaw Mountains]. The Tontos and Pinals and other southern Injuns goin' north pass thru the same points.

The best clues about the ancestral lands of the Yavepe, Northeastern Yavapai Indians, come from archaeologists like Connie L. Stone. Stone reported that the Yavepe were actually divided into two regional bands: The Wikenichapa, or Crown King band, were believed to occupy the southern half of the Bradshaws and range southward into the Sonoran Desert; and the Wikutepa, or Granite Peak band, occupied a territory that ranged from Granite Mountain southward across the Sierra Prietas into the northern end of the Bradshaw Mountains. In *People of the Desert, Canyons, and Pines,* Stone wrote of the seasonal journeys that the Wikutepa made in order to gather food; one particular trek Stone described would, under the best of conditions, be an arduous 60-mile journey across the rugged Bradshaws: "In mid-June, groups made a long journey to Cave Creek in the Southeastern Yavapai Territory. After remaining there for the two weeks of the early saguaro harvest, they returned north, harvesting saguaro fruits and mesquite along the way. In late summer and early autumn, they harvested manzanita berries, acorns, walnuts, and juniper berries in the Granite Peak area." Stone also reported that "spirits . . . were said to inhabit Granite Peak," indicating that the Wikutepa may have considered Granite Mountain sacred.

No doubt, Arizona's Indians developed their own style of mountaineering, among other reasons, to elude military troops in the vicinity of Granite Mountain and elsewhere across territorial Arizona. Archaeological evidence found elsewhere in the southwest in the form of cliff dwellings, "Moki steps," precarious footbridges, granaries, and other cliff-borne artifacts indicate that many early Native Americans were strong, fearless rock climbers; one can only imagine where they might have climbed on Arizona's foremost climbing crag.

But things didn't actually get nailed down on Granite Mountain until the late 1960s and early 1970s, which were the formative years of Prescott College and its nationally acclaimed Outdoor/Action and Adventure/Discovery programs. Largely developed by Britons Roy Smith and Rusty Baillie, and patterned after England's Outward Bound Program, Prescott College's outdoor programs were tailored to college students with aspirations—and achievements—ranging from sea kayaking the entire Gulf Coast of the Baja Peninsula to making successful ascents of 20,320-foot-high Mount McKinley in Alaska and 17,058-foot-high Mount Kenya in Africa. But few students left for Baja, or for the "dark continent," without first being introduced to climbing through the school's 3-week-long wilderness initiation program, called Orientation, and later through intensive, monthlong courses in rock climbing, mountain rescue, and winter mountaineering. Most rock climbing and related courses were taught in part on Granite Mountain and nearby Granite Dells, and as a result, many of the area's first ascents were made by Prescott College professors and students.

Most prolific among these climbers, perhaps, were instructor Rusty Baillie and student David Lovejoy (who now teaches). Baillie had a formidable list of climbing achievements before he ever set foot on Granite Mountain, including ascents of the deadly North Face of the Eiger in Switzerland and of Norway's ice-plastered, largely overhanging, mile-high Troll Wall. Lovejoy took part in so many high-standard first ascents on Granite Mountain that he literally wrote the book on it; called *Granite Mountain: A Pocket Guide to Rock Climbing in Granite Basin*, this classic guide (unfortunately out of print) included detailed descriptions of the first fifty-odd routes put up the southwest face of Granite Mountain. At the time the book was first published in 1973, Lovejoy and Baillie, together with Flagstaff-based climbers Scott Baxter and Karl Karlstrom, were responsible for many of the first ascents on the mountain and formed the core of what was then known as the Syndicato Granitica. Classic among their routes (which ranged from moderate and well protected to difficult face-, crack-, and aid-climbs) were the Beginner, Hassayampa, Magnolia Thunder Pussy, Coatimundi Whiteout, Candyland, "The Good, the Bad, and the Ugly," The Classic, Dream Weaver, Bleak Streak, and Jump Back Jack Crack.

Perhaps most noteworthy of the Syndicato's achievements was the difficult and dangerous "Dragon Route" that the four made up Colorado's imposing Painted Wall in the Black Canyon of the Gunnison River in 1973, a grade VI, 5.9, A-4, that took 9 days of oftentimes desperate climbing to complete. With their successful ascent, the group proved—as did successive waves of Prescott College students—that rock-climbing skills honed on Granite Mountain could successfully be used to push the frontiers of climbing around the globe.

But putting up bold new routes on Granite Mountain wasn't just the work of Syndicato members, or of Prescott College students; Jonathan Bjorklund and Phoenix climber Larry Trieber, together with their climbing partners, were responsible for developing many of the mountain's other early routes, including Green Dagger, Said and Done, Cats Pajamas, The Nose, and Granite Jungle, to name a few. Now, two decades later, climbers from all over the United States come to test their skills on the mountain's immaculate, sun-drenched, granite wall. Fortunately, the heart of this pristine climbing sanctuary has been officially protected under the 9,700-acre Granite Mountain Wilderness.

Directions
From the Courthouse Square in downtown Prescott, drive west on Gurley several blocks to Grove Avenue; turn north on Grove Avenue, which becomes Miller Valley Road. Continue north on Miller Valley Road to the strangest intersection this side of Times Square; turn left (west) on Iron Springs Road and follow the route of the old Prescott-to-Phoenix stage 3 miles to the turnoff for Granite Basin Lake. Turn right and follow the Granite Basin Road, USFS Road 374, a little more than 5 miles to the Granite Mountain Trailhead No. 261.

Granite Mountain Trail Log
For nonclimbers. If you're not a rock climber, don't let that prevent you from taking one of the prettiest hikes in the Prescott National Forest. From the Granite Mountain Trailhead to Blair Pass, Trail No. 261 parallels a mile-long leg of Granite Creek. It's usually dry, but during one freak October monsoon several years ago, climbing instructor David Lovejoy and a group of Prescott College students were reportedly marooned near the trailhead by a flash flood that swept down Granite Mountain. It was estimated to run as high as 27,000 cfs, reportedly pinned down the experienced wilderness travelers overnight, and completely buried a pickup truck and house trailer that other campers had parked nearby in a "dry" wash.

From Blair Pass, turn right and head up toward Granite Mountain Saddle on Trail No. 261; the Climbers Trail to the foot of the main wall turns out of a switchback off this well-maintained trail less than half a mile from Blair Pass. For hikers, it's another mile to Granite Mountain Saddle, and a mile beyond that to fine views from the ponderosa-pine-covered summit at 7,185 feet.

Climber's Approach

When you first pull into the Granite Mountain parking lot, the quickest way to the foot of the wall appears to be cross-country from your vehicle. It's not that far; besides, you can warm up by bouldering most of the way to your first climb. Right? If you get sucked into this character-building option, be sure to wear long pants and a long-sleeved shirt; take plenty of water and a long stick to move the rattlesnakes out of the way; and don't forget your headlamp, just in case you don't make it back to your vehicle by Miller Time.

For those who prefer the standard climber's approach, turn off at Trail No. 261 less than half a mile above Blair Pass; the Climber's Trail turns right (east) out of a switchback, crosses a small drainage, then climbs abruptly to the foot of the main wall. Sections of steep, nonmaintained trail lead the way between boulder piles, while cairns guide you around and over them. Be attentive along ths route, both for its course and for rattlesnakes in season.

The Southwest Face

The Swamp Slabs.   Undoubtedly named for the water that streams down this lowly face during snowmelt and summer monsoons, the Swamp Slabs comprise the western portion of Granite Mountain's southwest face and range from 150 feet to 300-plus feet high. Whether you're a beginning rock climber just learning how to lead, or an old-timer who's had his shoes in the mothballs too long, the Swamp Slabs area is the perfect place to warm up before moving on to more challenging routes on the main cliff. Starting on its uppermost end with a crack- and face-climb called The Beginner (5.4), you can work your way right around Swamp Slabs and move up incrementally to solid, well-protected routes like Debut (5.5), Greenhorns and Weenie Roast (5.6), and Tread Gently (5.7). Of all the routes on the Swamp Slabs, the 4-pitch crack-and-groove climb called Weenie Roast has one of the most underrated last pitches on Granite Mountain; although it's rated a weeny 5.6, grown men have been seen whimpering on its interesting finish.

Middle Section. Lovejoy calls this part of the Southwest Face, from Tread Gently (5.7) east to the start of The Classic (5.7), the Middle Section — and it offers the longest, most challenging routes on the mountain. Beginning with 5.6 routes like the Magician and Chim Chimney and the enlightening roof traverse at the top of Hassayampa (5.8), highlights of the Middle Section include the crotch-ripping first pitch on Magnolia Thunder Pussy (5.8 or 5.9, depending on how tall you are), the life-saving oak tree on Green Saviour (5.8), the Big Wall–style Sorcerer (5.10-plus), the must-do multiple pitch lines like Coatimundi Whiteout (5.8) and Candyland (5.9), and, finally, the best aid-climb on the Mountain, "The Good, the Bad, and the Ugly" (Grade III, A-3, 5.3).

Right side. Even if you don't climb any other route on the mountain, you must climb The Classic; rated Grade II, 5.7, The Classic was first climbed in 1968 by Scott Baxter, Karl Karlstrom, and Lee Dexter, and it represents the best of what the Southwest Face has to offer, from well-protected chimney- and crack-climbing to its breathtaking finish called High Exposure Exit. According to climber and writer Larry Coats, the blank face that the last pitch of The Classic traverses "had eluded several strong attempts when in January of '71, [Phoenix climber] Erik Powell, on his first trip to the Mountain, spied the aid bolts of earlier parties. Assuming the slab went free, Erik edged his way past the bolts and led on to the top of the wall, producing High Exposure Exit." Leading High Exposure Exit for the first time in a 35-mile-per-hour wind — without getting blown off — will bring out your fly-on-the-wall skills. But The Classic, with its High Exposure finish, is only a taste of the other exciting routes that lie east of it. Try finessing The Coke Bottle (5.7), or polish your finger- and toenails on the immaculate face of Bleak Streak (5.8), or wrestle and grunt your way up Jump Back Jack Crack (5.10), or dance up any of the lines that fall in between.

Ad-infinitum. There are so many fine and difficult new routes in between these classic lines that you should get a copy of Jim Waugh's *A Topo Guide to Granite Mountain* and contact David Lovejoy to see if he either has reprinted *Granite Mountain* or is currently distributing photocopies of the guide. Write to David Lovejoy, c/o Prescott College, 220 Grove Avenue, Prescott, AZ 86301.

In *Argonaut Tales*, Edmund Wells painted an enduring picture of Granite Mountain: "Looking off to the east, the full round moon hanging in the cloudless sky, had climbed up over the highest peaks. . . . In the background stands rough and rugged Granite Mountain pushing its bald peak into the

Rock climber Tony Mangine devotes all his attention to the next thin move on The Classic's "High Exposure Exit." Photo by John Annerino.

upper clouds, its sides and slopes beset with crags, immense boulders and steep faces of cliffs, spotted with the green of cedar and pine trees hanging in the air like miniature groves and parks."

   As of this writing, the Prescott National Forest had issued a permit to pulverize Granite Mountain for the few odd grains of gold they hope to find. So be sure to come see 'rough and rugged Granite Mountain' before the town fathers allow one of Prescott's greatest treasures to be turned into a slag heap.

Travel Notes
• **Mileage.**

   Granite Mountain Summit: Approximately 3½ miles each way.
   Climbing Area: Approximately 2 miles each way.

• **Elevation gain.**

   Granite Mountain Summit: 2,000-plus feet to summit 7,626.

Climbing Area: 1,500 feet from the trailhead to the top of the face (of which 150 to 500 feet will be up the face).

• **Water.**   No perennial water en route; snowmelt in season.

• **Emergencies.**   For climbers, there's a litter on the mountain near the Front Porch; while the rock on Granite Mountain is probably the best in Arizona, you should acquaint yourself with its location. For rescues, contact Yavapai County Sheriff's Department (911) or Prescott College (778-2090).

• **Nearest supply point.**   Prescott.

• **Managing agency.**   Prescott National Forest.

• **Backcountry information.**   Permits not required.

• **Biotic communities.**   Montane conifer forest, juniper pinyon woodland, and interior chaparral.

Northern Arizona

Car Tours

The Perkinsville Road

Jerome to Williams

Landform

The paved northern half of the 47-mile-long Perkinsville Road begins at the 6,783-foot level near Williams and, like nearby Sycamore Canyon, which it parallels, slides off the forested western end of the Mogollon Rim; after bottoming out at the Verde River 3,000 feet below, the rugged southern half of this old wagon road crawls back up the steep northern flanks of 7,834-foot-high Woodchute Mountain and tops out in the historic mining town of Jerome at 5,400 feet.

Historical Overview

Antonio de Espejo's sixteenth-century prospecting expedition to the vicinity of Jerome was a bust (see entry for Sycamore Canyon, Central Arizona), but that didn't prevent a mining boomtown of fifteen thousand from being hacked into the side of Woodchute Mountain 300 years later; in its heyday, four groceries, six lodging houses, eleven restaurants, seventeen watering holes, and umpteen cathouses clamored to serve the needs of fever-struck prospectors who, when the dust finally settled 72 years later, had dug up a reported $800 million in copper, gold, and silver ore. Once the richest copper mine in the world, the Billion Dollar Copper Camp was, according to Jerome historian James W. Brewer, Jr., a place "of hard rock, hard work, hard liquor and hard play."

One of the hardest jobs facing the United Verde Copper Company was getting its rich ore to market. The solution, in 1894, was in the construction of the United Verde and Pacific Railroad. For reasons that will become apparent as soon as you venture along the historic bed of this narrow-gauge railroad, the United Verde and Pacific earned a reputation as "the crookedest railroad in the United States."

But the "crookedest railroad in the United States," and the hard dollars that grubstaked it, only account for the southern half of the Perkinsville Road; the story behind the northern half had more to do with tourists and timber. Established in the 1880s as a lumber and railroad town, Williams was named after Bill Williams, a mountain man whom few people actually saw and who, as legend had it, was forced to eat his knife scabbard and leather gun case during a grueling midwinter trek to New Mexico. Hard to swallow? That depends on how hungry you've been. The fact is, Williams soon became known as the "Gateway to the Grand Canyon" because its Grand Canyon Railroad Company carted tourists to the South Rim for a fraction of what it cost to make the same journey by stage. In *The Story of Man at the Grand Canyon*, writer and historian J. Donald Hughes wrote: "The first scheduled train to travel from Williams to the Grand Canyon made its historic trip on September 17, 1901. . . . A relatively smooth rail journey of less than three hours, costing $3.95, replaced the jouncing all-day stage ride which cost $20."

To maintain Williams' reputation as a stepping-stone to one of the Seven Natural Wonders of the World, the Williams-Clarkdale cutoff was proposed. In a February 8, 1921, letter to S. L. Williams, Chairman of the Grand Canyon–Phoenix Highway Committee, the U.S. Forest Service endorsed the original 1919 proposal to build the Williams-to-Clarkdale Road. Among other reasons the proposal cited, "the road would mean more people from the south motoring to the Grand Canyon, where they can either camp or secure hotel accommodations." At the time, the route from Clarkdale to Williams was 115 miles over a rough wagon road; the Williams-Clarkdale Road would shave 67 miles off that circuitous journey. By the time it was finally completed 15 years later, it would also open up the largest stand of virgin ponderosa pine in the Tusayan District

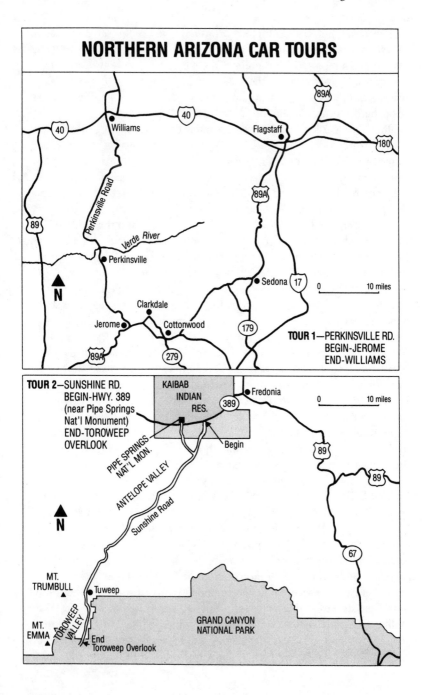

NORTHERN ARIZONA CAR TOURS

of the Kaibab National Forest to logging, and provide residents of the Verde River Valley with a more direct means to escape its blistering summers.

Pickup Truck Country. That the southern half of the Perkinsville Road was never paved stems from the fact—as one Arizona Highway Patrolman pointed out—that it lies in another county altogether (Yavapai, not Coconino), and that the funds Yavapai County originally allocated for the project were reportedly reappropriated. It's a good thing, too; otherwise, you'd be jockeying for position like a water spider on another narrow State Scenic Route crowded with lumbering road whales (RVs). As it now stands, the southern half of the Perkinsville Road is ideal pickup-truck country. There's just something about driving this lonesome dirt track in a pickup that brings out the wild blue yonder in all of us. As Detroit and Japan have long since learned, a pickup is the one link most Americans still have with their romantic vision of the Old West: when a cowboy rode horseback through belly-deep snow, skin-burning heat, and blood-curdling lightning storms chasing "doggies" into the next crimson sunset; when he rolled out his bed under star-filled heavens and was serenaded to sleep by a crackling mesquite fire and howling coyotes; and, just to get the outfit going before sunup again, when he sucked down boiled black coffee so strong it felt like it was going to burn a hole in his stomach "big enough to throw a cat through." Few one-lane adventures will get you back in the saddle of those horseback days, short of mounting up better than the Perkinsville Road.

Directions
From Jerome, the Perkinsville Road begins at the first hairpin turn climbing out of town. The spot is marked by a candy-apple red 1928 4WD flatbed truck "used to plow snow from Prescott to Crown King on the Senator Highway until the 1940s."

Road Log
Begin. Like few other roads in Arizona, this turnoff will lead you across a fairy-tale mural of peaks, mesas, and canyons that has mesmerized people since they first started hanging a mining town off the side of Woodchute Mountain in the late 1800s, back when the cyclorama formed by the San Francisco Mountains, the Mogollon Rim, Sycamore Canyon, and the Verde River Valley was simply called "The Million Dollar View." Except possibly during summer monsoons and winter snows, you won't really need a pickup to drive through this Million Dollar View; if you're careful, a four-door with good

rubber will make the grade. But just in case a gully washer hits the next hairpin before you do, pack a shovel. Stuff your picnic basket full of good grub, like the deep-dish apple cobbler or the Southern bar-b-qued ribs you can get down on Main Street at the Candy Kitchen Cafe. And don't forget your map, a thermos full of stout coffee, and your honey.

Mile 0 to 1. From Big Red, follow the Gold King Mine signs up the pavement and across the tracks to the Gold King Mine and Museum, open seven days a week, "9:00 A.M. till people quit coming." Stop and take the nickel tour of the mine and its huge 1894 stamp mill. If you've arrived in Jerome too late to head out on the Perkinsville Road, you can bed down for the night at the nearby Ghost Town Campground. But if the wild blue yonder still calls, head back to the Gold King Mine intersection marked by a sign with a prospector trying to jump off of it. Hang a left there and snake your way up the first couple of switchbacks. For all practical purposes, this is the original line of the United Verde and Pacific Railroad, constructed in 1893 to haul ore to the Santa Fe railhead at Prescott.

Mile 6. Six miles out from Jerome, you should have a pretty fair idea why the United Verde and Pacific Railroad was nicknamed "the crookedest railroad in the world." You'll have squeezed through the first of three one-lane bridges between Jerome and Williams and seesawed through many of the old narrow gauge's 126 curves before coming to a roadrunner stop at the marked road cut gouged into this steep, fluted arm of Woodchute. This first stretch is also the official 10-kilometer course for the Jerome Hill Climb held each August for fleet-footed lizards who like nothing better than running uphill as fast as they can in the summer heat.

If you're not a runner, look beyond the golden bear grass sweeping the breeze and the century plants poking their gnarly stalks at the blue sky, and gaze at the summit of Woodchute. Now imagine what it looked and sounded like when 30-foot sections of ponderosa pine logs came thundering down off the top of Woodchute and barreled into Jerome 5 miles and several thousand feet below; those logs were used to stoke Jerome's smelters.

Mile 6 to 7.6. Slip through the portal beyond the Road Cut into the yawning embrace of Horseshoe Canyon—an apt description for this section of the Perkinsville Road as it careens through 45-degree turns down and around the lower flanks of Woodchute past USFS Road Junction 155 to Junction 318A. (If you veer west on 318A, you can pick up Woodchute Trail No. 102 at Sheep Camp and hike 3 steep miles to the northern summit of 5,700-acre Woodchute Mountain Wilderness, which offers the most spectacular view of the Verde River Valley.)

Mile 7.6 to 15.5. From the junction of 318A, the highest mountain you see on the western horizon is the 9,341-foot-high juggernaut of Bill Williams Mountain; it marks your destination in Williams. And as you sled down the north side of Woodchute on USFS Road 318, you should also be able to pick out (left to right) cone-shaped Kendrick Peak; the rolling, hog-tied mass of Sitgreaves Mountain; the delicate summit crest of the San Francisco Mountains; and the dark, gaping mouth of Oak Creek Canyon etched into the southern brink of the Coconino Plateau. Even if you can't identify each of these northern Arizona landmarks, you'll feel as though you're driving through an oil painting, with the pinyon and juniper brushed onto the landscape with the stroke of Gauguin.

Mile 15 to 18.5. About 1876 a Montana prospector named James Baker built himself a ranch with ten thousand head of cattle and settled the area now grazed by the Perkins Ranch; USFS Road 318 ends at that ranch, which in 1925 was called Perkinsville. Here you can pick up USFS Road 354, head past the picket-post corral, and creep across a one-lane steel bridge. According to the National Register of Historic Places, the Perkinsville Bridge was originally called the San Carlos Bridge, because when the multispan truss was first built in 1913, it spanned the Gila River 250 miles southwest of here. But a flood in 1915 washed out part of the bridge, and 2 decades later, sections of it were re-erected across the Verde River and Walnut Creek under a Forest Service labor project designed to employ a "vast army of unemployed transients." According to the Historic American Buildings Survey, the Perkinsville Bridge and the Walnut Creek Bridge "are technologically noteworthy as the earliest examples in the state of one of the most common vehicular truss type [bridges] built in America."

Bear left after you cross the cottonwood-tree-lined Verde River, cross the Santa Fe railroad tracks (which still serve as a vital link between Flagstaff and Prescott), and start climbing the westernmost escarpment of the Mogollon Rim (which splices northern and central Arizona like a slip in the earth's crust). If you look to your right, you can see the neopolitan cross section of red and white limestones stained by Supai Sandstone, which forms the craggy mouth of Verde River Canyon immediately below the Perkins Ranch.

Mile 18.5 to 23.8. About 3.5 miles out from the Verde River you'll get into the kind of country you know you should be hiking—or riding horseback—through, chasing your dreams into another pinyon-studded sunset. There's a turnoff here, marked USFS Road 181, which, 13 miles later, will take you to the stone-silent western entrance of the Sycamore Canyon Wilderness Area. If you don't plan to explore Sycamore this trip, stay on

USFS Road 354 as it crosses the mouth of Government Canyon and saunters up to the Sand Flat turnoff 2.5 miles beyond. Hang yet another left onto USFS Road 492, breeze past Mexican Quarry Tank, bounce across the only two-lane bridge on the Perkinsville Road, and stay on Road 492 until you reach the redtop pavement.

Mile 23.8 to 39.3. Cruising up the redtop through bristling green stands of Ponderosa will seem like winged flight after galloping across the outback for the last couple of hours. But don't turn on your radar detector just yet. An unmarked scenic pullout 15.5 miles up the pavement looks back all the way to Jerome on the route you've just driven. So get out, stretch your legs, suck in the crisp mountain air, and take a little time to scan the horizon for Woodchute Mountain, the Bradshaws, the lights of Prescott (if it's near sundown), and hulking Granite Mountain.

Mile 41.4. Summertime, the Whitehorse Lake turnoff 2.1 miles beyond this scenic vista is a good road into the heart of the South Kaibab National Forest. You can spend the night camping on this 60-acre lake and listening to the frogs croak before you explore the headwaters of Sycamore Canyon Wilderness Area the next day. Paradise Forks, as it's known to Flagstaff area climbers, offers hundreds of crack climbs on columnar basalt.

Mile 45.5 to 47.1. Wintertime, though, you can turn off the redtop 4.5 miles beyond the Whitehorse Lake junction and downhill or cross-country ski at the Benham Snow Play Area before skidding into Williams for a hot toddy and a cozy bed.

Travel Notes

• **Primary access.** Via Jerome or Williams.

• **Mileage.** 47.1 (paved road for 23 miles; dirt, 24-plus miles).

• **Traveling time.** 3 to 4 hours.

• **Seasons.** Spring through fall are best.

• **Maps.** South Kaibab and Prescott National Forest Recreation Maps.

• **Nearest supply points.** Clarkdale, Jerome, and Williams.

• **Managing agencies.** U.S. Forest Service.

• **Biotic communities.** Plains and desert grassland, interior chaparral, juniper pinyon woodland, and montane conifer forest.

Sunshine Road

The Arizona Strip, Pipe Springs National Monument to Toroweap Overlook

Landform

The 60-mile-long Sunshine Road traverses the loneliest, most desolate corner of land in Arizona – the untamed, 11,000-square-mile Arizona Strip. Four natural barriers have virtually cordoned off the northwest corner of the state from the rest of modern Arizona: Marble Canyon and Echo Cliffs form what once was an impenetrable double-border to the east, while the long, broken walls of Vermilion Cliffs form a more hospitable border to the north; to the west, Grand Wash Cliffs and the 8,012-foot-high Virgin Mountains plug the gap between Arizona and Nevada, and to the south lies the most formidable barrier of all, the Grand Canyon of the Colorado River. Few highways breach any of these colossal landforms; the ones that do either go by way of Nevada or practically take you to Utah before bringing you back to Arizona.

Still home to an estimated three thousand people, this Massachusetts-sized corner of Arizona is comprised of four major plateaus: East to west, they are the Kaibab, Kanab, Uinkaret, and Shivwits. The Sunshine Road follows a natural depression formed by Antelope and Toroweap valleys between the Kanab and Uinkaret plateaus, and ends abruptly at the edge of the Grand Canyon. This end, known as Toroweap Overlook, is the most isolated vista of the Grand Canyon, but it's also one of the most spectacular.

Historical Overview

One of the earliest recorded traverses of the Arizona Strip via this approximate route was made by Maj. John Wesley Powell September 14–22, 1870. Ostensibly, Powell had two pressing reasons for exploring what he described as "that difficult region": He wanted to investigate the fate of Seneca and O. G. Howland and William Dunn, three men who had abandoned his first Colorado River expedition at Separation Canyon in 1869; and he wanted to explore the possibility of establishing resupply caches for his second expedition down the Colorado River in 1871. (See entry for Colorado River.)

However, while Powell was a respected explorer, adventurer, and mapmaker in his own right, he hired Mormon missionary Jacob Hamblin to act as his liaison with the local Paiute Indian guides who would lead them through this uncharted region. Of those guides Powell wrote: "I have prided myself on being able to grasp and retain in my mind the topography of a country, but these Indians put me to shame. . . . they know every rock and ledge, every gulch and cañon." Powell was describing the Kaibabbits, or Kaibab Paiutes, one of several bands of southern Paiute Indians who survived on their austere ancestral lands largely through horticulture, hunting, and gathering. Without the Kaibabbit's intimate knowledge of this expansive terrain—and its precious hidden water pockets, known as tinajas in central and southern Arizona—it's doubtful that Powell would have survived the 60-mile return trip from the Colorado River to the last reliable waterhole of Pipe Springs.

Following an ancient track that roughly parallels much of the Sunshine Road, Powell's group took 3 days to reach the rim of the Grand Canyon west of Toroweap Overlook. There the Kaibabbits talked long into the night of an Indian legend, *The So-kus Wai-un-ats*. It was a mythical dream within a dream, and of it Powell recalled: "When they had journeyed two days and were far out on the desert all the people thirsted, for they found no water, and they fell down upon the sand groaning and murmuring that they had been deceived, and they cursed the One-Two."

Foreshadowing his own journey ahead, Powell and his men dropped off the rim of the Canyon early the next morning and headed down to the Colorado River somewhere below Lava Rapids, perhaps via Whitmore Canyon. En route the old Paiute Indian, who Powell described as a "withered guide, the human pickle," led them to a water pocket so rank the horses wouldn't even drink from it. Soon the descent became so difficult that they had to tie up their horses in order to continue. But the black pall of night fell upon them long before they reached the river, so Powell and his men uprooted agave and used them as torches to light the rest of the way. By the time they finally reached the booming Colorado River, they were half-starved and exhausted; they "fell down upon the sand" and gulped the same waters that had nearly done in his expedition the year before. If his second Colorado River expedition needed to be resupplied, a now-weary Powell surmised, the Kaibabbits could be hired to make the food drop for them.

Powell's thirst-ravaged adventure was only beginning. Early the next morning he found a trail back to the horses. But after being hobbled all night without water, the horses were, as Powell wrote, "mad with thirst"—so thirsty that when the party later reached the putrid water pocket it had passed up the day before, the horses now eagerly drank the same scum. For some reason, Powell didn't carry any water, or at least not enough, back up from the Colorado River to get all the way out of the canyon. After watering the horses, he wrote, "We carefully strained a kettle for ourselves. . . . We boiled our kettle of water and skimmed it; straining, boiling and skimming made it a little better, and plenty of coffee took away the bad odor, and so modified the taste that most of us could drink it. Our little Indian, however, seemed to prefer the original mixture."

Powell's 'little Indian' no doubt saved his life, and those of his men; though he didn't even acknowledge it. Obviously, it was a close call because they took September 19 off to recuperate, and that night held a council around a roaring fire among Powell, his interpreter, Jacob Hamblin, the Kaibab-bits, and the Shivwits band of Paiutes. Yes, the Shivwits admitted, they had killed Powell's three men the summer before; in fact, they had riddled them with arrows—but only after an Indian from the other side of the river had told the Shivwits that several drunken miners had killed one of their women. Since no Indians had seen anyone else come down the river, they could only assume that Powell's men were responsible.

But Powell learned something else that evening. Incredibly, he could now trust his life to these very "murderers." Said their chief: "When you are hungry you may have our game. You may gather our sweet fruit. We will give you food when you come to our land. We will show you the springs and you may drink."

Directions
From Pipe Springs National Monument, drive 5.1 miles east on Highway 389 to a well-marked turnoff on the right; this turnoff is 6 miles west of Fredonia.

Pipe Springs National Monument Road Log
When Powell first rode into Pipe Springs via an Indian trail on September 13, 1870, he said, the Indians knew it as "Yellow Rock Water." To Mormon militiamen who fortified themselves from those same Indians by building an adobe fort there in 1868, it was called Pipe Springs. From the dawn of civilization, this historic way station has been the most dependable water source for anyone journeying across the Arizona Strip. And to this day, Pipe Springs National Monument—which, in a deft twist of fate, the Kaibab Paiutes now lease to the white man—still makes the best jumping-off spot for your own adventures across the Arizona Strip.

Mile 0 to 2.2. Highway 389 to Two Seeps Wash. You'll be driving south across Antelope Valley, a vast sweep of Great Basin desert scrub devoid of any real surprises except for fleeting glimpses of pronghorn antelope.

When Powell ended his second expedition down the Colorado River at the mouth of Kanab Creek in 1872, he planned to map the rest of the Grand Canyon by descending to the river from the rim above. While Powell did return to the area in 1875, the mapping wasn't completed until 1881, by Powell's protégé, Clarence E. Dutton. Dutton became a renowned cartographer for producing a remarkable report on his travels through the region in 1871–1872, called the *Tertiary History of the Grand Canyon District, With Atlas.* One of Dutton's own routes closely parallels that of the modern Sunshine Road to the brink of the Grand Canyon; shortly after leaving Pipe Springs, he noted: "To the southward stretches the desert, blank, lifeless, and expressionless as the sea." From a nineteenth-century cartographer's perspective that may have been true, but today many points interest the experienced desert traveler. For one, you can still make out 8,029-foot-high Mount Trumbull 50 miles to the southwest, and to the southeast you can readily see the great Kaibab Plateau, just as Dutton noted it more than a century ago.

Mile 2.2.   Two Seeps Wash. Dutton made no mention of this seemingly inconsequential wash, but several miles below the road it becomes Bitter Seeps Wash, which drains into Kanab Creek.

Mile 7.7.   Bulrush Wash. According to the 1913 paper "The Arizona Strip: Report of Reconnoissance of the Country North of the Grand Canyon," former president William Howard Taft made Bulrush Wash a public watering place; that may explain the dilapidated wooden bridge on the left side of the road at this milepost. What's of greater interest is the fact that Bulrush Wash becomes Burnt Canyon several miles below this rustic trestle. Bitter Seeps Wash and Burnt Canyon both drain Pipe Valley, which lies immediately to the west of the road. And from this vantage point approximately 7 miles southwest of what was once the last outpost of Pipe Springs, it seems only natural that prospectors who rushed down to the Colorado River during the 1872 gold rush used either Bitter Seeps Wash or Burnt Canyon—or both—to get in and out of Kanab Creek. (See entry for Kanab Canyon.)

Mile 18.   Sunshine Ridge. After passing CCC Trail Reservoir, the road contours around the northern end of Sunshine Ridge. Wild Band Reservoir is located half a mile to the north. According to Dutton, "The Wild

Band pockets have received their name from the fact that they are the resort of bands of wild horses that roam over these deserts, far from human haunts, ranging from spring to spring, which they visit by stealth only at night." While Dutton made no mention of actually seeing wild horses at the Wild Band pockets, Frederick S. Dellenbaugh, an artist with the second Powell Expedition, reported that he had seen twenty wild steeds storming across the plains near here in 1872, some 10 years before Dutton first camped here.

From the Wild Band pockets, Dellenbaugh reported following a "moccasin trail" toward Mount Trumbull; once you turn south from this point the road follows the western foot of Sunshine Ridge all the way to the Hack Canyon turnoff. This historic—perhaps prehistoric—route to Mount Trumbull was first called the Sunshine Road in the "Report of Reconnoissance of the Country North of the Grand Canyon," and no doubt it took its name from 5,000-foot-high Sunshine Ridge.

Mile 20.3.   Hack Canyon Wilderness turnoff on the left. This road leads to one of the principal trailheads and tributaries of the Kanab Creek Wilderness. The Atomic Energy Commission reportedly first upgraded the Sunshine Road to an all-weather road as far as Hack Canyon during the uranium rush of the mid-1950s.

Mile 27.7.   Three-way Fork. Take the middle fork. The grass-and-lava-covered hills immediately to the north are 5,855-foot-high Findlay Knolls and 5,878-foot-high Heaton Knolls. Heaton Knolls take their name from the Heatons, a pioneer family who ranched Pipe Springs at the turn of the century.

Mile 37.8.   Aborigine Rock Pass. At this point, the road climbs over a small ridge covered with pinyon juniper. This may have been what Dutton described when he wrote: "Just before reaching the basaltic mesa we must make our choice between two routes to the Toroweap, the one direct, the other very circuitous." Certain of water at Witches Pool, Dutton chose the direct route; in doing so, he differed from Powell, who meandered to the edge of the Canyon and relied on water pockets on the opposite side of Mount Trumbull.

From this point on, the Sunshine Road heads south into Toroweap Valley along the western foot of Toroweap Cliffs, which form a great band of limestone cliffs to the east, while the dark, wooded flanks of Mount Trumbull hover above Toroweap Valley to the west. There's little doubt that Dutton's route followed this valley between Toroweap Cliffs and Mount

Trumbull, because he wrote, "The left side has become a wall 700 feet high, while the other side, somewhat lower, is much broken and craggy."

Mile 40.4. Mount Trumbull and Colorado City turnoff on the right. Sometimes called Short Creek, Colorado City has been a holdout for Mormon polygamists since the turn of the century.

Mile 43. An unnamed 5,921-foot hill a mile west of the Sunshine Road marks the vicinity of the Witches Water Pocket, perhaps the most storied pocket on the Arizona Strip. Dutton described the location perfectly when he wrote: "About a mile from the valley we find the Witches Water Pocket. In every desert the watering places are memorable, and this one is no exception. It is a weird spot. Around it are the desolate Phlegraean fields, where jagged masses of black lava still protrude through rusty, decaying cinders." When Dellenbaugh stopped there with Powell on November 5, 1872, a Kaibab Paiute named Chuar said the Indians called the waterhole Innupin (or Oonupin) because witches haunted the area. But that didn't stop anyone from drinking. Wrote Dellenbaugh: "The water in the pocket was clear and pure, but it was full of small 'wigglers.' We tried to dip up a pail which should be free from them. The Major, seeing our efforts, took a cup and without looking drank it down with the nonchalant remark, 'I haven't seen any wigglers.'"

Mile 46.7. Mount Trumbull turnoff on the right. Go left to reach Toroweap Overlook. Much of the early history of Mount Trumbull and the Uinkaret Mountains dates back to 1874 when Mormon lumbermen first logged the area in order to build a temple in Saint George, Utah. It took oxen teams 2 weeks to transport the lumber 80 miles over the Temple Trail to Saint George. Today the 7,900-acre Mount Trumbull Wilderness remains the smallest and most remote wilderness area in the state; yet it protects an untrammeled vista that has been admired since its first recorded ascent on September 22, 1870. Wrote Powell: "made a long hard climb to its summit. And there, oh!, what a view was before us. A vision of glory! Peaks of lava all around below us; the vermillion cliffs to the north, with their splendor of colors . . . and away beyond, the San Francisco Mountains lifting their black heads into the heavens." Two years later Dellenbaugh and three other men spent the night on the summit of Mount Trumbull after riding horses to the top. Like Powell, Dellenbaugh also wrote of the summit vista: "a magnificent view in every direction, as far to the south-east as Mount San Francisco." Today the 1.5-mile cross-country hike to the summit of Mount Trumbull still makes a memorable ascent.

The 14,600-acre Mount Logan Wilderness can also be reached via the Mount Trumbull Road; an enjoyable 1.5-mile cross-country route also leads to the summit of this ancient volcano.

Mile 48.7. Schmutz Ranch on the left. According to Elinor Lin Mrachek, "Grandpa and Grandma Schmutz, Marc and Annie, were the [area's] earliest homesteaders, 1914." The Schmutzes came from Switzerland and settled in the area while Mr. Schmutz was working as a sawyer on Mount Trumbull. Located below the mouth of Paradise Canyon, the Schmutz place looked as fine as any to settle in the Toroweap Valley.

Mile 53.2. Toroweap International Airport on the right, established on federal land by the Bureau of Land Management and National Park Ranger John Riffey. The airport has a dirt airstrip and no facilities.

Mile 53.6. Toroweap Ranger Station on the left. "It has been described as the wettest, coldest, hottest, driest place on earth—it sometimes seemed that way too." That's one of the ways the late John Riffey summed up life at Toroweap. He was speaking on camera to his niece, Elinor Lin Mrachek, who wrote and produced a documentary film for her master's thesis at Michigan State University in 1977, called "A Man and a Place: Park Ranger John Riffey at Tuweep, AZ." Riffey was speaking from experience; he lived at Tuweep, as Toroweap was then called by locals, for 38 years while working for the National Park Service. Established on December 22, 1932, Grand Canyon National Monument then comprised some 300 square miles north of the Colorado River and west of Kanab Creek. As the only park ranger, Riffey single-handedly patrolled this vast area from his lonely outpost in his Super Cub airplane he nicknamed Pogo. In 1951 Riffey was promoted to Superintendent of Grand Canyon National Monument. Yet, much to the chagrin of his superiors over at the South Rim, he seldom wore his uniform. According to Mrachek, one official NPS memo to Riffey said: "At least wear your hat." Riffey replied: "There isn't any way for a man to get down under a truck and fix the brakes with a Park Service hat on."

While Riffey rarely wore his official Smokey the Bear hat, but he was said to wear many others: from mechanic to administrator, from ambulance driver to pilot. When Grand Canyon National Monument was incorporated into the park in 1975, Riffey's title changed, but his job remained the same: managing the most rugged and spectacular section of the Arizona Strip—single-handedly. Riffey died at the age of 69 while hauling water from Nixon Springs at the foot of Mount Trumbull. Fortunately his niece had finished her master's thesis before he died; Mrachek's work is a fine history of both the man and the place.

Mile 54.7.   Lava Falls Trail turnoff on the right. This is your last chance to hike the steepest, blackest, and hottest trail in Arizona. Continue left and proceed to Toroweap Overlook.

Mile 60.   The Edge of the Brink. This is one of the only places in Grand Canyon National Park where you can get out of your car, lie on your belly, and stare over 3,200 feet straight down to the Colorado River. If the water looks sluggish here, that's because the river is pooled up behind the most famous rapid in North America. Lava Falls is located more than a mile downstream from Toroweap Overlook, but on a stone-silent day you can actually hear it. You can also hear the incessant drone of single- and twin-engine air-tour operators barnstorming this section of the Canyon not long after sunup each day—the only sound to interrupt the incomparable silence and solitude. Except for half a dozen primitive campsites, which may or may not be occupied, you will be alone to study the Canyon's most alluring features. To the east, you can make out 5,434-foot Mount Sinyala, first climbed by a University of California–Los Angeles team in 1958; it reigns over the ancestral lands of the Havasupai Indians. To the south . . . well . . . bring a map. Bring several. Specifically, bring the old Grand Canyon National Monument Map and the 1892 Reconnaissance Map of Mount Trumbull. Compare today's map with those used not long after Powell and Dutton charted the area and see if you can identify any features or landmarks that they might have missed.

Of this vantage point, Dutton wrote: "The scenery here becomes colossal." Come see for yourself. While here, try to pinpoint the spot 1,500 feet below Toroweap Overlook where Henry Covington hid one of his wives circa 1917. According to Mrachek: "Henry Covington, miner and polygamist, kept one of his wives in an old Indian cave near his mine. The cave, about ten feet deep, carved by wind and water erosion out of the red sandstone rock of the Esplanade, was large enough to hold a bed, stove, a small plank table, and a bench." Some honeymoon suite. Then again, Covington probably would have told you this isn't the South Rim. Standing alone on the edge of this canyon desert, you'll be glad it isn't . . . as long as you've brought enough water to make it back to Pipe Springs.

Travel Notes

• **Primary access.**   Via Highway 389, near Pipe Springs.

• **Secondary access.**   Via two primitive roads. Route 2 is 90 miles along the Temple Trail from Highway 91 near Saint George, Utah; Route 3 is 55 miles from Highway 389 near Colorado City.

- **Mileage.**   60 miles each way (improved dirt road for 54 miles; unimproved dirt, 6 miles).

- **Traveling time.**   3 hours each way.

- **Suggested campsite.**   Toroweap Campground (primitive).

- **Season.**   The dry spells of spring through fall.

- **Map.**   American Automobile Association Road Map; Indian Country in Arizona, New Mexico, Utah and Colorado.

- **Nearest supply points.**   Kanab, Fredonia, and Pipe Springs, Arizona; Hurricane and Saint George, Utah.

- **Managing agencies.**   Kaibab Paiute Indian Reservation, Bureau of Land Management, and Grand Canyon National Park.

- **Biotic communities.**   juniper pinyon woodland, plains and desert grassland, and Great Basin Desert scrub.

River Expeditions

Colorado River

Grand Canyon, Lee's Ferry to Diamond Creek: whitewater rafting

Landform

Many early river runners began their epic voyages through the canyons of the Green and Colorado rivers at Green River, Wyoming. But, technically speaking, the headwaters of the Colorado River are formed on the west slope of the Continental Divide at 10,175-foot La Poudre Pass in Colorado's Rocky Mountains; en route to the Gulf of California some 1,400 miles downstream, the Colorado River descends more than 10,000 vertical feet and drains an area close to 244,000 square miles. The most famous segment of the Colorado River, however, is the 277-mile stretch that cuts its way through the Grand Canyon. From Lee's Ferry at Mile 0 to Pierce Ferry at Mile 277, the Colorado River drops 1,900 feet (an average of 8 feet per mile), creating 160 rapids that still thrill river runners today.

Historical Overview

One of the first men to test the Canyon's turbulent waters was James White. To this day, his simple story remains the most exciting—and controversial—chapter in the exhaustive history of the Colorado River.

First through the Grand Canyon?   On or about September 7, 1867, a sunburnt and emaciated trapper and prospector named James White drifted up to the banks of Callville, Arizona, on a crude log raft, claiming to have spent 2 weeks floating down the Colorado River in a desperate attempt to escape hostile Indians. Two and a half weeks later he wrote a letter to his brother describing his remarkable escape:

> Navigation of the Big Canon
> >   A Terrible Voyage
> >   Calville   September 26 1867.
> >   Dear Brother . . . soon after i rote i Went prospeCted with Captin Baker and gorge strole in the San Won montin Wee found vry god prospeCk but noth that Wold pay then Wee stare Down the San Won river wee travel down a bout 200 miles then Wee Cross over on Caloreado and Camp We lad over one day Wee found that Wee Cold not travel down the river and our horse Wass Sore fite and Wee had may up our mines to turene baCk When Wei Was attaCked by 15 to 20 utes indis they Kill Baker and gorge Strole and my self tok fore ropes off from our hourse and a ax ten pounds of flour and our gunns Wee had 15 millse to woak to Calarado Wee got to the river Jest at night Wee bilt a raft that night Wee had good Sailing fro three days and the Fore day gorge strole Was Wash off from the raft and down that left me alone i thought that it Wold be my time next i then pool off my boos and pands i then tide a rope to my wase I wend over falls from 10 to 15 feet hie my raft Wold tip over three and fore times a day the thurd day Wee loss our flour flour and fore seven days i had noth to eat to ralhhide nife Caber the 8. 9 days i got some musKit beens the 13 days a party of indis frendey they Wold not give me noth eat so i give my pistols for hine pards of a dog i ead one of for super and the other breakfast the 14 days i rive at Callville Whare i Was tak Care of by James ferry i was ten days With out pants or boos or hat i Was soon so bornt so i Cold hardly Wolk the ingis tok 7 head horse from us Joosh i Can rite yu thalfe i under Went i see the hardes time that eny man ever did in the World but thank god that i got thrught saft i am Well a gin and i hope the few lines Will fine you all Well i sned my beCk respeCk to all Josh anCe this When you git it.
> >   DreCk yo letter to
> > Callville, Arizona
> >   James White

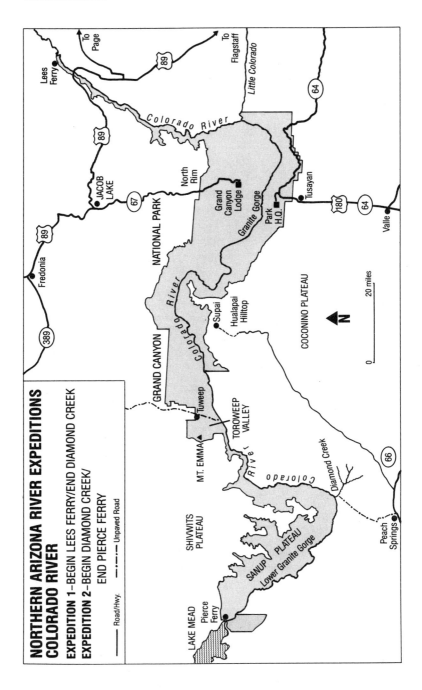

NORTHERN ARIZONA RIVER EXPEDITIONS
COLORADO RIVER

EXPEDITION 1–BEGIN LEES FERRY/END DIAMOND CREEK
EXPEDITION 2–BEGIN DIAMOND CREEK/
END PIERCE FERRY

——— Road/Hwy.   —·—·— Unpaved Road

If his incredible tale were true, the 30-year-old White woud be credited as the first man in history to have navigated the Colorado River through the Grand Canyon (albeit accidentally) 2 years before Maj. John Wesley Powell's first successful voyage in 1869. Early admirers like Gen. William J. Palmer and Thomas F. Dawson embraced White as a hero – believing that yes, indeed, he had come through the "Big Cañon."

But White's most famous detractor, railroad engineer and promoter Robert Brewster Stanton, said it was impossible for a man to negotiate more than 500 miles of rapids-strewn waters on a hastily constructed raft in the time that White claimed. In his book, *Colorado River Controversies*, Stanton spent ninety-three pages trying to discredit White's story. In the process, however, he included an eye-opening piece of information: that White's letter was published in the February 1869 edition of *The Rocky Mountain News*. Maj. John Wesley Powell didn't depart Green River, Wyoming, for what many people believed would be the first voyage down the Green and Colorado rivers until May 24 of that same year. Whether Powell read about White's traverse in *The Rocky Mountain News,* or heard about it from Samuel Bowles at Middle Park, Colorado, during the winter of 1868 (as Thomas F. Dawson suggests at the end of his enlightening June 4, 1917, Senate Resolution No. 79, "First Through the Grand Canyon"), evidence suggests that Major Powell knew James White had traversed the Colorado River before he embarked on his first successful run.

While White's adventure was by no means a scientific one – as was Powell's – if White did successfully navigate the Colorado River through the Grand Canyon in 1867, then Powell was not the first man through, and Stanton deserved less credit than he gave himself for being the first man to run the Colorado River after Powell's second expedition in 1871. For powerful men like Powell and Stanton, that made a big difference. Wrote Dawson:

> Knowing, then, that the canyon had been navigated from end to end; knowing that it no longer was entirely untraveled, and knowing especially that it was without high waterfalls, Powell might well enter upon his survey, appreciating the danger of the undertaking, but still willing to take the risk for the further advancement of the world's welfare and the promotion of his own fame. He accomplished both of these worthy purposes. But in his great achievement he had a way shower in the person of James White. And to James White belongs whatever glory there is to be awarded the First Through the Grand Canyon – one of the most marvelous adventures of all time.

To this day, detractors who believe Powell was the first dispute White's vague descriptions. But in the Autumn 1959 issue of *Arizona and the West*, renowned anthropologists Robert C. Euler and Henry F. Dobyns reviewed Richard E. Lingenfelter's *First Through the Grand Canyon* and concluded that "James White was the first man to float through the Grand Canyon."

What would settle the matter once and for all, I thought, would be to duplicate James White's adventure. On August 17, 1983, Richard W. Marks, Superintendent of Grand Canyon National Park, sent me a letter, which read, in part: "Dear Mr. Annerino: We have received and reviewed your proposal to run the Colorado River in the manner of James White to determine the feasibility of running the canyon as White claimed. Although the proposal is not strictly for scientific research, we believe your work will add a significant piece of evidence to the long-standing controversy. . . . Enclosed is your Research Certification for the 1984 James White Expedition."

Not long after I received the superintendent's letter, I began working out the logistics for the expedition. But it soon became apparent that the 1984 James White Expedition would be more similar to Powell's and Stanton's heavily equipped expeditions—with support rafts, rescue kayakers, a documentary film crew, and so on—than to a lone man trying to float through the Grand Canyon on a raft made of three cottonwood logs.

Why couldn't I run the river solo, as White had done? There were two overriding reasons. First, when Glen Canyon Dam was built in 1963, among other things, it drastically changed the temperature of the Colorado River; water released 230 feet below the surface of Lake Powell is now a heart-stopping 46 to 54 degrees Fahrenheit, instead of the 75 to 85 degrees White might have experienced in September during predam days. Consequently, I would need a dry suit in order to survive prolonged immersion in frigid water, and rescue kayakers to drag me out and revive me if necessary. Second, because the Colorado River now runs through a National Park, I couldn't simulate White's other experiences—like living off the land; nor could I build roaring fires to rewarm myself, as John Daggett and Bill Beers did when they floated down the Colorado River on black rubber Army boxes in April 1958.

Theoretically, I could still try to prove that White could have made it through the Canyon within the window of time claimed, but the style and spirit of White's adventure would have been lost on the expedition's size and constraints. In climbing terms, it was the difference between Himalayan tactics and alpine-style tactics, and I didn't want to siege the river. Furthermore, Daggett and Beers had "swum" 277 miles from Lee's

Ferry to Pierce Ferry in 26 days, spending half the time that White claimed to have spent on the river each day, and the 1951 Rigg and Rigg Expedition had rowed a Nevill's Cataract boat from Lee's Ferry to Pierce's Ferry in 53.5 hours. That settled the matter for me.

Other voyages down the Colorado. Dan Davis, former director of the Arizona-Sonora Desert Museum, wrote an unpublished paper called "Voyages Down the Colorado" during his early years as a ranger at Grand Canyon National Park. Among the many expeditions that Davis wrote about, several stand out as mileposts in the history of navigating the Rio Colorado:

• On May 25, 1889, Robert Brewster Stanton, chief engineer of the Denver, Colorado and Pacific Railway, and railroad president Frank M. Brown left Green River with six boats and a crew of sixteen "to survey the canyons for a practical route for a railroad." The expedition was abandoned after Brown and two other men drowned; none of the members had life preservers. Undeterred, Stanton organized a second expedition in 1889, this time including cork life preservers, and succeeded in boating all the way to the Gulf of California; Stanton's was the first expedition to "reach tidewater." (Powell's first expedition officially ended several hundred miles upstream at the Rio Virgen, while his second expedition ended even further upstream at the mouth of Kanab Creek.)

• On September 15, 1896, Nathaniel Galloway left Henry's Fork, Wyoming, in the company of his son and another trapper, William Richmond. Galloway had revolutionized boating the year before when he had rowed from Green River to Lee's Ferry, facing downstream so he could see and avoid oncoming hazards. Using this same technique during his second expedition in 1896, Galloway and Richmond rowed beyond Lee's Ferry all the way to Needles, which they reached on February 10, 1897, " . . . mainly for the hell of it." Most Grand Canyon oarsmen still use Galloway's technique.

• On September 8, 1911, brothers Emery and Ellsworth Kolb left Green River with the express purpose of taking the first moving pictures of boating the Colorado River. They arrived in Needles on January 18, 1912, and in 1920 The Macmillan Company published a book-length account of their adventures, *Through the Grand Canyon: From Wyoming to Mexico*, illustrated with seventy-two photographic plates. The movie played to packed houses in the East, as well as to many eager tourists who crowded into the Kolbs' South Rim studio over the years.

• On June 27, 1927, the Clyde Eddy Expedition left Green River, Utah, and became the first expedition to take a bear (!) all the way through the Grand Canyon. One passenger wrote: "Only the Grace of God is bringing us through, never have I been on such a slip-shot camping trip. I don't understand how any one man could assume such responsibility with so little knowledge of what he is doing." After losing one boat in Dubendorf Rapid, the group arrived in Needles on August 8.

• On October 20, 1928, newlyweds Glen and Bessie Hyde left Green River, Wyoming; they reached Bright Angel Creek on November 15, but they never made it to Needles. What happened to them between those two points has been at the center of another Colorado River controversy ever since. Some have speculated that Bessie shot her husband for bullying her into continuing on a honeymoon that she had grown weary of and walked out at Diamond Creek; if that's true, Bessie was the first woman to run the Colorado River and get away with murder in the Grand Canyon. But the television program "Unsolved Mysteries" recently offered other theories. Most interesting of all was the rumor going down the river several years ago that one old woman had told her boatman at the end of a trip that she was Bessie Hyde.

Today's river adventurers.   River running has come a long way since Norman Nevills first started taking paying customers down the Colorado in the late 1930s. In fact, before 1950, fewer than one hundred people were known to have run the Colorado River and, according to P. T. Reilly's article "How Deadly is Big Red," at least thirty-eight had died trying. But now some twenty-two thousand people raft all or part of the Colorado River every year, in everything from oar-powered Avon Spirits to 38-foot motor rigs.

Fortunately, Arizona boatman and outfitter Rob Elliott introduced paddle rafting to the Grand Canyon in 1971, and now modern river runners can relive some of the same challenges and adventures that early river runners faced. Hired by Colorado Outward Bound in 1968, Elliott was assigned to develop a rafting program on the Green and Yampa rivers that would incorporate Outward Bound's participatory philosophy. The son of American River Touring Association founder Lou Elliott, Rob was no stranger to river running: he knew that the best way to participate in river running was in a paddle raft. But while paddle rafting was becoming popular on short, technical rivers in the East, running small paddle boats on the West's big water had been an unknown. Elliott's paddle program was such an overwhelming success that now many other outfitters in the Southwest offer paddle rafting, which still forms the core of Outward Bound's river program in Dinosaur National Monument. The reason was simple: Passengers no longer sat idly by while bronze river gods rowed boldly into the churning depths of some dark canyon; instead, paddlers were part of a crew, responsible for navigating the river. In short, paddle rafting linked the modern river runner to the adventure-filled past — only no one had to drown in the process.

Since Elliott formed Arizona Raft Adventures in 1974, it has become internationally known for offering the most exciting and innovative expeditions down the Colorado River, from fully catered motor trips to traditional oar-powered raft trips. Says Elliott: "Paddling a raft together, you and I . . . work with, learn from, and discover a connection with the very force and spirit of the river — outside of us, and inside of us. That is what we speak of when we say, 'The river is in our blood.'" That philosophy — together with AZRA's paddle-craft expeditions and seasoned guides who provide encouragement when you're about to drop into Lava Falls at 35,000 cfs — contribute to the company's renown.

(Organizing a 2-week private river trip through the Grand Canyon can be a frustrating and costly undertaking for the uninitiated; you may find it more rewarding to go with a commercial outfitter. For a complete list of Colorado River outfitters, and private permit information, write: River Subdistrict Office, Grand Canyon National Park, P.O. Box 129, Grand Canyon, AZ 86023.)

Marble Canyon River Log

Mile 0. Lee's Ferry (elevation 3,100 feet). First settled in 1871 by Mormon polygamist John D. Lee (see entry for Buckskin Gulch/Paria Canyon), Lee's Ferry was the only practical place to establish a ford across the Colorado River between Green River, Utah, and Pierce Ferry near the head of steamboat navigation at Mile 277. According to J. Donald Hughes' *Story of Man at the Grand Canyon,* in 1923 the United States Geological Survey designated "Lee's Ferry [as] the point from which distances were measured [downstream] by the government surveys along the river in the Grand Canyon." To this day, the USGS system is the most practical way to measure your daily progress through the Grand Canyon. (Lee's Ferry, at Mile 0, is the put-in [or official launch site] for trips through the length of the Grand Canyon; Crystal Rapid, at Mile 98, is one of the most feared rapids in North America; Diamond Creek, at Mile 225, is the standard take-out for most trips down the Colorado River;

and so on.) For Bob Marley and Robert Cree, however, Lee's Ferry marked the end of a 55-day trek along the Colorado River from Diamond Creek in 1980; faced with climbs of up to 800 vertical feet to avoid precipitous drops along river's edge, the pair was reportedly the first to complete the arduous journey upstream.

Mile 1. Paria Riffle. On the right, Paria Canyon empties its silt-laden waters into the Colorado River; during periodic flash floods, the Paria River changes the color of the Colorado from a relatively clear, postdam green to the chocolaty soup known to early river runners during the heyday of the unbridled Rio Colorado River (Red River) in predam days: "Too thick to drink, and too thin to plow." Mile 1 also marks the point at which the river cuts through the Kaibab Limestone; the river cuts through the Toroweap Formation at Mile 1.7 and the Coconino Sandstone at Mile 3.9. To help river runners memorize nine of the geological formations the Colorado River penetrates, AZRA boatman Kevin Johnson developed a mnemonic: Kissing Takes Concentration; However, Some Require More Breath And Tongue: Kaibab, Toroweap, Coconino, Hermit, Supai, Redwall, Muav, Bright Angel, Tapeats.

Mile 4-plus. The Navajo Bridge spans the Colorado River 467 feet above; built during the 1920s at a cost of $350,000, the Navajo is the only bridge for driving across the Colorado River between Glen Canyon Dam near Page and Hoover Dam outside of Las Vegas. As you drift lazily beneath the bridge, try to envision the "bungee people"; in the early 1980s, a group of champagne-sipping adventurers dressed in top hats and tails jumped one at a time off the Navajo Bridge for the wild bounce at the end of a giant bungee cord.

Mile 5.2. The river cuts through Hermit Shale here.

Mile 8. Badger Creek Rapid (15-foot drop). According to Dan Davis' unpublished manuscript, "A Traverse of the Colorado River from Lee's Ferry to Lake Mead": "Jacob Hamblin killed a Badger on one of these creeks; it was carried to another creek and put on a fire to boil. . . . instead of stew, the alkalai in water and the fat from the badger had resulted in a kettle of soap—hence the names Badger and Soap Creeks." While Badger Creek is a dead end for hikers, Jackass Canyon on river left offers a 3-mile hike to Highway 89A.

Mile 11.2. Soap Creek Rapid (17-foot drop). With the possible exception of James White, no one ran Soap Creek Rapid until at least 1927, when Clyde Eddy did, according to his book *Danger River: Being an Account of the Only Successful Attempt to Navigate The Rapids of the World's Most Dangerous River.* Everyone else, from John Wesley Powell in 1869 and 1871 to Claude Birdseye's USGS expedition in 1923, had either portaged or lined the rapid. Frank M. Brown drowned in the tail waves of Soap Creek after portaging the rapid during Stanton's aborted expedition in 1889, while the Kolb brothers flipped both their boats when they tried to run it in 1911. The river cuts through the Supai Formation at this point.

Mile 14. Sheer Wall Rapid (8-foot drop). Tanner Wash enters from the left.

Mile 17. House Rock Rapid (10-foot drop). Rider Canyon enters from the right; a precipitous trail on river left offers photographers the best place from which to photograph this exciting rapid. When Powell's second expedition laid over at Lee's Ferry during the winter of 1871, some of his men named House Rock while surveying the country from above the river. Wrote Frederick S. Dellenbaugh: "About sunset we passed two large boulders which had fallen together, forming a rude shelter, under which Riggs or someone else had slept, and then jocosely printed above with charcoal the words 'House Rock Hotel.' . . . We called it the same."

Mile 20 to 31. North Canyon Rapid (12-foot drop) to South Canyon. Entering from the right, North Canyon creates the first of eleven named rapids between Mile 20 and Mile 31. Many river runners call this stretch the Roaring Twenties because of the excitement it offers and because it includes the likes of 24.5-Mile Rapid, where Henry C. Richards and Peter Hansbrough drowned during the tragic 1889 Stanton Expedition, and Cave Springs Rapid, where the 1923 Birdseye Expedition lost a canvas boat called the *Mojave*. Redwall Limestone first appears at Mile 22.6.

Mile 31. South Canyon enters from the right. Stanton aborted his disastrous 1889 expedition by climbing out South Canyon, then called Paradise Canyon, and heading to Kanab; later that same year, during Stanton's second expedition, photographer F. A. Nims broke his leg and had to be carried out South Canyon to a wagon driven cross-country from Lee's Ferry. Today, avid trout fishermen hike down South Canyon (via the House Rock Valley Road) to fish one of the best stretches on the Colorado River.

Mile 31-plus. Vasey's Paradise. If the tempo of the river slows down after the Roaring Twenties, there's still plenty to see and do in the thirties—

like visiting Vasey's Paradise. Powell named this beautiful double water-fall "in honor of the botanist who traveled with us last year"; a paradise to most, it was also the resting place of yet another Colorado River victim who died under mysterious circumstances. During the 1934 Frazier-Eddy Expedition, Alton Hatch made the following entry in his diary: "Stopped at Vasey's and went exploring, found pottery and rock houses and dug up a skeleton of a man. He had dark hair and wore buckskin clothes, had both legs broken and still had a bad odor to him. This was the top cave of the two caves." A favored water stop for most river runners, Vasey's Paradise is also one of two known places along the river where poison ivy grows; the other is downstream from Deer Creek Falls near Mile 136.

Mile 33. Redwall Cavern on the left. While fifty thousand people would have a difficult time squeezing into this immense cavern – as Powell claimed was possible – Redwall Cavern does offer outstanding acoustics for orchestras that periodically journey down the river. Muav Limestone appears below Mile 34.

Mile 41. Buck Farm Canyon enters from the right. You can take a 2-mile round-trip hike up Buck Farm, or look for Bert Loper's boat down-stream on river right; Loper's boat washed up near here when the 80-year-old river runner reportedly died of a heart attack after his boat capsized in 24.5-Mile Rapid on July 8, 1949.

Mile 43. Anasazi Footbridge. Long before the Kaibab Bridge was built across the Colorado River near Mile 87, the Anasazi constructed a crude footbridge in order to reach the river at this point. Boatman and -woman Kenton Grua and Ellen Tibbits reportedly free-climbed out this ancient route on river right to Point Hansbrough.

Mile 43-plus. President Harding Rapid (4-foot drop). According to Dan Davis, this rapid got its name when the 1923 USGS Birdseye Expedition reached it the day that President Harding died. Davis also reported that Peter Hansbrough was buried here by the Stanton Expedition on January 17, 1890, as was Boy Scout David Quigley, who drowned in Glen Canyon on June 26, 1951.

Mile 52. Nankoweap Rapid (25-foot drop). One of the most spectacu-lar and abrupt drops along the Colorado River is the 3,000-foot-high wall formed by the rim of the Desert Facade and the left bank of Nankoweap Rapids. Nankoweap Canyon enters from the right and offers, among other things, two popular hikes: the short, steep climb up to the Anasazi granaries, and the 8- to 10-mile-loop trek along the Butte Fault and Kwagunt Creek to Kwagunt Rapid (7-foot drop) at Mile 56. The 14-mile Nankoweap Trail, constructed by Powell and his men in 1882, is usually hiked from rim to river and back and is not recommended as a river hike. Bright Angel Shale appears at Mile 51.8, and Tapeats Sandstone at Mile 59.

Mile 61. Little Colorado River enters from the left. First kayaked by hair-boaters Brad Dimock and Tim Copper in 1976, the Little Colorado River Gorge also offers an outstanding 57-mile-long multiday trek from Cameron on Highway 89 to the Little Colorado's confluence with the Colorado River. Once you reach the river, you'll have to trek another 19 miles along the Beamer Trail, river bank, and Tanner Trail to reach a car shuttle at 7,288-foot Lipan Point atop the South Rim.

The Hopi Indians first ventured into the Little Colorado River Gorge via Salt Trail Canyon in order to gather salt from their sacred deposits in the Grand Canyon centuries ago. Spanish missionary Francisco Tomas Garces called this river the Colorado Chiquito in 1776; most modern river runners call this favorite lunch stop the Little C.

Upper Granite Gorge

When the 1869 Powell Expedition struck camp below the mouth of the Little Colorado River on August 13, Powell called the river beyond "The Great Unknown." Wrote Powell: "We have an unknown distance yet to run; an unknown river yet to explore. What falls there are, we know not; what rocks beset the channel, we know not; what walls rise above the river, we know not. Ah, well! we may conjecture many things." So will you, if you haven't rowed or paddled a boat into the dark Upper Granite Gorge before—because what wet your paddles in the Roaring Twenties and the rest of the 65-mile-long Marble Canyon is only a taste of the legendary "big drops" awaiting you in the Inner Gorge. From the 20-foot drop through Tanner Rapid at Mile 68, the river builds momentum, dropping another 25 feet through wall-hugging Unkar Rapid at Mile 72 and 15 feet in Nevills Rapid near Mile 75 to Hance Rapid near Mile 77.

Mile 77. Hance Rapid (30-foot drop). Scout from river left. Hance Rapid is named after "Captain" John Hance, who first entertained tourists at his South Rim guest ranch at the turn of the century. Dan Davis reported that the 1923 USGS Birdseye Expedition was the first to run all of its boats through this long, technical rapid without lining, portaging, or flipping.

Mile 78. Sockdologer Rapid (19-foot drop). If you manage to maneuver through Hance Rapid rightside up, wait till you drop into what the Powell Expedition called the Gates of Hell. Wrote Dellenbaugh: "We could look down on one of the most fearful places I ever saw or ever hope to see under like circumstances—a place that might have been the Gate to Hell. . . . We were near the beginning of a tremendous fall. The narrow river dropped suddenly and smoothly away, and then, beaten to foam, plunged and boomed for a third of a mile through a descent of from eighty to one hundred feet, the enormous waves leaping twenty or thirty feet in the air and sending spray twice as high." If this is your first time through what the Powell Expedition also called the "Sockdologer of the world," you will probably also overestimate the vertical drop this classic rapid makes.

Mile 75 to 87-plus. From the tailwaves of Sockdologer to Bright Angel Creek, the only rapid of consequence is Grapevine Rapid (18-foot drop) below Mile 81, though you should pull over on river right at Mile 84 and hike up Clear Creek to see one of the most unusual waterfalls in the Grand Canyon.

Midstroke, river runners brace for a wild run through Hance Rapid during a 12-day, Arizona Raft Adventure's paddle expedition from Lee's Ferry to Diamond Creek. Photo by John Annerino.

Mile 87-plus. Bright Angel Creek enters from the right. Veteran river runners have mixed emotions about stopping at Phantom Ranch. While the historic site is a destination for thousands of hikers and mule-riders each year, many boatmen are loathe to interrupt the tranquility of a 2-week Grand trip by stopping at this bustling, inner-Canyon tourist's mecca. On August 16, 1989, boatman Kevin Johnson summed up the feelings of many veteran Grand Canyon river guides when his passengers asked him if they would be stopping here and he told them "The only things of interest at Phantom Ranch are flies, mules, and cowboys." But when you spend 3 to 4 months working on the river every year, as Johnson does, there's no other place from which to mail a letter to your honey—even if it *is* carried out by a mule!

Mile 89. Pipe Creek enters from the left and forms Pipe Creek Rapid. Pipe Creek, however, is best known among river runners as the "interchange," a 2- to 3-hour layover where passengers signed on only for the upper half of a trip are dropped off, and where passengers booked only for the lower half are picked up. In either case, you'll need to make a 9-mile hike up or down the Bright Angel Trail.

But a Grand Canyon river trip is the adventure of a lifetime, so if you're seriously considering one—*go the distance!* Booking half a river trip may seem more economical and less time-consuming, but it's never as rewarding. People who hike out after rafting the upper half usually do so with a long face; they have just established a bond with the river—and with their new friends—when suddenly their magic carpet is jerked out from under them. Then they have to hike uphill, in the heat! On the other hand, the eager beavers who hike in for what is billed as the wildest half of the river often remain outsiders to some extent, unable to break into the group dynamics formed during the upper half.

Mile 90 to 98. If you've just hiked in for the lower half and haven't been down the river in a small boat before, you're in for what may seem like an unimaginably wild ride your first day out. Horn Creek Rapid, below Mile 90, drops only 10 feet, but, depending on the river flow, it's rated between 8 and 10 on the Deseret 1 to 10 Scale; Dan Davis reported "Park Rangers Sturdevant and Johnson drowned here in 1929." Granite Rapid, below Mile 93, drops 17 feet and seems as if it will pile-drive you into the wall on river right. Hermit Rapid, on the other hand, is a classic wave train, dropping 15 feet and offering river runners and swimmers (wearing double life vests) a roller-coaster ride; the grave on river left is that of San Diegoan George Jensen, who reportedly drowned upstream from Hermit Rapid during the 1950s. Named after hermit Louis Boucher, who "rode a white mule and told only white lies," Boucher Rapid is located 1.5 miles above Crystal Rapid and is the last benign-looking rapid you'll navigate before entering the Jaws of Death.

Mile 98. Crystal Rapid (17-foot drop). Go back! If you can't go back, portage around this rapid. If you can't do either, and if the water's high, take an air bag and a bedpan with you when you scout it. Unlike Lava Falls, and the seventeen other Grand Canyon rapids with drops of 15 feet or more, Crystal Rapids was formed relatively recently. James White was given a pass from the Big Guy on this one, as was Powell and everyone else who followed in their wake—until 1966. That's when the beast was born.

Rapids are principally formed by one of three variables: constriction, or how narrow the river channel is; gradient, or how abruptly the river drops; and debris, or how many rocks and boulders have been permanently deposited in the river channel by tributary drainages. While Crystal's 17-foot drop is only about half that of either Hance or Lava, the debris in it has turned it into a killer. According to the scientific paper "Effects of the Catastrophic Flood of December 1966, North Rim Area, Eastern Grand Canyon, Arizona," by M. E. Cooley, B. N. Aldridge, and Robert C. Euler, the North Rim was hammered by a storm of such intensity that it created a flood that "removed all evidence of previous floods" going back to A.D. 1050 to 1150. In *The Big Drops: Ten Legendary Rapids,* Robert Collins and Roderick Nash reported "fourteen inches of water fell in a period of only thirty-six hours. One consequence was the almost instantaneous creation of a Big Drop." But Crystal was different; tons of huge boulders deposited in the main stem of the Colorado River by this Biblical flood created a gaping, almost unavoidable whitewater maelstrom. During the record year of postdam runoff in 1983, when 92,000 cfs roared through the Grand Canyon, Crystal flipped and ate bus-sized motor rigs; people were killed and entire parties had to be evacuated by helicopters before the river subsided.

Even during average annual flows of 15,000 cfs, the hole in Crystal is not to be trifled with. So if you're rowing through on a private trip and haven't been here before, wait for another party that has—because if you flip in Crystal, and there's no one waiting down below to drag you out, there's a strong chance you'll end up swimming Tuna Creek Rapid a mile downstream as well . . . and anybody that's in cold Colorado River water for that long will be in trouble.

Mile 99 to 107-plus. The Gems. Between Tuna Creek Rapid and Bass Rapid is a series of moderate rapids called the Gems; in descending order, they are: Agate, Sapphire, Turquoise, Jasper, Jade, Ruby, and Serpentine. Davis reported that Powell's 1869 expedition "Portaged Sapphire and Turquoise, ran Ruby and [swamped the] EMMA . . . in Serpentine."

Mile 107-plus. Bass Rapid (4-foot drop) to Shinumo Rapid (8-foot drop). Bass Rapid was named after William Wallace Bass, who came to the Canyon for his health in 1884; during the ensuing 50 years, the enterprising Bass was responsible for, among other things, building the 7-mile-long South Bass Trail from the South Rim down to the river. Bass constructed a cableway across the river from the foot of the South Bass in 1908 in order to ferry tourists across to his camp and orchard in Shinumo Creek. Shinumo Creek, on river right, provides access to the North Rim via the rugged, seldom-hiked, 14-mile-long North Bass Trail. With limited hiking time, however, river runners generally focus their wanderings at the waterfall near the mouth of Shinumo Creek or on the historic site of Bass' Camp several miles up Shinumo Creek.

Middle Granite Gorge

Mile 110 to 130. 110-Mile Rapid to Bedrock Rapid. After running Crystal and the Gems, people start looking forward to laying over a day or two at Tapeats Creek, where they can hike Thunder River; however, there are plenty of worthwhile diversions en route. Named with the Havasupai Indian word for Colorado River, Hakatai Rapid was the location of Bass' second cable crossing, which he used to reach his asbestos mine in Hakatai Canyon. The 15-foot drop in Waltenberg Rapid below Mile 112 is one of the steepest drops on the river; in 1937 Haldane "Buzz" Holstrom reportedly hit the rocks on river right, but that didn't stop him from becoming the first man to row solo from Green River, Wyoming, through the Grand Canyon to Boulder Dam, which he reached on November 25. The trickling waterfall in Elves Chasm below Mile 116 is another must-see for passengers, though boatmen who have grown weary of the crowds sometimes use the time to dash off letters to other boatmen and leave them in a hidden mailbox near Elves.

Carved in the convoluted folds of Tapeats sandstone, Blacktail Canyon, below Mile 120, is undisputedly one of the prettiest short canyons and lunch stops on the river. Another grave near Forster Rapid is reportedly that of H. M. Nelson, whose body was found and buried there by the 1955 Rigg Expedition; Nelson drowned while trying to swim across the river near the Kaibab suspension bridge. After running Fossil Rapid (15-foot drop) at Mile 125, everybody starts thinking about Bedrock Rapid, because an unsuccessful run of Bedrock generally means one of two things:

getting sucked into the toilet-bowl eddy on river left, or wrapping or flipping a boat on the condominium-sized rock sitting squat in the middle of the river. Boats stuck in the eddy have to be lined out with ropes, while boats that hit Bedrock wrong will roll over and flip—as did a 37-foot motor rig in 1973.

Mile 131-plus. Duebendorf Rapid (15-foot drop): Seymour S. Duebendorf was a member of the 1909 Galloway-Stone Expedition; according to Davis, he "was violently upset in this rapid." The pullout on river right below this long, wild rapid provides access to a wonderful waterfall and seldom-seen Anasazi granaries several miles up Stone Creek.

Mile 133-plus to 136. Tapeats Rapid to Deer Creek. After sitting in a boat for days on end, there are few better ways to get your land legs back than by hiking 4 miles up Tapeats Creek to Thunder River—a cataract that streams out of the Muav Limestone; while it's been one of the most popular destination hikes from both the river and the North Rim (8 miles via Bill Hall Trailhead), a growing number of river runners are now continuing to hike over Surprise Valley from Thunder River to a shuttle boat waiting below Deer Creek. Veteran guides and cavers have explored .5 mile into Thunder River cave, while Deer Creek Narrows is also an exciting diversion, if you're properly equipped with ropes. The river in between Tapeats and Deer Creek is highlighted by Helicopter Eddy near Mile 135. According to *The Colorado River in Grand Canyon*, by Larry Stevens, the 76-foot-wide portal at this point is the narrowest the Colorado River flows through. Watch for poison ivy at Deer Creek.

Mile 143. Kanab Rapid. Powell terminated his second expedition in 1871 at the mouth of this 60-mile long canyon, the scene of a desperate gold rush in 1871–1872. (See entry for Kanab Canyon.)

Mile 146 to 148. Olo to Matkatamiba. Due to the increasing popularity of Matkatamiba, Olo Canyon has become an alternative to stopping at "Matkat." However, unlike the easy scramble along water-polished Muav Limestone into the natural amphitheater above the mouth of "Matkat," the entry into Olo requires a 25-foot climb up a free-swinging rope ladder to the mouth of this delicate side canyon. Over the years, a number of people have suffered serious injuries when they peeled off the rope ladder; as of the summer of 1989, the rope had been cut down by park rangers.

Mile 156-plus. Havasu Rapid. The stretch below Upset Rapid near Mile 150 is one of the most marginal yet sought-after camping areas on the Colorado River; names like Ledges, Last Chance, and Absolutely Last Chance describe the crowded rocky shelves on which entire river parties will camp on in order to be the first to pull into the mouth of Havasu early the next morning. And the pull-in at Havasu is everything. If you're new to the river and you missed the wall-hugging pull-in at Matkat, chances are you'll also miss the pull-in at Havasu unless you have your bowline ready to toss to a waiting boatman. Once you've made the pull-in, the mouth of Havasu will look like a parking lot. *Everybody* wants to stop and hike Havasu. On a busy summer day, it's common to see as many as twenty boats stuffed in the mouth of this tributary drainage, from kayaks and wooden dories to fleets of neoprene rafts sandwiched in by motor rigs, all strung together with a spaghetti of nylon bowlines.

Next to Paria Canyon, the Little Colorado River Gorge, and Kanab Creek, the 50-mile-long drainage formed by Cataract Canyon and Havasu Creek is one of the longest tributaries feeding the Colorado River; but unlike its upstream counterparts, Havasu has a mouth that is narrow and sheer walled. Consequently, this is not the place to tie up in the midst of a summer monsoon. Many a horror story has been told by boatmen who have tried to second-guess the weather – and the flash flood potential – and lost, only to be engulfed by a wall of angry brown water if they couldn't cut their bowlines fast enough. During less threatening weather, Havasu Creek provides a popular access to Beaver Falls via a 4-mile upstream hike; swimming into the subterranean cave called the Green Room and jumping 40 feet off the Accelerator are two of the more exciting pastimes at Beaver Falls. Those who don't hang out along the creek between the river and Beaver Falls, head up either to Mooney Falls or to the Havasupai Indian village of Supai 6 miles away.

Mile 179-plus.   Lava Falls (37-foot drop). On the Deseret 1 to 10 Scale, Lava is always a 10. From Havasu on down, you're only marking time until you reach this cataract first named by Powell's 1869 expedition on August 25. The river slows down, the boatmen grow serious for the first time since Crystal, and the passengers begin wondering just exactly what it is that they've gotten themselves into. Sure, you *can* walk around the falls – but not many elect to. Because after all the posturing and the chest beating, after the "Well, I did this on the Middle Fork last summer" and the "You should have seen the hippos in the Bio-Bio this winter," Lava Falls is the one great equalizer. It is to river running what El Capitan is to rock climbing. Boatmen, paddlers, and passengers must all reckon with it. And after a week to 10 days of howling on the river with new friends, baking in the heat, and freezing in the rain, who would suddenly admit to their peers that they're not going to run Lava? Few.

Still, with an awesome, 37-foot drop, Lava is a rapid that requires inspiration. Of all the legendary boatmen who have faced the untamed Colorado River, and all the self-appointed legends who have run the river since it was plugged by Glen Canyon Dam in 1964, the greatest inspiration still comes from the story of that humble prospector James White. In *The Big Drops*, Collins and Nash said it best: "Think of a weakened, dazed man, looking up from his logs at the line across the river, listening to the boom of Lava, and thinking, in desperate condition, that he might as well hang on and hope for the best. Then the sickening first drop and brown water tearing at his body and smashing it against the wood and, finally, the calm below and the wondering how much more could he take before death. He took enough to get out barely alive and tell a tale nobody would, at first, believe. We do." So do I.

Mile 180 to 225.   Beyond Lava to the Diamond Creek take-out. Once you have faced and run Lava, and recovered from the long night of post-Lava revelry, reality rears its ugly head in the form of one of the most perplexing questions asked on the river: "Is this the real world, or is the real world outside the Canyon?" Many boatmen will tell you the Canyon *is* the real world, and as long as you're on the river there's no disputing that. It has marked you for life. But the closer you get to Mile 225, the more you begin to wonder what's going on in . . . well . . . the *real* world. What tragedy has befallen our nation? What has happened to all those unfinished tasks you left behind? If, as boatman Robb Elliott suggests, you've "Learned from, and discovered a connection with the very force and spirit of the river," you'll walk into your own real world changed forever. And that's the power and the beauty of the Grand Canyon of the Colorado River.

Travel Notes

• **Primary access.**   Lee's Ferry.

• **Secondary access.**   Pipe Creek via South Kaibab and Bright Angel trails; also, boatmen and river runners have rendezvoused with river parties by hiking into the river via the Tanner Trail and Havasu Creek.

• **Elevation loss.**   1,800 feet.

• **Mileage.**   225 miles, Lee's Ferry to Diamond Creek.

• **Escape routes.**   See *Hiking the Grand Canyon,* by John Annerino.

- **Seasons.**   June through August are most popular, though the weeks before Memorial Day and after Labor Day are less crowded. From a photographic standpoint, the summer monsoon season of late July and early August is the most dramatic.

- **Maps and guides.**   *Grand Canyon River Guide,* by William Belknap; *The Colorado River in Grand Canyon: A Guide,* by Larry Stevens; *Guidebook to the Colorado River, Parts I and II,* by W. Kenneth Hamblin and J. Keith Rigby; *A River Runner's Guide to the History of the Grand Canyon,* by Kim Crumbo; and *Rivers of the Southwest: A Boater's Guide to the Rivers of Colorado, New Mexico, Utah and Arizona,* by Fletcher Anderson and Ann Hopkinson.

- **Managing agency.**   Grand Canyon National Park.

- **Backcountry information.**   Permit required for all river expeditions.

- **Biotic communities.**   (along river's edge): Great Basin Desert scrub and Mojave Desert scrub.

Lower Colorado River

Western Grand Canyon, Diamond Creek to Pierce Ferry: whitewater rafting

Landform

Between Diamond Creek at Mile 225 and Gneiss Canyon Rapid at Mile 236, the free-moving Colorado River drops more than 100 feet through the Lower Granite Gorge, where it begins to pool up in the sluggish waters of Lake Mead. Created by the construction of Hoover Dam in Black Canyon when the last of the concrete was poured on March 23, 1935, the impounded waters of Lake Mead have since buried all the rapids between Gneiss Canyon and Pierce Ferry at Mile 279, including two of the most treacherous rapids that early river runners faced: Separation Rapid below Mile 239 and Lava Cliff Rapid at Mile 246.

Historical Overview

Even before James White and Maj. John Wesley Powell headed down the Colorado River toward these fearsome cataracts in the 1860s, others, like Lt. Joseph Christmas Ives, struggled *up* the river from the Gulf of California in hopes of surmounting such unforeseen obstacles. Only Ives didn't try to navigate the Colorado River in a small boat or on a log raft; his military reconnaissance would attempt the first upstream run of the river in a 58-foot-long steamboat.

Lieutenant Ives had been assigned by the War Department to search out the head of steamboat navigation so that military forts along the river could be resupplied by steamboat. On January 11, 1858, the steel-hulled *Explorer* left Fort Yuma with two dozen men under Ives' command. But after struggling against the powerful currents for nearly a month, the wood-burning *Explorer* had covered only 150 miles to Fort Mojave. Undaunted, the Ives Expedition steamed on toward the mouth of Black Canyon, another 100 miles upstream, which they finally reached on March 8. Piloted by Captain Robinson, the hulking *Explorer* ascended a rapid spewing through the mouth of Black Canyon—only to run aground on a submerged boulder at the head of the rapid. In his "Report Upon the Colorado Rivers of the West," Ives wrote: "The concussion was so violent that the men near the bow were thrown overboard. . . . and it was expected that the boat would fill and sink." The boat didn't sink, but it took 3 days to repair the damage. Fearing that another wreck further upstream would drown the lot of them, Ives thought he would stand a better chance of finishing his reconnaissance in a small skiff and left the *Explorer* where it was for the return journey. As he quickly discovered, however, dragging a small skiff against the current wasn't much easier: "Rapids were of frequent occurrence, and at every one we were obliged to get out of the skiff, and haul it over. . . . The constant getting out of the boat, and the labor of dragging it through these difficult places [rapids], made our progress exceedingly tedious and fatiguing." On March 12, Ives threw in the towel; upstream navigation beyond Black Canyon, even in a skiff, was impossible. For all practical purposes, the *Explorer* marked the head of steamboat navigation.

Nonetheless, Ives pushed on. Led by Ireteba, a Mojave Indian Scout, the Ives Expedition headed cross-country and reached what may have been the climax of the expedition when Ives became—so far as is known—the first non-Indian to reach the bottom of the Grand Canyon. Several days before reaching the mouth of Diamond Creek, however, he described the scene from the head of Peach Springs Canyon, through which Ireteba would guide him down to the Colorado River: "The famous 'Big Cañon' was before us; and for a long time we paused in wondering delight, surveying that stupendous formation through which the Colorado and its tributaries break their way."

As vivid as Ives' reporting was, the Army refused to accept the fact that the head of steamboat navigation was the mouth of Black Canyon. According to *The Grand Colorado*, edited by T. H. Watkins, the Army "needed a head of navigation far up into the Colorado canyons to supply its troops in the region, and it was determined to have it." Enter Lt. George Montague Wheeler, Corps of Engineers. Where Ives failed to reach Diamond Creek by sticking solely to the river, Wheeler's 18-man expedition eventually succeeded on October 20, 1871.

At least two other upstream voyages followed these first two. On July 12, 1960, New Zealander Jon Hamilton reached Lee's Ferry after piloting a jet boat upstream through the Grand Canyon from Pierce's Ferry. Perhaps even more remarkable was the All Canoe Up River Expedition that became the first expedition to navigate the Colorado River upstream under its own paddle power in 1981; where steamboats and jet boats had to take the full brunt of a rapid head on, the canoes were able to eddy-hop the upstream currents created by many rapids.

Nobody used Diamond Creek as a launch site to attempt downstream navigation until October 1894, when 1st Lt. Charles L. Potter of the U.S. Army was "ordered to make an examination of the Colorado River from the mouth of the Virgen River to Yuma." Lieutenant Potter figured it would be "cheaper and quicker" to ship his boat overland to Peach Springs and boat down to the mouth of the Rio Virgen near present-day Pierce Ferry than to struggle upstream from Yuma. In *In and Around the Grand Canyon*, George Wharton James highlights the ensuing adventure: "They had difficulty in letting the boat down over the first rapids [Diamond Creek], and then, in accordance with what someone had told them, who knew less of the river than they did, they settled down to enjoy seventy-five miles of smooth water. When nightfall came they had had several narrow escapes and had shot fifteen rapids." But the group "shipwrecked seventeen miles below the mouth of Diamond Creek and had to walk sixty-five miles to Hackberry. They are satisfied to do their boating on some other river now."

Once a daunting stretch of river for early adventures, the 53-mile-long Diamond Creek run is now only a shadow of its former self. Gone are the rapids that once struck fear in the hearts and minds of men like White, Powell, and Ives. Yet what remains—10 miles of rapids, followed by 40-odd miles of "lake"—continues to lure both inexperienced and veteran river runners into the depths of the Western Grand Canyon. As Ives wrote, its timeless appeal lies in "that stupendous formation through which the Colorado River and its tributaries once broke their way."

Directions
From the junction of Route 66 and the Diamond Creek Road in Peach Springs, turn right (north) at the office of the Hualapai River Runners. Follow the Diamond Creek Road 21 miles north to the Colorado River.

Lower Granite Gorge River Log

Mile 225. Diamond Creek Rapid (25-foot drop). Nicknamed Stakeside Rapid in 1983, when a hellacious flash flood swept a river party's stakeside flatbed truck into the Colorado River, Diamond Creek was first called Arroyo de San Alexo by Padre Francisco Garces when he visited the region on July 17, 1776. But because Garces' exact location is difficult to pinpoint, Lieutenant Ives is generally credited with being the first non-Indian to reach the bottom of the Grand Canyon and the mouth of Diamond Creek, which he named on April 5, 1858. (See entry for Diamond Peak.)

Mile 229. Travertine Canyon and Rapid. At one time, the beach on river left below Travertine Rapid was a popular campsite for river runners who liked to spend as much time hiking above the river as they did floating down it. So if you drive to Diamond Creek on a Friday morning and don't put on the river until that afternoon, Travertine still makes an excellent first camp—though you'll have to break out of the tailwaves to make the tricky pull-in on river left. Even if you don't camp here, Travertine Falls is considered a must-see for river runners. For hikers, a stiff half-hour climb above the falls will gain the Tonto Platform.

Mile 231 to 235. 231-Mile Rapid to Bridge Canyon. In his unpublished chronology of early river runners, titled *A Traverse of the Colorado River: From Lee's Ferry to Lake Mead,* Dan Davis reported that Powell camped at Mile 231 on August 26, 1869. Wrote Powell: "We have a royal supper— unleavened bread, green squash sauce, and strong coffee. We have been for a few days on half rations, but now have no stint of roast squash." Three rapids in quick succession, 231-, 232-, and 233-Mile Rapids, offer the most wallop on the Diamond Creek run. Author and veteran guide Kim Crumbo speculates that honeymooners Glen and Bessie Hyde might have drowned in 232-Mile Rapid.

Mile 235. Bridge Canyon Rapid. Pull over on river left above 235-Mile Rapid and consider the following: If the Bridge Canyon Dam had been built here in the late 1960s, the impounded waters would have backed up into the Grand Canyon and flooded—among other things—Lava Falls. In one of the finest coups in conservation history, the Sierra Club stymied congressional approval of the Bridge Canyon Dam, and of the Marble Canyon Dam at Mile 39, by taking out full-page advertisements in *The Washington Post* and *The New York Times:* "NOW ONLY YOU CAN SAVE GRAND CANYON FROM BEING FLOODED—FOR PROFIT." Costing $15,000, the advertisements created an avalanche of mail from an outraged public denouncing the proposed dams. Today, fortunately, nearly 300 miles of river (albeit heavily controlled and regulated) still separate Glen Canyon Dam from Hoover Dam.

For hikers, it's 15 minutes up to the Tonto Platform, from which you can trek several miles west to Separation Canyon.

Mile 236. 236-Mile Rapid. This is where you slide off the river into the lake.

Mile 237. The first successful downstream run from Diamond Creek probably didn't push off until December 25, 1928; that's when Ellsworth and Emery Kolb, accompanied by park ranger James Brooks, put in at Diamond Creek in hopes of finding Glen and Bessie Hyde. A search plane launched from March Air Force Base discovered floating near Mile 237 a boat, which Emery identified in a subsequent flight as that belonging to the missing honeymooners. The quickest way to Mile 237 was via Diamond Creek, but none of the would-be rescuers had a boat at their immediate disposal. In *River Runners*, David Lavender reported that Brooks and the Kolbs built a boat on the spot out of a shack they ripped down, then rowed down to Mile 237. Wrote Lavender: "The scow, floating peaceably at Mile 237, seemed to confirm the conjecture."

Mile 239. Separation Canyon. Now buried by Lake Mead, Separation Rapid created a deadly rift among Powell and his men during his 1869 expedition. Of the rapid, Powell wrote: "We find that the lateral streams have washed boulders into the river, so as to form a dam, over which the water makes a broken fall 18 or 20 feet; then there is a rapid, beset with rocks, for 200 or 300 yards. . . . Below, there is a second fall; how great, we cannot tell." William Dunn and O. G. and Seneca Howland, no longer willing to bet their lives on the great unknown, climbed out Separation Canyon hoping to reach the nearest Mormon settlement 75 miles away; Powell, on the other hand, was determined to finish his exploration and pushed on with his remaining crew, only to discover after his successful expedition that Dunn and the Howlands had been killed. (See entry for Sunshine Road.) The 1934 Frazier-Eddy Expedition put up a plaque, now overlooking a benign stretch of flatwater on river right, to commemorate Dunn and the Howland brothers.

Nightfloat. Many raft parties tie their boats together and float the long, sluggish miles into the lake at night. The only thing likely to interrupt your star-filled reverie is the ominous sound of boulders falling off the towering black cliffs—and just missing your boat. Not to worry, though; actually, the unnerving "keplunk"s are made by beavers.

Mile 246.   Spencer Canyon. At one time Lava Cliff Rapid was considered the wildest rapid on the Colorado. On March 14, 1890, Stanton called it Rapid No. 477: "This to me is the most dreadful rapid we have met. It does look like destruction to run it." Stanton and his men lined it, as Powell had done 10 years earlier. But one of Powell's men, G. Y. Bradley, accidentally ran it on sight. Positioned in the boat, Bradley decided to cut one of the lines rather than drown if the boat broke apart at the top of the falls. Wrote Powell:

> With perfect composure Bradley seizes the great scull oar, places it in the stern rowlock, and pulls with all his power (and he is an athlete) to turn the bow of the boat downstream. . . . One, two, strokes he makes, and a third just as she goes over, and the boat is fairly turned, and she goes down almost beyond our sight, though we are more than a hundred feet above the river. Then she comes up again on a great wave, and down and up, then around behind some great rocks, and is lost in the mad white foam below. We stand frozen with fear, for we see no boat. Bradley is gone! so it seems. But now, away below, we see something coming out of the waves. It is evidently a boat. A moment more, and we see Bradley standing on deck, swinging his hat, to show he is alright.

According to Davis, Spencer Canyon was named after "Charlie Spencer, who married a Hualpai Squaw and lived with them in 'Wickty-Wizz' canyon (Meriwitica) until he was murdered."

The Tow Out.   Unless you're paddling a kayak, chances are you'll have to either be towed the rest of the way across Lake Mead or use a small outboard engine. En route, on river right below Mile 266 you'll see the remains of the Bat Cave where $1 Million was reportedly invested by the U.S. Guano Corporation to "recover bat guano," and on river left below Mile 274 you'll see Columbine Falls tucked into a cul-de-sac. Most of the history below Spencer Canyon, however, lies on the bottom of Lake Mead. Callville, where James White first climbed off his log raft, for example, is about where you'll motor into Pierce's Ferry.

Travel Notes
• **Primary access.**   Diamond Creek.

• **Elevation loss.**   100-plus feet.

• **Mileage.**   53-plus miles from Diamond Creek to Pierce's Ferry.

• **Escape routes.**   See *Hiking the Grand Canyon*, by John Annerino; also, there is much upstream motorboat traffic to the foot of 236-Mile Rapid.

- **Seasons.**   All year. Summer busy with motorboats; late spring and early fall can be most pleasant.

- **Maps and guides.**   Same as previous chapter. Also see "Colorado River: Its History in the Lower Canyons Area," a Ph.D. dessertation by Melvin T. Smith.

- **Managing agency.**   Hualpai Tribal Government. Fee and permit required. Hualpai River Runners, P.O. Box 168, Peach Springs, AZ 86434; (602) 769-2216.

- **Biotic communities.**   (along river's edge): Great Basin Desert scrub and Mojave Desert scrub.

Canyoneering

Kanab Canyon

Arizona Strip, Fredonia to the Colorado River

Landform

Of the seventy-seven major tributaries that drain into the Grand Canyon, Kanab Creek is one of the longest, second only to the 57-mile-long Little Colorado River Gorge. The headwaters of the Little Colorado River are formed by 11,403-foot Mount Baldy more than 200 miles upstream from its entrance into the gorge at Cameron; the headwaters of Kanab Creek are formed on the 9,000-foot-high slopes of Utah's Paunsaugunt Plateau 90-odd miles north of Fredonia. The fact that the deep, rugged 60-mile stretch of Kanab Creek from Fredonia to its confluence with the Colorado River is still called a creek on most maps—including modern USGS topographical maps—and not a canyon is puzzling. Kanab Creek and its canyon form a natural boundary between the eastern and western halves of the remote 11,000-square-mile Arizona Strip country; in its lowest reaches more than 3,500 feet deep! Of the twenty named tributaries that drain into Kanab Creek, fifteen are canyons and one other is called a gulch but is really a canyon.

Historical Overview

At least Kanab Creek is no longer called a wash, as it was in 1872 by Stephen Vandiver Jones and Walter Clement Powell. Both with Maj. John

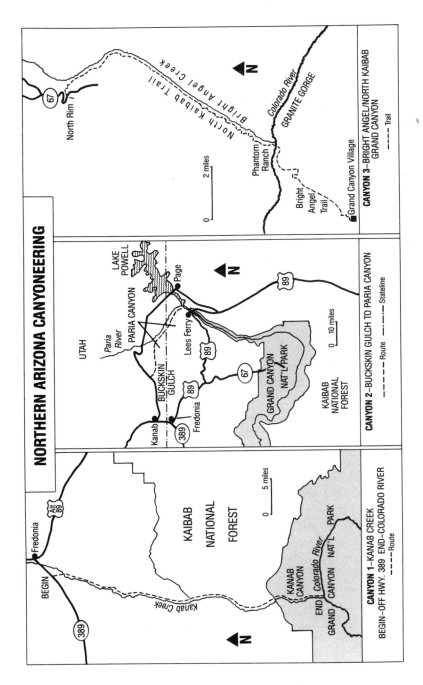

NORTHERN ARIZONA CANYONEERING

CANYON 3—BRIGHT ANGEL/NORTH KAIBAB
GRAND CANYON

----- Trail

North Rim

Bright Angel Creek

North Kaibab Trail

Colorado River

GRANITE GORGE

Phantom Ranch

Bright
Angel
Trail

Grand Canyon Village

N

0   2 miles

CANYON 2—BUCKSKIN GULCH TO PARIA CANYON

----- Route   —·—·— Stateline

LAKE POWELL

Page

UTAH

Paria River

PARIA CANYON

Lees Ferry

BUCKSKIN GULCH

Kanab

Fredonia

89

89

67

389

GRAND CANYON NAT'L PARK

KAIBAB NATIONAL FOREST

N

0   10 miles

CANYON 1—KANAB CREEK
BEGIN—OFF HWY. 389 END—COLORADO RIVER

----- Route

Fredonia

BEGIN

Alt 89

389

KAIBAB NATIONAL FOREST

Kanab Creek

KANAB CANYON

END Colorado River

GRAND CANYON NAT'L PARK

N

0   5 miles

Wesley Powell's second expedition down the Colorado River, Jones and Walter Powell noted the 1871–1872 gold rush that lured some 550 prospectors down Kanab Wash to the banks of the Colorado River. Major Powell's first cousin Clem best described those desperate times in a letter to the *Chicago Tribune*:

> Miners report every trail to the Colorado Cañons crowded with men seeking the new Eldorado. The washes leading down, such as Pipe Springs, Kanab, and Grand Wash, are the only practicable routes to the river. Some come in wagons, some on horseback, muleback, afoot, and one in a donkey-cart. Anything on wheels is utterly useless beyond this point. . . . They expected the rich leads of that never-to-be-forgotten year of '49. The excitement broke out so suddenly, the fever ran so high, that people crowded to the auriferous shore without food, without knowledge of mining, without proper implements. After prospecting for a time, and getting but a few fine grains of gold, provisions run out, hopes fall, starvation stares them in the face.

According to *Utah Historical Quarterly* editor Charles Kelly, after the taxing 60-odd-mile trek to the river from the last outpost of Pipe Springs most struggled back out of Kanab Creek half-starved and empty-handed. The mother lode they had hoped to strike in the depths of the Grand Canyon existed more in the minds of men than in the coarse sands of Big Red.

Prospectors weren't the only ones lured into trekking down the length of Kanab Creek from the vicinity of Pipe Springs. Clem started down on January 16, 1872, with John "Bonney" Bonnement and a cumbersome wet-plate camera he called an "infernal mountain howitzer"; he hoped to make his mark as a photographer. But the bitterly cold, 3-week-long expedition was a bust; not one of Clem's pictures developed. He was certain that E. O. Beaman, the original Powell Expedition photographer he was to assist, had sabotaged his chemicals. And if that wasn't enough to discourage a fledgling photographer from ever thinking about trying to take another picture again, on the way back up Kanab Creek one of the pack horses fell on Clem's camera. "In going over one bad place Riley's Horse, 'Doc,' fell off of a rock down some 11 or 12 feet. We all thought that he was killed at first, but falling square on his back saved him . . . [but] My camera was smashed to 10,000 pieces by the fall."

The most famous trek up or down Kanab Creek, however, took place later that same year, and it wasn't for the promise of fame or fortune; it was as an escape. Having nearly run the Colorado River through the length of the Grand Canyon for a second time, Major Powell was faced with a serious decision: If the expedition succeeded in running the dangerously high water below Kanab Creek in boats that were on the verge of falling apart, there was still the rumored threat of being ambushed by the Shivwits Paiute; on the other hand, if Major Powell called it good at Kanab Creek, he could finish mapping the rest of the canyon by hiking down at various points along the far western North Rim. Wrote Stephen Vandiver Jones: "the Major told me that owing to the shattered condition of the boats and the high stage of the water that we could leave the river here."

Major Powell and his expedition members took 4 days to walk and ride out Kanab Creek—and that's how long it will take you to follow in their footsteps.

Directions

From Fredonia, drive west on Highway 389 6 miles to an unmarked turnoff on the left (south); this is the Riggs Flat Road, approximately half a mile east of Milepost 27 and passable with a 2WD vehicle in dry weather. Follow this dirt track 2.8 miles to Nagles Crossing, the start of this end-to-end canyon trek. Theoretically, you can follow Kanab Creek right out of sleepy Fredonia, but starting at Nagles Crossing half a dozen miles downstream will help you avoid the fenced-off private land immediately to the south of Fredonia.

Canyon Log

(all mileages approximate)

Mile 0 to 5. Nagles Crossing to Booze Crossing. Coming from Kanab via the vicinity of modern Fredonia, it's difficult to pinpoint exactly where Powell's men entered and left upper Kanab Creek. On January 16, 1872, Clem wrote: "Our way led over the bottom till we struck the entrance of the canon." That could be anywhere in this sprawling land of Great Basin desert scrub, but Nagles Crossing seems like the logical place because men and horses could get fresh water at Quickwater Spring, a good alternative to silt-laden Kanab Creek water.

The first leg of Kanab Creek is actually a ditch, heavily lined with willows and tamarisk. Even Powell's men had to wrestle with dense stands of willows; avoid turning this leg of your adventure into a jungle experience by walking along the base of the silt-and-mud cliffs. About 2 miles below Nagles Crossing is a good Moenkopi terrace. And below Point 4580 (on your Fredonia, AZ quadrangle) you'll see the first of many fine cottonwoods that line Kanab Creek en route to the Colorado River.

Mile 5 to 11. Booze Crossing to Clear Water Spring. According to
Bureau of Land Management (BLM) archaeologist Rick Malcolmson, Booze
Crossing was used by Mormon pioneer and explorer Jacob Hamblin to
ford Kanab Creek during his travels through the area in the 1860s. Ironically, the only thing that still indicates this historic crossing is the 760-
kilovolt transmission lines that span the gap Kanab Creek has cut through
the Kaibab Limestone. Booze Crossing also approximates the point at which
you leave the Kaibab Indian Reservation and enter the 39,242-acre Kanab
Creek Wilderness Study Area. In the 1986 Arizona Strip Wilderness Study
Areas report, the BLM recommended "the entire Kanab Creek WSA as
nonsuitable for wilderness designation. The unit cannot be managed to
preserve wilderness character because of continuing mineral exploration
and interest in future mine development." Still searching for the mother
lode in the depths of Kanab Creek after all these years—only this time,
it's uranium. And only time will tell whether we'll all be drinking radioac-
tive water, because Kanab Creek drains into the Colorado River, which
we tap through the Central Arizona Project, among other ways.

Between Booze Crossing and Clearwater Spring, you'll spend much of
your time avoiding the tammies and willows; you'll make better progress
if you follow the benches above Kanab Creek proper.

The mouth of the drainage formed by Bitter Seeps Wash and Burnt
Canyon looks enticing; it was probably one of the key access points into
Kanab Creek from Pipe Springs for Powell's men and for prospectors during the 1871–1872 gold rush. Clem Powell's February 2 entry reads: "We
camped in the forks of two cañons, one which we came down." That could
be the confluence of Bitter Seeps and Burnt Canyon, or it could be the
mouth of those two canyons where they enter Kanab Creek. The area
is 8 to 10 miles southeast of what was once the last outpost of Pipe Springs;
that mileage corresponds to the frequent mention of an Eightmile Spring,
which might be the spring called Clear Water Spring today.

Mile 11 to 19. Clear Water Spring to Water Canyon. Clear Water
Spring is where it's indicated on your Fredonia, Arizona, quadrangle, and
whether or not it's the Eightmile Spring Clem Powell talked about, it's
a key water source for modern canyoneers. This freshwater spring, however,
is not fenced off, cattle have the run of it, and it's everything but clear.
So take your chances or try Birthday Spring.

About half a mile below Clear Water Spring, an unnamed drainage on
the right (west) comes off of Burnt Canyon Point; during this trek, a spring
located in this drainage above its confluence with Kanab Creek was reached

on expedition member Mike Young's fortieth birthday. The water percolating out of Birthday Spring is sweet, and the watercress growing around
it indicates it may be perennial. Birthday Spring is the pivotal water source
you need to find in order to reach Cedar Water Pockets 16 miles downstream.

From Birthday Spring, stay on the terrace above Kanab Creek on its
right (west) side until you're about half a mile below the mouth of Rock
Canyon. A trail threads the notch on the west side of the knob in the
NE ¼ section of Section 28; once you've gone through the gate, the trail
hugs the rimrock of Hermit Shale on the right (west) side of Kanab Creek.
There are two exposed sections along this stretch of Hermit, which seems
to correspond with Clem Powell's January 17 entry: "The cañon walls
growing higher, about 1500 feet high, and remind one of the cañons on
the river. We had a rough time of it, the trail being bad and ever anon
we had to force our way through the dense willows and again over some
steep rocky point where a single misstep would send a horse and rider
100 feet below among the rocks." Beyond this exposed traverse are several
comfortable spots to scramble back into Kanab Creek, now lined with
cottonwoods and Russian olive trees.

Mile 19 to 26-plus. Water Canyon to Snake Gulch. We didn't find
any water in Water Canyon during our August 5-8, 1988, trek, but as
Mike Young said, "If the truth be known, there's probably a tank on damn
near every one of these drainages." There is, and according to a route description by author Steve Aitchison in *The Hiker's Guide to Arizona,* "The riparian
or streamside vegetation has suffered in the upper reaches of Kanab due
to diversion of Kanab Creek by farmers in Fredonia and overgrazing."

Mile 26. Snake Gulch. Once you reach the vast arm of Snake Gulch,
it's much easier to pinpoint the movement of Powell's men all the way
to the river. In his well-written account of Powell's second expedition,
The Romance of the Colorado River, Dellenbaugh wrote: "We called it [Snake
Gulch] Shinumo Canyon because we found everywhere indications of the
former presence of that tribe." Stephen Vandiver Jones reported that he
and Major Powell "went up Shinimos Cañon 4 or 5 miles" on September
11, 1872, before returning to Kanab Canyon to complete their trip out
from Powell's second Colorado River expedition.

One of the most striking things you will see on this trek is the snake-
shaped rock alignment above the confluence of Snake Gulch and Kanab
Creek; at first, it looks like an exposed section of basalt several hundred
yards long, but in reality, it's a stone fence built by early cattlemen to

Two days into a four-day trek down the length of Kanab Canyon, canyoneer Mike Young uses a plastic baggie to fill his gallon water jug from this shallow tinaja (rain pocket). Photo by John Annerino.

fence off what must have been a lush grazing area. The only other places in the Southwest known to have this kind of stonework are the Mexican and Mormon farming villages outside of Juan Mata Ortíz, Chihuahua, where this type of fence is still in use today.

If you have the water but don't have the snap to make it another mile to the Cedar Water Pockets, the confluence of Snake Gulch and Kanab Creek is a good place to camp on your second day. Snake Gulch also marks the southern end of the BLM's Kanab Creek Wilderness Study Area and the northern boundary of the Kaibab National Forest's 77,100-acre Kanab Creek Wilderness Area.

Mile 26 to 36. Snake Gulch to Hack Canyon. From Snake Gulch you can see the wide bench of Supai Sandstone immediately to the south; in order to reach the Cedar Water Pockets, stay atop this mushroom-shaped platform on the left (east) side of Kanab Creek until you're approximately 1 mile south of Little Spring Canyon. To locate this key water source, scan the wide, shallow depressions in the white rock capping the red Supai for that life-sustaining reflection. Powell's men frequently mentioned these historic water pockets, referring to them as the "cedar tree." Wrote Dellenbaugh on September 10: "A trifle before sunset we arrived at the cedar tree, a short distance below the mouth of Shinumo Canyon, where our party had camped the previous March. The pockets were full of clear, fresh water, and we had plenty for horses as well as men. Not far off some human bones were found, old and bleached. We thought they must be the remains of the Navajo raider who escaped wounded from the Mormon attack near this locality."

From the Cedar Water Pockets, you can continue walking the rimrock on the east side of Kanab Creek until you're about 1 mile below Jensen Canyon. Here, in the main stem of Kanab Creek, the tammies begin to thin out and you can make good time walking the gravel beds or well-worn cattle trails paralleling either side of the creek all the way to Grama Canyon, and to Hack Canyon another 1.5 miles below.

Mile 36 to 44-plus. Hack Canyon to Jumpup Canyon. A towering rock spire marks the confluence of Hack Canyon, one of the most extensive canyon systems draining into Kanab Creek. Scientist Edwin McGee descended Hack Canyon in 1941 in order to fill the gap in the ancient Cambrian-age Grand Canyon rocks he felt could only "be filled by going down Kanab Canyon." Among other things, McGee discovered "that travel down the narrow steep-walled inner canyon was full of . . . excitement. One felt completely shut off from the world."

Under the BLM's All Wilderness Alternative, the 63,682-acre Hack Canyon Wilderness Study Area would become a wilderness area. But if mining interests sway the votes, only 12,531 acres of Hack Canyon would become a wilderness. During their 2-week-long exploration of Kanab Creek in the early 1960s, the husband and wife team of Rosalie and Melvin Goldstein entered Kanab Creek via Hack Canyon, In an account of their adventure, called "The Wrinkled Pink Walls of Kanab Canyon" and published in the July 1964 issue of *Arizona Highways Magazine*, the Goldsteins described the remains of mining exploration in Hack Canyon: "Disappointment has not obliterated an old tale of a lode of gold. There is an abandoned machine up in Hacks for grinding quartz. Uranium hunters looked in here, too." The trail the Goldsteins took down Hack Canyon was built by Pres Swapp and Bob Riggs, two Arizona Strip stockmen; it is one of the key access points for canyoneers wishing to explore the heart of Kanab Creek.

From Hack Canyon to the Colorado River 21 miles downstream is a deep, narrow confines, one of the most awesome tributary canyons in Arizona; while Paria Canyon matches Kanab's sublimity, only the Little Colorado River Gorge can match its stature. Chamberlain Canyon enters these head-craning narrows at Mile 40, where the Goldsteins described finding "an old prospectors' camp near its entrance. A coffee pot and fry-ing pan still rest on a rock ledge. The rats have eaten everything but a box of polished rice." The area immediately below Chamberlain still makes a fine campsite, though you shouldn't camp near Kanab Creek—particularly in these narrows—during summer monsoon season. At the time we were there, flash floods perhaps 2 weeks earlier had bowled over a 100-yard-long swath of willows and uprooted two giant cottonwoods, breaking them like matchsticks.

Mile 44-plus to 57. Jumpup Canyon to the Colorado River. Next to Hack Canyon, Jumpup Canyon at Mile 44-plus also provides pop-ular access for modern canyoneers into Kanab Creek. But as in Hack Canyon, all trails and routes leading into this remote wilderness are long and rugged and require time-consuming vehicle shuttles and in-novative logistics. Stephen Vandiver Jones wrote in his journal that he and his party "headed for Stewart's Ranche in a canon in the Kaivav," which, according to journal editor Dr. Herbert E. Gregory, is modern-day Jumpup Canyon.

Standing at the mouth of Jumpup Canyon near the 3,100-foot-level, you get the feeling you're staring into the mouth of a bottomless rock crusher that would first pulverize you, then drown what's left of you if a flash flood ever roared down off 6,000-foot-high Fishtail Mesa. If the going seemed fairly easy above Jumpup, the boulder hopping begins in earnest at this confluence.

The last key water source you need to find is located approximately 1.5 miles below the mouth of Jumpup; it's a series of freshwater springs that gurgle out from Kanab's muddy waters. A second series of springs is half a mile below these, about a quarter-mile upstream from an unnamed canyon entering from the left (east). The spring comes right out of the base of the Redwall and creates a short rivulet of fresh water that you can quaff right from the source. Three desert bighorn (one small ram and two ewes) curiously watched us from 100 feet above as we filled our water jugs from this unnamed spring.

Located near Mile 49, Shower Bath Spring was described by no fewer than three of Major Powell's expedition members, including Dellenbaugh, Jones, and Clem Powell. But Dellenbaugh's September 9 entry best describes it today: "The water charged with lime had built out from the wall a semi-circular mass covered by ferns, which was cut away below by floods till one could walk under in the sprinkling streams percolating through it. . . . This we called Shower-Bath Spring." After spending a day and a half tromping down the willow- and tammie-choked upper reaches of Kanab Creek, you will do well to follow Dellenbaugh's lead.

The difficulties of descending and reascending Kanab Creek seem to be concentrated immediately below Shower Bath Spring; while the obstacles are not insurmountable, they undoubtedly provided many toil-filled hours for early travelers trying to negotiate the streambed with a pack string.

Just below Shower Bath Spring, two deep pools of water can be negotiated by swimming or boulder scrambling, or avoid them altogether by gaining the ledge on the left (east) side of Kanab Creek until you can safely descend back into the creek bed. Immediately below this first cluster of boulders, several other house-sized boulder slides can also be negotiated without much difficulty. Dellenbaugh described the difficulty of negotiating these boulder slides with horses: "A small stream ran in the bottom, and this formed large pools amongst numerous ponderous boulders that had fallen in from the top of the walls some three thousand feet above our heads, the bottom being hardly more than sixty to seventy-five feet wide. It was with considerable difficulty that we got the animals past some of these places, and in one or two the pools were so long and deep they had to swim a little."

The Redwall Ledges. Approximately 1.5 miles below Shower Bath Spring, near Mile 50.5, pooled-up water collects in Kanab Creek's most dramatic drop. If you don't have flotation to negotiate this section, or if the air temperature is too cold, you can contour around this drop by ascending a faint trail several hundred vertical feet to the top of the Redwall Ledges on the left (east). Assuming you've been wearing tennis shoes to hike in the creek bed, you'll have to use extreme care in following the top of this broken ledge system until you can see the abrupt, elbow-shaped turn that Kanab Creek makes to the south. The steep talus slope that will take you safely back down to the creek bottom is upstream from this elbow-shaped bend; do not try descending off this rotten ledge system before you locate this key talus slope and see that it clearly connects the Redwall Ledges with the creek bottom.

Once safely across the Redwall Ledges, you'll realize how difficult it was for Jones, Dellenbaugh, and Clem Powell to negotiate Kanab Creek below Shower Bath Spring with their pack horses. While doing so on January 22, Clem Powell wrote: "The trail is now so bad that at a great many places [we] are compelled to lead our horses over one by one." From the bottom of the Redwall Ledges, you'll boulder hop and creek wade for approximately 6 miles before you reach the Colorado River. But the scenery is stunning, so take time to stop now and again to let it all settle in; you've earned it.

270 *Adventuring in Arizona*

Once you do reach the Colorado River at about Mile 57, you'll face the same problem all early travelers faced at this point: How do I get back to civilization? During the 1870s, the answer was simple. You struggled back the way you came, either to Pipe Spring or Kanab. Today, however, you have half a dozen options. You can trek back out to Nagles Crossing, in which case you should have cached some food during your descent. You can hike out to a prearranged car shuttle at the top of Hack or Jumpup canyon. You can crawl the 7 thankless, boulder-strewn river miles upstream to Deer Creek and take the Surprise Valley and Thunder River trails to a vehicle shuttle atop the North Rim—an option frequently chosen by canyoneers. (For a description of Thunder River Trails, see *Hiking the Grand Canyon*, by John Annerino.) Or you can avoid the problem altogether, spend a day and a half baking in the sparse shade of a lone tammie, try to hitchhike—then beg—a ride on a riverboat down to the mouth of Havasu Creek, and hike out to Hualapai Hilltop.

Travel Notes

• **Primary access.** As described, via Nagles Crossing. Access also via Snake Gulch, Hack Canyon (see entry for Sunshine Road), Jumpup Canyon, and Colorado River.

• **Elevation loss.** Approximately 2,700 vertical feet.

• **Mileage.** 57 miles one way from Nagles Crossing to the Colorado River, though you'll probably trek more than 60 miles when all is said and done.

• **Water sources.** Clear Water Spring, Birthday Spring, Cedar Water Pockets, the springs below Jumpup Canyon, Kanab Creek (if allowed to settle overnight before treating), and the Colorado River.

• **Cache points.** If you're returning via Nagles Crossing, consider caching food near the above-mentioned water sources.

• **Escape routes.** Give serious thought to this before descending Kanab Creek. If you have a shuttle vehicle parked atop Hack or Jumpup canyon and you're closer to either of these canyons than to the Colorado River, then that may be your best bet. However, if you're within a few miles of the Colorado River and it's river-running season, you might be better off going to the Colorado River and flagging down a commercial river outfitter.

• **Seasons.** The dry seasons of fall and spring would be most enjoyable. Winter can be downright cold and summers can be unforgivingly hot— or flood-swept.

- **Maps.** Fredonia, Jumpup Canyon, and Kanab Point quadrangles (15 minute).

- **Nearest supply points.** Fredonia and Kanab.

- **Managing agencies.** Kaibab-Paiute Tribal Council (Tribal Affairs Building, Pipe Springs Road, Fredonia, AZ 86022; 602-643-7245); Bureau of Land Management (Arizona Strip District Office, 196 East Tabernacle, Saint George, UT 84770; 801-673-3545); North Kaibab Ranger District (P.O. Box 248, Fredonia, AZ 86022; 602-653-5895); Grand Canyon National Park (Back Country Reservations Office, P.O. Box 129, Grand Canyon, AZ 86023; 602-638-2474).

- **Backcountry information.** For permission to use Nagles Crossing, contact the Kaibab-Paiute Tribal Council. For permits to camp overnight in Grand Canyon National Park, contact the Backcountry Reservations Office.

- **Biotic communities (along streambed).** Great Basin Desert scrub and Mojave Desert scrub.

Buckskin Gulch and Paria Canyon

Colorado Plateau: day hikes and extended treks

Landform

Of the four major tributaries that drain into the Grand Canyon between Lee's Ferry and Lake Mead, Paria Canyon is the shortest — but many would say it's the most spectacular. While the Little Colorado River Gorge, Kanab Creek, and Havasu and Cataract canyons are longer and perhaps more rugged, 35-mile-long Paria Canyon is a deep, twisting labyrinth that forms a natural boundary between the Paria Plateau to the southwest and the Kaiparowits Plateau to the northeast. For all practical purposes, Bryce Canyon forms the headwaters of the Paria River, which drains into the Colorado River near Lee's Ferry some 90 miles downstream. According to an early geographical reconnaissance of the Kaiparowits region conducted by the U.S. Geological Survey, the entire Paria River drains 935 square miles. But it's the lower gorge of this flash-flood–swept drainage that created the most intimidating obstacle for early travelers.

Historical Overview

Ancient petroglyphs adorning Paria Canyon's slick sandstone walls suggest it was a well-traveled route through the Pueblo Indians' ancestral lands;

according to archaeologists, these Indians inhabited the area around A.D. 1100. However, except for their puzzling and fascinating rock art, the Pueblo left few clues as to what difficulties—and discoveries—they encountered while traveling through Paria Canyon. The first men to provide any information were Francisco Dominguez and Silvestre Escalante in 1776; trapped like dogs on the west side of the Colorado River, the Spanish padres ventured only 2.5 miles up Paria Canyon before their guide found a route through the imposing rim of Echo Cliffs. (See entry for Echo Cliffs.)

The first recorded descent of Paria Canyon, however, didn't take place until polygamist John D. Lee arrived on the scene in 1871. According to W. L. Rusho and C. Gregory Crampton's *Desert River Crossing,* Lee had been excommunicated from the Mormon Church for his alleged participation in the Mountain Meadows Massacre; he and fifty other Mormon men—along with their Paiute allies—had played a role in murdering a wagon train full of 122 emigrants in September of 1857. Lee was subsequently ordered by the church to establish a reliable ford on the Colorado River.

But first Lee had to get to the river from Saint George, Utah. The only practical trail across the Arizona Strip, via Pipe Spring, was the route Dominguez and Escalante had pioneered in 1776; it headed south down Houserock Valley on the west side of the Paria Plateau before turning east along the base of the Vermilion Cliffs. Perhaps sensing a "shortcut" around the east side of Paria Plateau, Lee decided to head straight down Paria Canyon from the Mormon settlement of Pahreah. By today's canyoneering standards, that might not seem like such an improbable undertaking, but Lee drove sixty head of cattle to Pahreah and then embarked on one of the most outrageous cattle drives of all times.

Fortunately, Lee kept a diary, later edited by Juanita Brooks and Robert Cleland in *A Mormon Chronicle: The Diaries of John D. Lee: 1848–1876.* On December 3, 1871, Lee wrote,

> We concluded to drive down the creek, which took us Some 8 days of toil, fatuige, & labour, through brush, water, ice, & quicksand & some time passing through narrow chasms with perpendicular Bluffs on both sides, some 3000 feet high, & without seeing the sun for 48 hours, & every day Some of our animals Mired down & had to shoot one cow & leve her there, that we could not get out, & I My Self was under water. Mud & Ice every day. We finally reachd within 3 ms. of the mouth with 12 head, leveing the remander to feed some 10 ms. above. 4 days had Elapsed since our provisions had exasted, Save Some beef that we cut off the cow that was Mired.

Lee succeeded in reaching the mouth of Paria Canyon, and with the support of his seventeenth wife, Emma, established the first reliable ford across the Colorado River; it soon became known as Lee's Ferry, but Emma referred to it as Lonely Dell because she considered it a stark outpost in which to raise nine children. To make matters worse for Emma and the children, Lee was executed by a firing squad for his part in the Mountain Meadows Massacre just 6 years after he and his brethren made their remarkable cattle drive down Paria Canyon; for some reason, he had been pegged the sole scapegoat and was issued his death warrant at Mountain Meadows 2 decades after the massacre took place. Ironically, Lee had reportedly killed no one because his gun misfired.

Hardly a year had passed since Lee's first successful descent of Paria Canyon when another party tried to go *up* the canyon. According to an article in the 1881 bulletin "United Service: A Monthly Review Of Military And Naval Affairs," a military expedition met with horrible disaster deep within the confines of Paria Canyon. The author, identified only as T. V. B., described the ordeal in "An Episode of Military Explorations and Surveys." According to T. V. B., the eleven-man party, led by Lt. W. L. B. of the Army Corps of Engineers, was assigned to explore the "rim of the Great Basin of Southern Utah, thence go to the Colorado River, ascend and explore the cañon of Paria, and return." Of what strategic importance Paria Canyon held T. V. B. did not disclose; what he does say is that, while en route to the mouth of Paria Canyon during October of 1872, the expedition found the nights so cold that the men "would pile up half a dozen dead pine-trees and start a fire that lit up the pine woods for miles." No doubt, the old saying "White man builds big fire, stands back; Indian builds little fire, huddles close" grew from this expedition, because that's essentially what the group's Pah-Ute Indian guide tried to tell the men before abandoning the expedition, concluding "whitey man big fool!"

When T. V. B. and the nine remaining men started up Paria Canyon on November 20, they were under the impression that no one had ever gotten through the canyon before. The Mormons they'd met at Paria either were unaware of Lee's success, or wanted to keep the fugitive's whereabouts unknown; they told the expedition members only that "a flock of geese . . . had swam through the cañon" before. If that was some kind of cryptic warning, the expedition members failed to heed it. They spent much of the first day digging out their mules, which repeatedly got stuck in quicksand; consequently, they made only 10 miles.

The second day was undoubtedly worse. The mules fought the bit every time the men tried to ride them through "caverns dark as night"; by night fall, the men were nearly hypothermic after the day's struggle and camped on a "peninsula of rocks."

Day 3 marked the last for the expedition's German cook, identified only as Kittelman. After getting stuck belly deep in quicksand, Kittelman's mule rolled over and fell on him. Somehow, two men managed to hold the mule's head out of the frigid water, while the others frantically dug the struggling animal out. In the process, Kittelman got thrashed badly, but he survived. Kittelman must have been a proud German, though, because later that afternoon he volunteered to lead the others through a deep, ice-covered pond, after Lt. W. L. M. had failed to do so. Assuming the expedition covered 10 miles on the second day, and at least half that on the third day, it would have been in the vicinity of the confluence of Buckskin Gulch and the Paria's narrows, where deep pools 50 feet across are known to form. Of Kittelman's honorable attempt, T. V. B. wrote:

> Kittelman, though shivering with cold and scarcely more than half conscious . . . [said] that he was not afraid to ride his horse where any other man was willing to go. The animal entered the pool without hesitation, and had gotten nearly half-way across when, as if sucked down, man and horse disappeared. In about twenty seconds the man's head again came to the surface, as well as that of the horse, Kittelman no longer on the horse but evidently still clutching the bridle—his gaze vacant. After a few seconds, to our horror, man and horse disappeared and . . . [were] about to perish before our very eyes—almost within reach of our hand—and we utterly powerless for help, for who would plunge into that ice-covered pool, occupied as it was by a horse struggling for life?

Lieutenant W. L. M. would, and 15 seconds later he surfaced with the cold, limp, but still-breathing Kittelman. However, all efforts to revive Kittelman failed, and the following morning expedition members stuffed his body into a crevice a dozen feet above low water before heading out of Paria Canyon for good.

Directions

Three popular trailheads provide access into Paria Canyon; which you choose depends on the kind of trek you're planning. You can day hike in from Lee's Ferry at the mouth of Paria Canyon, or from either White House or Wire Pass at Paria's upper end. If you're planning to trek the length of Paria Canyon—as most people do—the most popular access point is White House Trailhead; Wire Pass Trailhead runs a close second. Another option is to hike down Buckskin Gulch from Wire Pass and up Paria

Canyon to White House; this route avoids what some less-seasoned canyoneers consider a tiresome slog below the confluence of Buckskin and Paria to Lee's Ferry, and it takes you through fantastic scenery. Described here is the route from Wire Pass to Lee's Ferry.

Lee's Ferry Trailhead. (About where Dominguez and Escalante, and the disastrous Kittelman Expedition, entered Paria Canyon.) From Flagstaff, drive north on Highways 89 and 89A 110 miles to Marble Canyon; turn north at the Lee's Ferry turnoff and drive 6 miles to the Historic Site of Lee's Ferry. The trail passes the cemetery and goes straight up the mouth of Paria Canyon on its west side.

White House Trailhead. (Near where John D. Lee entered Paria Canyon.) From Page, drive west on Highway 89 28 miles to the White House turnoff; the trailhead is located 2 miles south on this dirt road. The BLM's Paria Canyon entrance station is also located on this road; you can pick up your permits there and get up-to-date weather information — your most important consideration before heading toward the same narrows that proved Kittelman's undoing.

The Wire Pass Trailhead.   (Where this adventure begins.) From the White House turnoff, drive another 5 miles west on Highway 89 to the Houserock Valley Road. Turn south and drive 8.3 miles to the Wire Pass Trailhead.

Car Shuttles.   Unless you're going to walk all the way to Paria Canyon from parts unknown, you'll need a car shuttle; the only way to avoid one is by day hiking or by doing an out-and-back overnighter. You can work out the logistics with your hiking partners, or hire a shuttle driver.

Canyon Log

Mile 0 to 1.5.   Wire Pass to Buckskin Gulch. A tributary drainage of Buckskin Gulch, Wire Pass forms the beginning of the longest, narrowest, and perhaps darkest canyon known to man. Not long after you enter this slot canyon, you'll feel as if you're walking through the eye of a needle. At two points you'll probably need to take your pack off in order to proceed: The first obstruction is a chockstone wedged between baby-slick walls, a warm-up for those awaiting you down below in Buckskin Gulch; the second point is where the walls pinch closely together.

Mile 1.5 to 6.3.   Buckskin Gulch to Middle Trail. Buckskin Gulch is not shown on the earliest maps of the region: it was commonly known

as Kaibab Gulch, but somewhere along the way the name got changed.
The earliest recorded exploration of Kaibab Gulch was made during the
summer of 1922 by H. E. Gregory and L. F. Noble, two scientists making a stratigraphic reconnaissance of the region. In his 1928 report, Noble
wrote: "So far as we could ascertain the region around and just north of
Kaibab Gulch is the only area within or along the borders of the Kaibab
Plateau where both the upper and lower contacts of the Kaibab limestone
are exposed." Their recon would place them somewhere above the
confluence of Wire Pass and Buckskin Gulch, because at this point Buckskin Gulch cuts through the Navajo Sandstone, which is frequently no
more than 15 feet wide.

But the word *fissure* would more accurately describe this landform than
the word *gulch*, because trekking through Buckskin Gulch is like traveling
through a giant crack in the earth whose undulating, overhanging walls
often block out the sky completely. On sunny days—the only time you
should hike through this natural storm drain—a warm, ambient light refracts
off its golden walls, and incandescent shafts of light occasionally penetrate
the depths. You only have to look at the logs jammed between the walls
of this fissure 50 feet overhead to realize that Buckskin Gulch is not the
place to be on a cloudy day; you would need a headlamp to see where
you were going, and a life jacket wouldn't do any good if a flash flood
roared through this tunnel. Historian P. T. Reilly wrote that Buckskin
and Paria were "deeply incised . . . intaglio[s] in sandstone impossible to
cross for man or beast." After you hop over your first dead coyote lying
on the floor of Buckskin Gulch, you'll see how right he was. In order
to reach the foot of the Middle Trail, you'll also have to climb over log
jams and giant chockstones before you wade through a dank, mucky sump
of stagnant water called the Cesspool near Mile 5.8.

Mile 6.3 to 11.8. Middle Trail to the Confluence of Paria Canyon.
You've heard that old wives' tale, "If you want to know what the weather's
doing, just look out the window." Well, the short scramble out of Buckskin Gulch via the Middle Trail offers you the only way to do that before
continuing downstream. So if you have any worries about flash floods,
climb out the Middle Trail and try to second-guess the *Farmers Almanac*.
The pinyon-covered mesa at the top of Middle Trail, known as the West
Clark Bench, makes a good destination for an overnight trek; it is also
the only practical place to photograph Buckskin Gulch from above.

Known to geologists as an "inclosed meander," Buckskin Gulch, from
the foot of the Middle Trail down to the confluence of Paria Canyon,

was aptly described in *The Kaiparowits Region: A Geographic And Geologic Reconnaissance Of Parts Of Utah And Arizona*; wrote H. E. Gregory and Raymond C. Moore: "All the [Colorado Plateau] canyons are sinuous to a degree very much greater than indicated on topographic maps. Close-set meanders with horseshoe curves and goosenecks are common, and the traverse of many a canyon involves passing to right and left about towering buttresses with turns approaching 180 degrees."

At Mile 10.1 you'll encounter the Boulder Slide, the 30-foot tumble that Buckskin Gulch takes over several house-sized rocks. There should be at least one stout rope anchored in place to safeguard your descent; if there's not, lower your pack on the short piece of nylon rope, or shroud line, that you brought along as insurance before downclimbing modern "Moki Steps" undoubtedly hacked into place by a retired miner.

Mile 11.8. The Confluence of Buckskin Gulch and Paria Canyon forms the heart of the Paria River Narrows. The Narrows, however, are about 40 to 50 feet wide, and after emerging from Buckskin Gulch, you'll suddenly feel as if you're in Big Sky Country—albeit with 1,500-foot walls towering overhead. The Narrows should never be underestimated; there's no place to run in the event of a flash flood, and large, deep pools form here after heavy winter precipitation and summer monsoons. This seasonal "lake," as some canyoneers call it, can be floated with an air mattress during the late spring and early fall, though it should be avoided during cold weather, as the Kittelman tragedy so vividly illustrated.

If you turn north up Paria Canyon at the confluence, it's 7 miles to the White House Trailhead parking lot; if you turn south down Paria Canyon, it's 25 miles to the Lee's Ferry Trailhead. The following description highlights Paria Canyon between the confluence and Lee's Ferry.

Mile 11.8 to 22.3. The confluence south to Judd Hollow. In the parlance of geologists, Wire Pass, Buckskin Gulch, Paria Canyon—and Colorado Plateau canyons like them—are all considered *inclosed meanders*; Gregory and Moore further described them in *The Kaiparowits Region*: "In the canyons that enter the Colorado from the north and from the south closely pressed curves and almost right-angled turns mark the course of parallel canyon walls; straight sections are rare, and in few places is it possible to see both walls for half a mile ahead." From the confluence all the way to Judd Hollow, these are the dominant characteristics of this serpentine labyrinth.

As to what you'll be walking on, wading—perhaps swimming—through, and scrambling over, that's another matter awaiting your discovery. Just below the confluence you'll leave Utah and cross into Arizona. Freshwater springs and seeps are found throughout this section, and they're preferable to settling, straining, and purifying Paria River water. Apparently John D. Lee and his family did not treat Paria River water before they drank it; according to P. T. Reilly's "Historic Utilization of Paria River," the Lees, among others, "suffered frequently from dysentery and related illnesses."

Mile 20.3. The Adams Trail. Water-born bacteria didn't stop ranchers like Johnny Adams from trying to tap this dependable source of water. According to Reilly, the Arizona Strip faced a severe drought during the Depression era of the 1930s that forced pioneer stockmen like Adams to take imaginative steps to get water to their stock. Adams had no other choice; his cattle range lay atop the 6,000-foot-high Paria Plateau. Once known as the Sand Hills, the Paria Plateau was a veritable desert for early cattlemen and Pueblo Indians who, during parched conditions, traveled back and forth to existing springs near the base of the Vermilion Cliffs. To this day, no perennial springs exist atop this sweeping, sand-blasted mesa of pinyon and juniper; the few dependable natural water sources before stock tanks were developed were shallow pockets of rainwater that evaporated quickly between seasonal rains. Reilly wrote: "As these water-holes dried up and the carcasses of his cattle littered the landscape, Adams decided during the winter of 1938–1939 that his operation could not survive another waterless summer."

Enter Johnny Adams' Pipe Dream. Adams had his men forge a trail off the rim of the Paria Plateau into Paria Canyon, but this "trail" was so dangerously steep and rugged that horses couldn't be ridden down it. So the water pump, along with 2,000 feet of pipe, had to be lowered ledge by ledge from the rim of the Paria Plateau into Paria Canyon. Incredibly, the drought broke just as Adams' men reached the floor of Paria Canyon, so this feat of cowboy engineering was never truly tested.

Others apparently wanted to try out the pump, because Adams' setup changed hands several times throughout the next decade until, finally, Gerald Swapp bought it and moved it. Swapp's range was across Paria Canyon, on the opposite rim; so the entire operation had to be dismantled and lugged 2 miles downstream to Judd Hollow, where an additional 2 miles of pipe would be needed to reach the Echo rim. But Gerald Swapp died on March 28, 1949, and his range never bore fruit from Adams' Pipe Dream, either.

Today, an experienced canyoneer can still follow what remains of the Adams Trail to the top of Paria Plateau near Mile 20, and remnants of Swapp's labor can still be seen at Judd Hollow near Mile 22.3.

Mile 22.3 to 41.6. Judd Hollow to Lonely Dell. Few modern canyoneers would trade all of Glen Canyon for Paria Canyon – basically one
of Glen Canyon's tributaries. Ironically, it wasn't until Congress sanctioned
Glen Canyon Dam in 1956 that the upper end of Paria Canyon suddenly
became accessible to modern travelers. According to Reilly, that's when
Highway 89 was rerouted between Page and Kanab, Utah, and when the
first "backpackers" trekked down the length of Paria. That's also about the
time that Wrather Arch was discovered. Located near Mile 25.3, Wrather
Arch is a short hop up Wrather Canyon; fresh water emanates from a
spring below this thick, flying span of Navajo Sandstone – though you should
avoid camping in this wonderfully delicate area.

Not long after passing the mouth of Wrather Canyon, Paria Canyon
chisels its way through the Kayenta and Moenave sandstones at Mile 27.
At Mile 31.4, Bush Head Canyon enters from the south; it's the last major
tributary drainage you'll encounter before Paria Canyon lays open and
turns southwest near Mile 34. According to author Michael Kelsey, eighteen
desert bighorn sheep were transplanted here from Lake Mead in July 1984;
Kelsey wrote *Hiking and Exploring the Paria River,* the most comprehensive guide to the Paria River drainage and a must for canyoneers interested
in treks other than a tromp down Paria Canyon from one end to the other.
While poking into many nooks and crannies, the well-traveled Kelsey discovered a route below the mouth of Wrather Canyon that leads up to
Paria's North Rim; near the top of this route, Kelsey found several panels
of petroglyphs that corresponded with those he found above Wrather Arch
on the opposite rim. He surmised that this was an old Indian trail and
that it was "perhaps the only place in this canyon where you can go from
rim to rim, via the river in between." During the summer of 1968, archaeologists from the Museum of Northern Arizona surveyed sections of
Houserock Valley and the southwest corner of the Paria Plateau and discovered several descent routes leading from ancient Pueblo dwellings atop
Paria Plateau to perennial water sources at the foot of the Vermilion Cliffs.
Their report suggests that Kelsey may indeed have pieced together an ancient Indian route across what has long been considered the only natural
course of travel through the Paria and Kaiparowits plateaus: down the
spectacular but narrow, brushy, and boulder-choked streambed of Paria
Canyon.

So if about Mile 33 you're beginning to think you're slogging down
the river of no return, you can now look at canyoneering through Paria
from a different perspective: Its soaring walls have natural lines of weak-
ness undoubtedly scaled 1,000 years before John D. Lee first herded cattle

through what may have also seemed like an endless gorge to him. But no one knows which routes the Pueblo took to reach Paria's silt-laden water, or which routes may have offered them the best means of escape from its worst flash floods. A record flow of 19,000 cfs ripped through Paria Canyon on September 12, 1958; to put that in perspective, the BLM considers anything over 39 cfs dangerous for canyoneers. The Kittelman Expedition certainly didn't realize there were any routes out of Paria, other than up- or downstream. Wrote T. V. B.:

> We were upon a peninsula of rocks, just large enough to accommodate the party; beside us flowed the dark stream; over us rose to a vertical height of over three thousand feet of rocky walls of the chasm, but a few stars being visible. The body of Kittelman lay a few feet from the fire, covered by a blanket. The glare of the fire served only to intensify the weirdness of the scene. Added to this was the knowledge that should to-morrow be an unusually warm day the snow would melt in the mountains, the stream would rise, and we should be drowned like rats in a cage before the end of the cañon could again be reached.

Travel Notes

•**Primary access.**   For the route described, Wire Pass.

•**Secondary access.**   White House Trailhead and Lee's Ferry. Because it's difficult to predict the weather—or the flash flood potential—in upper Paria from the mouth of Paria Canyon, it's best to use the Lee's Ferry Trailhead only as a departure point for day hikes, not end-to-end treks.

•**Elevation loss.**   Approximately 2,500 vertical feet.

•**Mileage.**   Approximately 42 miles from Wire Pass to Lee's Ferry.

•**Water sources.**   Paria River; sinkholes in Buckskin Gulch; freshwater springs near Mile 14.5, at Mile 17, up Wrather Canyon at Mile 25.3, at Mile 26.8, at Mile 30.1, and half a mile up Bush Head Canyon at Mile 31.4.

•**Cache points.**   None on this point-to-point trek.

•**Escape routes.**   Depending on the nature of the emergency, whichever trailhead you're closest to: your vehicle at Wire Pass, the White House ranger station, or Lee's Ferry.

•**Seasons.**   See chart. The dry months of May to June and September to October are generally best.

• **Quicksand.** You've seen it in the Old West movies: A lone cowhand tries to pull a wailing calf out of the muck; in the struggle, he falls in and begins sinking helplessly out of sight, when, out of nowhere, the trail boss lassoes him with a rope and drags him out with his horse. Well, those are the movies. While John D. Lee and the Kittelman Expedition both had problems with quicksand, it proved troublesome basically for their stock. Fortunately, most of us are built differently than a 1,200-pound animal supported by four skinny legs. And unless you encounter the Vacuum Monster lying in wait at the bottom of one of Paria's sinkholes, you'll really have to work at sinking more than thigh deep.

• **Flash floods.** What should be of greater concern to you are flash floods; never anything to take lightly, they are particularly dangerous in Wire Pass, Buckskin Gulch, and the slot canyon sections of Paria. The chart put out by the Bureau of Land Management should help you plan your trip during the optimum season.

• **Maps.** Buckskin Mountain and Paria; Utah-Arizona; Paria Plateau and Lee's Ferry, AZ (all 15 minute).

• **Nearest supply points.** Page, Marble Canyon, Cliff Dwellers, Vermilion Cliffs, Jacob's Lake.

• **Managing agency.** Bureau of Land Management, 320 North First East, Kanab, UT 84741; (801) 644-2672.

• **Other emergency contacts.** Lee's Ferry National Park Service Ranger Station (602-355-2234); Kane County Sheriff (801-644-2349); and Coconino County Sheriff (602-645-2461).

• **Backcountry information.** Permits required for overnight camping; campfires allowed.

• **Biotic communities.** Juniper-pinyon Woodland and Great Basin Desert scrub.

Bright Angel and North Kaibab Trails

Grand Canyon: rim-to-rim hike

Landform

Smaller than Barranca del Cobre (Copper Canyon) in Chihuahua, Mexico, and shallower than Oregon and Idaho's 7,900-foot-deep Hell's Canyon, the Grand Canyon still ranks as the most awesome single-canyon complex on Earth. Comprising an estimated 2,000 square miles of northern Arizona, the Grand Canyon is 2 to 18 miles wide and, near the head of the Nankoweap Trail, almost 6,000 feet deep. Between Lee's Ferry at River Mile 0 and Pierce Ferry on Lake Mead at Mile 279, more than seventy-seven major tributary drainages still feed the once-mighty Colorado River, which cut its way through the Grand Canyon, some estimate, 5 to 20 million years ago.

Historical Overview

In *The Grand Colorado*, anthropologist and author Robert C. Euler wrote of the first canyoneers to use many of those tributary drainages as routes into and out of the Canyon: "Four thousand years before Major Powell's men tumbled through the Grand Canyon in their wooden boats, before geologists and archaeologists investigated its lessons and records, before photographers adjusted their focus and tourists stood on the south rim in awe—four thousand years before all this, human beings had wandered the Canyon's depths."

Ostensibly, these prehistoric canyoneers trekked into the heart of the Grand Canyon in quest of food. Hunters and gatherers, the ancient people of the desert culture scattered evidence of their seasonal wanderings in some of the Canyon's remote Redwall caves. Euler suggests that these crude, woven figures, called split-twig figurines, were effigies for a successful hunt, though no one knows for certain if this is true. But archaeological evidence unearthed at Unkar Delta indicates that the Anasazi (ancient ones) did trek into the Canyon more than 800 years ago to tend to small farms near the Colorado River. In *The Mountain Lying Down*, Euler paints a vivid picture of what the Anasazi might have looked like:

> The year was 1143 A.D. It was a raw spring day and a cold southwesterly
> wind was blowing as the two people slowly made their way up a precarious route from the canyon depths to the north rim. Each carried a large
> basket supported by a trumpline over the forehead, containing food—
> dried meat and the cooked and edible portion of the century plant—
> and skins filled with water. The man and woman were warmly dressed
> in loosely fitting cotton clothing covered with downy feathered robes.
> They wore heavy sandals made of yucca fibers. . . . It had taken them
> two days to walk out of the canyon.

In 1540, García López de Cárdenas tried to descend into the Grand Canyon, but his 3-day effort was a bust. Undoubtedly the sheer scale of the Canyon

Shuttle Services:

The following provide commercial shuttle service from Lee's Ferry to Paria Canyon trailheads:

Rona Levein Clark
Marble Canyon, AZ 86036
Phone: (602) 355-2262

Marble Canyon Lodge
Marble Canyon, AZ 86036
Phone: (602) 355-2225

Howard Clark
Vermillion Cliffs Lodge
Box HC 67-12
Marble Canyon, AZ 86036
Message Phone: (602) 355-9206

Sue Larson
Highway 89A
Marble Canyon, AZ 86036
Phone: (602) 355-2238

Richard Clark
Box HC 67-12
Marble Canyon, AZ 86036
Phone: (602) 355-2281

Ken Berlin
Box 13
Marble Canyon, AZ 86036
Phone: (602) 355-2286

Lake Powell Air Service
P.O. Box 1385
Page, AZ 86040
Phone: (602) 645-2494
(for persons arriving by air to Page, Arizona)

Kelley Louise
Vermillion Cliffs Lodge
Marble Canyon, AZ 86036
Phone: (602) 355-2215 (wk)
(602) 355-2282

overwhelmed him—as it continues to overwhelm modern canyoneers. Said Cárdenas: "What appeared to be easy from above was not so, but instead very hard and difficult." It wasn't until June 20, 1776, that Spanish missionary Francisco Garces became the first non-Indian to reach the bottom of the Grand Canyon. According to J. Donald Hughes' excellent and soundly researched *The Story of Man at the Grand Canyon* (updated and revised as *In the House of Stone and Light*), Garces descended "into a deep canyon of the 'Rio Jabesua' (Havasu or Cataract Creek) by traveling down a very precipitous trail. . . . Its canyon, he noted, was so deep that the sun did not rise until 10:00 A.M., and its red soil, watered by the creek, grew trees, grass and rich crops." Garces had discovered the lost paradise of the Havasupai Indians.

Paria River Canyon Information for Hikers

Flash Flood (1) Frequency		Water Level (2) Number of Days per Month			Water Temperature			Air Temperatures		Precipitation
		0-19cfs	20-39cfs	Over 39cfs	High	Low	Average	Mean Maximum	Mean Minimum	(inches)
1/5	Jan.	15.7	11.4	3.9	50	33	36.6	47	25	.38
1/10	Feb.	10.7	10.0	7.3	54	34	44.3	57	31	.47
3/10	Mar.	19.9	7.4	3.7	72	36	53.0	66	39	.49
0	Apr.	25.6	3.0	1.4	77	47	53.7	77	48	.39
1/10	May	28.4	1.7	0.9	90	50	68.3	86	56	.31
0	June	28.6	0.5	0.9	94	63	75.1	96	64	.24
1.9	July	24.4	2.1	4.5	90	70	79.0	103	72	.73
3.0	Aug.	18.2	3.7	9.1	91	64	75.0	100	70	1.18
1.4	Sept.	23.7	2.8	3.5	83	55	69.0	94	61	.51
3/10	Oct.	28.7	1.3	1.0	79	40	61.9	79	49	.42
1/2	Nov.	22.6	5.0	1.5	60	36	48.8	61	35	.39
3/10	Dec.	17.1	11.6	2.3	53	33	36.7	49	27	.44

(1) A flash flood is defined as a rise in daily runoff of 50 cfs or more. The actual rise in runoff rate will normally occur over a short period of time and be maintained for 1-4 days. 200-400 cfs rises in river level are periodically recorded. A frequency of 1/5 indicates a flash flood will occur during this month once in 5 years. 3.0 indicates an average of 3 flash floods during this month each year. 0 indicates there have been no flash floods during this month in the 10-year record used for computing this chart.

(2) Water Level. 0-19 cfs is considered comfortable for wading and hiking. 20-39 cfs is considered uncomfortable, but not dangerous. Over 39 cfs is considered DANGEROUS.

Data extracted from U.S. Geological Survey records for Les Ferry, Arizona.

According to Byrd H. Granger's *Grand Canyon Place Names*, the peace-loving Havasupai originally lived far to the east in the Little Colorado Valley until hostile neighbors drove them into the Grand Canyon's secure, verdant niches like Havasu. Undoubtedly, Bright Angel Creek also offered the Havasupai a safe haven, because as late as 1900, George Wharton James observed evidence of the Havasupai's occupation there. In *In and Around the Grand Canyon,* James wrote: "This — as were all the trails from the Little Colorado River to Havasu (Cataract) Canyon — was used first long ages ago by the Havasupai Indians, and, in the heart of the side canyon down which the trail goes, are still to be seen the rude irrigating canals which conveyed the large volume of water that flows from a near-by spring to the so-called Indian Garden, the richness of whose verdure is one of the great attractions to the tourist who gazes down from the rim." James wasn't a rim-bound author or tourist; he spent 10 years traveling many of the Grand Canyon's remote vistas and inner trails, and consequently came to know the Canyon as the "most sublime spectacle of earth." Along the Bright Angel Creek, named by John Wesley Powell during his first Colorado River expedition in 1869, the Bright Angel Trail was improved by Ralph and Niles Cameron between 1890 and 1891; the Camerons called it the Cameron Trail and, until Coconino County wrested control of it in 1928, charged tourists a buck a head to use it.

According to a paper on file at Grand Canyon National Park, called "Chronology of Grand Canyon Trails," Dan Hogan and Henry Ward became the first white men to hike the Canyon rim to rim in 1891; they descended the Cameron Trail to Indian Gardens, then followed lower Pipe Creek Canyon to the Colorado River before climbing out Bright Angel Canyon to the North Rim. Although Hogan and Ward's was the first recorded rim-to-rim trek using that route, Powell and his men first hiked up Bright Angel Canyon 55 years before the North Kaibab Trail would link the South and North rims; on August 16, 1869, Powell wrote: "Early in the morning the whole party starts up to explore the Bright Angel River, with the special purpose of seeking timber from which to make oars."

François Emile Matthes, the USGS cartographer responsible for surveying and making the first topographical map of the Grand Canyon in 1902, made the first recorded descent of Bright Angel Canyon. The route he and his men used to cross the Canyon from the North Rim descended the short northern arm of Bright Angel Canyon and crossed Bright Angel Creek ninety-four times before reaching the Colorado River. According to *The Story of Man at the Grand Canyon,* the day the expedition descended Bright Angel Canyon Matthes and his men were "startled to see 'two hag-

gard men and a weary burro' emerge from the depths at that point." A
year later, Kanab businessman E. D. Wooley formed the Grand Canyon
Transportation Company to lure tourists across the Canyon from the South
Rim's Santa Fe Railroad depot in hopes they'd visit the isolated North
Rim. Wooley's trail would essentially follow the same route that Matthes
had used the year before, but serious trail construction didn't begin until
1924. And when the entire cross-canyon Bright Angel–North Kaibab Trail
link was finally completed in 1928, "The total cost rim to rim was approximately $147,500," according to Frank J. Taylor and M. R. Tillot-
son's *Grand Canyon Country*, "exclusive of the Kaibab Suspension Bridge,
which added another $39,500." No small piece of change, even by to-
day's standards.

Today, the heavily used Bright Angel Trail ranks as one of the planet's
premier hiking trails – and, next to Phoenix's Squaw Peak, one of the most
heavily used trails in Arizona. When combined with the modern North
Kaibab Trail, it also offers the most popular canyoneering adventure in
the Grand Canyon region.

Directions

To reach the South Rim and the head of the Bright Angel Trail, drive
north from Flagstaff on Highway 180 for 82 miles; from Williams, drive
north on Arizona 64 28 miles to Highway 180 and follow Highway 180
another 32 miles to the South Rim.

To reach the North Rim, drive south 44 miles from Jacob's Lake on
Highway 67.

Bright Angel Trail Canyon Log

(All mileages counted down.) Hiking rim to rim is not much more difficult
than hiking down to the river and back, though it does require a car shuttle or arrangements with the Bright Angel Transportation Desk ([602] 638-
2631) to ride the North–South Rim shuttle bus. Hiking into the Grand
Canyon is the reverse of mountain climbing; first you descend a vertical
mile into the canyon and get tired; then you have to climb an incredibly
rugged mountain to get out. So in rim-to-rim trekking, you may find it
easier to hike down the North Kaibab Trail, which is longer and steeper
than the Bright Angel Trail, and come out the Bright Angel – though from
an esthetic standpoint, the subalpine forests of the North Rim make a far
more pleasant destination than does the crowded South Rim.

While many runners have made the rim-to-rim crossing in a single day, hikers saddled with groaning, knee-buckling backpacks generally take 2 to 3 days to complete the 23-mile journey. From an environmental standpoint, the trek is equivalent to hiking from Canada to Mexico and back. If you start on the North Rim, for instance, you leave the spruce-alpine fir forest around 8,000 feet, descend through the montane conifer forest and juniper-pinyon woodland, cross the Great Basin desert scrub (which comprises much of the Tonto Formation below both rims), and reach the Mojave Desert scrub near river level. On the way out, figuratively, you climb back up from Mexico to Canada. Rim-to-river trails generally fall into one of two categories: ridge trails or drainage trails. Trails like the South Kaibab and the Boucher are considered ridge trails because they follow ridges and offer exposed hiking en route; trails like the Bright Angel and the North Kaibab, on the other hand, are drainage trails confined to the bottoms of drainages—they don't offer the breathtaking vistas the ridge trails do. The 9.1-mile-long Bright Angel Trail follows the Garden and Pipe Creek drainages to the Colorado River, while the 14-mile-long North Kaibab Trail follows Bright Angel Canyon all the way to Roaring Springs before making an abrupt ascent out of Roaring Springs Canyon.

Beginning just west of the South Rim's Bright Angel Lodge, the Bright Angel Trail is well marked all the way to the river, though some of its highlights aren't as obvious:

Mile 1.6. Mile-and-a-Half House is a stone rest house built by the Civilian Conservation Corps in the 1930s; you'll find water there in the summer. This is an excellent stretch for seeing—and photographing—a band of seemingly tame Desert bighorn sheep.

Mile 2. Two Mile Corner is the site of petroglyphs dating back to A.D. 1300, when the trail was first reportedly used.

Mile 3. Three-Mile House, built by the CCC, also has water in the summer.

Mile 4.7. Indian Gardens. Here you will find a ranger station, a helipad, a campground, a corral, toilets, and, most importantly, water and shade; the massive cottonwood trees clustered around what was once a prehistoric spring can be seen from as far away as Shiva Temple on the North Rim. Indian Gardens is a good turnaround point for a day hike, as is the well-marked 1.5-mile trail out to Plateau Point. Called Angel Plateau by George Wharton James, Plateau Point offers a spectacular view of the Colorado

River swirling far below; it also marks the approximate vicinity of the first successful airplane landing in the Grand Canyon in 1922. In *The Grand Canyon: Early Impressions,* edited by Paul Schullery, author A. Gaylord wrote of British Royal Flying Corps Commander Thomas' remarkable landing on the Tonto Plateau: "The motor slows down. Thomas waves his hand to the people gathered along the rim high above him. The nose of the plane shoots up. One wing drops. Then the nose topples over and the plane shoots down. The tail wiggles and twists. Down, down, down; five hundred feet, one thousand feet — the plane is plunging and whirling to the bottom at a terrifying speed. Suddenly the motor begins to roar again. The plane has straightened out and now is flying on a level course. The most dangerous and yet the most useful stunt known to aviators has been executed for the first time in the very bowells of the earth!" No doubt, many of today's canyoneers, annoyed by the relentless drone of scenic over-flights, would take exception to Gaylord's assessment that this was "the most useful stunt known"; still, you can't help but admire the moxie and flying skill that Commander Thomas used to land on — and take off from — the rugged Tonto Plateau.

Mile 5 to 7.5. Tonto Trail Junction to River Trail. This junction provides access to the eastern half of the serpentine, 72-mile-long Tonto Trail, which follows the Tonto Plateau east to west through the Canyon. The South Kaibab Trail can be reached by hiking 4.1 miles east, while the Hermit Trail can be reached by walking 12 miles west from Indian Gardens. To reach the Colorado River and the foot of the North Kaibab Trail, slide through the convoluted folds of Tapeats Narrows before hammering your knees descending the Devil's Corkscrew to the River Trail.

Mile 7.5 to 9.1. Colorado River to Phantom Ranch. Follow the River Trail another 2 miles to Bright Angel Campground and Phantom Ranch on the opposite side of the river. (See entry for Colorado River.)

North Kaibab Trail

To reach the head of the North Kaibab Trail, drive 2 miles north of the North Rim's rustic Grand Canyon Lodge. Like the Bright Angel Trail, the North Kaibab is easy to follow. Aside from its length and steepness, the only difficulties you may encounter are rock slides, which periodically bury sections of the trail during torrential summer monsoons or when the snow melts. Dedicated cross-country skiers sometimes use the North Kaibab to reach the South Rim after ski-touring 40 miles into the snow-bound trailhead from Jacob's Lake.

Mile 0 to 4.7. Trailhead to Roaring Springs. This is the steepest section of the North Kaibab, where the trail drops 3,400 vertical feet down Roaring Springs Canyon to its confluence with Bright Angel Canyon. At Mile 1.8 is the Coconino Overlook and Supai Tunnel; at Mile 2.7 you'll find the breathtaking Redwall Bridge; and at Mile 3.6 is the Eye of the Needle.

Mile 4.7. Roaring Springs. Here you'll find a Park Service residence, lemonade stand (in summer), helipad, and campground. According to *The Story of Man at the Grand Canyon,* the Union Pacific Railroad built the Roaring Spring Pumphouse in 1928 because the North Rim had a problem obtaining enough water to fulfill its needs; Hughes wrote that enough electricity was generated by Bright Angel Creek "to pump the water 3870 feet upward to the North Rim."

The Old Kaibab Trail originally came down Bright Angel Canyon near its confluence with Roaring Springs Canyon; seasoned canyoneers can still locate the head of this abandoned trail by following the Ken Patrick Trail 3.5 miles east along the North Rim from the North Kaibab Trail parking lot.

Mile 6.9. Cottonwood Campground was established in 1927.

Mile 8.3. Ribbon Falls Trail Junction. This trail and the waterfall it leads to make the prettiest side trip on your rim-to-rim crossing. According to *Grand Canyon Country,* "The lime-impregnated waters of Ribbon Creek have piled up a large stalagmite or 'altar' of travertine at the base of the falls. . . . 42 feet high." Because it's usually in the shade, this otherwise beautiful 150-foot-high waterfall can be difficult to photograph.

Mile 12. Clear Creek Trail Junction. The CCC built the 9-mile-long Clear Creek Trail in 1935 to provide access to Cheyava Falls; according to *Grand Canyon Place Names, cheyava* is a Hopi Indian word for "intermittent"; Ellsworth Kolb named the falls when he first visited it with his brother Emery in 1903. The Clear Creek Trail also provides access to Angel's Gate, Brahma Temple, and Zoroaster Temple. (See entry for Brahma and Zoroaster Temples.)

Mile 13. Phantom Ranch. Designed by Mary E. Jane Colter, this canyon-bottom dude ranch was built by the Fred Harvey Company in 1922 for $22,000. You may want to bed down at this historic site, with a natural setting as idyllic as when John Wesley Powell first visited the spot on August 16, 1869; in *Explorations of the Colorado River and Its Canyons,* Powell wrote: "Early in the afternoon we discover a stream entering from the north—a clear, beautiful creek, coming down through a gorgeous red canyon. We land and camp on a sand beach above its mouth, under a great overspreading tree with willow shaped leaves. . . . We have named one stream [the Dirty Devil] away above, in honor of the great chief of the 'Bad Angels,' and as this is in beautiful contrast to that, we conclude to name it 'Bright Angel.'" Whichever trail you take to reach Bright Angel Creek, when you finally soak your trail-weary feet in its cool, soothing waters, you'll undoubtedly agree with Powell's choice of names.

Travel Notes

• **Primary access.**

–*North Kaibab Trail:* North Rim and Phantom Ranch.

–*Bright Angel Trail:* South Rim, Tonto Trail, and River Trail from Phantom Ranch.

• **Elevation.**

–*North Kaibab:* 8,241 feet at North Rim trailhead to 2,425 feet at Colorado River.

–*Bright Angel:* 6,860 feet at South Rim trailhead to 2,400 feet at river.

• **Elevation loss and gain.** (round-trip):

–*North Kaibab:* 5,816 vertical feet each way.

–*Bright Angel:* 4,460 vertical feet each way.

• **Mileage.**

–*North Kaibab:* 14 miles each way.

–*Bright Angel:* 9.1 miles each way.

• **Water.**

–*North Kaibab:* Roaring Springs, Cottonwood Camp, Bright Angel Creek (emergency), and Bright Angel Campground.

–*Bright Angel:* 1.5- and 3-Mile rest houses (in summer), Indian Gardens, Colorado River (emergency), and Bright Angel Campground.

• **Cache points.** (for round-trip hikes):

–*North Kaibab:* Secluded areas of Roaring Springs area and Ribbon Falls Trail Junction.

–*Bright Angel:* In the shade and seclusion of Tapeats Narrows.

•**Escape routes.**

–*North Kaibab:* North Rim, Roaring Springs, Cottonwood Camp (in summer), or Phantom Ranch.

–*Bright Angel:* South Rim, Indian Gardens, or Phantom Ranch.

•**Seasons.** Fall and spring. Winter can be either ideal or bitterly cold; summer, especially June, is a terrible time to hike in and out of this monumental oven.

•**Map.** Bright Angel quadrangle (15 minute).

•**Nearest supply points.**

–*North Kaibab:* Fredonia, Page, Jacob's Lake, and North Rim General Store.

–*Bright Angel:* Flagstaff, Williams, Cameron, and Babbitts General Store.

•**Managing agency.** Grand Canyon National Park (Backcountry Reservations Office, P.O. Box 129, Grand Canyon, AZ 86023; (602) 638-2474.

•**Backcountry information.** Permits required for all overnight hiking; fires not allowed.

•**Biotic communities.** Spruce-alpine fir forest, montane conifer forest, juniper-pinyon woodland, Great Basin Desert scrub, and Mojave Desert scrub.

•**Additional information.** For more information on canyoneering and hiking opportunities throughout the Grand Canyon region, see the Sierra Club Totebook *Hiking the Grand Canyon,* by John Annerino.

Trekking

San Francisco Mountains

Coconino Plateau: peak ascent

Landform

At 12,633 feet high, Humphreys Peak is the highest mountain in Arizona; it, together with Arizona's other two highest summits, nearby 12,356-foot-high Agassiz Peak and 11,969-foot-high Fremont Peak, form the tundra-covered summit crown of the San Francisco Mountains. Yet un-like southeast Arizona's 10,720-foot-high Pinaleno Mountains—whose base was formed near the 3,000-foot level and which has the greatest vertical relief of any mountain range in Arizona—the San Francisco Mountains have a base formed atop northern Arizona's 7,000-foot-high Coconino Plateau. According to William J. Breed's "The San Francisco Peaks: A Geologist's Perspective," when the mountain erupted between 1.8 million and 400,000 years ago, it may have reached a "maximum height of perhaps up to 15,600 feet." Today, the San Francisco Mountains comprise an estimated 22.5-square-mile area in a 2-million-acre volcanic field that has—among its sprawling, cobalt black flows of lava and ash—four hundred cinder cones. The region's early Franciscan explorers first named the mountains after Saint Francis of Assisi in 1629.

Historical Overview

In the late Peter Boardman's eloquent book on climbing three of the world's highest, most sacred mountains, called *Sacred Summits,* he wrote: "The mountains, the trees, rocks and springs of Europe were respected . . . as sacred places. Man had felt his links with them, but then had broken with his heritage and had buried this delicate magic of life." Here in Arizona, Native Americans joined forces in the 1970s to fight a long, disheartening legal battle against the white man to prevent him from desecrating their most sacred mountain by maintaining a ski resort on the peaks. The Indians tried to explain that these "mountains are our father and our mother. We come from them; we depend on them . . . each mountain is a person. The water courses are their veins and arteries. The water in them is to their life as our blood is to our bodies." Arizona's marginal ski industry, supported by the U.S. Forest Service, would have none of it. Once powerful former Navajo Tribal Chairman Peter McDonald said it as poignantly as any traditional Navajo elder could have: "Many outsiders look upon our religion as a superstition. They who worship in man-made churches, condemn and ridicule us who worship on mountains—the handiwork of God, Himself, and the Holy ones."

To the Navajo Indians, the San Francisco Mountains are known as Dok'o'sliid, (the Sacred Mountain of the West); to the Hopi it is Nuva-teekia-ovi (the Place of Snow on the Very Top); and to the only permanent residents of the Grand Canyon, the Havasupai, they are Huchassahpatch (Big Rock Mountain). If members of the prehistoric Sinagua culture didn't first climb the San Francisco Mountains between A.D. 600 and A.D. 1100,

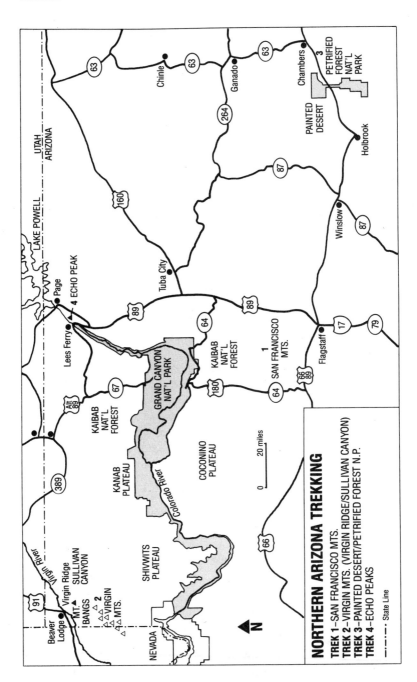

NORTHERN ARIZONA TREKKING

TREK 1–SAN FRANCISCO MTS.
TREK 2–VIRGIN MTS. (VIRGIN RIDGE/SULLIVAN CANYON)
TREK 3–PAINTED DESERT/PETRIFIED FOREST N.P.
TREK 4–ECHO PEAKS
------- State Line

members of the Hopi, Havasupai, or Navajo tribes undoubtedly made the
first ascent during a sacred pilgrimage sometime before Padre Francisco
Garces named them the Sierra Napoc in 1776.

The first recorded ascent of the San Francisco Peaks probably predates
early surveyors who traversed the Coconino Plateau in hopes of forging
a route for settlers to California along the 35th parallel. According to author
Platt Cline, Baldwin Möllhausen, an artist and topographer attached to
the 1853 Whipple Expedition, wrote: "We looked up at the sublime summits of the San Francisco Mountains, and needed no temple made with
hands wherein to worship our Creator."

Still other early settlers of Flagstaff thought the "Peaks" were the most
beautiful mountains on earth and a tonic for all ills that plagued mankind;
in *A Land of Sunshine: Northern Arizona and Flagstaff in 1887,* George
H. Tinker wrote: "One of the most pleasing and advantageous features
of the climate is the opportunity it offers of camping out in the midst of
the finest natural scenery to be found in the world. . . . As a sanitarium
the neighborhood of the San Francisco Mountains has no equal in the
health-giving regions of the whole Rocky Mountain range, and when this
fact becomes thoroughly understood thousands of lives will be prolonged
and an incalculable amount of human suffering alleviated."

What the perfectly sculpted, and benign-looking peaks lack in sheer vertical
relief, land mass, and route-finding challenges—in comparison to climbing
the Pinalenos from the bottom—they make up for in weather. Winds are
fickle and can quickly reach gale force, creating winter weather as unforgiving as in any mountain range in the Southwest. Consequently, the winter
slog up the peaks through knee-deep snow has become the most popular
"high altitude" climb in Arizona. Unfortunately, more than one unsuspecting
desert alpinist has perished near the summit in the throes of a fierce winter
storm.

The first known climbers to successfully tackle the San Francisco Mountains in the dead of winter were pioneer Arizonans Lilo Perrin and Milton "Crimpy" Farnsworth, who reached the summit of Humphreys Peak
on February 12, 1912. With a recent ascent of Switzerland's 13,642-foot
Jungfrau under his belt, Lilo roped up with Crimpy and set off for the
summit of Humphreys Peak at midnight. After making rapid progress,
Crimpy took over the lead; according to an article by Dermont Wilson
Melick, published in the May 27, 1982, edition of the *Williams News,*
"[Crimpy] took about six steps on the crust of snow and disappeared. He
had broken through the crust and was buried in about ten feet of soft
snow accumulated in the canyon. He would have certainly smothered to
death were it not for the rope attached to Lilo. . . . Other than this 'tight

spot,' Lilo says the climb went off as planned and he and Crimpy reached the top of Humphreys Peak at 6:35 a.m."

Because Crimpy and Lilo climbed through what was undoubtedly a stone-dark, bitterly cold night, they probably had little time to recognize the five life zones they climbed through. According to Stewart W. Aitchison's "The San Francisco Peaks: A Biological Sky-island," C. Hart Merriam developed his unique life zone concept on the Peaks in 1889: "His so-called 'laws of temperature control' supposedly governed completely the distribution of plants and animals." When Crimpy and Lilo made their midnight ascent, they undoubtedly began—as many modern mountaineers and hikers do—between the 7,000- and 8,000-foot level, about where the ponderosa pine forest of the Transition Zone wraps its way around the base of the San Francisco Mountains. Still groping upward in the dark, Crimpy and Lilo climbed through the mixed conifer forest of the Canadian Zone between the 8,000- and 9,500-foot level, before clambering over the snow-covered blowdown in the spruce-fir forest of the Hudsonian Zone at the 9,000- to 10,500-foot level. Finally, they began to break out of the thinning timber and gnarly stands of ancient bristlecone pines in the Subalpine Zone, before climbing atop the only patch of genuine Alpine Tundra in Arizona.

According to respected biologist Dr. Steven W. Carothers, the "1,200-acre island of tundra above the 11,400 foot elevation contour . . . has been isolated from other tundra habitats long enough for several species of plants to evolve into unique forms. . . . Found nowhere else in the world, the [threatened San Francisco] groundsel is imperiled by human foot traffic in the tundra during the summer season when the protective blanket of snow has disappeared."

Regular ascents of the peaks—and the accompanying assault on the fragile tundra summit cap—began more than 100 years ago, most often originating in Flagstaff. Pioneer rancher John Weatherford built a road up to the rim and to a point below the summit of Mount Humphreys. Today, the Weatherford Road is off-limits to vehicular traffic. But that won't stop you from climbing what George Wharton James described in 1917 as "the most beautiful and inviting mountain clusters in the United States"; three challenging routes lead to the summit of this supernal mountain wilderness.

Directions

To get to Kachina Peaks Trail from Flagstaff, drive 7 miles north on Highway 180 to the Snowbowl turnoff; take USFS Road 516 7 miles to the ski area. Signs will lead you to the foot of the Kachina Peaks Trail.

To get to the Weatherford Trail from Flagstaff, drive 2 miles north on Highway 180 to the Schultz Pass turnoff; follow USFS Road 420 4 miles to Schultz Tank. The trailhead is located north of the road.

You will need three maps (see the list at the end of this section) to find the start of Philomena Spring Trail, an elusive, seldom-used mountain track — but it's worth the trouble if you like the solitude and the challenge of backcountry orientation. From Flagstaff, drive 20 miles north on Highway 180 to the White Horse Hills turnoff; take USFS Road 151 3 miles to 418B, and follow 418B to the end. That should put you in the NE ¼ of Section 24, T.23 N., R.6 E., about where you can begin what some flatlanders have called "a wild-goose chase."

Kachina Peaks Trail Log

Built in 1984 when the 18,200-acre Kachina Peaks Wilderness was first established, the 4.5 mile-long Kachina Peaks Trail is easy to follow all the way to the 11,800-foot saddle between Humphreys and Agassiz peaks, near the 3.5-Mile mark; the only time you'll have any problem following this steep forest trail is when it's buried under deep snow. From the Humphreys-Agassiz Saddle, it's a mile north to the summit of Humphreys and a little less than a mile south up Agassiz. But hiking up Agassiz is temporarily prohibited due to the impact that hikers — coming up from the top of the chair lift at the 11,608-foot level — have had on the tundra.

Weatherford Trail

The 10-mile-long Weatherford Trail is a long, tiring slog compared to the brisk ascent you can make of the peaks by climbing the Kachina Peaks Trail. In large part, that's because the trail follows the old Weatherford Road, and when you're on a road — fenced off or not — you don't have that same intimate feeling of the environment that you get when you follow a narrow forest path. Once you reach 10,800-foot-high Fremont Saddle near Mile 5, your perspective will change as you're suddenly on the rim of the Inner Basin. The 1.5-mile leg to 11,354-foot Doyle Saddle is covered with fallen trees blown over by strong winds; once you reach Doyle Saddle, you'll see the remains of the old Weatherford Cabin, which provided rude overnight accommodations for adventuresome locals during the 1920s. It's another 1.5 miles to the Humphreys-Agassiz Saddle; en route you may see the giant rotor of a helicopter that crashed on the east face of Agassiz years ago.

Philomena Spring Trail

The history behind this trail is purely speculative, but the big clue is the rusted, 4-inch diameter steel pipe and wooden support trestle that carried this one-man water-supply project to Philomena Spring on the northwest slope of Humphreys Peak near the 11,600-foot level. It's safe to bet that one of Flagstaff's more ambitious cowboys hauled at least 2 miles of steel pipe, one section at a time, behind a good cutting horse by tying a stout lariat to his saddle horn. Assuming you find this old waterline, it's about 2.5 miles to Philomena Spring and another thigh-burning, lung-heaving half-mile to the summit of Arizona, also known as Humphreys.

Inner Basin Routes

Due to the new cross-country restrictions above timberline, once-classic ascent lines that climbed directly out of the Inner Basin to the summit of Humphreys Peak are now off limits.

Summit View

While the San Francisco Mountains are Arizona's highest—high and steep enough to have tree-snapping avalanches periodically rumble down their heavily forested flanks—they don't offer the unrestricted 360-degree panoramas found on lesser peaks like nearby 10,120-foot-high Kendrick Peak or its southern Arizona counterpart, 9,453-foot-high Mount Wrightson. To the south, Agassiz blocks much of the view from Humphreys, while Humphreys blots out Agassiz' northern horizon. Still, the view from Humphreys from the southeast swinging north around to the southwest is a memorable one—if the wind doesn't have you crawling around on all fours. The Grand Canyon, of course, is the most obvious landmark—a statewide gash in the earth 75 miles north. More difficult to identify is 10,388-foot-high Navajo Mountain just over the Utah line 125 miles northeast, now a mirage lost in the haze of the Navajo Power Plant. What seems to command the most attention, however, is the eastern horizon, perhaps because the late afternoon light beams down on it, or perhaps because much of what can be seen is the sacred land of the Navajo. Known as *dinetah*, "the land," the traditional Navajo's universe is encompassed by four sacred mountains in Arizona, New Mexico, and Colorado: 13,225-foot-high Hesperus Peak was, according to Navajo religion, fastened to Earth by a rainbow; 14,317-foot-high Blanca Peak was fastened to Earth by lightning; 11,389-foot-high Mount Taylor was fastened to Earth by a great flint knife; and the San Francisco Mountains were fastened to Earth by a sunbeam.

Within these four cardinal points is Earth Mother, where the largest tribe of Native Americans lives, works, and reveres Her through ceremonial sings, or chantways. Scattered throughout this Earth cap of forested mountains, sandstone monoliths, and sand-swept mesas of the Painted Desert are, according to Edith L. Watson's *Sacred Places*, no fewer than 240 other sacred mountains, mesas, buttes, rocks, lakes, and streams that have been identified on the Navajo Land Claim list. But, because of their sanctity, their locations are known only to a handful of Navajo medicine men.

Sitting on the peaks, you begin to understand why traditional Navajo, as well as Hopi and Havasupai, have come to revere the land. The breadth of this vast land rolls out from the foot of these magnificent peaks like a great wave for 100 miles in every direction. At night, when you can look out and see nothing but the stars above and a thousand tiny lights crawling through the black landscape below, you're reminded of your own fragile attachment to life on Earth. The late great Indian photographer Edward Curtis said it best in 1905: "Alone with my campfire, I gaze on the completely circling hill-top crested with countless campfires around which are gathered the people of a dying race. The gloom of the approaching night wraps itself about me. I feel that the life of these children of nature is like the dying day drawing to its end; only off in the west is the glorious light of the setting sun, telling us, perhaps, of light after darkness."

Travel Notes (for Kachina Peaks Trail)

• **Primary access.** Kachina Peaks Trailhead.

• **Total elevation gain and loss.** 3,033 vertical feet each way.

• **Mileage.** 9 miles round-trip.

• **Water sources.** No perennial water en route; snow to melt in winter.

• **Cache points.** 11,800-foot Humphreys-Agassiz Saddle.

• **Escape routes.** Either back the way you came, or straight down the ski run from the Humphreys-Agassiz Saddle.

• **Seasons.** All year. Depending on your interests and background, you may want to hike up on a clear June day, or during a warm Indian summer day in the fall when the aspens are turning colors. Lightning can be a hazard during the July-August monsoons, and during the wintertime you need to be fully prepared for cold alpine conditions.

• **Maps.** Humphreys Peak and White Horse Hills quadrangles (7½ minute) and Coconino National Forest map.

• **Nearest supply points.** Flagstaff and Williams.

• **Managing agency.** Coconino National Forest (Flagstaff Ranger District, 1100 N. Beaver, Flagstaff, AZ 86001; 602-527-7450).

• **Backcountry information.** Fires or camping are not allowed above timberline, generally around 11,400 feet; permit not required.

• **Biotic communities.** (C. Hart Merriam's Designations): ponderosa pine forest (Transition Zone), mixed conifer forest (Canadian Zone), sprucefir forest (Hudsonian Zone), subalpine (Timberline), and Alpine Tundra.

• **Caution.** Do not molest ceremonial bundles sometimes left by Native Americans during sacred pilgrimages up the Peaks!

Mount Bangs

Virgin Mountains: day hike, peak ascent, or canyon trek

Landform

Located in the northwestern-most corner of Arizona, the 8,000-foot-high Virgin Mountains knife their way between two physiographic provinces— the Colorado Plateau to the east and the Basin and Range to the west; thus situated on the western edge of the 6,000-foot-high Colorado Plateau, the Virgin Mountains make a screeching, mile-long drop into the Mojave Desert on their awesome western front. More than 40 miles long and 10 to 17 miles wide, this northeast-trending range claims high points in two states: 8,075-foot-high Virgin Peak is the highest summit, situated in Nevada on the southwestern end of the range, and 8,012-foot-high Mount Bangs, located in Arizona near the northeastern end of the Virgin Mountains, is the high point of the 35,092-acre Paiute Primitive Area. As intimidating a barrier as the Virgin Mountains might have been, most early travelers simply avoided them.

Historical Overview

As in central Arizona's imposing Sierra Estrellas (see entry for Sierra Estrellas) early explorers who rode and trekked across the northwestern corner of territorial Arizona were compelled to follow a river route around the northern end of the uncompromisingly rugged Virgin Mountains; their route of choice was along the Virgin River, which forms the natural boundary between the northern end of the range and the 5,060-foot-high Beaver Dam Mountains. Perhaps the most famous of this hardy breed was mountain man Jedediah Smith; in 1826 he pioneered the Virgin River route, which Arizona historian T. E. Farish believed he used as "the first white man to enter Arizona from the north."

But Smith had a larger claim to exploration than crossing a snippet of Arizona; from Bear Lake, Idaho, he embarked on an incredible journey of exploration from the Great Salt Lake across the Mojave Desert to the port of San Diego, then up to northern California, where he turned east back toward the Great Salt Lake; upon his arrival in Salt Lake, Smith wrote: "we had but one horse & one mule remaining, which were so poor, that they could scarce carry the little camp-equipage which I had along.—the balance of my horses, I was compelled to eat as they gave out."

It was during the early stages of this epic journey that Smith and fifteen men followed the course of the Virgin River around the foot of the Virgin Mountains. But details of this leg of the expedition are as lean as jerked beef. In a July 12, 1827, letter written to Gen. William Clark, Superintendent of Indian Affairs, the mountain man wrote:

> I passed over a range of Mountains running S.E. & N.W. and struck a river running S.W. which I called Adam's River, in Compliment to our President. The water is of a muddy cast, & is a little brackish—the country is mountainous to the east—towards the West, there are sandy plains, and detached Rockey Hills. Passing down the river some distance, I fell in with a Nation of Indians, who call themselves Pa Ulches. these Indians, as well as those last mentioned, wear rabbit Skin robes.—who raise some little Corn. & Pumpkins. the Country is destitute of Game of any description except a few Hares here.

Others, like George C. Yount and John G. Fremont, followed Smith's route through the Virgin River Gorge before it became better known as the Mormon Road in the 1860s. But no one made any mention of actually going into the Virgin Mountains—until Powell's men arrived in 1872. Even their reports provide few clues as to their actual route up Mount Bangs. Of the journals kept by Dellenbaugh, Clem Powell, and Almon Harris Thompson, Dellenbaugh's is most descriptive. Wrote Dellenbaugh: "After several days of feeling our way about in the rugged and dry region below St. George, we finally discovered a good water-pocket, from which Prof. and I made a long, hard ride and climb, and about sunset camped at the base of what is now called Mount Bangs, the highest peak of the Virgin Mountains, for which we were aiming. The next day we climbed an additional eleven-hundred feet to its summit, and completed our work in time by swift riding to get to our main camp at the water-pocket by half-past six."

A 1-degree reconnaissance map of the area, called the Mt. Trumbull Sheet, shows the old trail from Saint George, Utah, to Pierce Ferry on the Colorado River; assuming Dellenbaugh's party followed this trail south-southwest for approximately ·30 miles, they would have been in the vicinity of Black Rock Spring. Black Rock Spring is the first water source shown along this trail on the April 1886 edition of the Mt. Trumbull map; it's located at the 5,400-foot level 8 miles east-northeast of Mount Bangs. Furthermore, Dellenbaugh said his group camped at the base of Mount Bangs before making a 1,100-foot climb to its summit the next day, which means that the party could have camped in the upper end of Cottonwood Wash more than 1,000 feet below the summit. If that's true, then the modern drive into and day hike up Mount Bangs may very well follow the route that Dellenbaugh's party used to make the first recorded ascent in late April 1872.

But that remains to be substantiated, and the words of Jedediah Smith still hold true: "My situation here, has enabled me to collect information respecting a Section of country which, to the citizens of the U. States, has hitherto been veiled in obscurity." To this day, the rugged and remote Virgin Mountains remain "veiled in obscurity." The Bureau of Land Management estimates visitation figures at a paltry eight hundred to one thousand user days per year (one visitor per one day); that total includes picnickers, hikers, backpackers, hunters, and whitewater enthusiasts who run the Virgin River Gorge for a few weeks each spring.

So if you want to explore this wildly beautiful mountain range still overlooked by most modern explorers, the 55-square-mile Paiute Primitive Area, you have three principal choices. The easiest is to day hike up Mount Bangs. If you're fond of canyons, you may prefer to backpack into Sullivans Canyon, from either top or bottom. Or, if you want to tackle one of the most challenging and spectacular mountain climbs in Arizona, you can trek up Mount Bangs along the crest of the Virgin Ridge from the Virgin River Gorge.

Directions

To get to the beginning of the Mount Bangs day hike from Saint George, Utah, drive 2.2 miles west on I-15 to the Bloomington Exit; drive south through the Bloomington Hills development on Quail Hill Road 26 miles to Wolf Hole, reputed stomping grounds of the late Edward Abbey. Turn west at Wolf Hole and drive approximately 20 miles to Mesquite, Nevada, and then another mile to the junction of the Elbow Canyon Road and the Cottonwood Wash Road; turn north on the Cottonwood Wash Road and park near Cougar Springs or shift into granny gear to drive a mile closer to the official trailhead. The 2-mile trek up Mount Bangs begins at the Littlefield Reservoir and follows a bulldozer trail up the southeast side of the mountain; approximately 500 vertical feet below the summit, you'll have to leave the dozer trail and scramble through dense clusters of manzanita and chaparral to reach this craggy summit. The Littlefield Reservoir also provides access into the head of Sullivans Canyon.

To get to the Sullivans Canyon trek and Virgin Ridge peak ascent from Saint George, Utah, drive 20 miles west in I-15 to the Virgin River Canyon Campground. This BLM recreation area is perched on the shoulder of Interstate 15 in a shadeless expanse of creosote, staghorn cholla, and Joshua tree. Fortunately, the roar of traffic is muffled by the playful yelps of coyote pups tearing the heads off of slow lizards and by the Rio Virgen pulsing 100 yards below.

Trek Log

Mile 0 to 2.   Virgin River Canyon Campground to Sullivans Canyons (all mileages approximate.) To reach the mouth of Sullivans Canyon, or the foot of the Virgin Ridge, try following the BLM trail to Migrant's Cove; it begins on the west end of the campground but quickly loses itself in a maze of cattle tracks. So you may find it more practical to follow your own path west along the Virgin River.

When walking along the banks of this charming little river, it's easy to understand why the tracks of mountain men have now been followed by modern Interstate 15; Jedediah Smith's route through the Virgin River Gorge still offers the most natural line of travel between the Virgin Mountains and the Beaver Dam Mountains. What's more difficult to understand is why modern man hasn't left it at that. According to an article by Barry Burkhart in the October 12, 1988, edition of *The Arizona Republic*, "A joint conservation project between the U.S. Fish & Wildlife Service and Utah Department of Wildlife resources ended up poisoning as much as 60 miles of the Virgin River in Utah, Nevada, and Arizona." Biologists were trying to eliminate an exotic species of fish called a red shiner when they "lost control of the toxic agent rotenone" in what could only be described as a biological experiment run amok. As Burkhart reported, many native species were killed, "including the endangered woundfin, the threatened Virgin River spinedace and the Virgin River round-tail chub, which has been proposed for the federal endangered species list." As if this bureaucratic fiasco didn't raise enough havoc with the Virgin River's unique aquatic habitat, a 50-foot-high earthen dam recently collapsed near Saint

George, "resulting in a 20-foot-high wall of water [that] ripped down the Virgin River." Constructed in 1985 for $3 million, the 1,820-foot-long Quail Creek dam was reportedly built on a questionable geological foundation. In a special report for *The Arizona Republic,* Lance Gurwell quoted one geologist as saying: "There's no way that dike could have survived. . . . The geologic setting is so obvious, a beginning college student in Geology 1 should have been able to realize it."

Mile 2 to 3. Sullivans Canyon to Migrant's Cove. Sullivans Canyon is the second tributary canyon entering the Virgin River below the Virgin River Canyon Campground; Mountain Sheep Wash is the first. To reach Migrant's Cove, turn south into Sullivans Canyon and hike about a mile upstream to the first drainage entering from the west. Migrant's Cove is hidden somewhere among the rust-colored, cauliflower-shaped clumps of Supai Sandstone. According to BLM information, "This sandstone pocket was named for early hunting and gathering bands who migrated seasonally up and down these canyons." During May 1974, Brigham Young University made an archaeological survey of Sullivans Canyon and unearthed a Clovis-type projectile point, indicating that early man used the area between 15,000 B.C. and 10,000 B.C. In a report written for the BLM, Blaine A. Miller wrote: "The distinctive lanceolate projectile point used by Clovis hunters reflects their way of life which was primarily dependent upon killing large animals . . . such as the mammoth, bison, horse, and camel." Ancient habitation sites in Migrant's Cove indicate that it was a good place to roll out a buffalo hide and catch a little shut-eye. It still is, though you may prefer to use it as a turnaround point for a day hike or an overnighter.

From Migrant's Cove, you can climb Mount Bangs by following either Sullivans Canyon or the Virgin Ridge; the following section will highlight the trek up the Virgin Ridge to Mount Bangs and the descent down Sullivans Canyon.

Mile 3 to 15. Migrant's Cove to Littlefield Reservoir, via the Virgin Ridge. For all practical purposes, Migrant's Cove marks the northern end of the Virgin Ridge, where this ascent line begins in earnest; you can climb the Virgin Ridge right out of the Virgin River Gorge, but you'll use precious water—and time—negotiating the broken ridgeline between the Virgin River and Migrant's Cove. For rugged beauty and sheer topographical relief, climbing the Virgin Ridge is akin to trekking out of the Grand Canyon. What further contributes to its being one of the most challenging mountain climbs in Arizona—along with Mount Graham, from the bottom—is the fact there is no water en route, nor is there a trail to guide you. Consequently, an ascent of the Virgin Ridge demands key logistical planning and sound route-finding skills. For the most part, however, the crest can be followed with Stone-Age simplicity; just stay on the high point of the Virgin Ridge all the way to the northern end of the Virgin Ridge Trail (actually a dozer cut). The only time your route along the crest should vary is where you're confronted with several unnerving drop-offs and knife-edged hogbacks; then you'll have to decide when to follow the ridgeline and when to traverse beneath it on one side or the other.

About the time you've climbed out of the Mojave Desert and reached the pinyon juniper, you'll come to terms with the unrelenting nature of the Virgin Ridge. With the possible exception of the 9,412-foot-high Carrizo Mountains on the Navajo Indian Reservation, from no other vantage point in Arizona can you see into three other states (California, Nevada, and Utah). The only evidence that indicates you're not entirely alone on the Virgin Ridge are the bench marks strategically located along its crest; no doubt the United States Geological Survey climbed the Virgin Ridge at some point, though its brass caps are devoid of precise dates that would pinpoint exactly when.

Even if you leave at daybreak on a long spring day, chances are night will fall long before you reach the Littlefield Reservoir or Cougar Spring—so plan on camping somewhere along the upper end of the Virgin Ridge dozer cut. This wide "trail" begins near Mile 10-plus at the 6,500-foot level and follows the crest of the Virgin Ridge through cloud-sweeping stands of ponderosa all the way to the Littlefield Reservoir; but once you've followed it to Peak 7,555, near Mile 13, the climb is essentially over. Wherever you camp along this stretch, don't be surprised if you're awakened in the middle of the night by a mountain lion. This is truly wild, seldom-visited country, and if the lower half of the Virgin Ridge hasn't already imprinted that on you, the blood-curdling screams of a mother lion at two o'clock in the morning certainly will. But rest assured: Even in a controlled panic, you shouldn't have any problems following this dozer cut the rest of the way to the Littlefield Reservoir. In the dark. While looking over one shoulder.

Mile 15.   Littlefield Reservoir. Next to Cougar Spring, this stock pond is the only reliable water source this high up the mountain. That places greater pressure on it as a pivotal water source for wildlife, as well; so it's best not to camp near the reservoir and scare away the wildlife. Or the hunters. Incredible as it may seem, in the off-chance that you have problems identifying the largest man-made waterhole on the northern end of the Virgin Mountains, there are two hunting blinds within its fenced enclosure: One is a sit-down blind and the other is a tree blind. Evidently, they offer a "sporting chance" to local hunters who might not otherwise succeed in tracking a deer the-way ancient Paiute Indians once did here.

Summit View

Mile 17 (or Mile 2 if day hiking).   8,012-foot Mount Bangs. However you reach this gnarly, brush-covered granite summit cap, the 360-degree view is astounding; from this windswept island of Douglas fir, you can look straight down onto the Virgin River snaking its way southward across the Mojave Desert more than 6,000 vertical feet below. Clem Powell, who climbed Mount Bangs with the Powell expedition, described the view on April 25, 1872:

> Our objective was the highest peak of the range, Mt. Turner, 30 miles south of St. George. We crossed the Rio Virgen, and followed it for some 10 miles. It is a narrow, shallow stream, flowing, as do all the southern tributaries of the Colorado, over quicksands. It winds among hills, cliffs, and sage-encumbered plains. From the summit of a ridge, the village of Washington comes into view. For months, we have seen nothing but sand, and sage, and rock—gray desolate landscapes, with an occasional oasis of pine. Here, at our feet, is suddenly revealed something like civilization and human life.

Back to Civilization

From Mount Bangs, via the Littlefield Reservoir, there are several ways to return to civilization and human life. The easiest is to head straight down Sullivans Canyon or, some might argue, to have a shuttle vehicle waiting at Cougar Spring. If you want to keep things simple, however, head straight back down Sullivans Canyon to the Virgin River Canyon Campground. The route is approximately 15 miles long, and rugged, but it's beautiful; allow a full day. Like the Virgin Ridge, the "trail" into Sullivans Canyon isn't marked. Nothing is signed in the Paiute Primitive Area—not the trails, not the dozer cuts, nothing; so once you leave the dozer trail 1.5 miles north of (below) the Littlefield Reservoir, you're on your own again, just as Clovis man was when he roamed Sullivans Canyon 12,000 to 17,000 years ago. You can't ask for things to get much wilder or more primitive than that.

Travel Notes

•**Primary access.**   Virgin River Canyon Campground.

- **Elevation gain and loss.** 6,500-plus feet each way from the Virgin River Gorge.

- **Mileage.** Approximately 15 miles each way.

- **Water sources.** Virgin River, polluted; Littlefield Reservoir, Cougar Spring; Atkins Spring; seasonal springs in streambed between Littlefield Reservoir and main stem of Sullivans Canyon.

- **Cache points.** None.

- **Escape routes.** The easiest way back to the Virgin River Canyon Campground, unless you're closer to Cougar Spring, in which case you might find somebody at the ranch house south of there, but you can't count on it.

- **Seasons.** Fall and spring—though, during peak spring runoff, you may not be able to cross the Virgin River.

- **Maps.** Mount Bangs and Mountain Sheep Spring (both 7½-minute quadrangles).

- **Nearest supply points.** Saint George, Utah.

- **Managing agency.** Bureau of Land Management.

- **Backcountry information.** Permit not required.

- **Biotic communities.** Mojave Desert scrub, Great Basin Desert scrub, juniper-pinyon woodland, and montane conifer forest.

Painted Desert

Colorado Plateau: day hikes, moon walks, and trekking

Landform

Drained by the Little Colorado River, the Painted Desert is a 150-mile-long band of mile-high desert that extends roughly from Echo Cliffs on the north to Petrified Forest National Park on the south. First called El Desierto Pintado by Spaniards in 1540, this kaleidoscopic sweep of desert is still preserved in the 150-square-mile Petrified Forest National Park. Severed by Interstate 40 and bounded on all sides by the Navajo Indian Reservation, this isolated National Park boasts 50,260 acres of wilderness. The sprawling Painted Desert Wilderness lies north of I-40, while the narrow Rainbow Forest Wilderness is situated to the south.

Historical Overview

In *Mesa, Canon, and Pueblo,* onetime newspaper editor and adventurer Charles F. Lummis wrote: "It is a great 'bad lands' of sandy valleys and clay mounds and beetling mesas, across which lie sprawled the prostrate and shattered sections of giant trees, and around them a very kaleidoscope of their rainbow agate 'chips' – the most enchanted wood-pile one ever walked on." The indefatigable Lummis first walked across this corner of the Painted Desert in early January of 1885 during his epic *Tramp Across the Continent.* (See entry for Diamond Peak.) While he was chasing a deer somewhere in the Painted Desert, a ledge gave way and Lummis fell 20 feet; after reducing a ragged compound fracture, he made a forced march of 53 miles to Winslow in 30 hours. Of his tortuous, life-saving walk, Lummis wrote: "Cut and bruised from head to foot; that agonizing arm quivering to the jar of every footstep; weak with pain and loss of blood, with cold, wet feet slipping in the muddy snow – a thousand years could not drown the memory of that bitter 6th of January." But the years did drown those painful memories, and Lummis wrote of another walk through the Painted Desert.

Lummis wasn't the first to cross the Painted Desert; in fact, when he made his excruciating trek to Winslow, he walked along the Atlantic and Pacific Railway, which followed the 35th parallel from Fort Smith to Los Angeles and had been surveyed between 1853 and 1854, some 30 years before Lummis first visited the area. That's when Lt. Amiel Weeks Whipple and his party of surveyors first discovered petrified wood. Accompanying Whipple was a German artist and cartographer named Baldwin Möllhausen; in his *Diary of a Journey from the Mississippi to the Oasis of the Pacific,* Möllhausen describes how difficult it was to cross the Painted Desert along Lithodendran Wash: "The loose earth gave way continually beneath the hoofs of our mules, but between slipping and scrambling we got somehow to the bottom where we found the ground so broken by torrents of rain that our progress became still more difficult. . . . The valley is called by the Americans the Rio Secco, or Dry River, though at this part it might deserve the name of Petrified Forest." So it was named by Baldwin Möllhausen.

The December 2, 1853, entries in both Möllhausen's and Whipple's journals describe the wonderful discovery they made while looking for an easier route across the Painted Desert. It was largely because of the Whipple Survey that this forest of giant, petrified logs soon became accessible via rail service to tourists and scoundrels who oftentimes wore the same hats.

In *Some Strange Corners of Our Country,* Lummis talked of petrified logs being blown apart with black powder in Chalcedony Park, as locals referred to Petrified Forest in the 1880s: "In Tiffany's jewelry store, New York, you can see some magnificent specimens of polished cross-sections from these logs, which command enormous prices." According to one of Lummis' sources, it took days to saw through a petrified log with a steel blade and diamond dust—which was one reason for the high prices.

In 1906, President Theodore Roosevelt established Petrified Forest National Park to protect this national treasure. But the fact that it was a national park hardly deterred light-fingered visitors who, by the 1970s, were carting away an estimated 10 tons of petrified wood annually. That precedent dated back to the Whipple Survey when, as Möllhausen wrote: "We collected small specimens of all these various kinds of fossil trees, and regretted that as our means of transportation were so small we had to content ourselves with fragments." The Petrified Forest National Park brochure now warns that it's a federal offense to take so much as a sliver of "wood" out of the park; it is hoped that that law and the fact that commercial petrified wood can be purchased outside the park will serve as successful deterrents.

Directions

From Flagstaff, drive east in Interstate 40 90 miles to Holbrook; Petrified Forest National Park is another 25 miles east on I-40. Turn left onto the park road and stop in the Visitor Center. Primary access into the Painted Desert Wilderness is via Kachina Point, located several miles north of the Visitor Center.

The Painted Desert Wilderness Trek Log

In 1921, hunter and naturalist Charles Sheldon wrote: "But I will not forget these mystical nights, sitting alone here in camp in the moonlit desert. The calm, the silence, the radiance of the mountains, the softness of the light and the mystery pervading the scene." Sheldon was speaking of another time, in another desert—Mexico's El Gran Desierto 300 miles southwest of the Painted Desert. But he could have been describing an evening walk through the windswept Great Basin Desert, about where it fingers its way southward into the heartland of the Hopi and the Navajo. From the last outpost of civilization, I was probably no more than 4 or 5 miles out, at night, in the middle of the 43,030-acre Painted Desert Wilderness. I was a translucent shadow striding by the light of a full moon, along the northern edge of the Black Forest.

Germany, visions of medieval forests? Hardly. These trees (*Araucarioxylon arizonicum*) had turned to stone. To scientists and naturalists, they are related to *Araucarius*, conifers that thrive in South America, Australia, and elsewhere in the Southern Hemisphere. To U.S. Army Gen. William T. Sherman, who hauled one of these immense petrified logs back to Washington, D.C., in 1879, they were prize souvenirs. But with the light of the full moon rolling over them like an ethereal fog, they really did look to me more like the giant bones of the mythological *yietso*, reputed to have been slain by ancestral Navajos.

I had started this hike in Petrified Forest National Park with the goal of reaching Chinde Mesa 7 or 8 miles cross-country north by northwest from the Kachina Point. I had been to Chinde Mesa 5 years earlier and wanted to know if I could still see 11,403-foot Mount Baldy 90 miles to the south. With the advent of the coal-fired Four Corners and Navajo power plants, I wasn't sure if I'd still be able to see *dzil ligai*, "white mountain," the sacred mountain of the White Mountain Apaches. But as another hiker who had crossed this area not long before wrote, "for every hike we pick a destination. Often we don't make it." The further I walked, the more obvious it became that I would clearly not make my destination. I was enrapt, strolling through a lunarscape first roamed by 40-foot-long, 2,000-pound crocodile-like reptiles, where ancient man told time with solar calendars.

By day, this mile-high desert of strangely eroded badlands is home to the fleet-footed pronghorn antelope, which feed on abundant grasses and roam with carefree abandon, protected from all but the most tenacious of predators. Small mammals like black-tailed jackrabbits occasionally seek refuge from raptors that soar on summer thermals. In earlier times, the Hopi were reputed to run down the black-tailed jacks on foot—though there are no written records of the Hopi running antelope to death as one band of Southern Paiute Indians did. (Pursued for days by the strongest Paiute runners, the antelope would simply overheat and collapse.) But today, few people day hike or backpack the Painted Desert's gentle and beguiling wilderness; in all of 1985, hikers spent only approximately eight hundred user nights here. That's because Petrified Forest National Park suffers the fate of being little brother to the region's more ostentatious national parks, such as Canyonlands, Zion, and Grand Canyon. Yet it's hardly a deserving rap, because if you take the time to explore this desert on its terms—and that comes with walking—you'll feel the power of its subtle beauty.

I got an inkling of that not long after I crossed mud-caked Lithodendran Wash, and I decided this time night would be best for traversing an ancient boneyard. The footing was certainly conducive to nighttime walking; I heard a crunching underfoot like broken eggshells. Or maybe I was hearing the remnant echoes of a Lythodynastes, a 20-foot-long carnivore, still munching the bones of an ancient hunter caught too far afield from the communal fire. Nor did the terrain present any difficulties for nocturnal rambling. I could scramble along the fluted mounds of the sedimentary Chinle Formation, as Charles Lummis did when he took his agonizing spill, or I could stick to the flats, as I was doing now, and continue floating toward some nebulous spot on the starlit northern horizon. There I would camp, munch on a handful of food, and drink bottled water where no perennial water exists; then I would retire to a peaceful night of star- and moon-dusted reverie.

I continued walking the flats, held rapt by my own imagination. If a friend had accompanied me, there would have been nothing to say. The land did all the talking, whispering untold secrets from eons past. And like Sheldon, who spoke of another desert almost 100 years ago, I would never forget "the calm, the silence . . . the mystery pervading the scene."

Other Hikes and Considerations

From the Kachina Point entry, a trail will take you down to Lithodendran Wash; at that point, hiking is cross-country. You can follow the trail markers and cairns approximately 4 miles north to Standing Stumps and the nearby prehistoric ruins. This makes a good destination for a day hike, though you're not permitted to camp near the ruins. Chinde Mesa is another 3 or 4 miles cross-country, depending how true your course of travel is, but it's easily identifiable. Just remember when hiking anywhere in Petrified Forest National Park that the clean desert air makes landmarks appear deceptively close. You also have to carry all the water you need, and you should frequently look back along your route to familiarize yourself with the terrain and its key geographical features for your return.

The 7,240-acre Rainbow Forest Wilderness comprises much of Petrified Forest National Park south of I-40; because it's such a small wilderness, it's an excellent area in which to acquaint yourself with the rigors and peculiarities of cross-country travel and route finding. Primary access for the Rainbow Forest Wilderness is from The Flattops parking lot; if you plan to day hike or backpack the length of this wilderness area, start from the Long Logs parking lot and end at your shuttle vehicle at the Agate Bridge parking lot. These parking lots are clearly marked on the Petrified Forest National Park brochure you'll receive when you pay your entrance fee.

Travel Notes

- **Primary access.** Kachina Point Trailhead.

- **Total elevation gain and loss.** Depending on your hike, anywhere from 600 to 750 vertical feet each way.

- **Mileage.** Approximately 4 miles one way to the Standing Stumps area; another 3 to 4 miles one way to Chinde Mesa.

- **Water.** No perennial water en route; sometimes seasonal water can be found in Lithodendran Wash — as Baldwin Möllhausen first noted when he saw "a pool of bitter brackish water" there in 1853.

- **Cache points.** The high ground above Lithodendran Wash, or the midway point on a cross-country hike of your own design.

- **Escape routes.** Kachina Point via the most direct route.

- **Seasons.** Fall and spring are best. June can be extremely uncomfortable, though seasoned desert travelers may find the dramatic summer monsoons of July and August the most visually rewarding for hiking and photographing. Winter can be bitter, as Lummis discovered, in this wind-sheared high desert.

- **Maps.** Petrified Forest National Park (1:62,500).

- **Managing agency.** National Park Service, Petrified Forest National Park, Holbrook, AZ 86025; (602) 524–6228.

- **Backcountry information.** No campfires allowed. Overnight hiking by permit only.

- **Biotic communities.** Great Basin Desert scrub and plains and desert grassland.

Echo Cliffs

Colorado Plateau: day hikes and exploratory treks

Landform

Forming the western escarpment of the Kaibito Plateau, Echo Cliffs is a 50-mile-long band of Chinle and Navajo Sandstone. These northwest-trending, 6,000-foot-high cliffs are bordered on the west by the Painted Desert and, further to the west, by a deep gash in the earth called Marble

Canyon Gorge. For all practical purposes, a 5,500-foot-high pass called The Gap marks the southern end of Echo Cliffs near Hamblin Ridge, while the northern terminus is punctuated by Echo Peaks, a cluster of four wind-cleaved summits between 5,219 and 5,567 feet high. At 6,654 feet high, Red Point is the undisputed high point of Echo Cliffs, but the lower Navajo Sandstone summits of Echo Peaks underscore the dramatic, 2,000-foot vertical relief common throughout the northern half of this breathtaking escarpment.

Historical Overview

Fray Francisco Dominguez and Fray Silvestre Escalante made the first recorded ascent of Echo Cliffs on November 2, 1776. To the Spanish padres, Echo Cliffs presented an almost impenetrable wall—assuming they could ford the swift-moving Colorado River at Lee's Ferry. But they couldn't; Escalante's attempts to cross the river on a homemade raft failed, and *salsipuedes* ("get out if you can") became their rallying cry. According to the well-written, thoroughly researched *Desert River Crossing*, by W. L. Rusho and C. Gregory Crampton, one of Dominguez and Escalante's men found a route through Echo Cliffs about 2.5 miles above the confluence of the Paria and Colorado rivers. Wrote Escalante: "We spent more than three hours in climbing it because at the beginning it is very rugged and sandy and afterward has very difficult stretches and extremely perilous ledges of rock, and finally it becomes almost impassable." On January 2, 1777, Dominguez and Escalante finally returned to Sante Fe, New Mexico, from which they had embarked 5 months earlier on an unsuccessful attempt to pioneer a new route to Monterey, California.

Fittingly enough, the route of Dominguez and Escalante's enervating, steep sand slog through Echo Cliffs was later called Dominguez Pass; according to *Desert River Crossing*, repeat ascents of this short, difficult route were made by Mormon missionary Jacob Hamblin in both 1858 and 1859, by thirty-six Mormon militiamen in 1869, and by train robbers on the run from Prescott lawman William "Buckey" O'Neil in 1889. Frederick S. Dellenbaugh's account of his ascent on November 2, 1871, still serves as an insightful guide today; in *A Canyon Voyage*, Dellenbaugh wrote: "[A track] led us up the valley of the Paria, between great cliffs about three miles, and then we had another surprise, for it swung sharply to the right and climbed a steep, sandy slope towards the only apparent place where the two-thousand-foot cliffs could possibly be scaled by a horse." Evidently, Dellenbaugh was concerned about finding his Indian guide, "a single, ragged, woebegone, silent old man on as skinny and tottering a pony as ever I saw," and wrote about following "a very old Indian trail. When we had mounted to the base of the vertical rocks we travelled zig-zagging back and forth across the face of the precipice till presently the trail passed through a notch out upon the plateau. From an eminence we now scanned the whole visible area without discovering anything that apparently had not been there for several thousand years."

If you trek the incipient Dominguez Pass route today, you'll still find "little to discover that hasn't been there for several thousand years." Perhaps the best way to explore is to ascend the Charles H. Spencer Trail from Lee's Ferry, trek north along the crest of Echo Cliffs to Dominguez Pass, and return to Lee's Ferry via the Paria River. The Charles H. Spencer Trail was built in 1910 by the promoter and his mule Pete, and whether you use it to begin or end this historic loop, you'll be able to relive the challenges faced by early travelers while being rewarded with some of the most outstanding views of the area—assuming the nearby Navajo Power Plant hasn't laid down a depressingly bleak layer of smog over this sublime corner of the Colorado Plateau.

For the best view of the area, though, you'll have to scramble up Echo Peaks, as three of Major Powell's men did on October 21, 1871. Like the Spanish padres, Dellenbaugh, Francis M. Bishop, and Almon Harris Thompson chose a steep sand slope to ascend the then-unnamed peaks. Wrote Dellenbaugh: "In the morning Prof., Cap., and I climbed a steep slope of bright orange sand a little below our camp, a rather hard task as the sand was loose, causing us to slip backward at every step. After twelve hundred or fifteen hundred feet of this kind of climbing we reached the base of three rocky peaks several hundred feet higher." The three peaks were the 5,500-foot-high north summit, the 5,567-foot-high middle summit, and the 5,262-foot-high south summit. The southernmost summit of Echo Peaks, also unnamed, is 5,219-feet high and located immediately north of the CCC Pass described in the Trek Log of this section. According to Harvey Butchart's *Grand Canyon Treks II*, Powell's men climbed the northernmost summit of Echo Peaks, only managing to do so by helping each other to the top. Wrote Dellenbaugh:

> For amusement, I tried to shoot into the river [1.5 miles and more than 2,000 feet below] with Cap's .44 Remington revolver. As I pulled the trigger the noise was absolutely staggering. The violent report was followed by dead silence. While we were remarking [about] the intensity of the crash, from far away on some distant cliffs [the Vermilion Cliffs] northward the sound waves were hurled back to us with a rattle like

that of musketry. We tried again with the same result, the interval between the great roar and the echo being twenty-four seconds by the watch. We could call the place nothing but Echo Peaks, and since then the name has been applied also to the line of cliffs breaking to the south.

Directions

From the scenic pullout at the west end of Navajo Bridge on Highway 89A (120 miles north of Flagstaff), drive 1.8 miles south on Highway 89A to an unmarked turnoff on the left. Turn north and follow this nonmaintained one-lane track 2.1 miles along the base of Echo Cliffs to an unmarked pullout on the right.

The CCC Trail Log

According to *Desert River Crossing*, the CCC Trail was built in the 1930s as an alternative to the Buzzards Highline Trail, an ancient Indian trail that first provided access to the Colorado River via the northeast side of Echo Peaks. While little remains of Buzzards Highline Trail today, you can still easily follow the CCC Trail to the crest of Echo Cliffs.

Mile 0 to 1.5. Base of Echo Cliffs to its Crest. From your vehicle, walk cross-country toward a short, steep talus cone that ascends an obvious break in a cliff band; this is the contact point between the Moenkopi and Chinle formations. After you scramble up the 20-foot break, you'll come out on top of a broad terrace of Chinle. Head across this terrace southeast for several hundred yards until you pick up the CCC Trail coming in from the south. (You can pick up the CCC Trail a quarter-mile south of where your vehicle is parked, but where it ascends the Moenkopi it follows a drainage, and it's now so washed out that it would be like trekking up a steep, boulder-strewn trench.)

Once you pick up the CCC Trail, follow it as it climbs up to the crest of Echo Peaks. Near the top of the switchbacks, you'll be looking at a magnificent wall of what appears to be Chinle and Moenave, a tempting possibility for rock climbers interested in pioneering first ascents (as is much of Echo Cliffs). Beyond this wall, you'll have an uninterrupted view south along this seemingly endless band of cliffs until they turn due south near Red Point.

Immediately below the crest of Echo Cliffs is a short wall of stones that appears to be a trail shrine, reminiscent of those still found in unspoiled areas of the southwestern Arizona desert and the eastern California desert. Archaeologists believe that ancient Indians like California's Mojave and

Chemehuevi placed a stone along their route of travel each time they crossed the area on their prodigious journeys. This seems logical, as the CCC Trail was built to provide easier access to the Colorado River for Navajo Indians to water their stock.

Mile 1.5.   CCC Pass. At 4,800-plus feet and 1.5 miles out from your vehicle, this pass makes a good base camp or jumping-off spot for a variety of options well worth exploring. You can continue following the well-marked CCC Trail, which is easily visible from the pass, to the east. You can trek up the 5,436-foot-high bench mark a mile to the south and peer straight over the west wall of Echo Cliffs. Or you can make your way toward the base of Echo Peaks, though you may find it more practical to climb Echo Peaks as Dellenbaugh, Bishop, and Thompson did over a century ago—by slogging up one of the steepest sand spits in Arizona. If you opt to climb Echo Peaks from CCC Pass, head north cross-country and thread the pass formed by an unnamed knob at 4,998 feet and the crest of giant stone molars immediately to the east. But take your pack, because from Echo Peaks you can ski down much of the sandy west slope and loop south back to your vehicle once you hit the road.

One of the most exciting prospects for trekkers to consider from CCC Pass is a point-to-point traverse of the Echo Peaks crest. The 1891 Reconnaissance Map, called Echo Cliffs Sheet, doesn't show any ancient trails traversing this spectacular crest, but you can see the early wagon road that paralleled Tanner Wash and Hamblin Wash along the base of Echo Cliffs. This route was used by Mormon settlers on their way to the Little Colorado River Valley during the 1870s. It was well traveled then, and is now followed by modern Highway 89 and 89A.

Crest View

Few views of the Colorado Plateau rival the panorama from the crest of Echo Cliffs, or Echo Peaks; nowhere else in Arizona do such monumental landmarks converge. If Page, the Navajo Power Plant, and Lake Powell distract you from 6,900-foot-high Leche-E Rock and 10,388-foot-high Navajo Mountain to the east, you can still look to the west for a mesmerizing, largely unspoiled view of the Colorado Plateau. Northwest you can look straight into the mouth of 35-mile-long Paria Canyon, the natural boundary between Echo Cliffs and the Vermilion Cliffs (the only other band of cliffs outside of the Grand Canyon that rival the ones you're standing on). Further to the west, across sweeping Houserock Valley, is the nearly 9,000-foot-high Kaibab Plateau, called Buckskin Mountain about the time

Mormon settlers crossed it by way of the "Honeymoon Trail" from Saint George, Utah, to the Little Colorado River Valley. To the southwest you'll have what seems like a satellite view of Marble Canyon and all the tributary drainages that feed into that deep fissure, including Badger Canyon, Soap Creek, Tenmile Wash, and Rider Canyon, to name just a few. And immediately below, to the northeast, you'll be able to make out the rugged crust of Shinarump Conglomerate that climbs south from Lee's Ferry along the west slope of Echo Peaks; according to *Desert River Crossing*, "Veteran wagon drivers, well-acquainted with frontier roads, called Lee's Backbone the worst road they had ever traveled." If you come prepared, though, your trek along the CCC Trail will be one of the most rewarding.

Travel Notes

- **Primary access.** Via access road off Highway 89A.

- **Elevation gain and loss.** Approximately 1,400 vertical feet each way.

- **Mileage.** Approximately 1.5 miles one way.

- **Water sources.** Colorado River; ephemeral tinajas in season on crest.

- **Cache points.** CCC Pass if used as a base camp.

- **Escape routes.** Back the way you came.

- **Seasons.** Fall through spring, though Echo Peaks does catch snow in the winter.

- **Maps.** Lee's Ferry, AZ (7½ minute, Provisional Edition, 1985).

- **Nearest supply points.** Jacob's Lake, Cliff's Dwellers, Marble Canyon, Page, and Flagstaff.

- **Managing agency.** Navajo Indian Reservation.

- **Backcountry information.** Not required.

- **Biotic community.** Great Basin Desert scrub.

Climbing

Diamond Peak

Western Grand Canyon: peak ascent

Landform

Located in the Lower Granite Gorge on the west end of the Grand Canyon, 3,512-foot-high Diamond Peak is an isolated pyramid of Muav and Redwall limestone. A twin-summited peak, Diamond Peak thrusts itself out of this spectacular rugged terrain for more than 2,000 vertical feet; it occupies the natural triangle formed by the drainages of Two-Hundred-and-Twentyfour-Mile Canyon, the Colorado River, and the confluence of Diamond Creek and Peach Springs Canyon.

Historical Overview

Trying to nail down the first ascent of this remote Grand Canyon peak is a difficult task. Much of Diamond Peak's history is associated with Lt. Ives' journey down Peach Springs Canyon to the Colorado River on April 3, 1858. In *Report upon the Colorado River of the West,* Ives wrote of that descent: "The corresponding depth and gloom of the gaping chasms into which we were plunging, imparted an unearthly character to a way that might have resembled the portals of the inferno regions." The brooding woodcuts of the expedition artist evoke just that feeling; and in that light, you can only wonder what inspired Ives to name Diamond Creek—called Arroyo de San Alexo by Francisco Garces on July 17, 1775—after a precious stone.

Situated at the confluence of Diamond Creek and Peach Springs Canyon, the Diamond Creek Hotel provided overnight accommodations for tourists who ventured into the bottom of the Grand Canyon on the Farley Stage during the 1880s and 1890s. Diamond Peak would have been a natural objective for the more adventuresome tourists staying at the two-story hotel; one ascent was reportedly recorded in the hotel register, which was lost in a fire. An unsigned note from Grand Canyon National Park's climbing file supports the theory: "DIAMOND PEAK . . . Bottle with note in it dated 1894 found near summit. A man from Iceland and a woman had climbed it."

But Grand Canyon boatman and climber George Bain once heard that a barefoot Hualapai Indian was the first to climb Diamond Peak. And while that rumor has yet to be substantiated, the Hualapais probably did climb Diamond Peak first—though probably not barefoot, as the steep, broken east face is comprised of sharp, skin-ripping Redwall limestone.

And although he did not call the peak by its name, Charles F. Lummis probably ascended Diamond Peak as early as 1884, with his dog and a broken arm. In a commemorative book of his epic 3,507-mile walk from Cincinnati to Los Angeles, Lummis explained the reason for his transcon-

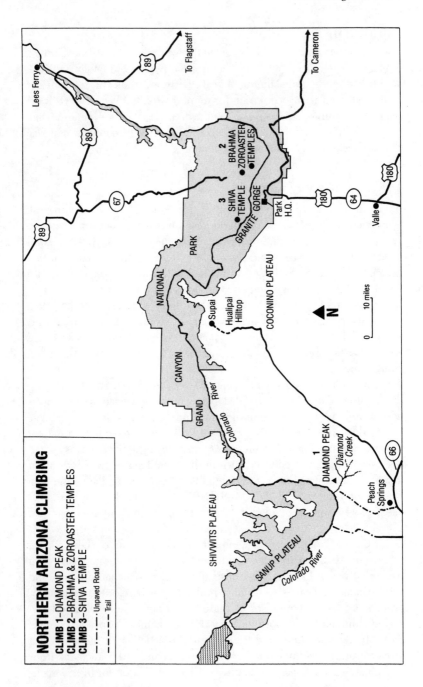

tinental walk: "Railroads and Pullmans were invented to help us hurry through life . . . I am an American and feel ashamed to know so little about my country as I do." One hundred and forty-three days after leaving Cincinnati, Lummis reached Los Angeles, where he immediately went to work as editor of a fledgling newspaper with a daily circulation of 2,700: the *Los Angeles Times*. Fortunately, Lummis took time to write about his cross-country adventure in a book called *A Tramp Across the Continent*. In this classic volume, he vividly recounts, among other hair-raising incidents, breaking his arm while deer hunting in the Painted Desert. (See entry for Painted Desert.) Far from medical help, he wrapped one end of a leather canteen strap around his wrist and the other end around a cedar tree and jumped backward to reset the bone.

Accompanied by his dog Shadow, Lummis detoured north when he reached Peach Springs and walked 23 miles down Peach Springs Canyon with his throbbing arm still in a sling to "visit the greatest wonder in the world—the Grand Cañon of the Colorado River." En route, he noted: "The wild majestic cliffs loomed taller, nobler, more marvelous, at every step, until the wash ran abruptly against a titanic pyramid of roseate rock, and was at an end, and we turned at right angles into the grander cañon of Diamond Creek." At this point, Lummis could only have been describing Diamond Peak, because from the confluence of Diamond Creek and Peach Springs Canyon, it clearly resembles a pyramid.

Lummis describes the ascent of Diamond Peak to a T. "Before daybreak next morning we were up and climbing one of the rugged terraced walls of a vast butte to get the view from its crest. It was a toilsome and painful climb to me, thanks to the arm, and at the easiest points it is no easy task for anyone. . . . The descent was ten times worse than the ascent—more difficult, more dangerous, and more painful . . . it was a great relief to stand again in that fantastic wash of Diamond Creek." That Lummis ended his descent in Diamond Creek further substantiates the probability that he climbed Diamond Peak, because the easiest and most natural approach to Diamond Peak is from Peach Springs Canyon via Diamond Creek.

Directions

From the junction of Historic Route 66 and the Diamond Creek Road, turn right (north) at the office of the Hualapai River Runners. Follow the well-maintained Diamond Creek Road 19 miles north to a ramada on the left side of the road above the confluence of Peach Springs Canyon and Diamond Creek. This is the best place to park your vehicle, above the periodic flash floods that scour Diamond Creek; in the stormy summer of 1983, a stakeside truck was swept into the Colorado River by a flash flood and several dozen river runners narrowly escaped with their lives.

The Approach

Mile 0 to 1. Ramada to Diamond Creek Pass. Walk several hundred yards due east from the ramada along a short bend in Diamond Creek until you reach the first obvious drainage, which runs northeast-southwest. You'll need a solid hour to pick your way along the boulders and climb 1,300 vertical feet to the pass below the east face of Diamond Peak. Keep your eyes open en route for the desert bighorn sheep that abound in the area; you may also hear the braying of a lone feral burro that outwitted the Park Service's eradication program in the early 1980s.

Located at the 2,600-plus-foot level, Diamond Peak Pass is an excellent campsite for late starters and offers a good view of the Colorado River 1.5 miles through the ocotillo to the northeast. Harvey Butchart, preeminent canyoneer who has made ascents of no fewer than eighty Grand Canyon temples, first called this pass Diamond Creek in the winter of 1966 when he trekked over it en route from Diamond Creek to Granite Park. Of his own earlier trek down Peach Springs Wash to the Colorado River on December 30, 1964, Butchart wrote: "About the most impressive view of this trip is the sight of Diamond Peak at the end of the straight stretch of Peach Springs Wash. It looks like something from Glacier National Park."

The East Face

From Diamond Creek Pass, you have to climb another 900 vertical feet to reach the main south summit of Diamond Peak; the 3rd and 4th Class route is broken down as follows.

• The Talus Slope: From Diamond Peak Pass, head west and ascend the obvious talus slope straight up approximately 400 vertical feet to the first prominent terrace.

• The Terrace: Traverse southwest (left) approximately 100 yards along this sloping terrace to a natural break; this break ascends a steep, broken gully filled with ocotillo and century plants on the left-hand side of an arête.

• The Gully: Scramble up a 20-foot step to the base of a 40-foot step. After scrambling up this 40-foot step on its left-hand side, scramble up a steep, rotten gully for approximately 80 feet. Surmount the short, exposed move at the top of this gully, which ends in a left-facing open book.

• The Zigzags: Follow the path of least resistance by angling diagonally up to the left for several hundred feet, zigzagging along several crumbly, exposed ledges to the main summit of Diamond Peak. Before you start panicking about how you're going to get down off this slag heap, spend a few moments to take in the view from the summit.

The Summit View

Of the summit, Lummis wrote: "The reward of that groaning, sore, skyward mile lay at the top. From that dizzy lookout I could see a hundred miles of the stupendous workshop of the Colorado River—that ineffable wilderness of flat-topped buttes threaded by windings of the vast cleft." You too will be able to make out the magnificent spires above Diamond Creek Narrows a mile and a half to the southeast. These spires of glass black Vishnu schist must have been what Lieutenant Ives referred to in 1858 as "apparitions of goblin-like figures perched in the rifts and hollows of the impending cliffs." Seen from the summit of Diamond Peak, these "goblins" beckon you to go explore the Narrows another time.

If you have designs on spending the night on the main summit, for either esthetic or photographic reasons, the only place to camp is in the 3-foot-deep summit fissure, which will sleep a party of three end to end. The roomy north summit is slightly lower but would make a better place to camp; it also provides the only up-river view, a breathtaking sight from the top of Diamond Peak, but to reach it requires several exposed moves on crumbly Redwall Limestone that are best protected by a belayer.

The Descent

Now that you're up here, how are you going to get down? A good question. Another question might be: How did Lummis climb down Diamond Peak with a broken arm and a dog? In *A Tramp Across the Continent*, Lummis described how he was forced to reverse one particularly hair-raising move he'd made easily during his ascent: "The descent was ten times worse than the ascent—more difficult, more dangerous, and more painful. . . . There were but two courses, to try to jump so as to land on the side of the cleft, or to hang on till exhausted, and then drop to sure death . . . with a desperate breath I thrust my whole life into a frantic effort, and sprang backwards into the air. If the Colorado Cañon ran all its seven hundred miles through cliffs of solid gold, I would not make that jump again for the whole of it." And you won't have to, either, if you bring a climbing rope to belay members of your party with and descend via your line of ascent.

Climber Dave Ganci approaches the summit of Diamond Peak, back-dropped by Diamond Creek and the Hualipai Indian lands of the western Grand Canyon. Photo by John Annerino.

Travel Notes

- **Suggested equipment.** One 150-foot rope; slings and carabiners for belay anchors; helmets.

- **Primary access.** Diamond Creek Road; George Bain climbed it from the Colorado River via Two-Hundred-and-Twentyfour-Mile Canyon.

- **Elevation gain and loss.** Approximately 2,200 vertical feet each way.

- **Mileage.** Approximately 1.5 miles each way.

- **Water sources.** Diamond Creek and the Colorado River.

- **Cache points.** Diamond Peak Pass.

- **Escape routes.** Back the way you came.

- **Emergencies.** Due to the inherent nature of Redwall Limestone, climbing parties should know their options in the event an emergency evacuation is needed. The Marine Corps Air Station, Yuma, would be the best rescue

team to pluck an injured climber off the east face of Diamond Peak. Call
Fleet Liaison Office at (602) 726-3558 with specific coordinates.

•**Seasons.** Late fall through early spring.

•**Maps.** Diamond Peak, AZ (7½ minute).

•**Nearest supply points.** Seligman, Peach Springs (if anything is open),
and Kingman. (In Seligman, treat yourself to a rootbeer float and a few
laughs at Delgadillo's Snow Cap on historic Route 66: "Slightly used Napkins
and Straws.")

•**Managing agency.** Hualapai Indian Reservation.

•**Backcountry information.** Permit required. Contact the offices of the
Hualapai River Runners, P.O. Box 168, Peach Springs, AZ 86434; (602)
769-2216.

•**Biotic community.** Mojave Desert scrub and Great Basin Desert scrub.

Brahma and Zoroaster Temples

North Rim, Grand Canyon: peak ascents via trekking and climbing

Landform

Of the 120-odd named temples within the Grand Canyon, few are more
striking than Zoroaster or Brahma. Comprised largely of Coconino Sandstone and Kaibab Limestone, these spectacular monoliths occupy a singu-
lar arm of Hermit Shale that extends southward from the North Rim into
the heart of the Grand Canyon. Named after the Persian deity of Zoroas-
trianism, 7,123-foot-high Zoroaster Temple is a flat-topped pyramid with
imposing walls of buff-colored sandstone more than 500 feet high. Brahma
Temple, at 7,551 feet high, was named after the Hindus' Supreme Creator. While it overshadows neighboring Zoroaster in sheer mass and height,
its walls are largely broken on its northern half, offering easier ascents for
nonclimbing canyoneers. Unexplored till December 1957, Zoroaster and
Brahma are now seen by more than 4 million visitors each year.

Historical Overview

Phoenix climbers Dave Ganci, Dick Ernst, and Jerry Robertson made the
first successful reconnaissance of Zoroaster from the South Rim in 1957.
Sliding down the steep, 7-mile-long Kaibab Trail with heavy packs was

not the biggest problem – though the knee-buckling vertical mile descent certainly added to the toil for anyone trying to reach the base of Zoroaster; nor was following the Clear Creek Trail 2.5 miles from Phantom Ranch to Sumner Wash. The crux to reaching both Zoroaster and Brahma lay between Sumner Wash and the base of Zoroaster almost 3,000 feet above; whoever pieced together the puzzling route through the grotesquely rotten Redwall Limestone and exposed ledges of Supai Sandstone would have the first crack at climbing the biggest plumb in the Grand Canyon. In the January 1959 issue of *Summit Magazine,* Dave Ganci wrote: "As we had guessed from pictures, the big problem would be the four prevailing rock walls that surround the temple and vary from three hundred to five hundred feet high. With amazing luck we found a route that led us to the base, somewhat beat for our efforts."

By the time Ganci returned to the inner Canyon to climb "Zoro's" Northeast Arête with Stanford student and climber Rick Tidrick on September 7, 1958, at least four other expeditions had failed. But Phoenix desert rats like Ganci and Tidrick knew a few things that California- and Colorado-born expedition members didn't; they knew the route, and they knew they couldn't carry enough water and their climbing gear to mount a successful summit bid in an inverted desert mountain range. So they launched their attempt in the wake of Arizona's summer monsoons, which periodically recharge the inner Canyon's ephemeral rain catchments, or tinajas.

After spending a drizzly night hunkered down at Phantom Ranch, Ganci and Tidrick forded the rain-swollen Bright Angel Creek early in the morning; the extended weather forecast called for rain the next 4 days, so they had little doubt that they could fill the empty 5 gallon metal jerry can they were humping up to Zoroaster. Consequently, Ganci and Tidrick carried only a gallon of water each – not enough water to climb 5,000 vertical feet to the summit of Zoroaster and back in the skull-numbing heat – unless the rains broke.

Still packing 65-pound loads, Ganci and Tidrick didn't reach Sumner Wash until noon. By the time they started up the nerve-wracking 4th Class chimney through the Redwall, dehydration brought on by 100-plus degrees Fahrenheit had taken its toll. It took the pair 3 hours to haul their packs to the top of the Redwall, where they were forced to camp in the Sumner-Zoroaster Saddle still 1,500 feet below the base of Zoroaster. Wrote Ganci: "Realizing we had drunk three quarts of our two gallons of water, we decided to start rationing the precious liquid, still expecting to collect rain. The clouds cleared that night and the starry night was an unwelcome sight."

After stoking up on a can of applesauce the next morning, Ganci and Tidrick made a break for Zoroaster carrying two ropes and a small rack of climbing gear. Providence was with them; they found two tinajas that held about a quart of water each—"and a generous supply of insect larvae"— in the Supai formation. Ganci added: "We tanked up and continued on to the base of the temple. We dropped our equipment at the crack I had seen the winter before, under the protection of a rattlesnake sunning himself at the base of the crack. We found two more water pockets and finished them off before heading back to base camp."

Too impatient to wait for the forecasted monsoons, Ganci and Tidrick decided to attempt Zoroaster at dawn the following day. But dehydration and fatigue caught up with them barely halfway up the Northeast Arête and they were forced to bivouac on a narrow ledge. Still stiff from what Ganci wrote was "a very uncomfortable bivouac," they negotiated an exposed, unprotected traverse the next morning and surmounted the Northeast Arête's crux summit crack. Shortly after 11 A.M. on September 23, 1958, Dave Ganci and Rick Tidrick reached the summit of Zoroaster Temple and built a 4½-foot-high cairn that, ideally, would be seen from the South Rim.

Out of water, a now-weary Gancy and Tidrick beat a hasty descent off Zoroaster via four shaky rappels to the half-gallon of water they still had stashed at its base. But it was barely enough to get them all the way down to Phantom Ranch the following day. Wrote Ganci: "Friday, after lowering all our equipment down the Redwall in the rain (our first rain since we left Phantom Ranch Monday morning) we returned to Phantom Ranch dead tired, thirsty, hungry . . ."

Nobody climbed neighboring Brahma Temple until almost 7 years after the Ganci-Tidrick ascent; until the 1957 Ganci-Ernst-Robertson recon, nobody—including eminent canyoneer Harvey Butchart—knew how to get through the Redwall and Supai bands. Perhaps Butchart was too busy pioneering a Grand Canyon lifetime total of 96 rim-to-river routes, 154 breaks through the Redwall, 15,000 miles of trekking, and 50 first ascents of less technical temples. At any rate, canyoneers Donald G. Davis and Clarence "Doc" Ellis made the first ascent of Brahma. At the time, Davis described Brahma as "one of the largest and most imposing Canyon summits yet remaining untested as to its accessibility without hardware." Yet it was because early rock climbers like Ganci, Tidrick, and Robertson had succeeded in employing modern rock-climbing techniques and astute routefinding skills on Zoroaster that "nonclimbing" canyoneers could reach a plumb like Brahma.

Davis and Ellis' lightning, 14-hour-round-trip first ascent of Brahma Temple from Phantom Ranch was impressive. Before they left Phantom Ranch on May 15, 1968, Brahma had repulsed no fewer than three earlier attempts, including one by Ellis and another companion in 1967. Success this time would depend largely on Davis and Ellis' ability to find the route the Ganci-Ernst-Robertson recon had pioneered through the Supai and to pick out and climb a 4th Class route up Brahma on sight. Carrying little more than a 150-foot ⅝-inch rope, two meals, a flashlight, and 1½ gallons of water apiece, Davis and Ellis left Phantom Ranch at 6:30 A.M. and made rapid progress, climbing to the top of the Redwall in 3 hours. The Supai ledges might have stopped them, as they had Ellis the year before, if Davis hadn't found "a rotting rappel slung around a tree, showing that the Zoroastrians had pioneered this route." Like the Ganci-Tidrick party, Davis and Ellis found water near the Supai—though it was only a trickle, which they didn't make use of.

From the Brahma-Zoroaster Saddle, Davis and Ellis figured their best chances lay on Brahma's broken west face. While contouring the foot of the West Face, Davis wrote, "we noticed a large block of fallen Coconino on which was preserved, tilted on its side, a several foot length of perhaps the best fossil brackway I have seen—the footprints of some lumbering . . . beast . . . the claw marks clearly on many prints. The feet were about three inches wide; the tail some ten inches."

Perhaps of greater interest than dinosaur tracks was the fact that no one had climbed Brahma before Davis and Ellis virtually sauntered up the west face and reached the summit only 7 hours after leaving Phantom Ranch. Considering the ease with which the two scrambled, it's interesting that Pueblo Indians hadn't beaten them to the punch 1,000 years earlier—as they had on Shiva Temple, Wotan's Throne, and Guinevere Castle, to name a few Grand Canyon temples first climbed by Indians. But Davis reportedly saw no Indian relics.

Dave Ganci described the view best while he bivouacked atop the Redwall before making the third ascent of Zoroaster with Jerry Robertson in 1959: "As the sun dropped over the west end of the canyon, the deep purple haze that is so characteristic of the canyon enveloped us. . . . it was then that the deep feeling of isolation and loneliness overcame us. We could see the far off specks of light from the El Tovar Hotel on the south rim. The immense silence, the awareness of being completely cut off from the civilized world and the close contact of nature made us realize how insignificant are the petty problems and anxieties of mankind. They meant nothing out here."

Directions

From Flagstaff, take Highway 180 50 miles north to the junction of Highway 64; drive north on Highway 64 27 miles to the South Rim of the Grand Canyon.

Trail Log

Mile 0 to 9.5. South Rim to Phantom Ranch. Descend the Bright Angel Trail 9.5 miles, or the South Kaibab Trail 6.7 miles, to Phantom Ranch. (See entry for Bright Angel and North Kaibab trails).

Mile 9.5 to 12. Phantom Ranch to Sumner Wash. Hike up the North Kaibab Trail to the junction of the Clear Creek Trail. En route to Zoroaster in 1958, Dave Ganci described the Clear Creek Trail as a "rarely used, unkept ranger's trail that would carry us above the first one-thousand-foot wall called the Granite Gorge." Today the Clear Creek Trail is a well-maintained sidewalk in comparison; it climbs out of Bright Angel Creek and contours the Tonto Formation 9 miles to perennial Clear Creek. An idyllic destination for hikers, Clear Creek is a pivotal water source for climbers en route to 6,400-foot-high Angel's Gate; also known as Snoopy and his Doghouse, Angel's Gate was first climbed in 1972 by Dave Ganci and fellow Phoenix climber Chuck Graff. Approximately 2.5 miles from Phantom Ranch along the Clear Creek Trail you'll come to a drainage below the east buttress of Sumner Butte that climbers call Sumner Wash; you can find fairly reliable tinajas seasonally in the Tapeats below the Clear Creek Trail near the bed of Sumner Wash.

Mile 12 to 13.5. Sumner Wash to the Sumner-Zoroaster Saddle. From Sumner Wash, head cross-country through the Bright Angel Shale and Muav Limestone up the left arm of Sumner Wash to an obvious break in the Redwall east of BM 5,468. If you're heavily laden, you may want to rope up or haul packs through the rotten 4th Class chimney above.

Mile 13.5 to 14.5. Sumner-Zoroaster Saddle to the Supai Band. A good place to cache water, the 5,200-foot-high Sumner-Zoroaster Saddle was used as a bivouac site and base camp by Ganci and crew during the first and third ascents of Zoroaster and also served as a campsite for Rick Tidrick and five members of the Colorado College Mountain Club when they made the second ascent of Zoroaster in 1959. From the Sumner-Zoroaster Saddle, trek up the main west ridge connecting Zoroaster and pick your way through intermittent ledges of Supai Sandstone to the main base of the Supai Cliffs.

Mile 14.5 to 15-plus. Supai Band to Zoroaster Base. The route through the Supai Band is below BM 6,321 on the north side; contour along the base of the Supai until you can eyeball a 4th Class route through it, usually marked by old rappel slings. Again, depending on your load, you may want to rope up for several short but exposed moves in the Supai. Once atop the Supai Band, front point up what George Bain accurately named the "Killer Talus Slope" to the base of Zoroaster.

Brahma Temple (for nonclimbers)

While an ascent of Brahma doesn't require the same technical expertise as one of Zoroaster does, you're still faced with a long, challenging climb from Phantom Ranch. To quote Donald Davis: "In terms of overall interest and challenge, I would rank these peaks . . . as equivalent to rather difficult trailless 14,000-foot [Colorado] Peaks."

The West Face. From the Brahma-Zoroaster Saddle, ascend the ridge of Hermit Shale north to the foot of the Coconino on Brahma's south side. Contour the foot of the west face two-thirds of the way north along Brahma until you reach its broken side. If you found the route to the foot of Brahma from Phantom Ranch, you shouldn't have any problems following the 4th Class route to the top of the Coconino, though you'll have to contour the base of the Toroweap on its north side to locate the easiest route to the top of this caprock.

Other 4th class routes. During our May 4, 1978, ascent of Brahma, expedition member Dave Ganci pioneered a new route up the east face in the same time it took photographer Christine Keith and I to scramble up the standard west face route; so there are other enticing 4th Class routes to pioneer on this monumental island of stone.

Descent route. Via the west face.

Suggested gear. For the standard west face route, you may want to bring a short climbing rope and some slings to belay members of your party up and down several exposed moves.

Zoroaster Temple (for climbers)

Once at the base of Zoroaster, you have several challenging options: You can climb the classic Northeast Arête or tackle the bold southwest face, or you can create a new route on Zoroaster's immaculate, still-unclimbed northwest or southeast face.

Northeast Arête. (Grade III, 5.7). The Northeast Arête is a classic summit in every sense of the term; six pitches of crack, friction, and chimney climbing—with several thought-provoking run-outs—lead to one of the most incredible summits in the Southwest. However, because of this route's northern exposure, you may encounter snow as late as May. Gary Ziegler wrote of this unexpected problem during the second ascent in 1959:

> Steve [Peacock], while moving up heavily laden with bivouac gear, lost his grip on a small nubbin handhold and slid out of the chimney, pulling me off my snow-covered belay ledge and leaving both of us hanging from my tie-in . . . Having reached the top of the chimney a dismal sight greeted us. The 150-foot crack that leads up to the summit plateau was filled with snow and ice. It was already late in the afternoon and the sun was almost down when Rick [Tidrick] started up the first segment. It was here that Rick made one of the most tremendous leads that I have ever seen. By amazing skill and determination, he was able to work his way up the icy crack onto a belay shelf. After bringing Joe [Ball] up, he tried several times to get started in the upper crack, but without any luck. Finally, by standing on Joe's sholders, he was able to drive in an angle [piton] and tension the remaining 40 feet to the top.

Southwest face. (Grade III, 5.9-plus). Seen by virtually everyone who visits the South Rim, the southwest face of Zoroaster Temple remained unclimbed until May 5, 1978; the primary reason was that no one had figured out how to climb through the largely overhanging bulge of Hermit that rims the bottom of the southwest face without employing artificial, or aid-climbing, techniques. Because the southwest face was recognized as such a prize, there was an unwritten code among veteran canyoneers that whoever did the first ascent should free-climb it, or use only natural hand- and footholds. When George Bain, Dave Ganci, and I first attempted the southwest face on May 3, we encountered the same problem that had stumped other parties—how to free-climb the Hermit. I was suffering from the first stages of giardiasis when I noticed a natural crawlway through the Hermit roof to the right of the pitch with which George was growing frustrated. But before we could use the crawlway for a serious attempt on the southwest face, we had to replenish our dwindling water supply.

On May 4, George descended all the way back down to the Sumner-Zoroaster Saddle to pick up several gallons of water he'd cached there 2 years earlier, while Christine Keith, Dave, and I refilled our water jugs from several tinajas we found atop the Hermit on the north side of Brahma. On May 5, George led through the crawlway, which put us onto the talus slope at the foot of the Coconino. From there, Dave, George, and

I alternated leads throughout a day of sunshine and whirling snow flurries. But darkness and the threat of a snowstorm were about to pull the carpet out from under us, still two full pitches below the summit. Faced with the option of retreating all the way back down the southwest face in the dark or shivering to death in a bivouac, we elected to climb through the night. Since Dave had just led a shaky 5.9 friction pitch in tennis shoes, George led the harrowing Twilight Traverse (5.10) and I led the Midnight Crack (a 5.7 squeeze chimney) with a flashlight in my mouth.

Stone cold, the three of us piled onto the summit of Zoroaster at 1:30 A.M., where we bivouacked around a small fire until sunup. In "Zoroaster at Midnight," Dave Ganci wrote: "Giggly with exhaustion and relief, we stood and gaped at each other in the growing light. Three scraggly looking characters on a temple-top in the middle of the Grand Canyon. Like the poet, here is where we longed to be . . . with front row seats, waiting for the curtain to rise on the world's greatest light show — a Canyon sunrise."

The northwest and southeast faces.   As of this writing, these two faces remain unclimbed, though both offer spectacular adventures on Coconino Sandstone. Be advised, though, that serious climbing on the Canyon's remote temples has more in common with mountaineering.

Descent route.   Via 3 rappels down the northeast arête.

Suggested gear.   For the northeast arête and the southwest face, take a minimum of two 150-foot ropes, a full rack, slings, and a helmet.

Travel Notes

• **Primary access.**   Via Phantom Ranch from the South Rim. It would seem that Brahma and Zoroaster, situated below the North Rim, could be approached with greater ease from the North Rim via 7,928-foot-high Obi Point. However, when George Bain and Joe Sharber attempted this approach during the mid-1970s, they were confronted with precipitous bands of Supai between 7,353-foot-high Deva Temple and Brahma Temple, and any advantage they might have had by using the shorter North Rim approach was negated by the fact that they would have had to fix ropes on the south side of Deva and climb 1½ pitches of Supai on the north side of Brahma. Donald Davis also pondered the possibility of approaching Brahma Temple from the North Rim and concluded: "If it were necessary to traverse below the top Supai cliff from Deva all the way to the break north of Zoroaster, the talus hopping might more than nullify any advantage in a North Rim approach."

• **Elevation gain and loss.** Round-trip, you will gain 10,000-plus vertical feet and lose 10,000-plus vertical feet.

• **Mileage.** (round-trip): Brahma Temple – 32-plus miles; Zoroaster Temple – 30-plus miles.

• **Water sources.** Phantom Ranch. Seasonal water can be found in Sumner Wash Tinajas, the Supai Seeps below Zoroaster, and the tinajas on the broad ledges of Hermit encircling both Brahma and Zoroaster temples.

• **Cache points.** Sumner Wash and the Sumner-Zoroaster Saddle.

• **Escape routes.** Back the way you came; signal mirrors to the South Rim.

• **Seasons.** Fall through spring.

• **Maps.** Bright Angel Point and Phantom Ranch (both 7.5-minute quadrangles).

• **Nearest supply points.** Babbitts Store/South Rim, Williams, and Flagstaff.

• **Managing agency.** Grand Canyon National Park.

• **Backcountry information.** Permit required for overnight camping; fires not permitted.

• **Biotic communities.** Great Basin Desert scrub and juniper-pinyon woodland.

Shiva Temple

North Rim, Grand Canyon: day hikes and peak ascent

Landform

At 7,646 feet high, Shiva Temple is a huge, blocklike massif jutting out into the heart of the Grand Canyon from the edge of the North Rim via a broad, mile-long ridgeline of Hermit Shale and Esplanade Sandstone. At 6,295 feet, Shiva Saddle marks the low point on this ridgeline, with 1,300 feet of vertical relief on Shiva's northeast corner. The temple's northern, southern, and eastern exposures offer the greatest vertical relief, dropping more than 3,000 feet to Dragon, Trinity, and Phantom creeks, which drain this wooded island in the sky on all fronts. With a summit area comprising some 275 acres, Shiva Temple has more in common with the Grand

Canyon's forested mesas and plateaus than with its more spectacular temples like Zoroaster. Because this "lost forest" seems to have been cut off from the North Rim by 20,000 years of erosion, Shiva Temple received its most publicized and controversial ascent on September 16, 1937.

Historical Overview

In "Summits Below the Rim: Mountain Climbing in the Grand Canyon," Harvey Butchart wrote: "Park Rangers suggested to Harold Anthony of the American Museum of Natural History that animal life on isolated mesas might have evolved into forms distinct from those on the rims." The Grand Canyon theory of evolution at the time was based on the fact that the inner Canyon desert acted as both a physical and a climatic barrier between the North and South rims; for example, the gray-tailed Abert's squirrel, which lives atop the South Rim, evolved differently from its cousin, the white-tailed Kaibab squirrel, which roams the subalpine forests of the North Rim. Telescoping this theory onto the isolated microhabitat of Shiva Temple, park rangers began wondering what existed on the sky island. No one knew, but Dr. Harold E. Anthony and expeditionary forces that looked ready to tackle a Himalayan giant were only too eager to find out.

And the press was only too willing to cover the expedition to "The Lost World of Shiva Temple." A September 11, 1937, Associated Press dispatch captured the essence of the drama that many hoped would unfold: "Two scientific parties waited near the brink of the Grand Canyon tonight, eager to scale unexplored Shiva Temple, the 'lost forest' separated from the mainland for untold centuries, in search of animal species dating from the last glacier age."

The problem was getting on top of Shiva Temple. Forerunner to today's helicopter, the autogyro, was first considered, but that option was quickly dropped after an aerial recon proved Shiva's summit was so densely wooded with virgin stands of yellow pine and pinyon juniper that a suitable helipad could not be found. There was another aerial option of sorts, though it was never seriously considered; according to Dr. Anthony, one man "volunteered to put on a football helmet and padded garments and, with a coil of rope in his arms, throw himself from a plane into the tops of the trees [atop Shiva]. Once on the top it would be easy to go to the rim and let the rope down over the cliffs to the party waiting below."

As much as the expedition may have wanted to base their operations out of the snug dwellings of the North Rim Lodge, there was no getting around it; Dr. Anthony and company would somehow have to climb Shiva

Temple in order to conduct a biological survey. Enter Walter A. Wood, Jr., of the American Geographic Society; his wife, Mrs. Wood; and Mr. Elliot Humphrey. According to Dr. Anthony, they were all veteran climbers, and they would be responsible for getting the scientists atop Shiva Temple.

During the aerial reconnaissance of Shiva's summit, expedition members had observed several possible routes that led directly up from Shiva Saddle through the broken cliffs on the temple's northeast corner. However, with little Canyon experience, they weren't certain what difficulties the climbing would present. They should have asked Emery Kolb: Having trekked all the way up to the base of Shiva Temple from the Colorado River in 1909, the Grand Canyon explorer and photographer already had a pretty good handle on the best way to climb Shiva and offered to lead the expedition to the summit. But Dr. Anthony rebuffed Emery's offer. (Some speculated that the press might get sidetracked reporting on the latest exploits of the veteran canyoneer, who had already become famous for boating the wild Colorado River all the way from Wyoming to the Gulf of California in 1911.

So Kolb quietly went about climbing Shiva Temple 2 weeks before the American Museum launched its ballyhooed "first ascent"; he underscored his point by climbing Shiva twice from the North Rim, the second time with his daughter. During one of those daylong ascents, Kolb marked the corners of Shiva Temple with cairns, thereby leaving irrefutable evidence that he had made the first modern ascent of Shiva Temple. But in his article for the 1937 issue of *Natural History*, "The Facts About Shiva—The Real Story of One of the Most Popular Scientific Adventures in Recent Years," Dr. Anthony wrote: "We had no knowledge that a white man had even climbed it."

Meanwhile, Park Superintendent Tillotson virtually paved the way for the Shiva Temple Expedition by having a spur road cut out to the edge of the North Rim across the bay from Tiyo Point. Dr. Anthony reported that expedition supplies were trucked out to the jump-off point for Shiva Saddle . . . but the expedition was hauling so much gear—including beds!—that it took almost a full day to cover the 2-mile descent down to Shiva Saddle. Dr. Anthony doesn't say exactly where "veteran climber" Walter Wood had accumulated his wealth of climbing experience; had that been reported, perhaps some light could be shed as to why seven expedition members roped together on two ropes near the base of the Coconino Sandstone in order to climb the northeast corner of Shiva. Incredibly, they did, and in the process a rock dislodged and hit Humphrey in the head and "cut through his hat and laid his scalp open."

Dr. Anthony's published route descriptions and photos indicate that the two ropes climbed the broken chimneys just to the left of Shiva's northeast corner. Had they explored the possibilities a hundred yards further to the south, they would have discovered a virtually unexposed route they could have walked dogs up; no doubt Pueblo Indians had made use of this route when they first climbed Shiva Temple almost 1,000 years before Kolb's first recorded ascent. For whatever reason, Dr. Anthony's party didn't use this route and consequently didn't reach the summit until noon on September 16. With inadequate provisions to feed the entire party, only Park Naturalist Edwin McKee and Dr. Anthony spent the first night on the summit; the others descended back to Shiva Saddle to coordinate the logistical support that would keep the scientists fat and happy throughout their biological survey. Before the first resupply arrived, however, Dr. Anthony and McKee let the outside world know that Shiva had finally been climbed. Of that first night, Dr. Anthony wrote: "We could see the lights of El Tovar shining on the South Rim, some nine miles distant; and we made a huge blaze of dry limbs on the south edge of Shiva which we felt sure would notify our friends that the expedition was finally on Shiva."

Over the next 10 days, Dr. Anthony and his assistant, George B. Andrews, were continually resupplied with both ground and air support; six Mormon lads from Kanab were hired to hump provisions to the top of Shiva, while aviatress Amy Andrews bombed the summit regularly with 10-gallon milk cans of water dropped from her bright red single-engine Stinson. Had Dr. Anthony planned his expedition either to coincide with late spring runoff or immediately after summer monsoons, he could have made use of the deep tinajas in Shiva Saddle just as the Pueblo Indians had when they harvested and baked mescal in nearby yanta ovens. But seasons—and the truth—be damned; this was a grant-fat scientific expedition with modern logistical support.

In all, Dr. Anthony baited between fifty and sixty traps on a daily basis, which, he wrote, kept him busy "skinning most of the day." His war chest of pelts soon included pack rats, wood rats, cottontails, and chipmunks, among other animals. While trapping and plinking away at hundreds of small defenseless animals in the name of science, Dr. Anthony couldn't help but notice antlers dropped by black-tailed deer, which migrated between the North Rim and Shiva Temple via the route on Shiva's south side, first seen by Kolb in 1909; he also found plenty of evidence—including flint chips, scrapers, spear points, and a yanta oven—that Pueblo Indians made use of Shiva's summit between A.D. 900 and A.D. 1100. But as far as earth-shattering biological discoveries were concerned, the expedition was a bust. A footnote at the end of Dr. Anthony's article summed up the scientific ruckus perfectly: "As this article goes to press [a] comparison has been made and reveals no noticeable differences between the animals of Shiva and those of the rim."

Directions

From Jacob's Lake, drive 40 miles south on Highway 67 to the Point Sublime Trail, actually a dirt road that provides immediate access to the Widforss Trailhead (as it's signed). From Highway 67, head west on the Point Sublime Trail 4 miles to the Tiyo Point turnoff, marked by a small wooden sign; once you turn south, it's another 6 miles to Tiyo Point. After you've taken in the panorama from this undeveloped vista, turn your vehicle around and drive 1.3 miles north back up the Tiyo Point Road and park. On your 7.5 Minute Bright Angel Point Quadrangle, you'll be approximately one-third of a mile north of BM 7,962.

The Descent

Mile 0 to 1.5. Tiyo Point Road to North Rim. From the Tiyo Point Road, head west-southwest cross-country through pristine stands of ponderosa for approximately 1 mile; east to west, you will cross a shallow depression and three deep ravines before you top out on a prominent ridgeline. Head southwest along this unnamed ridgeline for half a mile until you find the cairns that mark the descent into the steep ravine just east of BM 7,515. BM 7,515 is your key to finding this ravine, so refer to your map if you overshoot it; cairns mark the route through the mouth of the ravine out to BM 7,515.

Mile 1.5 to 2.5. North Rim to Shiva Saddle. From BM 7,515, follow the cairns and a faint trail one-third of a mile south along the Toroweap; once through the Toroweap, a steep, nonmaintained trail plunges through the Coconino Sandstone and Hermit Shale before you level out on the Esplanade Formation, which will take you south to the 6,295-foot low point in Shiva Saddle. There are tremendous tinajas, or water pockets, in this saddle, and an abundance of evidence that Pueblo Indians used the area to harvest and cook mescal in yanta ovens. You may also find historic trash left over from the 1937 Shiva Temple Expedition.

The Ascent

Mile 2.5 to 3.5. Shiva Saddle to Shiva Temple Summit. From Shiva Saddle, climb a short, unrelenting, steep talus slope through the Hermit Shale

*Grand Canyon climber and boatman George Bain peers over the edge of
Shiva Temple, backdropped by the North Rim, the twin-summited Isis
Temple, and the South Rim in the distance. Photo by John Annerino.*

to the base of the Coconino Sandstone on the northeast corner of Shiva Temple. Turn left and contour south along the base of the Coconino for approximately 75 yards until you find an easy break in the Coconino; based on their historical photographs, this is probably where the Shiva Temple Expedition turned right and started climbing the broken chimneys above. Continue heading south along this ledge for another 25 yards until you find a small cairn marking the ramp that zigzags north through the Coconino. If you're observant, you shouldn't have any problems following widely spaced cairns all the way through the Coconino; en route are two short boulder problems that you may have to haul your pack up, and one exposed move that you may prefer to crawl along. Once atop the Coconino, head up the ridgeline to Shiva's northeast corner; turn west and contour the base of the Toroweap until you find a steep, natural break you can scramble up to reach the 7,646-foot-high point of Shiva Temple.

Summit View

Two Phoenix Dairy milk cans left over from the Shiva Temple Expedition still mark Shiva's highest corner; during an August 18, 1963, ascent of Shiva Temple, Joseph G. Hall and his brother William discovered a species in one of these metal cans that had escaped Dr. Anthony's more elaborate traps 25 years earlier. Wrote Hall: "No sooner had we 'topped out' than we saw [Dr. Anthony's] rustic skinning table, and two ten-gallon milk-cans in which water had been parachuted to the expedition. Ironically, a spotted skunk, a species not recorded by Anthony, was found drowned in one of these cans which had been half-filled by recent rains."

While Dr. Anthony's original site may seem like the logical place to camp, the most spectacular spot is Shiva's southwest corner a mile west. From this airee, you can overlook Claude Birdseye Point, Osiris Temple, Tower of Ra, and Mencius and Confucius, to name just a few of the most prominent temples within sight; in the right light, you can also see the Colorado River near Tuna Creek to the southwest and the cottonwood trees below Indian Gardens to the southeast. Assuming the dirge from the Navajo Generating Plant hasn't enveloped the inner Canyon again, you can see far to the west—beyond Mount Huethawali on the South Bass Trail all the way to 8,028-foot-high Mount Trumbull on the Arizona Strip. On any given day, you should also be able to pick out several small "hills" 60 miles to the south; One is the dark blue pyramid of 12,633-foot-high San Francisco Mountains and the other is nipple-shaped Kendrick Peak, which cartographer François Matthes used as a key triangulation point for the first topographical map of the Grand Canyon in 1902.

But perhaps Clarence Dutton said it best; in 1882, the eminent Grand Canyon geologist wrote:

> Beyond the eastern Cloister, five or six miles distant, rises a gigantic mass which we named Shiva's Temple. It is the grandest of all the buttes, and the most majestic in aspect, though not the most ornate. Its mass is as great as the mountainous part of Mt. Washington [in New Hampshire]. . . . All around it are side gorges sunk to a depth nearly as profound as that of the main channel. It stands in the midst of a great throng of cloister-like buttes, with the same noble profiles and strong linaments as those immediately before us, with a plexus of awful chasms between them. In such a stupendous scene of wreck it seemed as if the fabled 'Destroyer' might find an abode not wholly uncongenial.

Travel Notes

•**Suggested equipment.** A 50-foot rope.

•**Primary access.** Via Tiyo Point Road.

•**Elevation loss and gain.** 3,000 vertical feet each way.

•**Mileage.** 6 to 7 miles round-trip.

•**Water sources.** No perennial water sources en route; seasonal tinajas in Shiva Saddle.

•**Cache point.** Shiva Saddle.

•**Escape routes.** Back the way you came.

•**Seasons.** Spring through fall, though some weeks during the summer can be warm.

•**Maps.** Shiva Temple and Bright Angel Point quadrangles (7.5 minute).

•**Nearest supply points.** North Rim and Jacob's Lake.

•**Managing agency.** National Park Service.

•**Backcountry information.** Permit required for overnight camping; no fires allowed.

•**Biotic community.** Mountain meadow, spruce-alpine fir forest, montane conifer forest, and Juniper-pinyon woodland.

Selected Bibliography

Annerino, John. *Hiking the Grand Canyon.* San Francisco: Sierra Club Books, 1986.

Annerino, John. *High Risk Photography: The Adventure Behind the Image.* Helena, Montana: American Geographic Publishing, 1991.

Annerino, John. *Running Wild.* Unpublished manuscript. Grand Canyon, 1991.

Annerino, John. *Path of Fire: Through America's Killing Ground.* Unpublished photo-documentary. Mexico and Arizona, 1991.

Barnes, William C. *Arizona Place Names.* Tucson: Univ. of Arizona Press, 1985.

Basso, Keith, ed. *Western Apache Raiding and Warfare.* Tucson: Univ. of Arizona Press, 1971.

Bolton, Herbert Eugene. *Anza's California Expeditions.* Berkeley: Univ. of California Press, 1930.

Bolton, Herbert Eugene. *Rim of Christendom: A Biography of Eusebio Francisco Kino, Pacific Coast Pioneer.* New York: Macmillan, 1936.

Bolton, Herbert Eugene. *Kino's Historical Memoir of Pimeria Alta.* 2 vols. Berkeley: Univ. of California Press, 1948.

Bourke, John G. *On The Border with Crooke.* New York: Charles Scribner's Sons, 1891.

Brickler, Stanley K.; Coss, Harold T.; Doyle, Jack D.; Garcia, Margot W.; Hartmann, Gayle; Jickling, David F.; Johnson, Robert C.; Moore, Steven D.; Sanders, Jeffrey M.; Tunnicliff, Brock; Utter, Jack; and Wilkosz, Mary E. *Natural Resources Management Plan for Luke Air Force Range.* Tucson: College of Agriculture, Univ. of Arizona, 1986.

Brookes, Juanita, and Cleland, Robert Glass. *A Mormon Chronicle: The Diaries of John D. Lee, 1848–1876.* San Marino, Calif.: Huntington Library, 1955.

Brown, David E., ed. *The Wolf in the Southwest: The Making of an Endangered Species.* Tucson: Univ. of Arizona Press, 1984.

Browne, J. Ross. *A Tour Through Arizona, 1864.* New York: Harper and Brothers, 1869.

Broyles, Bill. *Fifty Years of Water Management in Cabeza Prieta.* Unpublished manuscript. Arizona, 1991.

Broyles, Bill, ed. *El Camino del Diablo, The Devil's Highway: An Anthology.* Unpublished manuscript. Mexico and Arizona, 1991.

Bryan, Kirk. *Routes to Desert Watering Places in Papago Country: Arizona.* Water-Supply Paper No. 490-d. Washington, D.C.: U.S. Government Printing Office, 1922.

Bryan, Kirk. *The Papago Country, Arizona: A Geographic, Geologic, and Hydrological Reconnaissance with a Guide to Desert Watering Places.* Water-Supply Paper No. 499. Washington, D.C.: U.S. Government Printing Office, 1925.

Butchart, J. Harvey. *Grand Canyon Treks II: A Guide to Extended Canyon Routes.* Glendale: La Siesta Press, Calif. 1975.

Calvin, Ross, ed. *Lieutenant Emory Reports: A Reprint of Lieutenant W. H. Emory's Notes of a Military Reconnaissance.* Albuquerque: Univ. of New Mexico Press, 1951.

Cline, Platt. *They Came to the Mountain: The Story of Flagstaff's Beginnings.* Flagstaff: Northern Arizona Univ. and Northland Press, 1976.

Collins, Robert O., and Nash, Roderick. *The Big Drops: Ten Legendary Rapids.* San Francisco: Sierra Club Books, 1978.

Conner, Daniel Ellis. *Joseph Reddeford Walker and the Arizona Adventure.* Norman: Univ. of Oklahoma Press, 1956.

Coues, Elliott, trans. *On the Trail of the Spanish Pioneer: The Diary and Itinerary of Francisco Garces, 1775–1776.* New York: E. P. Harper, 1900.

Couts, Cave Johnson. *Hepah, California! The Journal of Cave Johnson Couts from Monterey, Nuevo Leon, Mexico to Los Angeles, California, during the Years 1848–1849.* Edited by Henry F. Dobyns. Tucson: Arizona Pioneer Historical Society, 1961.

Cozzens, Samuel W. *The Marvelous Country.* London: Sampson, Low, Marston and Searle, 1873.

Curtis, Edward S., and Andrews, Ralph Warren. *The North American Indian.* Seattle: Superior Publishing, 1962.

Davis, Goode P., Jr. *Man and Wildlife in Arizona: The American Exploration Period, 1824–1865.* Phoenix: Arizona Game and Fish Department, 1986.

Dawson, Thomas F. *First Through the Grand Canyon.* U.S. Senate Resolution No. 79, 4 June, 1917.

Dellenbaugh, Frederick S. *Romance of the Colorado River.* New York: G. P. Putnam's Sons, 1906.

Dellenbaugh, Frederick S. *A Canyon Voyage: The Narrative of the Second Powell Expedition down the Green-Colorado River from Wyoming, and the Explorations on Land, in the Years 1871 and 1872.* New Haven: Yale Univ. Press, 1926.

Dutton, Clarence E. *Tertiary History of the Grand Cañon District, with Atlas.* Washington, D.C.: U.S. Government Printing Office, 1882.

Farish, Thomas Edwin. *History of Arizona.* 8 vols. Phoenix, Ariz.: © Thomas Edwin Farish, 1915.

Forbes, Robert Humphrey. *Crabb's Fillibustering Expedition into Sonora, 1857.* Tucson: Arizona Silhouettes, 1952.

Fradkin, Philip L. *A River No More.* New York: Knopf, 1981.

Fuchs, James R. *A History of Williams, Arizona, 1876–1951.* Tucson: Univ. of Arizona, 1955.

Ganci, Dave. *Hiking the Southwest.* San Francisco: Sierra Club Books, 1983.

Ganci, Dave. *Desert Hiking.* 2d ed. Berkeley: Wilderness Press, 1987.

Ganci, Dave. *Desert Survival.* Merrillville, Ind.: ICS Books, 1991.

Gifford, Edward Winslow. *Northeastern and Western Yavapai.* Berkeley: Univ. of California Press, 1936.

Granger, Byrd Howell. *Grand Canyon Place Names.* Tucson: Univ. of Arizona Press, 1960.

Granger, Byrd Howell. *Arizona's Names: X Marks the Place.* Tucson, Ariz.: Falconer Publishing, 1983.

Gregory, Herbert Ernest, and Moore, Robert C. *The Kaiparowits Region: A Geographic and Geologic Reconnaissance of Parts of Utah and Arizona.* Washington, D.C.: U.S. Government Printing Office, 1931.

Grubbs, Bruce, and Aitchison, Stewart. *The Hiker's Guide to Arizona.* Billings, Mont.: Falcon Press Publishing, 1987.

342   *Adventuring in Arizona*

Harris, Benjamin Butler. *The Gila Trail: The Texas Argonauts and the California Gold Rush.* Edited and annotated by Richard H. Dillon. Norman: Univ. of Oklahoma Press, 1960.

Hartmann, William K. *Desert Heart: Chronicles of the Sonoran Desert.* Tucson, Ariz.: Fisher Books, 1989.

Henson, Pauline. *Founding a Wilderness Capital, 1864.* Flagstaff, Ariz.: Northland Press, 1965.

Hinton, Richard J. *The Handbook to Arizona.* Tucson: Arizona Silhouettes, 1954.

Hornaday, William T. *Campfires on Desert and Lava.* New York: Charles Scribner's Sons, 1908.

Hughes, J. Donald. *The Story of Man at the Grand Canyon.* Grand Canyon, Ariz.: Grand Canyon Natural History Association, 1967.

Ives, Joseph Christmas. *Report upon the Colorado River of the West: Explored in 1857 and 1858.* Washington, D.C.: U.S. Government Printing Office, 1861.

Ives, Ronald L. *Land of Lava, Ash, and Sand: The Pinacate Region of Northwestern Mexico.* Tucson: Arizona Historical Society, 1989.

James, George Wharton. *In and around the Grand Canyon.* Boston: Little, Brown and Co., 1900.

James, George Wharton. *The Grand Canyon of Arizona: How To See It.* Boston: Little, Brown and Co., 1910.

James, George Wharton. *Arizona, the Wonderland.* Boston: Page, 1917.

Kelsey, Michael R. *Hiking and Exploring the Paria River.* Provo, Utah: Kelsey Publishing Co., 1987.

Kolb, Emery L. *Through the Grand Canyon from Wyoming to Mexico.* New York: Macmillan, 1920.

Laird, Carobeth. *The Chemehuevis.* Banning, Calif.: Malki Museum Press, 1976.

Lavender, David Sievert. *River Runners of the Grand Canyon.* Grand Canyon, Ariz.: Grand Canyon Natural History Association, 1985.

Lingenfelter, Richard E. *First Through the Grand Canyon.* Los Angeles: Glen Dawson, 1958.

Lowe, Charles H. *Arizona's Natural Environment.* Tucson: Univ. of Arizona Press, 1964.

Lumholtz, Karl Sofus. *New Trails in Mexico: An Account of One Year's Exploration in Northwestern Sonora, Mexico, and Southwestern Arizona 1909–1910*. New York: Charles Scribner's Sons, 1902.

Lummis, Charles Fletcher. *Some Strange Corners of Our Country: The Wonderland of the Southwest*. New York: Century Co., 1892.

Lummis, Charles Fletcher. *A Tramp Across the Continent*. New York: Charles Scribner's Sons, 1892.

Lummis, Charles Fletcher. *Mesa, Cañon and Pueblo*. New York: Appleton-Century, 1938.

Mange, Juan Mateo. *Luz de Tierra Incognita: Unknown Arizona and Sonora, 1693–1721*. English translation of part 2 by Harry J. Karns et al. Tucson: Arizona Silhouettes, 1954.

Merrill, W. Earl. *One Hundred Footprints on Forgotten Trails*. Mesa, Ariz.: Lofgreen Printing Co., 1978.

Möllhausen, Baldwin. *Diary of a Journey from the Mississippi to the Coasts of the Pacific with a United States Government Expedition*. 2 vols. London: Longman, Brown, Green, Longmans, & Roberts, 1858.

Mowry, Sylvester. *The Geography and Resources of Arizona and Sonora*. San Francisco: A. Roman and Co., 1863.

Obregon, Baltasar de. *Obregon's History of 16th Century Explorations in Western America*. Translated, edited, and annotated by George P. Hammond and Agapito Rey. Los Angeles: Wetzel Publishing Co., 1928.

Ortiz, Alfonso, ed. *Handbook of North American Indians: Southwest*. Vol. 10. Washington, D.C.: Smithsonian Institution/U.S. Government Printing Office, 1983.

Pattie, James Ohio. *Personal Narrative of James Ohio Pattie of Kentucky*. Reuben Gold Thwaites, ed. Cleveland, Ohio: Arthur H. Clark Co., 1905.

Perez de Luxan, Diego. *Expedition into New Mexico Made by Antonio de Espejo, 1582–1583: As Revealed in the Journal of Diego Perez de Luxan*. Translated by George P. Hammond and Agapito Rey. Los Angeles: Quivira Society, 1929.

Pourade, Richard F. "Anza Conquers the Desert: The Anza Expeditions from Mexico to California and the Founding of San Francisco, 1774–1776." San Diego, Calif.: *Union Tribune*, 1971.

Powell, John Wesley. *Explorations of the Colorado River of the West and Its Tributaries: Explored in 1869, 1870, 1871, and 1872*. Washington, D.C.: U.S. Government Printing Office, 1875.

Power, Thomas Jefferson, and Whitlatch, John. *Shoot-out at Dawn: An Arizona Tragedy.* Phoenix, Ariz.: Phoenix Books, 1981.

Pumpelly, Raphael. *Across America and Asia: Notes of a Five Years' Journey Around the World and of Residence in Arizona, Japan and China.* New York: Leypoldt and Holt, 1870.

Pumpelly, Raphael. *Pumpelly's Arizona.* Edited by Andrew Wallace. Tucson, Ariz.: Palo Verde Press, 1965.

Reisner, Marc. *Cadillac Desert: The American West and Its Disappearing Water.* New York: Viking, 1986.

Ross, Clyde Polhemus. *The Lower Gila Region: A Geographic, Geologic, and Hydrological Reconnaissance, with a Guide to Desert Watering Places.* Washington, D.C.: U.S. Government Printing Office, 1923.

Rusho, W. L., and Crampton, C. Gregory. *Desert River Crossing: Historic Lee's Ferry on the Colorado River.* Salt Lake City, Utah: Peregrine Smith, 1975.

Schullery, Paul, ed. *The Grand Canyon: Early Impressions.* Boulder: Colorado Associated Univ. Press, 1981.

Sheldon, Charles. *The Wilderness of Desert Bighorns and Seri Indians: The Southwestern Journals of Charles Sheldon.* Phoenix: Arizona Desert Bighorn Sheep Society, 1979.

Sherman, James E., and Barbara H. Sherman. *Ghost Towns of Arizona.* Norman: Univ. of Oklahoma Press, 1969.

Smith, Melvin T. *The Colorado River: Its History in the Lower Canyons Area.* Provo, Utah: Brigham Young Univ., 1972.

Smith, Olga Wright. *Gold on the Desert.* Albuquerque: Univ. of New Mexico Press, 1956.

Stanton, Robert Brewster. *Colorado River Controversies.* Boulder City, Nev.: Westwater Books, 1982.

Stevens, Larry. *The Colorado River in Grand Canyon.* Flagstaff, Ariz.: Red Lake Books, 1983.

Stone, Connie. *Deceptive Desolation: Prehistory of the Sonoran Desert in West Central Arizona.* Phoenix, Ariz.: Bureau of Land Management, 1986.

Stone, Connie. *People of the Desert, Canyons and Pines: Prehistory of the Patayan Country in West Central Arizona.* Phoenix, Ariz.: Bureau of Land Management, 1987.

Summerhayes, Martha. *Vanished Arizona: Recollections of the Army Life of a New England Woman.* Glorieta, N.M.: Rio Grande Press, 1970.

Swanson, James, and Kollenborn, Tom. *Superstition Mountain: A Ride through Time.* Phoenix, Ariz.: Arrowhead Press, 1981.

Thrapp, Dan L. *Al Sieber: Chief of Scouts.* Norman: Univ. of Oklahoma Press, 1964.

Tinker, George H. *A Land of Sunshine: Flagstaff and Its Surroundings, 1887.* Glendale, Calif.: Arthur H. Clark Co., 1969.

Walker, Henry P., and Bufkin, Donald. *Historical Atlas of Arizona.* Norman: Univ. of Oklahoma Press, 1978.

Watkins, T. H. et al. *The Grand Colorado: The Story of a River and Its Canyons.* Palo Alto, Calif.: American West Publishing Co., 1969.

Wells, Edmund. *Argonaut Tales: Stories of the Gold Seekers and the Indian Scouts of Early Arizona.* New York: F. H. Hitchcock, 1927.

Wheeler, Lt. George Montague. *Preliminary Report Concerning Explorations and Surveys:* Principally in Nevada and Arizona. Washington, D.C.: U.S. Government Printing Office, 1872.

Wheeler, Lt. George Montague. *Report upon United States Geographical Surveys West of the 100th Meridian.* 7 vols. Washington, D.C.: U.S. Government Printing Office, 1875–1889.

Wilson, John P. *Islands in the Desert: A History of the Uplands of Southeast Arizona.* Unpublished manuscript. Tucson, Ariz.: Coronado National Forest, 1987.

Mountain Ranges of Arizona

Number	Name of Range	Name of High Point
1	Agua Caliente. Mtns.	Morris B.M.
2	Agua Dulce Mtns.	Quitovaguita B.M.
3	Aguila Mtns.	Eagle B.M.
4	Ajo Range	Mt. Ajo
5	Alvarez Mtns.	unnamed
6	Aquarius Mtns.	unnamed
7	Artesa Mtns.	unnamed
8	Artillery Mtns.	Eagle Point
9	Atascosa Mtns.	Atascosa Pk.
10	Baboquivari Mtns.	Baboquivari Pk.
11	Batamote Mtns.	unnamed
12	Bates Mtns.	Kino Pk.
13	Beaver Dam Mtns.	unnamed (AZ)
	————	West Mt. Pk. (UT)
14	Belmont Mtns.	Belmont B.M.
15	Big Horn Mtns.	Big Horn Pk.
16	Big Lue Mtns.	unnamed
17	Bill Williams Mtns.	unnamed
18	Black Mtns.	Mt. Perkins
19	Black Mtns.	Tres Alamos
20	Blackjack Mtns.	unnamed
21	Bradshaw Mtns.	Mt. Union
22	Brownell Mtns.	Brownell Pk.
23	Bryan Mtns.	San B.M.
24	Buck Mtns.	Buck B.M.
25	Buckhorn Mtns.	Crater B.M.
26	Buckskin Mtns.	Buckskin B.M.
27	Butler Mtns.	Lech B.M.

by Doug Kasian

Elevation	Quad Location	Land Status
1,240	Hyder SE 7½	PAT
2,850	Agua Dulce Mtns. 15	CPWR
1,800	Aguila Mtns. 15	BMGR
4,812	Mt. Ajo 15	OPNM/TOIR
3,419	Vamori 7½	TOIR
6,236	Cedar Basin 7½	AZSL
3,381	Sells East 7½	TOIR
3,480	Artillery Pk. 15	BLM
6,422	Ruby 7½	CRNF
7,734	Baboquivari Pk. 7½	BLM/TOIR
3,212	Sikort Chuapo Mtns. 15	BLM
3,197	Kino Pk. 15	OPNM
5,060	Mountain Sheep Spring 7½	BLM
7,680	West Mountain Pk. 7½	BLM
3,137	Belmont Mtns. 15	BLM
3,480	Big Horn Mtns. 15	BLM
7,160	Big Lue Mtns. 15	ASNF
2,700	Parker Dam 15	BLM
5,456	Mt. Perkins 15	BLM
4,293	Date Creek Ranch NW 7½	BLM
4,851	Haystack Butte 7½	TNF
7,979	Groom Creek 7½	PNF
3,573	Quijotoa Mtns. 15	TOIR
1,794	Granite Mtns. 15	CPWR
2,410	Buck Mtns. 7½	BLM
4,565	Garfias Mtn. 7½	AZSL
3,927	Alamo Dam 15	BLM
1,169	Tinajas Altas 15	BMGR

Number	*Name of Range*	*Name of High Point*
28	Cabeza Prieta Mtns.	Cabeza B.M.
29	Carrizo Mtns.	Pastora Pk.
30	Casa Grande Mtns.	unnamed
31	Castle Dome Mtns.	Castle Dome Pk.
32	Castle Mtns.	unnamed
33	Cerbat Mtns.	Mt. Tipton
34	Cerro Colorado Mtns.	Colorado B.M.
35	Chiricahua Mtns.	Chiricahua Pk.
36	Chocolate Mtns.	Twin B.M.
37	Chuksa Mtns.	Roof Butte
38	Cimarron Mtns.	unnamed
39	Connell Mtns.	unnamed
40	Copper Mtns.	unnamed
41	Cottonwood Mtns.	unnamed
42	Coyote Mtns.	unnamed
43	Crater Range	unnamed
44	Crooked Mtns.	unnamed
45	Date Creek Mtns.	unnamed
46	Diablo Mtns.	unnamed
47	Dome Rock Mtns.	Cunningham Mtn.
48	Dos Cabezas Mtns.	Dos Cabezas Pks.
49	Dragoon Mtns.	Mt. Glenn
50	Dripping Springs Mtns.	Scott Mtn.
51	Eagletail Mtns.	Eagletail Pk.
52	Empire Mtns.	unnamed
53	Gakolik Mtns.	Redondo B.M.
54	Galiuro Mtns.	Bassett Pk.
55	Gila Bend Mtns.	Woolsey Pk.
56	Gila Mtns.	Bryce Mtn.
57	Gila Mtns.	Sheep Mtn.
58	Goldfield Mtns.	Dome Mtn.

Elevation	Quad Location	Land Status
2,830	Cabeza Prieta Pk. 15	CPWR
9,407	Pastora Pk. 7½	NIR
2,350	Case Grande Mtns. 7½	MIL
3,788	Castle Dome Mtns.15	KNWR
3,140	Cimarron Pk. 15	TOIR
7,148	Mt. Tipton 7½	BLM
5,319	Cerro Colorado 7½	AZSL
9,759	Chiricahua Pk.´7½	CRNF
2,822	Tweed Mine 7½	YPG
9,820	Roof Butte 7½	NIR
3,145	Gu Achi 15	TOIR
6,412	Campwood 7½	PNF
2,888	Cabeza Prieta Pk. 15	BMGR
6,631	Valentine SE 7½	AZSL
6,529	Pan Tak 7½	BLM
1,838	Childs Valley 15	BMGR
2,660	Cimarron Pk. 15	TOIR
4,940	O'Neill Pass 7½	AZSL
3,372	Mt. Ajo 15	OPNM
3,316	Cunningham Mtn. 7½	BLM
8,354	Dos Cabezas 7½	BLM
7,500	Cochise Stronghold 7½	CRNF
5,096	Hot Tamale 7½	AZSL
3,300	Eagletail Mtns. 15	BLM
5,588	Mt. Fagan 7½	BLM
3,000	Sikort Chuapo Mtns. 15	TOIR
7,663	Bassett Pk. 7½	CRNF
3,171	Woolsey Pk. 7½	BLM
7,298	Bryce Mtn. 15	BLM/SCIR
3,156	Wellton Hills 7½	BMGR
3,381	Stewart Mtn. 7½	TNF

Number	Name of Range	Name of High Point
59	Granite Mtns.	Granite B.M.
60	Granite Wash Mtns.	Salome Pk.
61	Grayback Mtns.	Grayback B.M.
62	Growler Mtns.	Gro B.M.
63	Harcuvar Mtns.	Smith Pk.
64	Harquahala Mtns.	Harquahala Pk.
65	Hayes Mtns.	unnamed
66	Hieroglyphic Mtns.	unnamed
67	Hobble Mtns.	unnamed
68	Huachuca Mtns.	Miller Pk.
69	Hualapai Mtns.	Hualapai Pk.
70	John the Baptist Mtns.	unnamed
71	Juniper Mtns.	Juniper Mesa
72	Kaibab Mtns.	unnamed
73	Kofa Mtns.	Signal Pk.
74	Laguna Mtns.	Gila City B.M.
75	La Lesna Mtns.	unnamed (AZ)
		unnamed (MEX)
76	Las Guijas Mtns.	unnamed
77	Little Ajo Mtns.	Black Mtn.
78	Little Buckskin Mtns.	unnamed
79	Little Dragoon Mtns.	Lime B.M.
80	Little Harquahala Mtns.	Harquar B.M.
81	Little Horn Mtns.	unnamed
82	Little Rincon Mtns.	Forest Hill
83	Lukachukai Mtns.	unnamed
84	McAllister Range	unnamed
85	McCloud Mtns.	unnamed
86	McCracken Mtns.	unnamed
87	McDowell Mtns.	East End

Elevation	Quad Location	Land Status
2,490	Granite Mtns. 15	BMGR
3,991	Salome 15	BLM
5,133	Grayback Mtns. 7½	AZSL
3,293	Agua Dulce 15	CPWR
5,242	Smith Pk. 7½	AZSL
5,681	Gladden 15	BLM
5,332	Coolidge Dam 7½	SCIR
3,651	Garfias Mtn. 7½	BLM
7,454	Valle 15	CNF
9,466	Miller Pk. 7½	CRNF
8,417	Hualapai Pk. 7½	HMP
2,180	Ajo 15	BLM
7,100	Juniper Mtns. 7½	PNF
7,700	Jacob Lake 7½	KNF
4,877	Livingstone Hills 15	KNWR
1,080	Laguna Dam 7½	YPG
2,694	La Lesna Mtns. 7½	TOIR
3,445	La Lesna Mtns. 7½	
4,665	Cerro Colorado 7½	AZSL
3,008	Ajo 15	BLM
2,840	Alamo Dam 15	BLM
6,726	Dragoon 7½	AZSL
3,084	Hope 15	BLM
3,100	Little Horn 15	BLM
6,114	Happy Valley 7½	CRNF
9,466	Cove 7½	NIR
4,923	Minnehaha 7½	PNF
4,980	Hillside 7½	AZSL
3,926	Dutch Flat SE 7½	PAT
4,067	McDowell Pk. 7½	BLM

Number	Name of Range	Name of High Point
88	Maricopa Mtns.	unnamed
89	Mazatzal Mtns.	Mazatzal Pk.
90	Mescal Mtns.	El Capitan Mtn.
91	Mesquite Mtns.	Mesquite B.M.
92	Middle Mtns.	Los Angeles B.M.
93	Moccasin Mtns.	Moccasin B.M.
94	Mohave Mtns.	Crossman Pk.
95	Mohawk Mtns.	Mohawk B.M.
96	Mohon Mtns.	Mohon Pk.
97	Moquith Mtns.	Moquith B.M.
98	Muggins Mtns.	Mugg B.M.
99	Mule Mtns.	Mt. Ballard
100	Music Mtns.	unnamed
101	Mustang Mtns.	unnamed
102	Natanes Mtns.	unnamed
103	New River Mtns.	unnamed
104	New Water Mtns.	unnamed
105	North Comobabi Mtns.	Mt. Devine
106	Oro Blanco Mtns.	Fraguita Pk.
107	Painted Rock Mtns.	unnamed
108	Pajarito Mtns.	unnamed (AZ)
	————	Cerro el Ruido (MEX)
109	Palomas Mtns.	unnamed
110	Palo Verde Mtns.	unnamed
111	Patagonia Mtns.	Mt. Washington
112	Peacock Mtns.	Peacock Pk.
113	Pedregosa Mtns.	unnamed
114	Peloncillo Mtns.	Guthrie Pk. (AZ)
	————	Gray Mountain (NM)
115	Perilla Mtns.	College Pk. S.
116	Phoenix Mtns.	Squaw Pk.

Elevation	Quad Location	Land Status
3,272	Estrella 7½	BLM
7,903	Mazatzal Pk. 7½	TNF/PNF
6,568	El Capitan 7½	BLM
3,789	Chupan Mtns. 7½	TOIR
1,300	Middle Mtns. N 7½	YPG
6,623	Moccasin 7½	KIR
5,100	Crossman Pk. 7½	BLM
2,775	Mohawk Mtns. SW 7½	BMGR
7,499	Mohon Pk. 7½	AZSL
7,058	Kaibab 7½	KIR
1,908	Red Bluff Mtns. W 7½	YPG
7,370	Bisbee 7½	BLM
6,697	Music Mtns. NE 7½	BLM
6,469	Mustang Mtns. 7½	AZSL
7,540	Natanes Mtns. NW 7½	SCIR
5,936	Cooks Mesa 7½	TNF
2,536	Vicksburg 15	KNWR
4,783	Sil Nakya 7½	TOIR
5,369	Arivaca 7½	CRNF
1,510	Sentinel NE 7½	BLM
5,460	Alamo Springs 7½	CRNF
5,939	Alamo Springs 7½	
1,900	Palomas 15	YPG
2.121	Enid 7½	BLM
7,221	Duquesne 7½	CRNF
6,292	Peacock Pk. 7½	PAT
6,540	Pedregosa Mtns. W 7½	AZSL/CRNF
6,571	Guthrie 7½	BLM
6,928	Indian Peak 7½	BLM
6,388	College Pks. 7½	AZSL
2,608	Sunnyslope 7½	PMP

Number	Name of Range	Name of High Point
117	Picacho Mtns.	Newman Pk.
118	Pinal Mtns.	Pinal Pk.
119	Pinaleno Mtns.	Mt. Graham
120	Plomosa Mtns.	Black Mesa
121	Poachie Range	Poachie B.M.
122	Pozo Redondo Mtns.	Childs B.M.
123	Pozo Verde Mtns.	Pozora B.M.
124	Puerto Blanco Mtns.	Pinkley Pk.
125	Quijotoa Mtns.	unnamed
126	Quinlin Mtns.	Kitt Pk.
127	Rawhide Mtns.	Fools Pk.
128	Rincon Mtns.	Mica Mtns.
129	Roskruge Mtns.	Martina Mtn.
130	Sacaton Mtns.	Sacaton Pk.
131	Salt River Mtns.	Salt River Pk.
132	San Cayetano Mtns.	San Cayetano Pk.
133	San Francisco Mtns.	Maness Pk. (AZ)
	————	Aspen Mt. (NM)
134	San Francisco Mtn.	Humphreys Pk.
135	San Luis Mtns.	unnamed
136	Sand Tank Mtns.	Maricopa Pk.
137	Santa Catalina Mtns.	Mt. Lemmon
138	Santa Maria Mtns.	Hyde Creek Mt.
139	Santa Rita Mtns.	Mt. Wrightson
140	Santa Rosa Mtns.	Gu Achi Pk.
141	Santa Teresa Mtns.	Mt. Turnbull
142	Santan Mtns.	unnamed
143	Sauceda Mtns.	Sauceda B.M.
144	Sawmill Mtns.	Mt. Logan
145	Sawtooth Mtns.	unnamed
146	Sevenmile Mtns.	unnamed

Elevation	Quad Location	Land Status
4,500	Newman Pk. 7½	BLM
7,848	Pinal Pk. 7½	TNF
10,720	Mt. Graham 7½	CRNF
3,639	Quartzsite 15	BLM
4,807	Arrastra Mtn. 7½	BLM
3,097	Sikort Chuapo Mtns. 15	TOIR
4,701	Presumido Pk. 7½	AZSL
3,145	Kino Pk. 15	OPNM
3,940	Quijotoa Mtns. 15	TOIR
6,880	Kitt Pk. 7½	TOIR
3,000	Artillery Pk. 15	BLM
8,664	Mica Mtn. 7½	SNM
4,042	San Pedro 7½	AZSL
2,755	Sacaton 7½	GRIR
4,857	Salt River Pk. 7½	TNF
6,004	San Cayetano Mtns. 7½	PAT
8,280	Blue 15	ASNF
8,980	Bull Basin NM 7½	GNF
12,633	Humphreys Pk. 7½	CNF
4,797	Wilbur Canyon 7½	CRNF
4,084	Big Horn 7½	BMGR
9,157	Mt. Lemmon 7½	CRNF
7,272	Campwood 7½	PNF
9,453	Mt. Wrightson 7½	CRNF
4,556	Santa Rosa Mtns. 15	TOIR
8,282	San Carlos Reservoir 15	SCIR
3,115	Chandler Heights 7½	GRIR
4,118	Sikort Chuapo 15	BLM
7,866	Mount Logan 7½	BLM
2,630	Greene Reservoir 7½	BLM
6,415	Sevenmile Mtns. 7½	TNF

Number	Name of Range	Name of High Point
147	Sheridan Mtns.	unnamed
148	Sierra Ancha	Aztec Pk.
149	Sierra Arida	unnamed
150	Sierra Blanca	Rabia B.M.
151	Sierra de la Lechuguilla	unnamed (AZ)
———		unnamed (MEX)
152	Sierra de le Nariz	Border Mon. #160 (AZ)
———		unnamed (MEX)
153	Sierra de Santa Rosa	unnamed
154	Sierra Estrella	unnamed
155	Sierra Pinta	Pinta B.M.
156	Sierra Prieta	West Spruce Mtn.
157	Sierrita Mtns.	Keystone Pk.
158	Sikort Chuapo Mtns.	unnamed
159	Silver Bell Mtns.	Silver Bell Pk.
160	Silver Reef Mtns.	unnamed
161	Slate Mtns.	Prieta Pk.
162	Sonoyta Mtns.	unnamed
163	South Comobabi Mtns.	Como B.M.
164	South Mtns.	South Mtn.
165	Suizo Mtns.	unnamed
166	Superstition Mtns.	Superstition B.M.
167	Swisshelm Mtns.	Swisshelm Mtn.
168	Table Top Mtns.	Table Top
169	Tank Mtns.	unnamed
170	Tat Momoli Mtns.	unnamed
171	Tinajas Altas Mtns.	Tinajas Altas B.M.
172	Tortilla Mtns.	Antelope Pk.
173	Tortolita Mtns.	unnamed
174	Trigo Mtns.	Mojave Pk.
175	Tucson Mtns.	Wasson Pk.

Elevation	Quad Location	Land Status
3,264	Gu Achi 15	TOIR
7,748	Aztec Pk. 7½	TNF
1,780	Sierra Arida 15	CPWR
3,727	Quijotoa Mtns. 15	TOIR
1,860	Tule Mtns. 15	BMGR
2,402	Mina del Desierto 1:50,000	
2,688	Diaz Pk. 15	TOIR/MEX
3,199	Santa Rosa 1:50,000	
2,921	Pia Oik 7½	OPNM
4,512	Avondale SE 7½	GRIR
2,950	Isla Pinta 15	CPWR
7,180	Iron Springs 7½	PNF
6,188	Samaniego Pk. 7½	BLM
3,633	Sikort Chuapo Mtns. 15	TOIR
4,261	Silver Bell Pk. 15	AZSL
2,476	Silver Reef Mtns. 7½	TOIR
3,332	N. Komelik 7½	TOIR
2,313	Lukeville 7½	OPNM
4,547	Comobabi 7½	TOIR
2,720	Lone Butte 7½	PSMP
3,369	Tortolita Mtns. 15	AZSL
5,057	Goldfield 7½	TNF
7,185	Swisshelm Mtn. 7½	BLM
4,356	Antelope Pk. 7½	BLM
2,506	Engesser Pass 15	YPG
2,635	Vaiva Vo 7½	TOIR
2,764	Tinajas Altas 15	BMGR
4,547	Putnam Wash 7½	AZSL
4,696	Tortolita Mtns. 15	AZSL
2,768	Mojave Pk. 7½	YPG
4,687	Avra 7½	TMP

Number	Name of Range	Name of High Point
176	Tule Mtns.	unnamed (AZ)
———		unnamed (MEX)
177	Tumacacori Mtns.	unnamed
178	Tunitcha Mtns.	Matthews Peak
179	Uinkaret Mtns.	Mt. Trumbull
180	Usery Mtns.	Usery B.M.
181	Vekol Mtns.	unnamed
182	Virgin Mtns.	Mt. Bangs (AZ)
———		Virgin Pk. (NEV)
183	Vulture Mtns.	Vulture Pk.
184	Waterman Mtns.	Waterman Pk.
185	Weaver Mtns.	Weaver Pk.
186	West Silver Bell Mtns.	unnamed
187	Whetstone Mtns.	Apache Pk.
188	White Mtns.	Mt. Baldy
189	White Tank Mtns.	unnamed
190	Whitlock Mtns.	unnamed
191	Wickenburg Mtns.	Morgan Butte
192	Winchester Mtns.	Reiley Pk.
193	Yon Dot Mtns.	unnamed

Key to Land Status abbreviations:

ASNF – Apache-Sitgreaves National Forest
AZSL – Arizona State Land
BLM – Bureau of Land Management
BMGR – Barry M. Goldwater Range
CNF – Coconino National Forest
CPWR – Cabeza Prieta Wildlife Refuge
CRNF – Coronado National Forest
GNF – Gila National Forest
GRIR – Gila River Indian Reservation
HMP – Hualapai Mountain Park
KIR – Kaibab Indian Reservation
KNF – Kaibab National Forest
KNWR – Kofa National Wildlife Refuge
MEX – Mexico

Elevation	Quad Location	Land Status
2,307	Sierra Arida 15	CPWR
2,694	Mina del Desierto 1:50,000	
5,736	Tubac 7½	CRNF
9,550	Tsaile 7½	NIR
8,029	Mt. Trumbull NW 7½	BLM
2,972	Granite Reef Dam 7½	TNF
3,609	Kohatk 7½	TOIR
8,012	Mt. Bangs 7½	BLM
8,075	Virgin Pk. 15	BLM
3,658	Vulture Mtns. 15	BLM
3,820	Silver Bell Pk. 15	BLM
6,574	Weaver Pk. 7½	AZSL
3,100	Vaca Hills 15	AZSL
7,711	Apache Pk. 7½	CRNF
11,420	Mt. Baldy 7½	ASNF
4,083	White Tank Mtns. SE 7½	WTMP
5,682	Dry Mtn. 7½	AZSL
4,611	Morgan Butte 7½	PAT
7,631	Reiley Pk. 7½	CRNF
6,338	Bodaway Mesa 7½	NIR

MIL – Military Reserve
NIR – Navajo Indian Reservation
OPNM – Organ Pipe National Monument
PAT – Patented
PMP – Phoenix Mountains Preserve
PNF – Prescott National Forest
PSMP – Phoenix South Mountain Park
SCIR – San Carlos Indian Reservation
SNM – Saguaro National Monument
TMP – Tucson Mountain Park
TNF – Tonto National Forest
TOIR – Tohono O'Odham Indian Reservation
WTMP – White Tank Mountain Regional Park
YPG – Yuma Proving Ground

Border Travel Warning

Smugglers have been using remote border routes to run contraband and drugs out of frontier Sonora since the Gadsden Treaty of 1853; to this day, heavily armed *contrabandistas* continue to elude posses of law-enforcement officers along many remote sections of the U.S.-Mexico border, especially along the Arizona-Sonora border. Since the Colombian cartels have come under law enforcement in Miami, principal staging areas have been set up in remote regions of frontier Sonora. So you are herewith advised to use extreme caution and common sense when traveling remote border routes—such as the Ruby Road, El Camino del Diablo, Couts' Trail, Sycamore Canyon in the Pajarito Wilderness, and the Mohawk Sand Dunes—described in this book. Notify a reliable friend of your itinerary and exact route of travel; travel by day; travel with companions; carry a reliable CB radio when traveling by vehicle.

Index

Goodwin (C), 140
Graham, Col. James Duncan, 73
Graham, Maj. Lawrence Pike, 47, 48, 73
Graham, William H., 73
Grand Canyon (N), 2, 4, 5, 9, 18, 235;
exploration of, 255, 256; from Sunshine
Road, 227, 228; Mojave Desert at, 2;
National Monument, 10, 233; North
Rim, 249, 251, 263, 270, 323, 331;
rim-to-rim hikes and trails, 281–91;
South Rim, 11, 221, 327; to Colorado
River, 235; tributary canyons, 11–12;
western, 254–59, 316, 322. *See also*
Colorado River; Lower Colorado River
Grand Wash Cliffs (N), 227
Granger, Byrd H., 159, 285
Granite Dells (C), 15, 212, 213, 214
Granite Mountain (C), 211–19, 226; climb-
er's approach, 216; directions, 215;
historical overview, 212–15; landform,
211; southwest face, 216–18; trail log,
215–16; travel notes, 218–19
Granite Rapid (N), 248
Grapevine Rapid (N), 247
Great Basin Desert (N), 2, 16, 287, 308
Greene, Jerome A., 92
Gregory, Dr. Herbert E., 268, 276, 277
Groom, Col. Bob, 137
Groom Creek (C), 137
Growler Mountains, Pass, and Wash (S),
25–26, 27
Grua, Kenton, 245
Grubbs, Bruce, 206
Gurwell, Lance, 303

Hack Canyon and Wilderness (N), 231,
266–67, 270
Hakatai Rapid (N), 250
Hall, Andy, 156
Hall, Joseph G., and William, 337
Hamblin, Jacob, 227–28, 229, 243, 264, 312
Hammond, George P., 166, 174
Hance, "Captain" John, 246
Hance Rapid (N), 246, 247
Hank and Yank Spring (S), 43, 59
Hansbrough, Peter, 244, 245
Harlan, John and Mara, 105
Harquahala Plain and Valley (C), 205, 210
Harris, Benjamin Butler, 196
Harwell, Henry O., 190, 193, 195
Hassayampa Lake (C), 138
Hassayampa River (C), 117, 134
Hatch, Alton, 245
Havasu Creek (N), 252, 270, 283, 285
Havasu National Wildlife Refuge (C), 17,
154, 155, 159

Havasu Rapid (N), 251
Hawkins, Billy, 156
Hayden, Charles T., 147
Hayden, Sen. Carl, 53
Heald, Weldon F., 12
Heaton Knolls (N), 231
Hedrick, Larry, 130
Heliograph Peak (S), 73, 75
Henderson, Randall and Rand, 119
Hermit Rapid and Trail (N), 248
Hesperus Peak (N), 297
Hewitt, Henry "Hank," 43
Hidden Valley (C), 191–92
Hill, Louis C., 128
Hinton, R. J., 187
Hogan, Dan, 285
Holmlund, James P., 115
Holstrom, Haldane "Buzz," 250
Holusha, Rosemary, 137
Hooker Hot Spring (S), 67
Horn Creek Rapid (N), 248
Hornaday, Dr. William, T., 22, 88, 90,
95
Horse Mesa Dam (C), 131
Horsethief Basin Recreation Area (C), 141
House Rock Rapid (N), 244
Houserock Valley (N), 315
Howe, Sandra, 148
Howland, Seneca and O. G., 227, 258
Huachuca Mountains (S), 46, 48, 50
Hualapai Hilltop (N), 270
Hughes, J. Donald, 221, 242, 283, 289
Humphrey, Elliott, 333
Humphreys, Ben, 196
Humphreys Peak (N), 5, 13–14, 291,
294–95, 296, 297
Hunter, Capt. Sherold, 113
Hunter Trail (S), 113–14
Hyde, Glen and Bessie, 241, 257, 258

Indian Canyon (S), 123–24
Indian Gardens (N), 285, 287, 288, 337
Intermontane Province, 2, 4, 6–7
Ireteba, 255
Isis Temple (N), 336
Ives, Lt. Joseph Christmas, 1, 155–56,
158, 254–55, 317, 321
Ives, Ronald L., 89, 92–93

Jackson Cabin (S), 67, 68
Jaeger, Louis F., 23
James, George Wharton: and Apache
Trail, 127, 128; and Grand Canyon,
256, 285, 287; and Prescott, 136; and
San Francisco Mountains, 295; and
Sycamore Canyon, 164, 167, 168, 171

Nagera, Pedro Castenada de, 51–52
Nagles Crossing (N), 263, 270
Nankoweap Rapid (N), 245–46
Nankoweap Trail (N), 282
Nash, Roderick, 249, 253
Natanje, 130
Navajo Bridge (N), 243
Navajo Indian Reservation (N), 304, 306
Needles, The, 159
Nelson, Jerry, 184
Nevills, Norman, 241
Nevills Rapid (N), 246
Newton, Charles, 149
Nims, F. A., 244
Ninety-Mile Desert (S), 111, 112, 115
Niza, Fray Marcos de, 16, 51–52, 127, 144
Nogales (S), 39, 46, 47, 48, 50
Norris, Frank, 210
North Canyon Rapid (N), 244
North Kaibab Trail (N), 281–91; canyon log, 288–90; directions, 286; historical overview, 282–84, 285–86; landform, 281–82; travel notes, 290–91
Northern Arizona: *canyoneering*, 260–91; Bright Angel, 281–91; Buckskin Gulch, 271–81; Kanab Canyon, 260–71; North Kaibab Trail, 281–91; Paria Canyon, 271–81; *car tours*, 220–35; Perkinsville Road, 220–26; Sunshine Road, 227–35; *climbing*, 316–38; Brahma Temple, 323–31; Diamond Peak, 316–23; *river expeditions*, 235–60; Colorado River, 235–60; Shiva Temple, 331–38; *trekking*, 291–316; Echo Cliffs, 311–16; Mount Bangs, 299–306; Painted Desert, 306–11; San Francisco Mountains, 291–99; Zoroaster Temple, 323–31

Oak Creek Canyon (N), 225
Old Kaibab Trail (N), 289
Old Pueblo of Tucson (S), 108, 111
Olo Canyon (N), 251
Onate, Juan de, 9, 117
110-Mile Rapid (N), 250
O'Neil, Dave, 29
O'Neil's Grave and Pass (S), 29
Organ Pipe Cactus National Monument (S), 16, 19, 25, 26; hikes and treks in, 96–99; Sierra del Ajo, 88, 89, 90, 91, 92, 93–94
Oro Blanco (S), 44–45

Pack Saddle Pass (C), 195–96
Painted Desert and Wilderness (N), 2, 16, 298, 306–11; directions, 308; historical

overview, 307–8; landform, 306; other hikes, 310; travel notes, 311; trek log, 308–10
Paiute Primitive Area (N), 299, 301, 305
Pajarito Mountains and Wilderness (S), 39, 49, 51, 55, 57, 58, 61
Palace Station (C), 139–40
Palm Canyon and Trail (S), 119–21
Palmer, Gen. William J., 166–67, 169, 172, 238
Palo Verde Mountains (C), 189
Paloverde Trail (S), 96–97
Papago Indian Reservation (S), 89, 93–94, 99, 109–10
Papago Well (S), 28–29
Papagueria (S), 40
Paradise Forks (N), 15, 226
Paria Canyon (N), 12, 243, 271–81, 315; canyon log, 275–80; confluence of, 276–77; directions, 274–75; hiker information, 284; historical overview, 271–74; landform, 271; shuttle services to, 283; travel notes, 280–81
Paria Plateau (N), 271, 272, 278, 279
Paria Riffle (N), 243
Paria River Narrows (N), 277
Parker Lake Recreation Area (S), 53
Patagonia Mountains (S), 46, 47–48, 50, 54
Pattie, James Ohio, 63, 127, 146–47, 161
Peach Springs Canyon (N), 317, 319
Pearson, Frank and Myrtle, 44
Peeples, Abraham Harlow, 135
Peralta Canyon (C), 130
Perkinsville Road (N), 220–26; directions, 223; historical overview, 220–21, 223; landform, 220; road log, 223–26; travel notes, 226
Perrin, Lilo, 14, 294–95
Petrified Forest National Park (N), 2, 16, 306, 308, 309, 310
Phantom Ranch (N), 248, 288, 289–90, 324–27
Philomena Spring Trail (N), 297
Phoenix Basin (C), 188
Phoenix (C): air pollution, 11, 77, 121–22, 204; climate, 6; and Eagletail Mountain, 205; and Palm Canyon and Trail, 119–21; and Sierra Estrellas, 189, 190, 194, 196; and Sonoran Desert, 112; urban problems of, 10, 11, 52; water and, 10, 143, 153, 210
Phoenix Mountains (N), 15
Picacho Mountains (S), 111, 113
Picacho Pass (S), 111, 114–15
Picacho Peak (S), 111–16; directions, 113;